MARYLAND MORTALITY SCHEDULE

1850 AND 1860

Ruth T. Dryden

Heritage Books
2024

HERITAGE BOOKS
AN IMPRINT OF HERITAGE BOOKS, INC.

Books, CDs, and more—Worldwide

For our listing of thousands of titles see our website
at
www.HeritageBooks.com

A Facsimile Reprint
Published 2024 by
HERITAGE BOOKS, INC.
Publishing Division
5810 Ruatan Street
Berwyn Heights, MD 20740

— Publisher's Notice —
In reprints such as this, it is often not possible to remove
blemishes from the original. We feel the contents of this
book warrant its reissue despite these blemishes and
hope you will agree and read it with pleasure.

International Standard Book Number
Paperbound: 978-0-7884-2805-0

MORTALITY SCHEDULE OF MARYLAND

persons who died during the year ending 1 June 1850

COUNTY -Allegany   DISTRICT

name	age	mar wid	birth place	mon. died	Occupation	cause of death
Emma Buckey	0/12		Md	Jul		L.Compl.
Sarah A.Brown	2		Md	Aug		Comsap.
Mary C.Barr	1/12		Md	Aug		Measles
Marcellus Gordes	1/12		Md	Mar		none
Anna R.Walker	3		Md	Sep		none
Oliver P.Strong	6		Md	Jun		Fever
Ann J.Shuck	1		Md.	Aug		L.Compl
Maria Maneau	47	W	Md	Jun		consumpt.
Perry B.White	2		Md	May		Dropsey
Carmile Jarbo	1/12		Md	Oct		L.Compl.
Arthur Cowton	3/12		Md	Jul		L.Compl.
Josephene Hamlin	2		Md	Aug		Intermet.F.
Howard Hert	1/12		Md.	Aug		Scrofala
Mary Elliott	69	M	Pa	Oct		Typhoid
Godfrey Richards	87	M	Va	Sep	blacksmith	Old Age
Isaac F.Richards	1/12		Va	Aug		unknown
Sarah Breugh	2		Md	Jul		L.Compl
William Hildebrand	3/12		Md	Aug		L.Compl.
Ann R. Hose	1		Md	Jun		L.Compl.
Titus Slue	22		Germ.	Apl.	Waggoner	drowned
Levi Curtis	63	M	Va	Feb	Miller	Dropsy
Mary Timely	37	M	Irel.	Oct		unknown
Elizabeth Herring	28	M	Pa	Jan		consump.
Josephine Reitgete	2/12		Md	Aug		L.Compl.
Mary Stoves	16		Md	Aug	Seamstress	Cholora
Rachel A.P.Phelps	1		Md	Sep		unknown
Maryann Eckles	32		Md	Sep		typhoid
John Emerty	39	M	Irel.	Feb	Labourer	Interm.
Nancy Mitchell	40	M	Md	Jun		Consumpt.
Elizabeth V.Rye	2		Ohio	Oct		InftBow
Elizabeth Eldred	29	M	N.Y.	May		confinemt.
Charles F.B.Swans	24		Md	Jul	Physician	Typhoid
Marshall Gephart	1/12		Md	Sep		Spasms
Eleanor Wilson	1		Md	Jun		SmallPox
Margaret Burn	1		Md	Oct		SmallPox
Isaac Ravenscroft	1		Md	Nov		Diahera
Isaac Swartsingrover	3		Md	Jan		unknown
Elizabeth Zebough	24		Md	Apr		Typhoid
Jeremiah Custer	76	W	Md	May		fevers
Catharine Custer	30		Md	Mar		fevers
James C.Garlitz	4		Md	Jul		croup
Catherine Reikel	60	M	Irel.	Jan		Eps.ofHeart
James H. Fuller	8		Md	Mar		Palp.o.Ht.
Conrad Seikel	1/12		Md	Sep		suffocation
William F.Clammer	9		"	Jan		inflam.Brain
Rachel Frazer	1/12		Md	Nov		unknown
Mary Edwards	18		Md	Jun		Typhoid
Leonard Smith	60	M	Md	Jun	farmer	dropsy
Jackson Green	21		Pa	Feb		consumpt.
John Welburn	1/12		Md	Jun		croup
John Boyer	38	M	Va	Feb		unknown

1.

MORTALITY SCHEDULE OF MARYLAND

persons who died during the year ending 1 June 18_50_

COUNTY Allegany   DISTRICT

name	age	mar wid	birth place	mon. died	Occupation	cause of death
Mary E. Hinebaugh	1/12		Md	Oct		dropsy
Aamanda Sweitzer	1/12		Md	Dec		dropsy
Jacob Browning	45	M	Md	Jan	farmer	typhoid
Lloyd Browning	23		Md	Feb	laborer	typhoid
Hester Dew	40		Md	Dec		consumpt.
David Hoye	34	M	Md	Aug	farmer	unknown
Maryann Friend	28	M	Md	Sep		Liver Comp
Israel Friend	45	M	Md	Aug	hunter	unknown
Aza Friend	2/12		Md	Sep		L.Compl
Fred M.Fredlock	26		Germ.	Jul	sawyer	drowned
Joseph W. Riggs	23		Md	Apr	farmer	consump.
Sarah Irons	28	M	Md	May		unknown
Sarah Jane Baker	3/12		Md	Dec		Sc.Fever
Cath.Pagan	4		Md	Jan		Sc.Fever
Julia McDaniel	38	M	Irel.	Jun		Infl.lungs
John Connelly	3		Md	Jun		Sc.Fever
Thomas Clark	2		Md	Jun		unknown
Charles Sterted	1		Md	Jun		Sc.fever
Mary Seikel	1		Md	Sep		suffocated
Margaret Ann Garvey	2		Md	Aug		L.Compl.
Caroline Hughes	20		Md	Apr		typhoid
Isaac Startzman	15		Md	Apr	clerk	typhoid
James Callan	1/12		Md	May		diarrhia
John Sterrett	45	M	N.Ham.	Jul	ordinary keeper	dropsey
Jacob W.Sterrett	2		Md	Oct		Sc Fever
Mary J.Sterrett	2		Md	Oct		croup
Mary Boehm	1		Md	Jul		unknown
John Hoge	75	M	Md	Jun	LandJobber	old age
Henry Wilkins	1/12		Md	feb		unknown
William Elbert	1/12		Md	May		unknown
Mary E.Carter	3/12		Md	Jun		croup
John Jeffries	51	M	Md	Jun	farmer	crushed
George Long	62	M	Md	Nov	farmer	diarrhia
Samuel Flanagan	8		Va	Jan		croup
Elizabeth Stotler	48	M	Md	Sep		unknown
Ellen Welch	27	M	Pa	Jun		typhoid
John E.Welch	6/12		Md	Sep		unknown
Sarah Beale	84	W	Md	Oct		old age
Richard T.Bowden	5		Md	Oct		Sc.fever
Jeremiah Wolford	5		Md	Jul		Flun
Hiram Woolford	3		Md	Jul		Flun.
Cyrus Smith	3/12		Md	Aug		Sc.Fever
Flora Valentine	3		Md	Feb		croup
Christiana Rice	63	M	Md	Jul		typhoid
John Coney	20		Md	Jun		cholera
Bernard Sweitman	36	W	Irel.	Sep		old age
Mary Jane Sweitman	1		Md	Aug		unknown
Margaret King	4		Md	May		fever
Michael Nicaly	55	M	Md	Mar	farmer	H.Drunk
Henry Bevans	68	M	Md	Nov	farmer	unknown

2.

MORTALITY SCHEDULE OF MARYLAND

persons who died during the year ending 1 June 18_50_

COUNTY Allegany   DISTRICT

name	age	mar wid	birth place	mon. died	Occupation	cause of death
Jacob S.Reel	1/12		Md	Sep		Dysentry
Elihu S.Street	23		Md	Apr		Sc.Fever
James C.Duenny	19		Pa	Aug	laborer	Mer.Bow
Mary Black	67	M	Md	May		unknown
Margaret Murphy	30		Irel	May		typhoid
Catharine Conswick	76		Eng.	Sep		Palsy
George Burrale	59	W	Md	Jun	R.R.Hand	killd.byCars
Susan A.Dillon	2/12		Md	Jul		L.Compl
John Herbert	58	M	Md	Jun	carpenter	fever
John Canor	2		Md	Mar		Sc.Fever
Mordicai Glass	25		Pa	Aug	Laborer	consump
Levi Moon	39	M	Md	Mar	S.Mason	typhoid
Delila C.Baker	7		Md	May		fever
Mary E.Fitzpatrick	6		Md	Apr		Sc.Fever
Robert B. Crays	37	M	Md	Jul	Cabt.Maker	consump
David Young	24		Scot.	Jun	Engineer	typhoid
Archibald Young	13		Pa	Jul		typhoid
Elizabeth Jane Young	10		Pa	Jul		typhoid
Peter Hope	48	M	Pa	Jun	laborer	Infla.Lungs
Michael N.Nixon	50	M	Ire	Aug	laborer	typhoid
Elizabeth Dolan	3		Md	Dec		Sc.Fever
Margaret Mooney	1		Md	Jul		croup
Kesiah McDonald	2		Md	Aug		Chlorea
Benjamin Thomas	2		Md	Feb		unknown
Mary Wilhelm	55	M	Md	Jun		dropsy
Jonathan Wilhelm	25		Md	Dec	farmer	consumpt.
Harriet E. Crow	2		Md	Jul		Sc.Fever
David Thomas	4		Md	Jun		Sc.Fever
Maria Harden	3/12		Md	Mar		Water on Brain
Mary Brall	1		Md	Jul		cold
Elizabeth Camrod	1/12		Md	Feb		croup
Euphrates Stratton	1		Md	Apr		Infla.Lungs
Lotitia Merrill	2/12		Md	Aug		unknown
William Crosse	3		Md	Aug		croup
Daniel Brown	20		Scot	Aug	miner	Cinoke?
George W.Jackson	40	M	N.Y.	Apr	wagonMaker	Apoplexy
William Sutton	4/12		Md	Nov		unknown
Charles Sutton	1/12		Md	Nov		unknown
Ann Butler	16		Md	Nov		unknown
Emily Lewis	18		Md	Aug		Sm.Pox
Mary Ellen Lewis	1/12		Md	Aug		Conoulions
Nimrod Groves	1		Md	Jan		croup
Parson W.Kight	1		Md	Jul		unknown
Mary Greenwade	39	M	Va	Apr		consump.
Charity Greenwade	56	M	Md	Mar		unknown
Latitia Sigler	41	M	Md	Apr		unknown
Sarah Wingert	6		Md	May		Sc.Fever
Catharine Boose	73	W	Md	Aug		Palsy
John Cliao	1		Md	Mar		water on brain

3

persons who died during the year ending 1 June 18_50_

COUNTY -Anne Arundel   DISTRICT Howard District

name	age	mar wid	birth place	mon. died	Occupation	cause of death
Georgenia Thompson	2		Md	Aug		Dysentary
Mary J. Bation	22	M	Md	Mar		Perp.Fever
Sarah J.Tasher(black)	2		Md	Feb		unknown
Mary Treakle	71	W	Eng	Jan		Paralisis
Mary A. Hipsley	20	W	Md	Jul		consumpt.
Lithe King	48		Md	Dec		Puf.Rheumatism
Jeremiah McNeil	44	M	Md	Dec	farmer	Sore Throat
David Garner(black)	8		Md	Jun		Infl.Bowels
George Streaker	39	M	Md	Apr	farmer	infl.Bowels
John Baxley	80	M	Md	Jun	book keeper	Pleurisy
Harriet A.Tyler (black)	3/12		Md	May		overlaid
Allen Warfield	81	W	Md	Apr	farmer	cancer
Emeline Snider	17		Md	May		heart
Lewis Mason (black)	30		Md	Oct	laborer	killed
James S. Becraft	2		Md	May		Sc.Fever
Anna M.Miller	46	W	Md	Nov		pleurisy
Ellen Walker	20		Md	Apr		consumpt.
Achiah Hobbs (female)	65		Md	Sep		insanity
Samuel Caughey	53	M	Ire	Mar	laborer	plurisy
Mary Warfield	58	M	Md	Mar		consumpt.
Elizabeth Warfield	30	M	Md	Sep		Puer.Fever
Caleb Selby	44	M	Md	Jul	farmer	consumpt.
Allen Dorsey	72	M	Md	Oct	HotelKeeper	Hemorage Lungs
Elizabeth Dorsey	72	M	Md	May		parylasis
Alice Mantle	8/12		Md	Oct		Bilious Fever
John Gaither (mulatto)	2		Md	Mar		consumpt.
Hiram Hectrope	22		Md	Aug	tailor	consumpt.
Isaac Turner	50	M	Md	Mar	Millwright	Pneumonia
Mary France	28		Md	Feb		Dyspepsia
George Clark	6/12		Md	Jul		Cholera
Allen Reed	47	M	Md	Aug	laborer	consumpt.
Owen Oconner	52	M	Ire	Oct	laborer	Typhoid
Johannah N.Davis	23	M	Ger	May		Perp.Fever
Ann Stewart	51	M	Md	Aug		consumpt.
John Bland Mayo	9/12		Md	Sep		Cholera
Margaret E.Lowry	30	M	Md	Apr		consumpt.
Henry B. Childers	35	M	Va	Oct	stoneCutter	Consumpt.
William H.Childers	8		Md	Jul		drowned
Benjamin N.Childers	1		Md	May		consumpt.
Margery Jeans	65	W	Md	Jul		Dropsy
Delilah Heath	36	M	Mass	Oct		Dyspepsia
Henry T. Coale	1		Md	Jul		Sc.Fever
Mary E.Warfield	18		Md	Apr		Affec.Lover
George Louders	1		Md	Apr		teething
Mary J.Blue	19		Md	Oct		burnt
William H.Worthington	7/12		Md	Jul		Typhoid
George Cook	58	M	Baltimore	Oct	farmer	heart Disease
James Hughes	4		Md	Aug		brain
Jonathan Conner	36	M	Md	Dec	stoneCutter	Cholora
Basil Duvale	35	M	Md	Jan	Waggoner	convulsions
Mary A. Rider	17		Md	Dec		consumpt.

4.

MORTALITY SCHEDULE OF MARYLAND

persons who died during the year ending 1 June 18_50_

COUNTY Anne Arundel   DISTRICT Howard Dist.

name	age	mar wid	birth place	mon. died	Occupation	cause of death
Patrick Riley	55	M=	Md	Dec	weaver	Erysipelas
Edwin O.Patterson	1		Md	Oct		consumpt.
Thomas Kitzelberger	1		Md	May		dysentary
Amanda J.Cary	2/12		Md	Dec		croup
Eli Claggett	28	M	Md	Oct	farmer	Delirium Tr.
William D.Hammond	26	M	Md	Jan	sadler	Delirium Tr.
David Jones	82	M	Eng	Apr	baker	paralysis
James D.Thomas	29	M	Md	Dec	farmer	typhoid
James Hammond	67	M	Md	Sep	none	unknown
Daniel Lambourn	74	W	Pa	Mar	paperMaker	Pneumonia
Mary A.Walters	14		N.Y.	Mar		typhoid
Priscilla H.Harison	61	W	Md	Dec		cancer
Joseph Smallewood	84	M	Md	Jul	farmer	lungs
Francis K.Murray	10/12		Md	Mar		teething
Mary A. Murray	63	W	Md	Apr		Cancer
George Hoofnagle	60		Md	Mar	laborer	pleurisy
LaFayette Watkins	65	W	Md	May	blk.Smith	consumpt.
Ellen Dedent	91	W	Md	May		consumpt.
Emeline Owens	3		Md	Apr		Sc.Fever
Richard Bounds	20		Md	Nov	laborer	Dysentary
Emily L. Put	2		Md	Feb		burnt
Barnet Dean	78	M	Md	Sep	farmer	paralysis
John R.Nicholson	89	W	Md	sep	shoemaker	old age
Sarah E.Nicholson	9		Md	Jun		Sc.Fever
Reuben Johnson	24		Md	Feb	farmer	Pneumonia
Elzabeth Laley	16		Md	Sep		consumpt.
Henry Willing	10		Md	Aug		dysentary
Mary Willing	1		Md	Jul		sudden
William H.Bradford	27		Md	May	clerk	consumpt.
Charles T.Bradford	27		Md	May	clerk	consumpt.
Elizabeth Cross	71	W	Md	Oct		Sc.Fever
Isaiah O.Cross	4		Md	Oct		Sc.Fever
Sarah Flaherty	90	W	Irel	Aug		old age
James Edelin	6		Md	Jan		Inflam.Lgs.
James Edelin	35	M	Md	Dec	farmer	sudden
Indiana Maclin	11		Md	Nov		inflam.bowels
Anginina Moore	11		Md	Apr		Patar.fever
Henry C.Pindle	6/12		Md	Jun		Cholera
Nicholas Hardey	56	M	Md	Jan	farmer	Typhoid
Rachel Cole(black)	126		Md	Dec		old age
Peter Cole (black)	100		Md	Nov		old age
Georgiana Johnson	2		Md	Jan		cold
Edward Iglehart	87	M	Md	Jan	farmer	pneumonia
Reuben Johnson	28		Md	Dec	farmer	typhoid
Jonathan Thompson	78		Md	Jan	farmer	Dyssepsia
Henry Elliott	5		Md	Jun		Sc.Fever
Mary J.Strawbridge	9		Md	Jul		Consussion
Margaret A.Brown	29	M	Md	Nov		pregnancy
Edward Matthews	28		Md	May	laborer	consumption

4.a

MORTALITY SCHEDULE OF MARYLAND

persons who died during the year ending 1 June 18__50

COUNTY   Anne Arundel   DISTRICT   -Howard and 2nd.Dist.

name	age	mar wid	birth place	mon. died	Occupation	cause of death
Sarah E. Norton	2		Ohio	Aug		Dysentary
Jane Lakers Young	38	M	Md	Aug		Dysentary
Juliania Martin	7/12		Md	Oct		Whooping Cough
Reuben M.Hammond	41		Md	Oct	farmer	Mania Pt.
George R. Fort	5		Md	Feb		Sc.Fever
Phillip Rivers	26		Md	Nov	physician	consumpt.
Edwin P. Hayden	38	M	Md	May	CountyClerk	Heart
Juliana Stevens	17		Md	Oct		typhoid
Mary Jane Stevens	14		Md	Oct		typhoid
Sarah Ellen Stevens	11		Md	Dec		typhoid
James ALLEN	70	W	Pa	Feb	butcher	old age
John Hudson	49	M	Del.	Oct	laborer	typhoid
George Keffenberger	5/12		Md	Apr		Sc.fever
John W. Smoot	4		Md	Dec		croup
Eliza Fuller (Mullatto)	13		Md	May		consumpt.
Maria J. Selly	2		Md	Aug		Cholera
Joseph McBee	20		Md	Mar	farmer	Pneumonia
Rachel Flewhart	60	M	Md	mar		pneumonia
Samuel F.Burdett	31		Md	Mar	farmer	pneumonia
William Ohr	43	M	Md	Mar	garmer	pneumonia
Catharine Ohr	41		Md	Mar		pneumonia
Henrietta Shipley	71	W	Md	Apr		pneumonia
John Blakely	7		Md	May		Congest.Fever
Margaret Warfield	56		Md	Apr		Pneumonia
Louisa Hood	41	M	Md	Aug		cancer
Rebecca J.Peddicord	6		Md	Jul		Sc.Fever
Elizabeth Warfield	48	M	Md	Feb		Paralysis
Alexander Mitchell	1		Md	Apr		Water onBrain
James Walker	4		Md	Apr		infl.Brain
Thomas Gilliam	45		Irel	Jan	Blk.Smith	Pleurisy
George Hackett	1		Md	Aug		Pox
Rachel Day	3		Md	Apr		unknown
Ephraim Harden	40		Md	Sep	farmer	Abses.of Liver
Sarah E. Stack	9		Md	Aug		Dysentry
Walter Brown	75	M	Md	Sep	farmer	Belious Fever
Rinaldo W.Dorsey	37	M	Md	Mar	Collector	consumption
Elizabeth Howard	1/12		Md	Nov		Summer Compt.
Brice Worthington	34		Md	Nov	merchant	consumption
Jacob Waters	30	M	Md	Aug	farmer	dysentry (2nd Dis
Mrs.E.Woodward	78	W	Md	Mar		Dysentry
Sarah Hammond	80	W	Md	Mar		Dysentry
Stephen Chaney	4		Md	Aug		Dysentry
Andrew Harman	58	M	Md	Sep	farmer	consump.
Annette Shipley	4/12		Md	Jun		Dysentry
Emily Hord	3/12		Md	May		Whoop.Cough
Mordicai Jacob	1		Md	Feb		Whoop.Cough
John T. Biggs	3/12		Md	Jul		Diarhea
Sarah M.Bryant	4		Md	Sep		Sc.Fever
Aquilla Scurvey (black)	45		Md	Feb		consump.

MORTALITY SCHEDULE OF MARYLAND

persons who died during the year ending 1 June 1850

COUNTY Anne Arundel   DISTRICT -3rd Dist.and Annapolis
                                                            City

name	age	mar wid	birth place	mon. died	Occupation	cause of death
Joshua Solan	9mo.		Md	Jul		Scarlet Fev.
Beal Johnson	38		Md	Sep		consumpt.
John Tolinger	35		Md	Sep		pleurisy
Mary Bell	1		Md	Jul		unknown
Alice Hammon	1		Md	Aug		Dysentry
Cath.Carter	9		Md	Aug		Dysentry
W.S.Linthecul m	1		Md	Dec		Dysentry
Lame Perry	40		Md	Feb		Biloious
Thomas Perry	33		Md	Mar		paralysis
Peter Griffin	16		Md	Apr		accident
(female)Grimes	73	M	Md	Jul		Appoplexy
Mary E.Gambrel	20	M	Md	Oct		Choler
John Watkins	6		Md	Apr		Sc.Fever
George Sands	4		Md	Mar		Sc.Fever
Edward Sands	2		Md	Mar		Sc.Fever
John M.Collins	20		Conn	Sep	waterman	Sm.Pox
Fanny Sarah(black	18		Md	Apr		child br.
Edward H. Johnson	5		Md	Oct		Scarlet Fev.
Joshua Turner	62		Md	Nov	laborer	Pleurisy
Hannah Turner	2		Md	Nov		teething
Phillip Doyle	45		Md	Dec		Bilious
Mary Doyle	41		Md	Dec		Bilious
Ann Doyle	6mo.		Md	Dec		unknown
Eliza Sheckell	32		Md	Nov		Puer.Fever
Maria Sheckell	1mo.		Md	Nov		unknown
Margaret H.Thornton	4		Md	Sep		Whoop.cough
Lama Johnson	1mo.		Md	Feb		unknown
Vachel Sewell	45		Md	Dec	farmer	pleurisy
Rachel Johnson	25		Md	Jan		Bilious
Jacob Gray	40		Md	Jan		pleurisy
Cor.B.Crisp	29		Md	Sep	farmer	Pleurisy
A.(fem) Catetron	70		Md	Dec		Dysentry
George Franklin	3		Md	Mar	(city of	Scarlet Fever
Charlie Hunt	9mo.		Md	Jun	Annapolis)	Scarlet Fever
Florence Clayton	7		Md	Apr		Dec.of Heart
A.B.Swan (fem)	6		Md	Apr		Infl.brain
Julia Philips	1mo.		Md	Jul		Choe.Infant
Debora Magruder	10		Ill	Jan		Scarlet Fev.
James W.Bright	6		Md	Jul		Scarlet Fev.
James F.Bright	6mo.		Md	Jul		Cot.inLungs
Richard Parkinson	53		Md	May	carpenter	Bil.Pleurisy
Manten Brewer (fem)	2		Md	Nov		Small Pox
Wm.H.Brewer	1mo.		Md	Nov		Small Pox
William McParlin	72		Irel.	Mar	WatchMaker	Bil.Fever
Gideon Whittington	11		Md	Jul		Scarlet Fever.
Charles W.Whittington	4		Md	Nov		Scarlet Fever
William H. Basil	4		Md	Nov		unknown
Margaret Knighton	22		Germ.	Nov		Acep.Lungs
William Oldick	23		Vern	Apr	farmer	Small Pox

6.

MORTALITY SCHEDULE OF MARYLAND

persons who died during the year ending 1 June 18<u>50</u>

COUNTY   Anne Arundel   DISTRICT   City of Annapolis-1st.D.

name	age	mar wid	birth place	mon. died	Occupation	cause of death
William Dale	20		Md	Mar	laborer	Small Pox
C.Ramsey(male)	24		Md	Mar	laborer	Small Pox
J.McEley (male)	25		Irel	Jan	laborer	Small Pox
Mary Lutz	45		Germ.	Feb		Small Pox
James Mills	24		Baltimore	Feb		Small Pox
Mary Wilson	22		Md	Feb		Small Pox
Ann Harney	18		Md	Dec		Small Pox
Mrs. Lebby	41		Md	Dec		Small Pox
Mary Griffin	18		Irel	Oct		Small Pox
Helen Gowan	4		Md	Jul		Sc.Fever
Rebecca Colter	32	M	Annap.	Jan		Tetniss
John Norris	35	M	Annap.	Apr	tailor	consumpt.
W.N.Jacobs(male)	1		Annap.	Mar		Pleursy
W. F. Jacobs	1mo.		"	Oct		unknown
Josephine Jacobs	1mo.		"	Oct		consumption
William D.Hurst	25		pr.Geo.	May	shoemaker	Scarlet Fev.
J.L.Jones(fem)	3		Annap	Mar		Scarlet Fev.
Charles W.Jones	1		"	Mar		Scarlet Fev.
A.Cowan Taylor	5		"	Aug		Pneumonia
Sally Ireland	12		"	Aug		Scarlet Fev.
E.A.Davis(male)	7		"	Feb		Scarlet Fev.
Wm.Thos.Brewer	6		"	Feb		Scarlet Fev.
Lucretia Elliott	2		"	Jul		sudden
Ann Brown (black)	39		"	Nov		Bil.Fever
Rawlis Brewer	5mo.		"	Jul		unknown
George Dunn	52		"	May		sudden
George Wright	20		"	Jun	tailor	consumpt.
W.W.Thomas(male)	1		"	Jul		unknown
A. Thomas (male)	1		"	Aug		unknown
George Thomas	1mo.		"	Jul		unknown
Martin F.Revell	50		Va.	Aug	tailor	Bil.Fever
Charity B.Offer	1mo.		Annap.	May		Infla.Lungs
Earnest Snowden	1		"	Nov		con.brain
Millard F.Litle	2		"	Nov		Small Pox
Thomas Frazier	9		"	Sep		Scarlet Fev.
Ann Sewell	56		"	Feb		Parolitck
John W.Richardson	39		Md	Jul	Clergyman	pneumonia
Asabellia Weir	10		Md	Oct		scarlet Fev.
infant of CC Stewart	1mo.		Md	Jul		Bilious
Mrs.Mary Maxcy	63		Md	Jul		old age
William F.Dotson	2		Md	Apr		bilious
Martha C. Dotson	2		Md	Jun		bilious
Mary F. Stincel?	14		Md	Sep		Scarlet Fev.
Ann Nichols	40	W	Md	Sep		Dysentry
Daniel Knighton	7mo		Md	May	(1st.Dist.)	infl.lungs
Roger Tydings	2mo.		Md	Sep		Dysentry
John J.Dorsett	3		Md	Apr		Pneumonia
Daniel M.Brogden	14		Md	Oct		Infl.brain
Marthay Minay	55		Md	Apr		decline

MORTALITY SCHEDULE OF MARYLAND

persons who died during the year ending 1 June 18__

COUNTY Anne Arundel   DISTRICT 8th.Dist.& 1st.Dist.

name	age	mar wid	birth place	mon. died	Occupation	cause of death
William T.Loylis	22		Md	Sep	Doctor	Colery
Elizabeth Dove	14		Md	Aug		Bilious
Sarah Nite	22		Md	Nov		bilious
Joyce Allen	24		Md	Sep		Cholera
Ann P.A.Whittington	7		Md	Sep		Scarlet Fev.
Ealig A.Cunningham	9		Md	Mar		Scarlet Fev.
Susan A.Turgis?	49		Md	Jun		Cetues B.
Knuit Swormsteat	45		N.Y.	Sep	Merchant	sudden
Mary Jacobs	1		Md	Aug		croup
Lewis Luthan?	70		Md	Nov	Methodist Pars.	?
			1st.District			
Henry Purdy	45	M	Md	Oct		Strang.Hernia
Galon Purdy	5mo.		Md	Oct		Pneumonia
Galon Purdy	36	M	Md	Oct		Pleurisy
Emily Stewart	18		Md	Feb		Scarlet Fev.
Aaron Parrish	40	W	Md	Dec	fisherman	Mamia Pot.
Joshua Hood	60	W	Md	Oct		Appoplexy
James Hood	3		Md	Sep		Dysentry
George M.D.Hood	1		Md	Sep		Dysentry
Betty Menikin	60	W	Md	Aug		Dysentry
Joshua A.Hood	1mo.		Md	Aug		unknown-sudden
			2nd District			
William McCauley	2		A.A.Co	Aug		Dysentry
James B.Stewart	4		"	Oct		unknown
Margaretta Mezick	38	M	"	Jan		Cancer
Millicent Cook	28		"	Feb		Pleurisy
George Waring	6mo.		"	Jun		inflamation
Eliza Ann Pettibone	25		"	Jul		consumpt.
Thomas Warfield	14		"	Aug		dropsy
Nathan Weston	2		"	Jan		Whoop.cough
L.A.Meek(fem)	1		"	Jan		Dysentry
Mary Jones	8		"	Sep		Dysentry
Edward Jones	2		"	Sep		Dysentry
Thomas Basford	1		"	Jul		unknown
Edward Brown	5		"	Feb		unknown
Lydia Sewell	59		"	Jan		Appoplexy

8.

MORTALITY SCHEDULE OF MARYLAND

persons who died during the year ending 1 June 18<u>50</u>

COUNTY Baltimore   DISTRICT Baltimore City,1st.Ward

name	age	mar wid	birth place	mon. died	Occupation	cause of death
George Flanigan	1		Md	Jun		Cholera
M. Nollen(male)	4		Md	Feb		Scarlet Fev.
Martin Weitzell	1		"	May		Cholera
John Graty	2		Md	Jan		croup
Sarah E.Caldwill	2mo.		Md	Jul		Thrash
Joseph Kirth	1		Md	Mar		teething
Mark Butler	40	M	Md	Jun	clerk	Ship Fever
Henry Schotts	27	M	Md	Apr	Seaman	typhus Fever
John Poppins	80		Md	May	Seaman	old age
Kedi Raynis	4		Md	Aug		Whoop.Cough
Laura Raynis	4mo.		Md	Jun		Cholera
William E.Gray	20		Md	May		Fits
John Robinson	1mo.		Md	Mar		unknown
J.Casthwart (fem)	32		Md	Apr		Fits
Richard P.Disney	2mo.		Md	Jun		water onBrain
Mary A. Delgay?	20		Md	Oct		consumption
Charles A.Blake	6mo.		Md	Apr		water onBrain
Adelina Hoops	4		Pa	Jan		croup
Mary F.Milligan	5		Md	Jan		consumption
Martha Brown	34		Md	Sep		Typhoid
Eugenia H.Donnell	4		Md	Nov		fits
Richard J.Quinn	4		Pa	Jun		water on Brain
Milly A.Mitchell	60	M	Md	Jun		Diarrhia
Richard Walker	25	M	Md	Feb		consumption
Elizabeth Armstrong	30	M	Md	Nov		consumption
Thomas Parker	89	W	Scot.	Mar	Mariner	old age
Mary Parker	52	W	Md	Jul		dropsy
Thomas Trehey	1		Md	Aug		cholora
William Parlitt	1mo.		Md	Dec		unknown
Thomas Morran	30	M	Irel	Oct	Laborer	Dysentry
Sarah E.Boday	8mo.		Md	Dec		scrofula
Joseph V.Taylor?	34	M	Md	Dec	laborer	Frozin
Matilda Herzig	4mo.		Md	Jul		chlora
Catherine James	2		Md	Mar		Scarlt Fever
Mary A.Queen	11		Md	Oct		Enlarg.Heart
Henry Crey	1		Md	Jul		dropsy
Margaret A.Brown	1mo.		Md	Nov		croup
Ellen M.Connill	58	W	Md	Nov		consumption
William H.Fetch	2		Md	Feb		croup
Ann Young	38	M	Md	Aug		cholera
William Young	2		Md	Aug		cholera
Edward McLaughlin	10mo.		Md	Jul		water onBrain
Jacob Brown	17		Md	Jul		drowned
Randall Howden	2		Md	Feb		dropsy
George W.Johnson	3		D.C.	Apr		water onBrain
John Simmons	72	W	Md	Dec	carpenter	small pox
John Powell	27		Md	Sep	lawyer	Dysentary
Patrick Cooney	50	W	Irel	Sep	cooper	appoplexy
James Bowers	2		Md	mar		brain fever
John Hayes	10		Irel	Jun		drowned
Rosana Davis	4mo.		Md	May		water onBrain
			9.			

MORTALITY SCHEDULE OF MARYLAND

persons who died during the year ending 1 June 1850

COUNTY Baltimore   DISTRICT Baltimore City 1stWard

name	age	mar wid	birth place	mon. died	Occupation	cause of death
Margaret Flemis	16		Md.	Jun		water onBrain
Sophia Lath	11		Germ.	Jun		drowned
Michael Elwood	9		Md	Nov		consumption
J.G.Gillespie(male)	9mo.		Md	May		cropu
John McAllister	45	M	Md	Apr	laborer	unknown
Emily Sherwood	19	M	Md	Jul		consumption
Charles A.Wilson	4		Md	Jul		dysentary
Elijah Lyons	50	M	Md	Apr	carpenter	consumption
Henry Otten	8mo.		Md	Aug		water onBrain
John Lahwot	9mo.		Md	Aug		cholera
Mary Lahwot	1mo.		Md	Feb		cholera
Hannah Zimmany	35	M	Germ.	Jan		childbed
Conrad Herbert	1mo		Md	Oct		unknown
Phillip Quinn	23		Irel.	Mar	carpenter	R.R.accident
Harriet A.Minge	3mo.		Balt.Cty	Aug		summer compl.
James S.Arby	2		"	Jul		teething
Eskel Coleman	16		"	Apr		Bilious Fever
Tholmas Newman	40	M	"	Aug		consumption
Thomas W.Beam	6mo.		"	Jul		summer compl.
Robert E.Clark	10mo.		"	Jul		cholora
Elizabeth Daley	63	W	Md	Jul		heart disease
Elizabeth James	66	W	Md	Oct		Cong.Lungs
Sarah Bailey	2		Md	Jul		cholera
Mary T.Pully	19		Md	May		heart disease
Susan Hedwick	22		Md	Sep		consumption
Beatty Moore	1		Md	Sep		unknown
James Smith	10mo.		Md	Jan		scrofula
Charles K.Thomas	5mo.		Md	Nov		croup
Patrick Conner	1mo.		Md	Sep		Thrash
George W. Hodges	6mo.		Md	Jul		cholora
Ann L. Hodges	11mo.			Sep		water onbrain
Mary C.Atlin	2		Md	Mar		catarah Fev.
Harriet Hobbs	2		Md	Sep		cholera
Louisia Bowlin	19	M	Germ.	Oct		childbed
Ruben Andrews	57	M	Conn.	Jul		diarrhia
John E.Knowles	3mo		Md	Jun		water on brain
Frank Knowles	11mo.		Md	Sep		cholera
William Horney	25	M	Md	Jun	carpenter	cholera
Rose Deagan	50	M	Irel.	Jul		dysentary
Vinton Deagan	12		Md	Jul		dysentary
Thomas Hudson	10mo.		Md	Jul		cholera
Ann E.Hudson	3		Md	Sep		scarlet fever
Samuel Boaz	2		Md	Mar		scarlet fever
Catharine Kennard	5		Md	Sep		catarrah Fever
James Ludir (black)	50	M	Md	Jun	laborer	fits
William W.Clark	4		Md	Mar		Neuralga
Julia A. Green	21	M	Md	May		consumption
James Stevensen	6mo.		Md	Jan		Diarrhia
Mary E. Bacheler	1		Md	Jul		cholera

10.

MORTALITY SCHEDULE OF MARYLAND

persons who died during the year ending 1 June 1850

COUNTY Baltimore   DISTRICT -Baltimore City-1st Dist.

name	age	mar wid	birth place	mon. died	Occupation	cause of death
Ann E.B.Raynor	1		Md	Jul		cholora
M.E.Armstrong (fem)	2mo.		Md	Nov		weekness
Sarah Morgan	84	W	Va.	Jan		old age
Catherine S.Ramsey	6		Md	Jun	Erisipela	erxipela
Peter Cline	35	M	Pa	Oct		Typhoid Fev.
Mary S. Cline	2		Md	Sep		Billious Fever
Sarah D.Lloyd	7mo.		Md	Dec		fits
Jane Fredericks	2		Md	Jul		water onBrain
Kesiah Smith	67	W	Md	Oct		unknown
Winifred Kelley	50	M	Ireland	Jul		Diarrhia
John Kelly	10		"	Jan		water onBrain
Thomas Kelly	8		"	Jan		water onBrain
James McDonough	70	W	"	Jan		cramps
M. Corbet (male)	36	M	"	Feb		ague
L. Gernett	3mo		Md	Jun		small pox
Emma H.Brown	1		Md	Feb		inflam.lungs
Mary Kranff	1		Md	May		scarlet fever
Charles Lainhardt	2		Md	Sep		cholora
James Lainhardt	3mo.		Md	May		weakness
Laura Lainhardt	3mo.		Md	Jul		weakness
Mary A. Burns	19		Md	Oct		Typhus Fever
William Ward	72		Md	May		consumption
George R. Ayres	6mo.		Md	Oct		cold
John Frisby	18		Md	Dec		bodily Affliction
Mary A.Eaton	2		Md	Mar		water onBrain
Abigail Rieves	70	W	Pa	Aug		diarrhia
Sarah Gill	60		Md	Jul		consumption
Eugena Benz	3		Md	Jun		scarlet fever
John Smith	22		Md	Dec	mariner	drowned
John Myers	26		Md	Dec	mariner	mariner-drowned
Willaim Englewisher	25		Ger.	Dec	mariner	drowned
Edward Brown	20		Ger.	Dec	mariner	drowned
William J.Denny	24		Ger	Jun	plumbing	cholera
Stephen Williams	5		Md	Sep		dropsy
Matthew Waddle	32		Irel	Apr		drowned
Marcellus Jennings	2		Md	Jul		cholera
Annabella Jennings	4mo.		Md	Jan		unknown
Mary A.Murry	9mo.		Md	Jun		scarlet fever
Thomas Conoway	10mo.		Md	Jan		water on Brain
Margaret Green	61		Irel	Aug		heart
Antonin Brooks	2mo.		Md	Jan		cold
Sarah A.Shillings	4mo.		Md	Jan		water on Brain
Mary Thompson	1mo.		Md	May		unknown
Margaret A.Travin	21		Pa.	Apr		consumption
Edward Adams	7		Md	Aug		drowned
William N.Killin	9mo.		Md	Jul		dysentry
Adam Saltzir?	52		Ger.	Nov.	Butcher	consumption
Sidney N.Saltzir	4mo.		Md	Jul		cholera
Gustus Letcher	4mo.		Md	Aug		cholera
Catharine Gayle	29		Md	Apr		consumption
Christian Balster	17		Ger.	Jan		consumption

11.

persons who died during the year ending 1 June 1850

COUNTY Baltimore   DISTRICT   1st Ward

name	age	mar wid	birth place	mon. died	Occupation	cause of death
John Johnson	2mo.		Md	Jul		unknown
Peter Borwick	26		Ger.	Sep	seaman	drowned
A. Hutman	27		Ger	Dec	seaman	drowned
Richard Bell	28		Ger	Dec	seaman	drowned
Benjamin Zankin	23		Ger.	Dec	seaman	drowned
Mathias Zankin	29		Ger.	Dec	seaman	drowned
Rosanna Loons	7mo		Md	Unkn		teething
Thomas A. Seinin	40	M	Md	Unkn	Mariner	consumption
Frederick Schafer	2		Md	Unkn		Cholora
Caroline Adams	2		Md	Aug		Cholora
Allice E. Arvery	1 mo		Md	Jan		Choked
Alonzo Scheron	4		Md	Aug		unknown
John Kirby	1		Md	Apr		Scarlet Fev.
Henry Peterson	80	M	Md	Jul	Laborer	old age
Richael Peterson	50	W	Md	Sep		consumption
Gertrude Gasper	71	W	Md	Feb		unknown
John H. Reiner	3		Md	Dec		croup
Louisa E. Reiner	1		Md	Apr		croup
Margaret Green	51	W	Irel	Aug		appoplexy
William Harley	27		Md	Jul	carpenter	a fall
Bernard Schafer	2		Md	May		inflam.Lungs
John Lancer	11mo		Md	Aug		water onBrain
Edward White	14		Irel.	Apr		cold
James H. Buns	4		Md	Jul		water onBrain
Margaret Bradford	53	W	Dele.	Dec		consumption
William Parlet	1mo		Md	Dec		unknown
George Culpp	40	M	Ger.	Apr	grocer	consumption
George Staylor	1mo		Md	May		consumption
Lauar A. Russell	3mo		Md	Sep		cholora
Alfred Patterson	1		Md	Feb		fall on head
H.W. Jones	3mo		Md	Apr		spasms
Alexander B. Hanna	48	M	Md	Oct	mariner	consumption
Sarah A. Milholand	19	M	Md	Feb		scarlet fever
Benjamin F. Hall	15		Md	May		heart disease
Mary A. Hall	4		Md	Feb		croup
Francis Hill	71	M	Md	Jan	boat build.	consumption
Charles H. Roach	2mo		Md	Jul		lung.congestion
Robert Fox	30		Md	Jan	mariner	unknown
Charles Fox	55	W	Eng.	Jun		paralysis
Phillip Cramblitt	1mo		Md	May		unknown
Mary E. Springstell	1		Md	Jan		scarlet fever
Rosanna Gore	1mo		Md	Jul		unknown
Mary A. Bishop	42		Del.	Dec		heart disease
John Bradley	28		Del	Jan	shoemaker	comsumption
Ann Gunichis	6mo		Ire.	Mar		unknown
John Farrill	25		Md	Jul	clerk	consumption
John Mohlin	44	M	Md	Apr	Butcher	consumption
Crispin S.H. Turner	15		Md	Feb		Typhoid
Ann R. Cole	5mo		Md	Feb		croup
Charles R. Eagleston	1		Md	Feb		cholera
Edward Thompson	2		Md	Feb		scarlet fever

MORTALITY SCHEDULE OF MARYLAND

persons who died during the year ending 1 June 18 50

COUNTY Baltimore   DISTRICT 1st Ward

name	age	mar wid	birth place	mon. died	Occupation	cause of death
Joshua F.Shaw	4mo		Md	May		dysentary
Samuel Dawson	1		Md	Jun		brain disease
Ann E.Maloy	28	M	Md	Jan		consumption
Hellin Maloy	8mo		Md	Jun		consumption
William Ruther	1		Md	Jul		teathing
Henry Zinkard	50	M	Md	Mar	Laborer	drowned
Joseph S.Willis	3		Md	Feb		scarlet fever
Susan Hinton	21	M	Md	Jun		diarrhea
Ann E.Connilly	3		Md	Jun		diarrhea
Conrad Scharitz?	48	W	Ger.	Oct		unknown
Mary Scharitz?	28	M	Ger.	Aug		consumption
William Dunnington	24		Md	Jun		cholera
Elizabeth James	64	W	Md	Oct		lung congestion
Susan Thomas	1mo		Md	Jun		weakness
James H.Armstrong	7mo		Md	Jun		brain inflamat.
Henry Ward	2		Md	May		water on brain
Rosanna Underwood	3		Md	Jan		dropsey
James Peacock	1		Md	Jul		cholora
Ann R.Peacock	3		Md	Jan		scarlet fever
John M.Hartly	3mo.		Md	Jul		heart disease
Martha V.Meads	6		Md	Jan		croup
George R.Meads	2		Md	Nov		catarah fever
James P.Mahan	5mo		Md	Feb		water on brain
Mary J.Gilsey	2		Ire.	Aug		cholora
Bridget Cain	40	M	Ire.	Jan		consumption
Luke Victory	5mo		Md	Jun		water on brain
Martin Dinfelter	9		Md	May		drowned
Oliver Hubbard	7mo		Md	Jul		cholora
Patrick Shay	40	M	Ire.	May		unknown
Mary L.Kane	9		Md	Feb		scarlet fever
William H.Kane	5		Md	Feb		scarlet fever
Elizabeth J.Charles	17		Md	Jul		consumption
James Pickens	4		Md	Jul		cholora
Catharine Rickard	4mo		Md	Jun		cholora
Mary R.Shaw	10mo		Md	Feb		croup
Mary A. Kemp	20		Ger.	Aug		childbed
Georgetta Pugh	2		Md	Apr		Scarlet fever
					2nd Ward	
Elizabeth Weaver	1		Md	Jul		summer compla.
Chirstian Hoofman	1		Md	Mar		unknown
William Bowser	32		Md	Jan	laborer	consumption
Earnest Volante	1		Md	Jun		summer compla.
Samuel Islfelter	1		Md	Jul		summer compl.
Henery Meyers	8mo.		Md	Jul		croup
John G. Smith	3mo.		Md	Apr		small pox
Anton Sterbner	1mo		Md	Feb		heart disease
John Miller	5mo		Md	Jul		summer compl.
Peter Luckner	8mo		Md	Aug		summer compl.
Mary E. Braberry	5		Md	Mar		small pox
M. Deitzell	47		Ger.	Apr	laborer	small pox
Johanna Cannon	61		Md	Jul		appolexy
James Conner	40		Ire.	Jul	laborer	unknown

13

persons who died during the year ending 1 June 18 50

COUNTY   Baltimore   DISTRICT   2nd Ward in City

name	age	mar wid	birth place	mon. died	Occupation	cause of death
Jane Conner	35		Ire.	Nov		Colina Morb.
Sarah Walker	89		Eng	Oct		accident
Eliza Clayton	10		Md	Sep		Lung Hemmorage
Charles H.Williams	1		Md	Sep		consumption
Elizabeth Elliot	1		Md	Jul		catarrah fever
William Ruby	3		Md	Mar		dropsy
Thomas Finn	8mo.		Md	Jun		inflam.brain
Mathew Kance	45		Ire.	Mar		consumption
Hester Woods	14		Md	Jul		kings evil
Frederick Aimchest	29		Ger	Jul		accident
John D. Watson	1		Md	Aug		dysentary
Jacob Will	1		Md	Nov		summer complaint
Ann Gutwell	11mo		Md	Mar		croup
John Frederick	40	M	Ger.	Nov		accident
Augustus Watson	1mo		Md	Mar		spasm
Mary C. Nine	3		Md	Dec		dropsy
Augustus A.Nine	1		Md	Jun		dysentary
Harman Tabman	34		Md	May		consumption
Mary James	38	M	Md	May		small pox
Harman Dorman	45	M	Ger.	Feb		consumption
Henry Wilson	1		Md	Jun		whooping cough
Samuel Hopkins	48	M	Md	Jun	laborer	mania por.
Hester Cornish	50		Md	Jan		fits
Marcellus Jennings	2		Md	Jul		cholora
Margaret Jennings	6		Md	Jan		spine disease
Thomas Kinley	12		Md	Apr		consumption
Isiah Owen	57	M	Md	Jul		consumption
John R. Spurrier	28	M	Md	Nov	seaman	consumption
Jane Brooks	3mo		Md	Oct		kidney infect.
Frederick Heidline	80	M	Ger.	Nov		old age
John Davis	33		Eng	Sep	seaman	diarrhea
Mathew Anderson	38		Norway	Sep	seaman	diarrhea
William H.Thompson	1mo		Md	Jul		heart disease
John A. Schosler	8mo		Md	Mar		catarrah fever
John Kan	1day		Md	Mar		catarrah fever
Catharine Collins	9		Ire.	Nov		accident
Elizabeth Keoh	9mo		Md	Sep		unknown
Elizabeth Miller	2		Md	Nov		croup
John Setz	3		Md	Oct		water on brain
John Morrison	11mo		Md	Jul		diarrhea
Sarah A.Brown	20		Md	Jun		diarrhea
James H.West (black)	1mo		Md	unknow.		unknown
Edward Kerr	6		Md	Jul		bowel inflama.
Nancy Carter	46		Md	Jun		paralysis
Henry Kuster	12		Md	Mar		small pox
Rose Broachman	9mo		Md	Apr		small pox
Laura Vrihberger?	5		Md	Apr		small pox
Mary Seiber	41		Ger	Sep		cholic
Joseph Beck	3		Md	May		heart disease

MORTALITY SCHEDULE OF MARYLAND

persons who died during the year ending 1 June 18<u>50</u>

COUNTY   Baltimore   DISTRICT 2nd Ward in Bal.City

name	age	mar wid	birth place	mon. died	Occupation	cause of death
Catharine Beck	7mo		Md	Feb		catarrah fever
Elizabeth Reinheimer	10mo		Md	Jul		summer compl.
Mary Morrison	21		Ger.	Mar		fits
Joseph B.Lebkill	3mo		Md	Dec		croup
Margaret Sobel	1		Md	Oct		unknown
Clorine Johnson	9mo		Md	Apr		spine disease
James E.Smith	5mo		Md	Jul		liver compl.
Elias Smith	2mo		Md	Sep		summer compl.
Susan L.Jewett	1		Md	Jul		water on brain
David Lomax	5mo		Md	Jul		summer compl.
Edward Hopkins	9		Md	May		consumption
Elizabeth Knapp	36		Md	Aug		consumption
Cemitta? Bukenwald	2		Md	Jul		summer compl.
John Janeharper	9		Md	Jul		cramp
Catharine May	3		Ger.	Mar		scarlet fever
Frederick France	1		Md	Jul		dysentary
Conig Ramsey	2		Md	Jul		consumption
Ann Bakner	34		Ger	Jul		brain fever
George Rodger	68		Eng.	Jul		Mamac?
Elizabeth Furniss	5mo		Md	Jun		summer compl.
Mary Furniss	1		Md	Jun		small pox
Marksley Pfiester	21		Ger	Sep	laborer	erexpilas
Amelia Somer	9mo		Ger	Jul		cholora
Joseph Somer	6		Ger	Oct		scarlet fever
Henry Syinker	50		Ger.	Mar	laborer	drowned
Richard Hamilton	1		Md	Aug		dysentary
Thomas Holden	25		Md	Jun	seaman	diarrhea
John S.Holden	21		Md	Oct	seaman	drowned
Henry G.Latomme	1mo		Md	Jul		unknown
Ellen Conn	15		Md	Aug		St.Anthonys dance
Emma Fritz	6mo		Md	Jul		cholora
John Glass	51		Md	Sep	laborer	heart disease
Mary Kelly	9mo		Md	Aug		brain inflam.
John Simpson	18		Eng	Aug	laborer	fall
Joseph Heiple	2		Md	Aug		small pox
John W. Pfuke	2		Md	Aug		small pox
Frederick Kramer	1mo		Md	Aug		small pox
Mary A. Baker	21		Md	Aug		small pox
Aaron Bohner	22		Prussia	Aug	laborer	brain fever
Sarah Johnson	32	M	Md	Jul		diarrhea
Thomas Francis	1mo.		Md	Jul		diarrhea
Samuel West	10		Md	Mar		consumption
Mary Hadley	60	W	unkn.	Sep		old age
John Chase	63		Md	Jul	laborer	broken heart
Sarah J.Benson	38	M	Del.	Jan		consumption
David Keistner	44		Ger.	Dec		consumption
F.(fem.)Orendorff	1		Md	Dec		croup
Fillmore Scherlock	11mo		Md	Jul		teething
Samuel Edell	2mo		Md	Jul		whooping cough

15

persons who died during the year ending 1 June 1850

COUNTY Baltimore   DISTRICT 2nd & 3rd Wards, City

name	age	mar wid	birth place	mon. died	Occupation	cause of death
Ann R. Matthews	4mo		Md	Jun		weakness
Frances Matthews	1		Md	May		weakness
Robert A. Caldwell	2		Md	Mar		dysentary
James McNulty	39		Irel.	Sep	laborer	heat
Joseph Seidler	51		Md	Mar	shoemaker	dropsey
Catharine Entay	16		Ger.	Jun		catarrah fever
Maria Rietly	22		Md	Nov		consumption
Robinson Johnson(Mul)	31	M	Va.	Mar	hod carrier	small pox
Frederick Schumel	1		Md	Jan		scarlet fever
Christina Schumel	8mo		Md	May		teething
John C. Busch	52	M	Ger.	Apr	Tavern Keep.	Gravel
John Sulzer	1		Md	Aug		summer compl.
Josephine Wounder	1mo		Md	May		consumption
Edward Quinn	1		Md	Jun		Infla. Brain
Josephine Woodward	2		Md	unkn		summer compl.
Michael Shields	5mo		Md	Jul		brain inflam.
John Lupner	2		Md	Aug		cholora
Waldman Nirce	10mo		Md	Jul		teething
Elizabeth Knight	32	W	Md	Jun		consumption
William E. Small	1		Md	Dec		typhoid fever
Britania Robinson	20	M	Md	Apr		consumption
Edward Holt	7		Md	Feb.	at school	scarlet fever
Elizabeth Stevenson	27	M	Irel.	Dec		consumption
Mary C. Weaver	1		Md	Jul		brain fever
Margaret A. Hays	1		Md	Mar		spasms
Andrew Cheesebrough	47		Conn.	Nov	merchant	dropsey
Sarah Cheesbrough	77		Conn	Jun		heart disease
Sarah Middleton	1day		Md	Jun		unknown
Emily Albaugh	23		Md	Dec		childbed
Justina Albaugh	7mo		Md	Jul		summercompl.
William F. Sanner	14		Md	Nov		bowel inflam.
Sarah W. Edwards	20		Md	Aug		heart inflam.
Phillip Valentine	2		Md	Mar		small pox
Mary Getgenhorst	53	M	Ger.	Sep		billius plurisy
Henry Busch	20		Ger	Apr	laborer	gastric fever
Frederick Busch	1mo		Md	Sep		could not swallow
Genevia Pfister(male)	58		Ger.	Aug	laborer	weakness
Ann M. Boone	3		Md	Apr		scarlet fever
John B. Boone	1		Md	Apr		scarlet fever
Edward Goble	9		Md	Oct		fits
John Richstein	11mo		Md	Feb		croup
Elijah Nicholas (black)	40	M	Md	unkn	laborer	cold
John N. Noble	6		Md	Jul		cholora
Matthew Kelley	72		Irel	Mar	laborer	heart disease
George N. Jones	31		Md	May	laborer	water on breast
William Demby	78		Pa.	Feb	shipJoiner	old age
John Lunt	1		Md	Jun		summer compla.
Christian Waller	4		Md	Aug		wateron brain
Henry Gould	60		Md	Dec	ship carpen.	old age
Elizabeth Green	9mo		Md	Jul		summer compla.
Frederick Fanel	9mo		Md	Jul		dysentary
Hannah Hemler	1		Md	Jul		summer compl.

MORTALITY SCHEDULE OF MARYLAND

persons who died during the year ending 1 June 18_50_

COUNTY Baltimore   DISTRICT 2nd Ward in Bal.City

name	age	mar wid	birth place	mon. died	Occupation	cause of death
Amelia Elmore	3		Md	Aug		summer complan.
Eve Triase	57		Ger.	Aug		cholora
Elizabeth King	9mo		Md	Jul		summer complain.
Mary King	1mo		Md	Nov		unknown
Mary A. Mullen	61		Va	Nov		dropsy
Gotlieb Rupt	2		Md	Jul		scarlet fever
Catharine Wentzell	1		Md	Mar		croup
Conna Brown	6mo		Md	Feb		croup
Mary Hanlauf	28		Ger	Jul		small pox
Catharine Dowish	6mo		Md	Jul		cholora
Nicholas S.Chaffer	2		Md	Jul		small pox
William Meyers	3mo.		Md	Jul		cholora
Edward Brown	8mo		Md	Jul		scarlet fever
John Weaver	10mo		Md	Aug		dysentary
Jacob Miller	27	M	Ger.	Jun	laborer	bowel inflam.
Louisa Rowly	30	M	Ger.	Nov		child bed
Sophia Benny	1		Md	Jun		heat das.
Isabella Nime	19		Md	Aug		summer complain.
Elizabeth Neilson	7mo		Md	Jul		small pox
George Philner	1mo		Md	Jun		small pox
John Nepotite	21		Ger.	Mar	laborer	strangulation
Mary Goldsmith	1mo		Md	Apr		unknown
Richard Wise	86	M	Md	Apr	laborer	consumption
Julius Consella	4mo.		Md	May		crippled birth
William A.Brammel	4		Md	unkn		fits
Sarah A.Brammel	1		Md	unkn		consumption
Charles E.Cooper	6mo		Md	Jul		whooping cough
Michael Sayle	44	M	Ger	Nov	laborer	nervous fever
William Ehart	20		Ger	May		billious fever
Charles Bowen	3		Md	Nov		small pox
Michael H.Connor	3		Md	Jan		small pox
Patrick Tobin	6		Irel.	Jan		small pox
Henry Lee	33	M	Md	Apr		expsnsed?
George Culprina	8		Md	Sep		consumption
Therisa Rawlings	1		Md	May		small pox
Millay Haw	54	W	Md	Mar		consumption
John W.Smith	1		Md	Jul		summer complain.
Margaret Weilig	4		Md	Mar		small pox
Valentin Brown(male)	3mo		Md	Oct		consumption
Elizabeth Wolford	25		Md	Feb		liver complain.
Margaret Blake	22		Md	Feb		consumption
Howard Matte	26		Md	May		typhoid fever
Barbara Henkleman	5		Md	Mar		small pox
Theresa Henkleman	4		Md	Mar		small pox
Ann Emeringer	25		Md	Feb		bowel inflam.
Minta Chase	44		Md	Jul		consumption
William Roberts	4		Md	Jun		drowned
Lenora Fegeler	1		Md	Apr		small pox
Caroline Erfrenback	2		Md	Jul		scarlet fever
Fidilia C.Rudolph	9mo		Ger.	Jul		breast affection

persons who died during the year ending 1 June 18<u>50</u>

COUNTY   Baltimore   DISTRICT 2nd Ward

name	age	mar wid	birth place	mon. died	Occupation	cause of death
John Bunke	3mo		Md	Mar		croup
Nicholas Lanier	2		Md	Aug		teething
Thomas H.Mornan	10mo		Md	Jul		ships fever
Martha Wilson	15		Md	Jun		small pox
			3rd Ward			
Jermiah Frazier	67	M	Md	none		none listed
Rachel A. Tolley	21	M	Md	"		"
Ann E. Malley	33	M	Md	"		"
Frederick A.Frilac	35		Md	"		"
C.S.Budesley (male)	1		Md	"		
Isabella Smith	7		Md	"		"
Joseph Smith	1mo		Md	"		"
James S.Parkhurst	Omo.		Md	"		"
Emael Handy (black)	26		Md	"		"
John H.Fetting	3		Md	Feb		scarlet fever
Ann S. Fetting	6		Md	Feb		scarlet fever
Washington Hooper	10		Md	Jul		spine
Elizabeth A.Gilley	1		Md	Jul		bro.Inf.
William A.Thompson	8		Md	Oct		scarlet fever
Thomas P.Thompson	4		Md	Nov		scarlet fever
John W. Naivore	11mo		Md	May		teething
Benjamin Wimpsey	74		Md	Apr	farmer	old age
Thomas T.Norwood	1		Md	May		Lung infect.
Mary E.Ash	36	M	Md	Oct		thrast?
Thomas Newbold	1mo		Md	Jun		unknown
Harry Muller	6mo		Md	Oct		lung congest.
George Bagleman	3mo.		Md	Jul		consumpt.
Augustus Bagleman	6mo		Md	Aug		consumpt.
Anna Wiegart	2		Md	Feb		Scrofila
Grace Ericksen	1		Md	Aug		dysentary
Alex Lowe	4		Md	Oct		burnt
Thomas Atkinson	38	M	Md	Sep	sailmaker	consumption
Charlotte Matthews	61		Md	Sep		diarrhea
Adam C. Bloyd	17		Md	Mar	Mchinest	brain affec.
Eliza L. Evane	1		Md	Nov		gastric fever
John Davis	6		Md	Jun		dysentry
Margaret Oster	7		Md	Aug		dysentry
George Gale	2		Md	May		teething
Thomas Black	1mo		Md	Aug		unknown
Charles E.Cooper	1		Md	Aug		Y.Jaundice
John Marshel	6		Md	Oct		croup
William F.Marshel	4		Md	Nov		croup
Elizabeth Mills	67		Va.	Sep		Bile inten.
Elizabeth Rutter	1		Md	May		brain
Mary A. Cowman	5		Md	Jun		bronchitis
Mary Michaw	23	M	Prussia	Aug		typhoid fever
Albert Michaw	5mo		Md	Jan		consumption
Robert Davidsen	36		Md	Feb	potter	consumption
Catte Gallup	51		Md	Aug		cholora
Ann Dougan	6mo		Md	May		small pox

MORTALITY SCHEDULE OF MARYLAND

persons who died during the year ending 1 June 1850

COUNTY Baltimore   DISTRICT 3rd Ward, Baltimore City

name	age	mar wid	birth place	mon. died	Occupation	cause of death
Elizabeth Lenty	25		Ger.	Aug		dysentry
Virginia G. Ward	8		Md	May		infl. lungs
Harvey Hazlett	9mo		Md	Aug		Bil. Infl.
Georginia Lednum	2mo		Md	Aug		Cho. Ing.
Ludwell Summer	62		Ger	Aug	instrut. maker	consumption
John S. Lowrey	54		Md	Feb	waterman	brain inflam.
Sarah A. Delaney	6		Md	Nov		bils. Dysentry
Christopher Charles	6		Md	Jun		small pox
George W. Charles	3		Md	Dec		lung inflam.
Frances Slater	26	M	Md	May		consumption
Ann E. Slater	1		Md	Jun		bowel inflam.
Elizabeth Davis	3mo		Md	May		spine
John D. Davis	7		Md	Jul		dysentry
J.B. Wright (male)	5		Pa.	Mar		dysentry
Richard D. Edwards	49	M	Md	May	seaCaptain	liver
Frances Foose	2		Md	Jul		Cho. inf.
Hugh Davey	73	M	Md	Jul	seaCaptain	old age
Robert H. Dixon	28		Va	Jul	sailmaker	bowel inflam.
John C. Smith	2		Md	Jul		dysentry
Catherine Horning	23	M	Ger	Jan		child bed
Conrad Horning	1mo		Md	Jul		unknown
Elnora Berry	8mo		Md	Aug		poisoned
Elizabeth A. Davis	10mo		Md	Aug		cho. inf.
George Roberts	57	M	Md	Jun	waterman	lung inflam.
James H. Jenkins	2		Md	Jul		brain
William Jones	54	M	Md	Sep	storekeeper	Hemorage
Mary Inlois	96	W	Md	Aug		old age
Thomas T. Ashcroft	2		Md	Dec		water on brain
James Ashcroft	11mo		Md	Jul		brain inflam.
Adella Phillips	20	M	Md	Jan		brain congest
John R. King	2		Md	Jan		brain congest
Joshua B. Willis	1		Md	Jan		scalded
Thomas Davey	1		Md	May		scarlet fever
Henry Middleton	76	M	Md	Dec	bricklayer	dysentry
William F. Shedrick	1		Md	Dec		scarlet fever
Martha A. Trice	12		Md	Dec		consumption
Sarah Trice	36	M	Md	Nov		Arisyphilis
William Trice	1mo		Md	Jan		debitity
William H. Birch	8		Md	May		water on brain
James A. Sampson	4mo		Md	Jul		Cho. Inf.
John Francis	6		Md	Jul		whooping cough
Rachel Owens	50		Md	Aug		typhoid
James Thurlow	1		Md	Sep		bils. fever
John Johnson	2		Md	Feb		inflam. brain
Ann Lawson	11mo		Md	Aug		teething
Margaret O'Leary	14		Md	Sep		croup
Stern? Challe	69	M	Md	Sep	shoemaker	old age
Bridget Hogan	6mo		Md	Aug		teething
Phillip Miller	5		Md	Jan		scarlet fever
John Miller	3		Md	Jan		scarlet fever
Mary Miller	8mo		Md	May		cramp.
Ann Cathcart	61	W	Ire.	Feb		Rhumas.

MORTALITY SCHEDULE OF MARYLAND

persons who died during the year ending 1 June 18<u>50</u>

COUNTY Baltimore   DISTRICT 3rd Ward,Balt.City

name	age	mar wid	birth place	mon. died	Occupation	cause of death
Amanda O.Lynch	2		Md	Mar		scarlet fever
Marian V.Milburn	2		Md	Jul		dysentry
Hester A.Bartlet	5		Md	Jan		arixyphils.
Emily Cromwell	2		Md	Dec		scarlet fever
Frederick Bladder	10mo		Md	Mar		Cho.Inf.
Mary J.Bromwell	2mo		Md	Aug		water on brain
Eliza Kelso	1		Md	Jun		catarr.fever
John B.Robelet	9		Md	Nov		scarlet fever
Alveida Robelet	11mo		Md	Nov		scarlet fever
Mary C.Riely	2		Md	Jul		Head
Emily C.Reily	5mo		Md	Dec		bowel inflam.
Edward D.Halbert	42	M	Irel.	Jan	grocer	Plurisy
Hester F.Glenn	22		Md	Aug		bowel inflam.
Delia Shippard	57	M	Va	Aug		spine
Adolph s Spear	1		Md	Aug		cho.inf.
Margaret Reily	78	W	Md	Jan		old age
Mark Garman	1mo		Md	Jan		unknown
Thomas Sullivan	1mo		Md	Feb		cranif.
Sarah Ware (black)	20		Md	Apr		consumption
James H.Mason	1		Md	Nov		hooping cough
Susana Burke(black)	1		Md	Feb		Gastin.fever
Sarah E. Gray	10		Md	Aug		bils.Dysentry
Mary Reily	87	W	Pa	Dec		old age
Mary Macinhammer	20		Md	Apr		heart disease
John Mason	14		Md	Jul		scarlet fever
James S.Johnson	1		Md	Mar		scarlet fever
Alexander McKinley	29	M	Irel.	Mar		cirisouss.
Eliza J.Bouldin	3		Md	Mar		typhoid fever
Henry Lloyd	1mo		Md	Aug		unknown
Henrietta M.Lynch	80	W	Md	Feb		paralytic
Mary Watts	55	M	Md	Mar		consumpt.
Cathe.Kolp	1		Md	Sep		chol.inf.
William F.Smith	19		Va	Jan	sailor	lost at sea
August Myers	46	M	Germ.	Oct	tailor	bils.dysentry
John Flayton	3		Md	May		burnt
George W.Fisher	27		Va	Aug	shoemaker	cholora
Catherine Chambers	76	W	Md	Apr		debility
William Blacklar	53	M	Eng.	Apr	butcher	sucide
Charles Cemer	5		Md	May		Catanfes.?
Edgar Bruscuss	11mo		Md	Dec		consumption
Daniel Anthony	73	M	Md	Apr	shipCarpen.	old age
Elizabeth Taylor	83	W	Md	Apr		old age
Edwin Baker	7mo		Md	Aug		Pho.Inf.
Emily S.Waters	27	M	Md	May		consumption
George R. Jones	5		Md	Mar		scarlet fever
Jacob Miller	1		Md	Apr		chol.Inf.
Eliza Alexander	25		Md	Apr		consumption
Maria Roberts	35	W	Md	Nov		consumption
Maria D.Littig	1		Md	Apr		catarr.fever
E.Fenwick Small	31	M	Pa	Sep	clerk	Typhoid
Oakley Hadaway	64	W	Md	Jul	shipCarpen.	Paralytic
William Gardner	11mo		Md	May		brain fever

20

persons who died during the year ending 1 June 18<u>50</u>

COUNTY Baltimore   DISTRICT 3rd Ward, Baltimore City

name	age	mar wid	birth place	mon. died	Occupation	cause of death
Thomas Yearby?	39	M	Va.	Nov	waterman	Inflam.Rhum.
Mary C. Butle	1mo		Md	Nov		unknown
John Stallings	60	M	Md	May		abcess of lungs
George W. Long	3mo		Md	Jun		scarlet fever
Nathan Stevenson	5		Md	Aug		dysentary
Hellen Marr	1		Md	Sep		cholora
Sarah Scrivner	80	W	Md	Sep		old age
Elizabeth E.Jacobs	8mo		Md	Jun		water on brain
Mary J.Jacobs	8mo		Md	Jun		water on brain
Sophia Turner	55		Md	Sep		dysentry
Messra Vida	30		Ger.	Apr		typhoid
Eliza J. Metz	20	M	Md	Jul		consumption
Stanley Chister	25		Md	Apr	Caulker	consumption
Mary Griffin	59	W	Md	Jun		typhoid
Robert T.Wilkinson	2		Md	Oct		brain fever
Mena Branner	1		Md	Jan		croup
Louis Stout	2		Md	May		small pox
James H. Bangs	17		Md	Mar		Infly.Rhum.
Joseph Livermore	2		Md	May		Cho.Inf.
Andrew Gough	2		Md	Jun		Cho.Inf.
Isabella Joice	33	M	Md	Dec		consumption
Martha Hartford	53	W	Eng.	Dec.		dropsy
Elizabeth Sewell	24		Md	Jun		dysentry
Mary Barrett	11mo		Md	Jun		brain fever
Jacob Mezick	27	M	Md	May	hatter	bowel inflam.
Vriginia Diggs	2		Md	Aug		brain disease
Kerney Watts	10		Md	May		scarlet fever
John D.Watts	7		Md	May		scarlet fever
Eliza Stever	27	M	Md	Mar		consumption
Alice E. Vien	2		Md	Apr		water on brain
John Walmsly	50	W	Md	Jan	farmer	Gastric fever
Elizabeth Walmsly	36	M	Md	Dec		Bils.plelurisy
Maria L.Denis	1		Md	Mar		water on brain
Theodore J.Highman	23	M	Ger.	Oct		lost at sea
Henry J.Jurgens	35	M	Ger	Oct		lost at sea
Mary Harris	21	M	Md	Sep		consumption
Joseph Zinkle	9mo		Md	Apr		catarr.fever
Caroline V.Edwards	3		Md	Jan		croup
Elizabeth James	60	W	Md	Oct		cong.of lungs
Susan R. Benyon	2		Md	Mar		scalded
Ann M.V.Dunham	4		Md	Aug		bils.dysentry
Eugene L.McKay	1		Md	Aug		infl.brain
James Miller	35	M	Eng.	Jan	forageMaster	shot-accident
John J.White	3		Md	Apr		scarlet fever
Maria L. Chew	1		Md	Jun		cho.inf.
Asbury L.Chew	14		Md	Jan		killed
Julian Clark(female)	27		Md	Aug		bils.Dysentry
Emma C.Abraham	10mo		Md	Oct		heart
Benjamin Bixandine	32		Md	Jun	sailor	arditis
John Emery	40		Md	Aug		hydrecophilis

persons who died during the year ending 1 June 18<u>50</u>

COUNTY Baltimore   DISTRICT 3rd Ward.Baltimore City

name	age	mar wid	birth place	mon. died	Occupation	cause of death
E.A.Roe(male)	40		Mass.	Oct	physician	phunitis
George Armstrong	29		Pa	Oct	gailer	fever
James Hamilton	21		Irel.	Jan		consumpt
Samuel Fletcher	19		N.J.	Jan		pneumonia
Jane Gordon	27		Va	Feb		fistula
Mary J. Oram	38		N.C.	Feb		ptisis
Cyrus Bates	74		Md	Apr		old age
J.W.Mora(male)	32		Me.	Apr		typhoid
Joseph Hayes	36		Pa.	May	machinist	typhoid
Mary Longfellow	35		S.C.	May		phrenitis
Mary Stump	24	M	Md	Jun		consumption
Levinia Miller	4		Md	Mar		scarlet fever
Robert E.Arnold	5mo		Md	May		catarr.fever
Mary Reice	23	M	Md	Aug		consumption
Eugene Eckel	19		Md	Nov	clerk	consumption
Caroline Friedenrick	5		Md	Jan		scarlet fever
Daneil Anthony	73	M	Md	Jul	carpenter	cholora
James Holms	23		Md	Aug	miller	consumption
Benjamin Fuller	1		Md	Aug		cho.Inf.
Florinda Elmsworth	3		Md	Mar		hooping cough
Margaret Murphy	11		Ire.	Apr		consumption
John Liverman	36	M	Ger.	Dec	sawyer	killed
Charles J.White	3		Md	Apr		scarlet fever
Mary E.Schow	2		Md	Feb		scarlet fever
Ellen Flaherty	50		Irel.	May		scarlet fever
John H. Faber	4mo		Md	Jan		unknown
Frances O.Codel	4mo		Md	Nov		spine
Hissia Smith	67	W	Md	Oct		dropsy
Elizabeth Thomas	76	M	Germ.	Dec		pratytic
Jane Adams	42	M	Md	Mar		dropsy
Sebastian Sultzer	70	M	Md	Jul		dysentary
Isabella Wood	2		Md	Aug		dysentry
Sarah E. Darrough	1		Md	Aug		cho.inf.
Alexander J.James	39	M	Md	Aug	pilot	apoplexy
Temperance Jones	76	W	Md	Oct		consumption
Charles Watts	6		Md	Mar		scarlet fever
William B. Snow	8mo		Md	Mar		gastric fever
Jone L.Phinney	41	M	Md	Mar		debility
George W. Curlett	33	M	Md	May	sportsman	kidney disf.
Susana Grant	93	W	Pa	May		old age
John Merritt	2		Md	Sep		dysentary
Mary A. Cost	2		Md	Jun		dysentary
Frans.Sprankling	2		Md	Sep		consumption
Robert Laurence	7mo		Md	Dec		water on brain
Elizabeth A. Carter	8mo		Md	Jun		cho.inf.
James Fox	1mo.		Md	Jan		unknown
Sarah Frazier	1mo		Md	Jun		debility
Edward M. Johnson	25		Md	Jul	sailor	lost at sea
Charles H.Hopkins	1mo		Md	Aug		bils.dysentry
Bartholomew McCarthy	6mo		Md	Aug		cho.inf.
John Merris	40		Irel.	Jul	laborer	bils.fever

MORTALITY SCHEDULE OF MARYLAND

persons who died during the year ending 1 June 18<u>50</u>

COUNTY   Baltimore   DISTRICT 3rd Ward & 4th ward,City

name	age	mar wid	birth place	mon. died	Occupation	cause of death
John Williams	1mo		Md	Aug		unknown
Mary Schwartz	2mo		Md	Apr		small pox
Howart Baynis	1mo		Md	Jul		cho.inf.
Sarah M. Preston	11		Md	Feb		gastric fever
4th Ward						
Catherine Lide	53		Pa	Apr		consumption
George Betts	16		Md	Nov	turner	injuries
Levia Cathall (male)	60	W	Md	feb		consumption
Lizzy Redman	2		Md	May		convulsion
Nathaniel H.Thayer	2		Md	May		teething
Cordilia Billinger	1		Md	May		cho.inf.
Nantzy T.Crocker	61	W	Mass	Apr		asthma
George Stockett	7		Md	Aug		dysentry
Kate Caughers	5mo		Md	Jun		heart
Mary Askew	73		Md	Aug		old age
Henry C.Dunlevy	18		Md	Sep		typhoid
George A.Chapman	1		Md	Jul		cho.inf.
John Woods	36	M	Irel.	Nov	chandler	intenifier?
Matilda Robinson	8		Md	Feb		scarlet fever
Horace Robinson	4		Md	Feb		scarlet fever
Frederick Robinson	4		Md	Feb		scarlet fever
Grace Robinson	1		Md	Feb		scarlet fever
Mary E.Welsh	5mo		Md	Jun		catarr.fever
Levi Larkins	1mo		Md	Jun		spasms
Jacob Young(black)	60	M	Md	Jun	whitewasher	bowel.inflam.
Joel W. Hilbert	6		Ohio	Jul		infl.brain
James L.Riley	2		Md	Feb		infl.brain
Laura V.Pritchard	3		Md	Mar		small pox
Lucretia Kanklin	4mo		Md	Mar		cho.inf.
Maria Kanklin	2		Md	Jul		cho.inf.
Elizabeth Smart	25	M	Md	Sep		typhoid
Alice P.Phillips	10mo		Md	Apr		inflm.brain
Maria A. Setten	2		Md	Oct		cho.inf.
John Fink	1mo		Md	Jul		cho.inf.
John Holliday	42	W	Md	Dec		scrofula
Mary Jones	23		Mass	Sep		consumption
Eliza J.Ball	24		Md	Aug		typhoid
Isabella Barrows	24		Md	Nov		consumption
John P.Fowler	49	M	Md	Feb	carpenter	consumption
Denwood Barrows	2		Md	Feb		brain inflam.
Barthol DeGory	77	W	France	Jul		cancer
Ann A. Dowsan	47	W	Md	May		dropsey
Anna Grimes (Mul)	4		D.C	Jun		cho.inf.
Cathe B. Dobbin	18		Md	Dec		consumption
Elenna Scott	33		Md	Jan		dropsey
William H.King	6		Md	Oct		burnt
Ann Holbert	85	W	Irel.	Sep		diarrhea
Mary Landers	9mo		Md	Jun		cho.inf.
Susan DeSpeda	8		Md	Jul		dysentry
Charles DeSpeda	18		Md	Jan	bricklayer	shot
Elizabeth Asher	66		Md	Feb		aresyphilis
Edward Cook	50		Md	Jan	sailor	pleurisy

23

MORTALITY SCHEDULE OF MARYLAND

persons who died during the year ending 1 June 1850

COUNTY Baltimore   DISTRICT 4th Ward, City

name	age	mar wid	birth place	mon. died	Occupation	cause of death
Samuel Dukeheart	1mo		Md	Feb		unknown
Mary L.Abbott	6		Md	Feb		scarlet fever
William Mann	11		Md	Dec		typhoid
Peter Cornilius	88	W	France	Jun		old age
Louisa Hobbs	34		Md	Dec		consumption
Washington Sands	40	M	Md	Feb	tailor	consumption
Richard Sands	21		Md	Feb		consumption
Benjamin Buck	4mo		Md	Jul		brain fever
Reba Robinson	84	W	Md	Jul		old age
Charles E. Boehler	1		Md	Jul		cho.inf.
Thomas Tyson	28		Va	Jul	shoemaker	small pox
Rosabella J.Posey	4		Md	Feb		scarlet fever
Mary Lloyd	55	M	Md	Feb		apoplexy
Isabella Henry	6mo		Md	Jun		brain fever
Elizabeth Crouse	55		Pa	Mar		consumption
Daniel E.Reese	79	W	Pa	Mar	Minister	heart
Emma Jones	3mo		Md	Dec		whooping cough
Levin Jones	2		Md	Dec		whooping cough
Levin Fallen	28		Md	Aug	sailor	lung abcess
Mary V.Fallen	1		Md	Aug		diarrhea
Elizabeth Marine	6mo		Md	Jan		brain inflam.
John Graff	6mo		Md	Sep		cho.inf.
Louisa Getzer	48	M	Germ.	Dec		dropsy
William G.Steuart	7		Md	Dec		spine
George Palmer	9		Md	Aug		consumption
William F. Gray	6mo.		Md	May		cho.inf.
Susan C. Goodrick	3		Md	Jun		scarlet fever
Mary Middleton	36	M	Md	Mar		consumption
Mary Brewer	57		Md	Mar		cancer
Isabella Reany	65	M	Irel.	Dec		bil.dysentary
George Hewlett	35		Germ.	Nov	tailor	consumption
Mary Heisler	2		Md	Dec		brain fever
Sarah Goodfellow	1		Md	May		arespyhitis
Caroline Johnson	64	W	Eng.	Apr		dropsey
Margaret Detrick	30		Irel.	Mar		consumption
John H.Cornelius	3		Md	Nov		liver
William H. Wood	5		Md	Jul		cho.inf.
Joseph Rineheart	5mo		Md	Aug		cho.inf.
Emma C.Davis	6mo		Md	Jun		consumption
James Hughes(Mul)	36		Md	May	bricklayer	typhoid
Thomas T.Tucker	39		Md	Oct		broken heart
Adnus?Star (fem)	81	W	Pa	Jun		consumption
John Cole	31	M	Md	Jul	waterman	drowned
George Donaldson	1		Md	Aug		water on brain
John Cole	30		Md	Jul		aramia
Ellen Cloughley	11mo		Md	Jul		cho.inf.
Jane Maugham	80	W	Irel	Jun		rheumatism
Catherine L.Stapleton	60	W	Irel	Jul		consumption
Joseph Sills	55	M	Engl.	Nov	stationer	yellow fever
Enoch E. Lowry	44	M	Md	Nov	merchant	typhoid

24

MORTALITY SCHEDULE OF MARYLAND

persons who died during the year ending 1 June 18<u>50</u>

COUNTY Baltimore   DISTRICT 4th Ward

name	age	mar wid	birth place	mon. died	Occupation	cause of death
Mary Mason	24		Md	Jan		consumption
Kate Merideth	1		Md	Nov		croup
William F.Clark	10		Md	Mar		typhoid
Emet B. Root	6		Va	Aug		Dysentary
Maurice Baker	23	M	Md	Jul	merchant	dysentary
Edward Landen	1		Md	Jul		dysentary
Fanny Jones	2		Md	Aug		Scarlet fever
John Biddle	25		Md	Aug	sailor	cholera
Thomas Kennedy	28	M	Engl.	Sep	minister	diarrhea
Thomas Norton	6		Md	Oct		killed
Margaret Herring	1		Md	Jul		cho.inf.
Jacob Schliegh	48	M	Germ.	Jan		rheumatism
Christine Kemling	1		Md	Sep		cho.inf.
John A. Graham	6		Md	Aug		scarlet fever
Mary A. Horsely	51	M	Md	Nov		arisyphlia
James C.White	20		Pa	May	paperhanger	dropsey
Zunus M.Conway	6		Del	Sep		measles
David Ricketts	65	W	Md	Sep	flour inspect.	bil.fever
Elizabeth Frey	52	M	Ct.	Jan		pneumonia
Franklin Hickman	17		Md	Aug	stationer	bils.fever
Ellen Sutton	3		Md	Jul		brain fever
Mary A. Balbirnie	45		Md	Aug		cancer
Eliza Foreman	1mo		Md	Apr		unknown
Susan Perry	40	M	Md	May		arisephiles
Susana Waters	26	M	Md	May		chill
J.Deidrick Woldman	39	M	Germ.	Mar	tabocconist	consumption
Janis Adams	40	M	Md	Mar		paralytic
Jerome Rigger	1		Md	Nov		gast.fever
Rebecca Snow	59	M	Md	Sep		dysentary
Elizabeth Mimex	63	W	Md	Nov		consumption
Louisa Cannon	38	M	Md	Nov		consumption
Sarah A. Ruff	1mo		Md	Aug		cho.inf.
George F. Speitzer	65		Germ.	Aug	laborer	debility
Anna Flannigan	2mo		Md	Dec		catarr.fever
William H. Smith	1mo.		Md	Aug		consumption
Eve Drace	52		Germ.	Aug		cramp.
Chirstian Shuper	2		Md	Jun		cho.inf.
Joseph Oswinkel	40	M	Germ.	Jun	tailor	dropsey
Jane Hazel	50	M	N.Y.	Aug		bil.dysentary
Ellen McGinney	1mo		Md	Aug		hives
Hannah Porter	47	M	Pa	Jun		consumption
Ann M. Conaway	17		Md	Nov		typhoid
Mary Dunn	34		Eng.	Aug		cholora
John Anthony	3		Va	Aug		cho.inf.
Mary Anthony	1mo		Va.	Jul		tetter
Margaret H. Keys	10mo		Md	Sep		spasms
George Coffenbagger	9		Md	Oct		typhoid
Martin Manning	22		Md	Dec	laborer	cold
Isaac Holliday	24		Md	Dec		typhoid
George A. Smith	4		Md	Dec		typhoid
John B.Donaldson	3		Pa.	Oct		consumption

persons who died during the year ending 1 June 18<u>50</u>

COUNTY Baltimore   DISTRICT   4th Ward,City Baltimore

name	age	mar wid	birth place	mon. died	Occupation	cause of death
Florina Kelsey	1		Md	Sep		dysentary
Masha B.Shap(male)	49		Md	Jul		cancer
John Griffith	45		Md	Jun	SeaCapt.	lost
Ellen A. Keniss	50		Irel.	Mar		pneumonia
Mary Henderson	1		Md	Nov		brain fever
William B. Henderson	24		Md	Feb	marble Driper	consumption
Elizabeth Abbott	49		Md	May		stomach infect.
Charles H. Taylor	10		Md	Apr		typhoid
Emeline C. Mason	38		Mass	May		consumption
		5th Ward				
William T. Fill(black)	7mo.		Md	Jun		fever
Sally Ann Shippman	36		Del.	Jun		spinal Urolgy
Edward Joyes Cloud	4		Md	Feb		scarlet fever
A. Richard(male)	67	W	Switz.	Mar	watchmaker	typhoid
George W. Balderston	9		Md	Jul		diareah
C.S.Balderston(male)	1		Md	Jul		diareah
Martha Lancaster	39	M	Md	Nov		consumption
Edward Thurston	62	M	Verm.	Jun	lawyer	consumption
William L.Orchard	28		Md	May	rider	yellow fever
Edmund Lynch	72		Md	Mar	paint store	gout
Mary Stevenson	47	M	Md	Mar		consumption
Ann Smith	6mo		Md	Jun		summer compl.
T.Tyler(male)	3mo		Md	Apr		convulsions
William Ed.Mace	3		Md	Mar		unknown
S.Coleman(fem)	8mo		Md	Aug		unknown
Eliza Chesnut	50		Md	Mar		cancer
L.Sheldon (fem)	28	M	Md	Jan		diareah
Esther Fluttes	80	W	Md	Mar		old age
Charles Mould (black)	50	M	Md	Jan	wood Sawyer	Dropsey
Rachel Gross	39	M	Md	Oct		consumption
Mary T.Wilkins	6mo		Md	Aug		dysentary
Thomas Drum	14		Md	Jun		unknown
Jane Hasselett	26	M	Md	Jan		consumption
C.Michiel	44	M	Md	Jun	hotelKeeper	unknown
C.C.Michael (male)	5mo		Md	Aug		consumption
John Newneir?	73	M	Md	Jun	tailor	catarr.fever
L.K.Johnson (male)	3mo		Md	Dec		paralisis
Ann Wade	44		Md	Mar		lung congest.
Jacob Dobler	70	M	Germ.	Sep	tailor	interm.fever
L.Wynn (male)	8		Md	Jun		dropsey
Alexander McCormac	23		Va	Jun	trader	choloric Morb.
M.B.Hasselett (fem)	1		Md	Jul		unknown
Mary L.Meads	3		Md	Jan		brain disease
Lewis Ross	6		Md	Sep		cholora
Jane Story	10mo		Md	Jun		catarr.fever
C.W.Menkin(fem)	26	M	Md	Jul		consumption
William Woodell	8		Md	May		lockjaw
Henry Smith	7		Md	Apr		unknown
Henry W. Lehrol	9		Md	Mar		head compl.
Mary Smith	79	W	Md	Jun		unknown

26

MORTALITY SCHEDULE OF MARYLAND

persons who died during the year ending 1 June 18<u>50</u>

COUNTY Baltimore   DISTRICT 5th Ward.City Baltimore

name	age	mar wid	birth place	mon. died	Occupation	cause of death
Cath.Kolehart	4mo		Md	May		croup
Mary Wigas	4mo		Md	Jul		summer compl.
Caroline Pink	45		Engl.	unkn		inflm.Rheuma.
Maria Clampitt	20		Md	unkn		scarlet fever
Sarah Dempsey	12		Md	Jul		inflam.bowels
Rebecca Core	80		Md	Jun		paulsey
Henry B.Hands	2		Md	unkn		typhoid
Garrett Stack	5		Irel	Mar		consumption
William Bramble	63	W	Md	Jul	Huxter	cholora
Susan Bramble	28		Md	Feb		consumption
Elizabeth Read	67	W	Va	Sep		consumption
Jane Eltonhead	70	W	Engl	Jul		old age
Mary A.Hinds	64	W	Switz.	Jan		bil.fever
Catherine Fry	3		Md	Apr		burnt
Susan J.Emmerson(Mul)	1mo		Md	Apr		unknown
Emiline Merritt	35	M	N.Y.	Sep		consumption
William D.Brian	47		Irel.	Feb	larborer	consumption
Emma Moor	6mo		Md	May		catarr.fever
James White	27	M	Del.	Jul	seaman	drowned
John King	1		Md	Jul		summer compl.
Isaac N. Bowie	36		Md	Nov	Hatter	consumption
Francis McCaddin	6		Md	Jun		scarlet fever
Robert Waddle	34		Md	Feb	moulder	irasiphilas
George Brown	45	W	Md	Jul	collector	blood to head
Eliza Montgomery	none		Md	Apr		dropsey
Anna P.Mills	2		Md	Jan		dropsey
Robert White	4mo		Md	Feb		brain inflam.
H.A.Phillips(Male)	31		Va	Feb	merchant	fever
Perry Nicholls	3mo		Md	Feb		unknown
J.H.McShane(male)	3mo		Md	Feb		unknown
B. Mc Mackin	29	M	Md	Jun	shoemaker	unknown
E.J.Mortimer	4		Md	Dec		scarlet fever
Mastin Bedcoph	1		Md	Feb		scarlet fever
John H. Heiniken	48	M	Germ.	Aug	sugar refin.	bowel inflam.
Lewis Sommer	61	W	Germ.	Aug	storekeeper	diariah
Mary McAllister	6		Md	Oct		croup
Mary Kromiller	6mo		Md	Jul		summer compl.
Jacob Lafatra	72	W	N.Jers.	Aug	bootmaker	unknown
John O. Tarrington	1		Md	Jul		summer compl.
E.Chaney(fem)	46	M	Md	Mar		consumption
James Bowen	20		Pa	Mar	sailmaker	consumption
Martin Hatter	3		Md	Jul		gastric fever
John Brown	21		Pa.	Apr	clerk	suden
Michael Kirchner	46	M	Ger.	Jul	shoemaker	bowel inflam.
William Kelley	20		Md	Jan	plaster	consumption
Jane Adams	47	M	Md	Mar		lung Hemmorag.
Patrick Byrne	64		Irel.	Mar		eresypilas
Edwin D.Ball	2		Md	Nov		rash
Thomas T. Hooper	16		Md	Mar	mariner	yellow fever
Mary Davidson	6mo		Md	Dec		water on brain
Deborah D.Thompson	54		Md	Jul		consumption
William H. Brown	2		Md	Jul		brain fever

27

persons who died during the year ending 1 June 18_50_

COUNTY Baltimore   DISTRICT 6th Ward,City Baltimore

name	age	mar wid	birth place	mon. died	Occupation	cause of death
Susan Halbert	21		Md	Sep		consumption
Ann Halbert	87		Irel	Sep		old age
James Adams	26		Del.	Oct	couchsmith	consumption
John Holden	1		Md	Aug		summer comp.
Agnes Hooper	10mo		Md	Aug		summer compl.
Mary A. Gould	25	M	Md	Oct		dropsey
Martha A. Groom	19		Md	Jan		small pox
Samuel Hopkins	1		Md	Jun		small pox
John G. Murray	2		Md	Oct		catarr.fever
Mary Lloyd	45	W	Md	Feb		appoploxy
Solomon Lindall	77	W	Md	May	carpenter	old age
Mary A.Weitzell	25		Md	Dec		childbed
Sarah J.Deal	21	M	Md	Jul		sysentary
Martin Chlers	21		Ger.	Jan	shoemaker	consumpton
William Bable	2		Md	Apr		brain fever
Charles Schenk	7mo		Md	Sep		scarlet fever
Josephine Cole	7		D.C.	Apr		scarlet fever
Frederic Warren	1		Md	Aug		summer comp.
John Laudensleiger	7mo		Md	Aug		summer comp.
Mary M. Tappan	1mo		Md	Aug		cholora
Martha Y.Cross	87	W	Pa	Aug		dysentary
Samuel D.Cross	17		Md	Aug		dysentary
Patrick C.Magnin	39		Md	Jul	shoemaker	infl.brain
Julia D.Magnin	7mo.		Md	Jul		summer compl.
Samuel Hays	32		N.Y.	Aug	stonecutter	brain fever
Sarah H.Porter	15		Eng.	Oct		typhoid
Margaret Ball	1mo		Md	May		infl.brain
Mary Coe	31		Md	Oct		consumption
Daniel Carter	4		Md	Oct		croup
Emma R. Green	3		Md	Sep		whooping cough
John Chruch	4		Md	Jul		measles
Mary J.Church	11mo		Md	Aug		measles
Elizabeth Kinman	4mo		Md	Aug		summer compl.
William G. Lonigrove	1		Md	Jul		summer compl.
William Brady	30		Md	Nov	tailor	consumption
William Johnson	6		Md	Jul		scarlet fever
Thomas Bowin	6		Md	Apr		congest.brain
Eliza J. Arimons?	26		Md	Feb		consumption
Mary Askins	75		Md	Aug		old age
Ann M. Talbott (black)	32		Md	Sep		consumption
Alonzo A. Rodenmayer	5		Md	May		brain fever
Kinny Chilling(fem)	6		Md	May		brain fever
William Cole	50		Irel.	Jan	weaver	consumption
Morgianna Rinnons	21		Baltim.	Oct		consumption
Thomas Quinn	45		Irel.	Sep	bailiff	appoplexy
Joseph Alexander Stalling	1		Baltim.	Mar		typhoid
Mary Brown	49		Baltim.	Mar		typhoid
Julia Devine	2		"	May		dysentary
Edward Griffith	8mo		"	Aug		heart disease
Thomas G. Hill	56		Philad.	Jan	merchant	heart disease
Caroline Sondheimer	10		Md	Dec		lung disease
Samuel Harper	1		Md	Jul		cho.infl.

MORTALITY SCHEDULE OF MARYLAND

persons who died during the year ending 1 June 18<u>50</u>

COUNTY Baltimore   DISTRICT 6thWard-Baltimore City

name	age	mar wid	birth place	mon. died	Occupation	cause of death
Catherine Green	6		Md	Apr		Heart Disease
Frederic Green	43		Germ.	Jun		sudden
John A.Floyd	23		Irel	Mar		consumption
James G.Livingston	68	M	Pa	Jun	shoemaker	diariah
Ann Bradburn	50		Md	Nov		dysentary
Rebecca Mudd	75		Md	Mar		typhoid
Jane Helmsley	73		Md	Mar		typhoid
Mary Bradford	73		Md	Mar		typhoid
James H. Carlile	10		Md	Dec		liver compl.
Sarah A. Magniss	37	M	Md	Oct		dysentary
James Phillips	48	W	Md	Jul		heart disease
Laura V. Pritchard	2		Md	Mar		small pox
William Hiller	1		Md	Aug		dropsey
Phoebe Chamberlain	3mo		Md	Oct		diareah
Margaretta O.Mezick	35	M	Md	Jan		cancer
William Stribel	17		Md	Jul	chairpainter	Typhoid
Rebecca Harden	44	M	Md	Jul		childbed
Wolvierga? Fenwick(fem)	50	M	Ger.	Jun		cancer
Charles E.Brotherton	1		Md	Nov		small pox
Mary P.McLaughlin	37	M	Md	Aug		typhoid
John R.H.Berry	5		Md	Dec		unknown
Elizabeth Hammond	35	M	Md	Apr		cholora
Mary A. Tucker	42	M	Md	Aug		consumption
Edward J.Church	3		Md	Aug		cataarh.fever
Margaret McLain	1mo		Md	Sep		summer compl.
Alexander Raniy	50	M	Md	Jun	plasterer	cholora
John Aldridge	2mo		Md	Dec		infla.brain
James L.Riley	3		Md	Feb		lung inflam.
Joseph J. French	1		Md	Jul		dysentary
Christana Wilxox	52	M	Md	Oct		dysentary
Edwin Shaw	1mo		Md	Nov		spasms
Susan Lee	17	M	Md	Feb		sonsumption
Margaret Em Curdy	4		Md	Oct		diareah
Nancy Frank	1mo		Md	Sep		spasms
John G. Maddin	1		Md	Oct		brain inflam.
Mary Kuhn	67	M	Ger.	Mar		old age
John B. McCoutt	31		Md	Sep		consumption
Margaret Allen	65	M	Md	Oct		consumption
Grace E.Wilson	1		Md	Oct		typhoid
Noah Gill	6mo		Md	Jun		water on brain
Avarilla Foster	1		Md	Aug		dysentary
Christina E. Gephart	42	W	Ger.	Feb		cancer
Edward Henkel	4		Md	Apr		scarlet fever
Martin Whilan	1		Md	Aug		typhoid
Mary Decker	6		Md	Aug		bill.dysentary
Theodore Decker	4		Md	Dec		typhoid
Eliza Mitlee	42		Md	Feb		consumption
Karman Gilmore	7mo		Md	Aug		teething
Walter D. Smith	6mo		Md	May		scarlet fever

MORTALITY SCHEDULE OF MARYLAND

persons who died during the year ending 1 June 18<u>50</u>

COUNTY Baltimore   DISTRICT 6th Ward Baltimore City

name	age	mar wid	birth place	mon. died	Occupation	cause of death
John Miller	1		Md	Jan		cataah.Fever
Nehemiah B. Shorey	52		Mass.	Jan	Hatter	lung congest.
Virginia Roundtree	5		Md	Jul		influ.D.
Mary J.Lanbrach	1mo		Md	Jul		summer compl.
William Lindsey	64		Md	Sep	shoemaker	pleurisy
Elizabeth Hull	17		Md	Aug		childbed
Sarah J. Macauby	3		Md	Jan		whooping cough
Bridget Murray	8mo		Md	Jul		heart disease
Nathaniel Kirby	50		Md	Jul	trader	paraletic
Elizabeth West	33		Va	Nov		spine disease
Eliza Watson	16		Md	Nov		consumption
James Grant	5mo		N.Y.	Nov		croup
Mary M.Prescott	10mo		Md	Jul		bowel compl.
Jacob P. Hare	57		Md	Feb	chairmaker	consumption
William H. Mobley	36		Md	Aug	carpenter	consumption
Julia Williamston	1wk		Md	Aug		summer compl.
Ulrich B. Stammin	55		Md	May	painter	consumption
7th Ward						
William Lineberger	56	M	Md	Mar	tinner	liver compl.
Sarah E.Mullen	3mo		Md	May		c.Fever
Charles M. Donilee	3		Md	Feb		c.fever
John Bond	90	W	at sea	Feb	tailor	old age
Louis Donaldson	2mo		Md	Jan		infantile
Conradt Grader	1		Md	Jan		dysentary
Louisa Bremford	2mo		Md	Mar		liver compl.
William H. Arloe	3		Md	Aug		disentary
Mary Tull	79	W	Md	Mar		old age
Josephine Epson	6		Md	Aug		b.fever
Emma Elliott	10		Md	Jul		S.Fever
Stephen Hyland	40		Md	Feb	carpenter	dropsey
Asbury Taylor	39		Md	Feb	blacksmith	consumption
Zacheria Taylor	2		Md	May		consump.
Alfred Blakeney	36		Md	Aug	carpenter	not known
Hannah Emmart	63		Md	Apr		consumption
Sarah T.Emmart	1		Md	Jul		S.Fever
Felix Wilson	39		Md	Nov	plasterer	absess
Lewis Thorn	34		Eng.	Dec	vetinary Surg.	consumption
Samuel Cuney?	72		Md	Dec	farmer	old age
Samuel Bradburn	55		Md	Apr	carpenter	earsylphilis
Alexander J.W.Jackson	4		Md	Jan		S.Fever
James W.Elliott	5		Md	Sep		disentary
Laura J. House	3		Md	Oct		S.Fever
Mary J.Saunders	11mo		Md	Jul		dysentary
John S. Lusby	1mo		Md	Mar		not known
Smith Carmine	41		Md	Mar	laborer	S.Fever
Mary Green	103		N. C.	Dec		old age
William Davidson	43		Md	Mar		B.Colic
Rouberta Riston	1		Md	Sep		consumption
James Murrey	30		Va	Oct		Scalded
George Weis	44		Md	Jan		bronchites

persons who died during the year ending 1 June 18<u>50</u>

COUNTY Balitmore   DISTRICT 7th Ward-City Baltimore

name	age	mar wid	birth place	mon. died	Occupation	cause of death
Charles Montgomery	1		Md	Aug		colic infan.
Adolphus Haywood	3mo		Md	Sep		whoop cough
Emeline Deets	6		Md	Jul		consumption
James Addams	28		Md	Oct	coachsmith	consumption
James M. Lednum	39	M	Md	Mar	blacksmith	F. Fever
Martha S.Phillips	1		Md	Jul		colia infan.
Emily E. Beam	11		Md	Sep		dysentary
Winfield S. Hobbs	2mo		Md	Apr		inflam.lungs
Henry Wineman	50	M	Md	Apr	nightman	mania
Catherine E.Wineholts	51	M	Ger	Nov		dysentary
Levis A. Levering	1		Md	Feb		s.fever
Sidney Freeman	45	M	Va	Jun		not known
Susanna Simpson	1		Md	Apr		c.fever
Nancy A. Ware	42	M	Ire.	Jan		pleurisy
James McTagart	64	W	Scot.	Feb	gardner	pleurisy
John J. Baninger	1		Md	Jun		head disease
Richard Watts	1		Md	Nov		head disease
James Gardner	49	M	Pa	May	cooper	neuralga
Sarah Hews	87	W	Del.	Jan		pleurisy
Joseph Schettler	38	M	Ger.	Feb	tailor	g.Fever
Constantine Ewing	65	M	Ger.	Dec	painter	old age
Sophia Ewing	46	W	Ger	Jan		disentary
Elizabeth Morrison	9mo		Md	Jul		disentary
Mary E.C. Bassett	6mo		Md	Jul		bowel inflam.
Robert Clark	37	M	Irel.	Nov	laborer	dio?
John T.W.Kimeridge	7mo		Md	Mar		water on brain
Mary E. Dogged	1		Md	Nov		bowel inflam.
Nicholas U.Waller	1		Md	Sep		b.Disentary
Alexena Burnett	20		Md	Jan		consumption
James A. Blake	2		Md	Jul		disentary
Adam Yogle	17		Ger.	Apr	none	dropsy
Elijah Lawrence	57		Md	Apr	carpenter	consumption
Smith Carmine	51		Md	Mar	painter	S.fever
Georgean Gregory	27	M	Md	Apr		child bed
Harrison C.Sweaney	8		Md	Nov		s.fever
George Masure	2		Md	Jan		S.fever
Alexander Gibson	5mo		Md	Dec		croup
Jacob Weir	33	M	Ger.	Mar	baker	B.Bluncy
Mary Miller	2		Md	Jan		worms on brain
John C. Myron	16		Md	Jan	confectioner	dysentary
Lawrence Hanley	7mo		Md	Jul		summer compl.
Eliza J.Garrett	1		Md	Dec		S.fever
Alexander Newell	2		Irel	Apr		disentary
Edward Foreman	72	M	Md	Aug	none	disentary
Rachel Hamman	75	W	Md	May		parelilick
Francis D.Gable	2		Md	Jan		disentary
Blessena Bunch	27	M	Md	Mar		consumption
Mary Wolfell	3mo		Md	Apr		disentary
Martha E.White	2mo		Md	Aug		not known
John Bbrisco	61	M	Md	Oct	shoemaker	consumption

persons who died during the year ending 1 June 18<u>50</u>

COUNTY Baltimore   DISTRICT 7th Ward-Baltimore City

name	age	mar wid	birth place	mon. died	Occupation	cause of death
Alexander Reynolds	5		Md	Mar		brain fever
Lucretia B.Cruse	2		Md	Jan		s.fever
Mary C.Espy	4		Md	Feb		heart disease
Elizabeth Montgomery	14		Md	Jul		disentary
Christopher Wright	27		Md	Oct	bookbinder	consumption
William Morrow	9mo		Md	Aug		s.fever
Charles Riely	21		Md	Oct	shoemaker	s.fever
Conradt Smouse	1mo		Md	Jun		not known
Dina Hoffman	1		Md	Apr		cold
Mary Williams	3mo		Md	May		cold
Alice Barrenger	5mo		Md	Dec		consumption
George K.Batchelor	11mo		Md	Mar		head compl.
William T. Lee	3		Md	May		s.pox
Mary Steinman	75	W	Pa	Sep		old age
Alrick B.Steinman	55	W	Md	May		consumption
Sarah E. Delcher	3		Md	Dec		s.fev.
William George	1		Md	Dec		s.fever
John T.Sherwood	25		Md	Sep	storekeeper	disentary
Charles Beal	2		Md	Jun		s.fever
John T. Leitch	1		Md	Dec		s.pox
John H. Welch	1		Md	Jul		lung inflam.
Mary Swaitz	1		Md	Mar		fitts
Walter P.Brooks	53		Va	Jun		suicide
David McClester	28		Md	Dec		consumption
Mary C.McClester	6mo		Md	Apr		dropsey
Patsey Cromwell	58		Md	Apr		bronchitis
Benjamin Townsen	16		Md	Feb		lung inflam.
John C. Kemble	6mo		Md	Aug		disentary
Welden R. Norris	1		Md	Dec		b.Fever
Henrietta Dorsey	6mo		Md	Jul		colia morbus
James Gardner	48		Md	May		s.fever
Ellen Bud	22		Md	Oct		child bed
Mary A. Darling	10mo		Md	Feb		s.pox
Susanna Badfield	64		Md	Aug		heart disease
Elena Stewart	5mo		Md	Jun		dropsey
John Crosby	16		Md	Jul		fitts
William Crosby	7		Md	Jul		disentary
William S. Wright	2		Md	Apr		S.fever
Agness M.Snyder	6		Md	May		s.fever
Lemuel D.Peircy	2		Md	Apr		s.fever
William G.Piercy	1		Md	Apr		s.fever
Patrick Mooney	64	w	Irel	Nov	laborer	b.fever
Francis Connelly	6mo		Md	Apr		brain inflam.
James Parish	1		Md	Aug		s.fever
William P.Wilson	6		Md	Dec		typhoid
Catherine McClanihan	1		Md	Nov		teething
Laurance Cunningham	32		Ire.	Dec	laborer	mania
John T.W. Eleese	22		Md	Sep	shoemaker	dis.from Mexico
Hugh Donovan	1		Md	Aug		measels
Samuel Weir	25		Ire.	Jul	laborer	s.fever
Henry Curvell	43		Md	Aug	carpenter	mania

MORTALITY SCHEDULE OF MARYLAND

persons who died during the year ending 1 June 18<u>50</u>

COUNTY Baltimore   DISTRICT 8th Ward-Balitmore City

name	age	mar wid	birth place	mon. died	Occupation	cause of death
Phoebe Daub	61		Eng.	May		paralitic
Margaret E.Meisman	2		Md	Aug		Disintary
Elijah Dilman	16		Md	Feb	clerk	S.Fever
Francis M. Mahon	32	M	Irel.	Aug	grocer	lung inflam.
Casper Wernic	64	M	Ger.	Jul	cabinet maker	consumption
Catherine Haubel	10mo		Md	May		croup
Mary A. Bowen	25		Md	May		consumption
Resena Keene	2		Md	Aug		whooping cough
Fadinan Hess	40	M	Ger.	Feb	Paver	cold
Joseph E.Wiseman	4		Md	Aug		gastric fever
Margaret E.Link	2		Md	Nov		heart compl.
William Renn	41	M	Eng.	Jul	larborer	diarea
Susan Brown	2		Md	Nov		heart disease
Mary Dellaha	10mo		Md	Nov		whooping cough
Margaret Peihner	2		Md	Feb		small pox
Phillip Peihner	1		Md	Apr		small pox
Mary Peihner	2mo		Md	Feb		small pox
Christian Snyder	63	M	Pa.	Jun		Janders?
James Can	47		Irel	Aug	dray man	consumption
Ranoldph Bishop	1		Md	Dec		croup
John J.Lightner	7mo		Md	Dec		fitts
Mary A. Page	2mo		Md	Jul		liver compl.
Ocelia Doutee	11mo		Md	Apr		C.fever
Sarah J.Scarf	2		Md	Oct		bowel inflam.
Catherine Ubryough	2		Md	Jun		consumption
Mary Ubryough	5		Md	Jun		not known
Jane A.Thompson	35	M	Md	Aug		diarea
Stephen Armiger	10mo		Md	Aug		not known
Ganney Geabert	2		Md	Sep		disentary
Ann McCullough	3		Md	Jan		small pox
William Root	56	M	Pa.	Dec	blacksmith	consumption
Catherine Fonsler	2		Md	Oct		consumpiton
Sarah Kelley	63	M	Ire.	Jan		not known
Louisa Wilkinson	38		Va.	Feb		consumption
Lewis Wright	11mo		Md	Aug		disentary
Joseph Bower	8mo		Md	Dec		small pox
Robert S. Rollins	1		Md	Aug		colia inflam.
Geney Devalin	7mo		Md	Apr		caltran
James Bracken	1		Md	May		disentary
Mary J.Crummer	37	M	Md	Mar		cancer
John Filter	8mo		Md	Dec		small pox
Edward Ketterick	22		Md	Dec	sailor	S.Fever
Ann E. Rodgers	2		Md	Aug		water on brain
Ann E. Leddey	16		Md	Apr		consumption
James Leddey	15		Md	Aug	printer	consumption
Mary O. Naley	49	W	Ire.	Apr		pleuricy
Mary A. Fleming	3		Md	Feb		consumption
Catherine Cluhen	1		Ire.	Sep		whooping cough
Frances Flanigan	1		Md	Feb		not known
James M. Bains	8		Va	Mar		brain inflam.

33

persons who died during the year ending 1 June 18_50_

COUNTY   Balitmore   DISTRICT   8th Ward, Baltimore City

name	age	mar wid	birth place	mon. died	Occupation	cause of death
Henry Keys	22		Ire.	Jan	carter	consumption
Timothy L.Richards	72	M	Md	Jan	coachmaker	appoplexy
Martha G.Bromley	28	M	Md	Aug		disentary
Samuel S.Mumford	9mo		Md	Jul		disentary
Cornelius Lambert	44	M	Md	Aug		kidney inflam.
Mary A. Roach	2mo		Md	Jan		croup
Oscar Thompson	1		Md	Mar		S.Fever
Robert Gilmore	3		Md	Aug		disentary
John G.Connelly	3mo		Md	Jan		lung inflam.
Ann A. Carragan	1		Md	Jul		summer compl.
Florida Mohiser	3		Md	Dec		S.Fever
Lehina Gordon	1		Md	Jul		summer compl.
Mary Sholt	5		Md	Jan		s.fever
Mary Tenant	73	W	Pa.	Jan		pareletic
Mary Massa	13		Md	Nov		heart disease
Figney Davis (fem)	52	W	Md	Aug		colia
John Davis	2		Md	Dec		fitts
Mary Schreimer	4		Md	Jul		bowel inflam.
Cecelia M. Donaugh	71	W	Ire.	May		heart disease
George Curlett	36	M	Md	May	blacksmith	drop.kidneys
Catherine Deffendale	58	W	Md	Feb		consumption
Sarah Green	63	W	Va.	Dec		consumption
Sebastian Michael	2		Md	Feb		burned
James Galiece	30	M	Ire.	Jun	ironFinisher	colia
Jeremiah Hopkins	30		Md	Sep	carpenter	disentary
Michael Duffey	42		Ire.	Oct	blacksmith	disentary
Salem Pegg	33		Va	Feb	clerk	consumption
Charles Banenger	25		Ger.	Aug	none	disentary
George Clark	21		Md	Jun	painter	consumption
John Reddish	50		Md	Sep	brassFounder	disentary
Henry Boeman	24		Ger.	Sep	drayman	disentary
Frederick Weigold	24		Ger.	Nov	butcher	disentary
Jacob Mayentice	23		Pa.	Oct	engraver	disentary
Henry Moyer	72		Ger.	Jul	coachsmith	consumption
Independence Forman(male)	1		Md	Jun		colia.inflam.
Margaret Phyfer	10		Md	Jul		b.fever
William A. Pruett	5		Md	Aug		water on brain
Charles W.Reede	48	M	N.J.	Sep		liver compl.
Michael Coray	10mo		Md	Oct		consumption
Lydia O.Murphy	8		Md	Oct		head compl.
Charles F.Cronhardt	11mo		Ger.	Aug		infant.colia.
Thomas Cole	71	M	Md	Aug	tanner	paraletic
Elizabeth Robinson	18	M	Md	Mar		S.Fever
Ann Kidd	5mo		Md	Mar		not known
Sarah M. Fay	54	M	Md	Aug		pareletic
Elizabeth Wilson	52	W	Md	Dec		brain parelis.
Louisa Curtis	6		Md	Nov		accident
James Mooney	7		Md	Apr		small pox
William T. Ballard	44	M	Md	Jan	shoemaker	lung inflam.
Sarah P.Davis	1mo		Md	Jun		not known

MORTALITY SCHEDULE OF MARYLAND

persons who died during the year ending 1 June 18<u>50</u>

COUNTY Baltimore   DISTRICT 8th Ward-Baltimore City

name	age	mar wid	birth place	mon. died	Occupation	cause of death
Charles Pentz	18		Md	Apr	butcher	bowel inflam.
Edward Wrixon	23		Pa.	Apr	painter	consumption
Henry Wright	9		Md	Jul		s.fever
Margaret Ryan	1		Md	Sep		not known
William S.Calloway	3		Md	Sep		colia.infan.
Agness V. Taylor	1		Pa	Sep.		colia.infan.
Mary A.Darting	10mo		Md	Feb		small pox
Elizabeth Torrance	35	M	unkn.	Jun	died in	brain infl.
Malinda King	55		unkn.	Jul	Md.Hospital	"
Andrew Coulter	54		Md	Jul	for Insane	"
Marilda Thompson	23	M	unkn.	Jul	"	"
John C. Cayor	48	M	Md	Aug	"	"
Caleb Clark	50	M	Md	Dec	"	"
Hugh L. Macken	25		Md	Dec	"	"
Warner Scott	28		Md	Dec	"	"
William Jenkins	51		Md	Jan	"	"
Thomas M. Callak	38		Irel.	Feb	"	"
William M.Cullen	45		Md	Mar	"	"
			9th Ward			
Richard M. Hall	69	M	Eng.	Mar	clerk	consumption
Henry W. Hall	1		Md	May		small pox
Ann Ridout	54	W	Md	Feb		heart disease
Charles Young	3		Md	Jan		small pox
Lysetta Burger	30	M	Ger.	Jun		childbed
Lysetta Burger	4		Md	Oct		unknown
Dorthea Berg	6		Md	Oct		Vanolora?
James Oldham	93	W	Md	Jul	saddler	dropsy
James Kelly	1		Md	Jun		head disease
Alexander Elliott	62	M	Ire.	Jul	whitsmith	dropsey
Christian Createe	1		Md	Jan		summer compl.
Alice McDonald	64	M	Irel.	Feb		areasyplis
Michael McDonald	28	M	Md	Nov	blacksmith	lung inflam.
Franklin Williams	3m		Md	Jun		small pox
Owen Reilly	55	M	Irel	Sep	laborer	typhoid
Abraham Wyburg	2		Md	Jun		brain fever
Mary J.Collier	11		Eng.	May		epylepsis
John H. Baist	45	M	Ger	Feb	cooper	bowel inflam.
Elizabeth Torrance	35	M	Irel	Jun		unknown
Samuel Allen	9m		Md	Sep		brain fever
Nathan Frank	2		Md	Jan		scarlet fever
Morris Cohen	1		Md	Jun		whooping cough
Alexander Jordan	19		Md	Apr	clerk	accident
Isaac S.George	6mo		Md	Jan		catar.fever
Nelson R.Stockdale	1		Md	Jun		catar.fever
Catharine E.Carroll	1m		Md	Jul		brain fever
Ludwig W. Gerlach	1		Md	Mar		scarlet fever
Emily Flaman	2		Md	Mar		catar.fever
Frances Flaman	8mo		Md	Mar		catar.fever
Mary Mathews	45	M	Ire.	Mar		womb disease
Julietta Smith (mul)	2		Md	Feb		lung disease
James Lutts	7		Md	Jun		drowned

35

persons who died during the year ending 1 June 18<u>50</u>

COUNTY Baltimore   DISTRICT 9th Ward-Baltimore City

name	age	mar wid	birth place	mon. died	Occupation	cause of death
Isaac G. Cutler	30	M	Mass.	Jun	physician	cholera
William Boyle	9mo		Md	Aug		brain fever
James F.Rossiter	6mo		Md	Jul		bowel inflam.
William Devinnay	87	W	Irel	Jul	bricklayer	old age
Henry Scholes	29	M	Ger	Mar	tavernkeeper	unknown
John Walker	1		Md	May		summer compl.
Mary A. Brigman	35	M	Ger.	Apr		dysentary
Frederic Brigman	15		Ger.	Mar	none	brain fever
Joseph O. Larrabee	5		Md	May		screfula
Hannah Larrabee	2		Md	May		shot
Francis X.Lafevre	1		Md	Sep		dysentary
Emma Ward	36	M	Eng.	Jan		heart disease
Catharine Moore	22		Ire.	Jul		ship fever
Elizaberh McCann	4		Md	Jun		brain fever
John Morton	54	M	Irel	Jun	hardware	cholera
Edwin Brooks	27		Md	Dec		consumption
James Cave	58		Md	Feb	none	paralysis
Susanna Mills	76	W	Md	Apr		old age
John Shiel	2		Ire.	Dec		bowel inflam.
James Shiel	1		Md	May		bowel inflam.
John Dacey	65	W	Ire.	Mar	shoemaker	old age
John Kelly	50	M	Irel.	Aug	huckster	dysentary
Ann E. Byrne	3mO		Md	Feb		erysipelas
James Duncan	49	M	Ire.	Jan	trader	lung inflam.
Edward Roberts	33	M	Md	Oct	clerk	consumption
Mary L.Roberts	3mO		Md	Nov		brain fever
Owen Jones	19		Md	Oct	cabinetmaker	consumption
William Wills	26		Md	Aug	carpenter	typhoid fever
William Gibson	70	W	Pa	Dec	tinner	sudden
Christian Duncan	62	M	Ger	Aug	paver	consumption
Lydia Thomas	3		France	Mar		croup
Robert Stanling	4		N.Y.	Oct		scarlet fever
Marcilla Stanling	3		N.Y.	Oct		scarlet fever
Charles Stanling	1		Md	Oct		scarlet fever
David Emmart	4		Md	Feb		hydrophia
George W.Emmart	4mo		Md	Feb		brain fever
Olin Westwood	2		Md	Jul		summer compl.
Henry Marshall	12		Md	Jan		small pox
George T.Bishop	25		Md	Feb	boot-fitter	consumption
Francis A. Brown	3		Md	Oct		scarlet fever
William B. Pyfer	32	M	Md	May	broker	typhoid
Anna M.B.Moody	42	M	Md	May		bowel congest.
Frances Jenkins	9mo		Md	Nov		spasms
James R. Williams Sr.	69	M	Md	Oct	dyer	rheumatism
Kate S.Jameson	4		Md	Apr		head disease
S.Shepard (male)	39	M	N.Y.	Apr	lotery broker	typhoid
Septimus Dorsey	32		Md	Mar	physician	paralysis
Ann Baynard	29		Del.	Jan	seamstress	unknown
Robert G.King	43	M	N.Y.	Oct	actor	consumption
Amanda V. Kirk	22		Md	Feb		consumption
Isabella Duncan	24		Md	Oct		unknown
E.D.Cliffe(fem)	30	M	Md	Dec		typhoid

36

name	age	mar wid	birth place	mon. died	Occupation	cause of death
Rebecca Lindenberger	72	W	Md	Feb		inflam.fever
Ann Emory	76	W	Md	Feb		inflam.fever
Emeline Riley	1		Md	Dec		spasms
Joseph Hyland	1		Md	Oct		typhoid
James Mitchell	76	M	Md	Jun49	Hack Prop.	congest.lung
Virginia Curthrell	48	W	Va	Apr		bilious
Eleanor Clarke	104	W	Ire.	May		old age
Grace Jones	73	W	Eng	Mar		paralysis
Archibald P.Cook	1		Md	Sep		infantile
Floyd Shipley	30		Md	Dec	stable keep.	typhoid
Charles Hill	2		Md	Aug		summer compl.
Martha Harrod	38		Md	Aug		heart disease
Joseph Brown	41	M	Md	Oct	shoemaker	dropsy
Evelyn S.Vigurs	3		Cuba	Jun49		bowel inflam.
Almaide Larogue	19		Md	Jun49		typhus
Francis Ravigneaux	69	M	France	May	none	bowel inflam.
Charlotte Acker	5		Md	Nov		scarlet fever
Lawrence Rait	42	M	Irel	Mar	laborer	impost liver
Susan McGrath	62	W	Irel	Jun49		typhoid
George B. Morrison	4		Md	May		croup
Esther Brown	58	W	Md	Oct		heart
Susan Webster	2mo		Md	Mar		dropsy
Mary A. Fisher	47		Md	Jan		consumption
Susannah Fisher	5		Md	Feb		heart
Caroline E. Redwood	8mo		Md	Mar		catarrh
John Winder	8mo		Md	Jun49		teething
Andrew Meretti	12		Pa.	Aug		drowned
Christopher Hughes	67	W	Md	Sep	none	dropsy
Elisa Perkins	44		Mass	Feb		catarrh
Frederick Bredimeyer	50	M	Ger.	Jan	merchant	apoplexy
Thomas Cape	1mo		Md	Aug		summer comp.
Jos.Henry Cornish	11mo		Md	Jan		accident
Rachel Heidi	78	W	Md	Nov		lung inflam.
Henry M.Hurst	1		Md	Mar		neuralgia
Frances A.McLaughlin	49	M	Pa.	Dec		pulmonary
William C. Bowin	1		Md	Sep		croup
			10th Ward			
Eleanor Scott	33		Md	Jan	hat trimmer	dropsy
Jeremiah Burke	18		Ire.	May	cooper	erysipelias
Mary Catherine Duterly	10		Md	Feb		gastric fever
Amelia Mulhoffer	9		Md	May		spasms
Peter Francis Reidasil	6wk		Md	Jul		bowel consump.
Elizabeth Williamson	65	W	Ire.	Aug		dysentary
Jacob Waldsmith	8mo		Md	May		consumption
Henrietta E. Maclea	5		Md	Jul		croup
Thomas O'Brien	20		Irel.	Jul	laborer	cholera
Emile Volkman	1		Md	Dec		cutting teeth
Frances Collins	32	M	Irel.	Jan		puerperal
Eliza Wierterwitz	3		Ger.	Aug		croup
Isidore Kann	11		Md	Aug		infl.bowel
Elisa Ehlers	1		Md	Sep		unknown

persons who died during the year ending 1 June 1850

COUNTY Baltimore   DISTRICT 10th Ward Baltimore City

name	age	mar wid	birth place	mon. died	Occupation	cause of death
Samuel Brady	1		Md	Mar		teething
Amanda Tiralda	19d.		Md	Oct		heart disease
John Moekel	3d.		Md	Jan		fits
George Rosemer	1		Md	May		chicken pox
Thomas Hanbury	9mo		N.Y.	Jan		teething
Simon Wolf	1		Ger.	Feb		measles
Andrew Laing	11mo		Md	Jan		teething
Catherine Wierman	43	M	France	May		childbirth
Boniface Wierman	8d.		Md	May		D.
Margaret Rosendale	25	M	Ger.	Jun		childbirth
Henry Rosendale	10d.		Md	Jul		D.
Catherine P.Innis	1		Md	Sep		croup
Laura Emma Hughes	2		Md	Dec		whooping c.
Louis H. Gouley	59	M	France	Oct	BittersManuf.	sore throat
Charles Gouley	5		Md	Sep		emphagena
Anna M. Ridgely	36	M	Md	Apr		consumption
Mary A. Kidd	15		Md	Aug		consumption
			11th Ward			
Susan Smith(black)	7		Md	Mar		W.Cons.
Z.Taylor Blakely	5mo		Md	Jul		unknown
George Rhoads	44	M	Eng	Feb	C.F.Spinner	consumption
William Stine	29		Md	Sep		N.Fever
William F. Murdock	18		Md	Oct	clerk	not named
Margaret Hennick	60		Md	Jan		kidney dis.
Hester Watson	87	W	Pa.	Dec		dropsey
Mary A. Bromwill	36	M	Md	Feb		consumption
R.H.C.Bromwell(male)	9mo		Md	Feb		lungs
Rebecca Grant	72	W	Md·	Jan		consumption
Jane Hackitt	88	W	Md	Jan		old age
Mary J. Elder	3		Md	Jul		catarah
Rebecca Hayward	70	W	Md	Sep		dysentary
Henry Keighler	1		Md	Jun		W.cough
Richard Doyle	24		Md	Aug	merchant	dysentary
James Grady	38		Ire.	Oct	tailor	consumption
Wm. G. Clickman	1		Pa.	Sep		teething
Annie Nelson	12		Md	Oct		brain
J.C.Hoffman(male)	32		Md	Sep	merchant	consumption
Mary Gorman	7mo		Md	Jul		teething
Edward Benner	18		Md	Mar	carter	killed
Joseph Benner	15		Md	Dec		heart disease
Mary Creig	42	M	Ire.	Apr		dropsy
Samuel Short	9mo		Md	Jul		water on brain
Mary J. Banon	6mo		Md	May		disentary
Henry Porter	24		Md	Jan	carter	consumption
Lewis C.Hitchcock	1		Md	Jul		consumption
Hugh Boyd Scott	1d		Md	May		injuries
Wilson Hall	39	M	Md	Apr	laborer	injuries job.
John F.Wood	11		Md	Jun		scarlet fever
Anna Rosmoore	11mo		Md	Mar		chicken pox
Samuel Hays	23		Md	Aug	clerk	consumption

persons who died during the year ending 1 June 18<u>50</u>

COUNTY Baltimore   DISTRICT   11th Ward, Baltimore City

name	age	mar wid	birth place	mon. died	Occupation	cause of death
William Turnbull	11mo		Md	Aug		Scarlet fever
Owen Donelly	55	M	Ire.	Aug	grocer	unknown
John Gray	14d		Md	Jan		brain
Mary A. Donnelly	77	M	Eng.	May		old age
John McInhammer	8mo		Md	Jul		cholera inf.
George Spary	31	M	Eng	Aug	stoneCutter	heart
Dennis Reilly	30	M	Ire	Apr	grocer	consumption
Augustas Buck	4mO		Md	Jul		brain
Henry Wicall	7mo		Md	Apr		fits
Maria E.Whippel	5mo		Md	Jun		unknown
Edward Cockey	27		Md	Jul	clerk	d.ofHeart
Ann R. Reaner	5		Md	Feb		pleurisy
Isabella Reaner	7mo		Md	Feb		croup
Cristor Hartzog	43	M	Ger.	Jan	cabinetMaker	consumption
Nelson Scarf	24		Md	Jan	plasterer	typhoid fever
Cornelius G.Williams	2		Md	Jul		typhoid fever
C.Alfred Hush	7mo		Md	Jul		typhoid fever
George Peters	81	W	Pa	Mar	bricklayer	consumption
Elisha McConicken?	32	M	Md	Mar	tailor	eresipilus
Margaret Denk	3mo		Md	Oct		unknown
Andrew Hinkleman	4mo		Md	Nov		croup
Harriet Wright	25	M	Md	Feb		childbed
George Kolb	75	M	Md	Apr	butcher	kidneys
Jane Ennis	53	M	Irel.	May		typhoid
Sarah E. Winters	2		Md	May		dysentary
Henry Paterson	36		Md	May	grover	consumption
George P. Keirle	18		Md	Jan	tinner	cranh.
Emma Keirle	8		Md	Aug		brain
Eliza J. Brown	1		Md	Feb		head dis.
James A. Crouch	21		Md	Mar	teacher	apoplexy
Elizabeth G. Sutton	15		Md	Sep		typhoid
Bridget Radicey	10mo		Md	Aug		dysentary
John Radicey	2		Md	Aug		Wen.brain
Patrick Radicey	7mo		Md	Dec		croup
John Volker	4		Md	Jun		scarlet fever
Henry P.Cavenaugh	18		Irel.	Oct	Baker	unknown
Maria A.Cavenaugh	15		Irel.	Nov		decline
Martha Chister	8mo		Md	Jan		catarah
Thomas Wheeler	9mo		Md	Aug		dysentary
Elizabeth Ningerth	3		Md	Jun		measles
Harman Ningerth	2		Md	Jun		measles
Hugh Hergan	1		Md	May		croup
Margaret Hergan	2		Md	Jun		cysentary
Edward McColigan	6		Md	Oct		brain
Mary A. Jenkins	16		Md	Sep		heart dis.
Mary E. Burton	2		Md	Dec		brain
Ann Daley	5mo		Md	Oct		unkno wn
Lawrence W. Curlett	3		Md	Mar		scarlet fever
Mrs.T.King Carroll	46	M	Md	Jul		rheumatism
Ellen Nickell	11mo		Md	Nov		dysentary
Margaret Kenrick	60		Md	Jan		kidney

MORTALITY SCHEDULE OF MARYLAND

persons who died during the year ending 1 June 1850

COUNTY Baltimore   DISTRICT 11th Ward, Baltimore City

name	age	mar wid	birth place	mon. died	Occupation	cause of death
Eugene McColough	4mo		Md	Nov		lever compl.
Eliza Gramay	19		Md	Oct		dropsey
ElizabethMyers	10mo		Md	Apr		water onbrain
Arlinger Wittlig(male)	1		Md	May		consumption
Joseph Steinmaker	6mo		Md	Aug		dysentary
William Mitchell	37	M	Irel.	Dec	stonecutter	lung inflam.
James Cunningham	53	M	Irel	Mar		consumption
Eliza J.Mitchell	9		Md	Mar		Wen Brain
Catherine Myers	8		Md	Aug		liver compl.
Mary Speak	62	W	Md	Sep		bowel inflam.
Charles Conrad	1		Md	Feb		dysentary
Philis Ireland	4		Md	Feb		burnt
Darcus Joyce	95	W	Md	Feb		old age
Edward Ensey	20		Md	Feb	taboconist	consumption
Josephine Brady	2		Md	Sep		lungs
Francis Harwood	13		Md	Dec		scarlet fever
James D. Mallone	41		Irel	Dec	tailor	kidneys
Rachel Carr	29		Md	Apr		consumption
Lewis Barney	68	M	Pa	Apr	merchant	consumption
Mary McCanner	40		Irel.	May		sudden
John A. Conkling	49	M	Conn	Sep	seaCaptain	dysentary
Elizabeth L.Conkling	7		Md	Aug		dysentary
Charles Calvin	1		Md	Nov		brain inflam.
Jeanette Harrison	30	M	Md	Jun		consumption
Mary C.Harrison	4mo		Md	May		heart
Eliza Cristy	60		Md	Mar		diariah
George Luigerman	2		Md	Jul		w.brain
Sarah Parsons	87	W	Md	Dec		old age
Samuel Hamilton	14		Md	Sep		brain fever
Anna Hamilton	10		Md	Sep		brain fever
Mary C.Hamilton	1		Md	Jul		Wh.cough
Thomas Carr	4mo		Md	Jan		injuries
Margaret Bradinward	1mo		Md	Jul		unknown
Frederick Ballard	10mo		Md	Aug		head
Robert R. Pitts	1		Md	Feb		gastric fever
George E. Weaver	42	M	Md	Jul		liver disease
Edward Brown	28	W	Md	Aug	stonecutter	heart disease
Charles Duncan	42	M	Md	Jul	engineer	killed
John L. Duncan	2		Md	Apr		c.brain
Louise Medenger	18	W	Md	Feb		consumption
George W. Stallings	2		Md	Jan		scarlet fever
Mary E. Wilcox	14		Md	Sep		dysentary
Isaac Scarf	1		Md	Aug		dysentary
Daniel Sullivan	25	W	Irel.	May	laborer	dropsey
Edward M. Evans	3mo		Md	Dec		liver
Mary Hughes	9		Md	Jan		scarlet fever
F.F.Buckmiller	5mo		Md	Jan		fits
George W. Osler	4mo		Pa.	Jun		eresipelas
Elnora Weber	58	W	Ger.	Jan		Oebelitz

MORTALITY SCHEDULE OF MARYLAND

persons who died during the year ending 1 June 18<u>50</u>

COUNTY Baltimore   DISTRICT 12thWard,Baltimore City

name	age	mar wid	birth place	mon. died	Occupation	cause of death
John Smith	50	M	Md	Jul	stonemason	intest.fever
Ciline Moreun? (fem)	64		WestInd.	Nov		complic.
Mary Wins	4mo		Md	Aug		heart inflam.
Henry Siegel	2		Md	Feb		heart inflam.
Louisa Preston	64	W	Md	Apr		pneumonia
Charles Rogge	3mo		Md	Jul		Chola.infant.
Alex.Ferguson	29	M	Scot.	Jan	saddler	consumption
David Jones	52		Va	Feb	teacher	gastric fever
Charles Young	1mo		Md	Jun		sickness
Frederick Young	1mo		Md	Jun		sickness
Peter Macklet	51	M	Ger	Oct	shoemaker	consumption
William Binke	4		Md	Feb		scarlet fever
John F. Konig	53	M	Germ.	Mar	baker	unknown
John Higham	52	M	Eng	May	stonecutter	ereyseplus
John Pinniman?	31	M	Mass	Feb	paintor	lung inflam.
Sarah Dorsey	64	M	Md	Apr		consumption
Victoria Miller	10mo		Md	May		catarah.fever
Clinton Shipley	1		Md	Dec		lung inflam.
Jane McKinnie	83	W	Irel	Feb		Paralysis
Mary A. Bennyer?	20		Md	Jun		conges.brain
Sarah Wynick	32	M	Md	Jul		b. broken
Eliz.Stiles	6mo		Md	Jul		teething
Rebecah. McIntosh	27	M	Md	Jan		diareah
Eliz Weidner	33	M	Ger	Feb		small pox
Philis Frank	8mo		Md	Jun		chola.infan.
Fanny Sewell	5		Md	Feb		catar.Fever
Sarah McConnell	2		Md	Mar		scarlet fever
William Thompson	31	M	Scot.	Jul	saddler	consumption
Henrietta Thompson	29	W	D.C.	Jul		insane
Charles Steigers	58	M	Md	May	carpenter	consumption
H.L.Shockley(male)	9		Md	May		heart disease
Edward Newton	14		Md	May		typhoid
Samu el Smith	3		Md	Jun		scarlet fever
Susan Thomas	26	M	Md	Jul		dysentary
Henry Stansbury	1mo		Md	Jul		eursypilus
Mary Seipp	36		Md	May		heart disease
Frederick K.Price	6		Md	Aug		hoop.cough
Ellen Ireland	42	M	Pa	May		Sum. compl.
Anne Clifford	8mo		Md	Jun		liver
Josephine Rogers	6		Md	May		gastric fever
Elizabeth Gilpin	42	M	Md	May		child bed
Andrew Rogers	4		Md	Aug		dysentary
Margaret Elder	75		Md	May		brain fever
Margaret McGinn	68	M	Irel.	May		diareah
John Berryman	54		Md	May	clerk	pleurisy
Margaret Chambers	16		Md	Jun		lungs
Julia White	2		Md	Jul		dysentary
Lorenz Hoffman	58	M	Ger.	Jun	carpenter	consumption
John Chaisly?	68	M	Irel	Oct	none	oleum.
Elizabeth Alsford	64	W	Pa	Nov		dropsey
Celia Eberhart	2		Md	Jan		measles

41

MORTALITY SCHEDULE OF MARYLAND

persons who died during the year ending 1 June 1850

COUNTY Baltimore   DISTRICT 12th Ward, Baltimore City

name	age	mar wid	birth place	mon. died	Occupation	cause of death
Mary King	5mo		Md	Jul		chol.infan.
A.Brickamp(male)	37	M	Ger	Apr	cooper	ship fever
Mary Massey	8		Md	Feb		lung congs.
Ophelia Lowe	1		Md	Aug		sum.compl.
Joseph Richardson	3		Md	Nov		scarlet fever
George Norris	16		Md	May		consumption
Maria Blackburn	1		Md	Jan		lung inflam.
Sufaia McLaughton	4mo		Md	May		catarrah
Letitia McIntire	16		Md	Jun		Typhoid
Nicky Gassoway	22		Md	Jan	carpenter	lockjaw
Nicholas Gott?	66	W	Md	Apr	carpenter	consumption
Samuel Aguin	19		Md	Aug	clerk	dysentary
Helen Stanley	11		Md	Jul		dysentary
Bridgit Manning	18		Md	Oct		consumption
E.C.Ward (fem)	50	W	Md	Feb	(page dif-	consumptio n
Eliza Mariner	50	W	Ire.	Nov	ficult to	consumption
Emeline Juniss?	32	M	Md	May	read)	consumption
Frank Juniss	14		Md	Jul		consumption
William L.Steinmetz	56	M	Md	Feb	merchant	typhoid
L.Blaisdell(male)	90	W	Ire.	Oct		old age
Maria Sillig	63	W	Md	Jun		lung congest.
Isaac Baine	36	M	Md	Jul	clerk	gastric fever
Elmira Perkins	51	W	Pa	May		lung hemmor.
Julia Taylor	6		Md	Nov		B.fever
Edward Bradley	1		Md	Nov		dysentary
Mary E. Conolley	5		Md	Sep		lung conges.
Lorraine Miller	1		Md	Nov		water on brain
Frederick Kelton	1		Md	Nov		scarlet fever
Albert Elphamy	11mo		Md	Jul		chol.infant.
Margaret Gilks	36	W	Md	Mar		consumption
Owen Bouldin	40	w	Irel.	Jul	wheelright	sudden
Anne King	3		Md	Jun		typhoied
Margaret Gillespie	6mo		Md	Jun		thrush
Merrieba Cook	39	M	Md	Nov		consumption
John Francis	2		Md	Mar		stomach inflam.
James W. Brunlige	6		Md	Aug		dysentary
John Scott	76	W	Irel.	Aug		palsy
Ellinor Lynch	4		Md	May		lung inflam.
Alex.Brickamp	1		Md	Jul		consumption
William N. Blake	13		Md	Jul		drowned
			13th Ward			
David Schroeder	66	W	Ger.	Nov	shoemaker	asthma
Jacob Rimby	28	M	N.J.	Dec	moulder	consumption
Emma Rimby	9mo		Md	Mar		croup
John R. Pottinger	56		Md	Feb		heart disease
Henry Hett	1		Md	Jul		congesttion
Ann Moore	73	W	Md	May		erisipilas
Daniel Egan	39	W	Md	Sep	cabinetmaker	consumption
John Ewing	9mo		Md	Mar		teething
Mary E. Bird	26	M	Md	May		childbed
Alfred B.Cannon	5mo		Md	Jun		water on brain
John D.M.Cannon	19		Md	Jan	none	typhoid

42

persons who died during the year ending 1 June 18_50_

COUNTY Baltimore   DISTRICT 13th Ward, Baltimore City

name	age	mar wid	birth place	mon. died	Occupation	cause of death
John Young	3mo		Md	Jul		brain fever
Solloman Brittingham	49	M	Md	Feb	seaman	consumption
Ruben Sturgis	53	M	Md	Oct	shoemaker	consumption
Oliva Sturgis	19		Md	Nov		consumption
Emily Louisa Marcellas	18		Md	Jan		consumption
John G. Morris	3		Md	Jul		croup
Alphonse Brunn	8mo		Md	July		brain fever
Francis Brunn	8mo		Md	Jun		brain fever
John Mencken	64	W	Md	Jul	carpenter	consumption
John Hahn	62	W	Eng	Mar	none	unknown
Rebecca Davis	18		Va.	Oct		typhoid
Charlotte Sherwood	3		Irel.	Apr		gastric fever
David Tottle	2		Md	Aug		whooping cough
Mary Tottle	10mo		Md	Sep		whooping cough
Nathaniel Mitchior	26	M	Ger.	Nov	grinder	accident
Hellen Firchs	66		Ger	Dec		heart diseast
John E. Gross	7mo		Md	Mar		summer compl.
Catharine McGinnis	32		Md	May		consumption
Joseph Graber	36	M	Ger	Aug	larorer	unknown
Peter A. Keller	11mo		Md	May		fits
Hugh Kennedy	78		Irel	Sep	blacksmith	dropsey
Ann M.C.Ream	21		Md	unkn		unknown
Mary Chance	1		Md	Jun		chol.infant.
George A. Stamp	64	M	Md	Mar	clerk	heart disease
John T. Walker	60	M	Md	Jul	clothier	heart disease
John Cripner	43		Md	unkn.	porter	typhoid
Lewis Cole	36	M	Md	Sep	blacksmith	jaundice
Elizabeth Whitridge	2		Md	Apr		cat.fever
Fanny A.T.Mackall	1		Md	Apr		brain disease
Daniel Chalmers	79	W	Md	Jun		old age
Mary Robertson	77	M	N.J.	Jan		old age
Frederick C. Dannenberg	48	M	atSea	Mar	GermanFancy store	apoplexy
Albert L.Webb	11mo		Md	May		brain congest.
Jacob Eichhorn	24		Ger.	Nov	cooper	Agu.fever
Darius White	38		Md	Jul	shoemaker	heart dis.
Ellen Ford	45		Md	Mar		pneumonia
Samuel Warden	5mo		Md	Dec		catar.fever
Johanna Oliver	18		Md	Jul		spine disease
James R.Kurtz	1		Md	Feb		dysentary
Joseph M.Switzer	8mo		Md	May		catar.fever
Dorothy Woodward	41	M	Md	Nov		consumption
Francis Dorsey	43	M	Irel	Mar	marblepolisher	unknown
George Knoll	32	M	Ger	May	engraver	heart disease
Ema E. Thomas	75	W	Prussia	Jul		old age
Helen V. Beahan	1		Md	Mar		hepatitis
Christopher Boyer	29	M	Irel	Aug	porter	consumption
Rebecca Han	68	W	Md	Mar		hepatitis
Benjamin R. Buckley	7		Md	Apr		brain inflam.
Dinah Swallenberry	56	W	Ger	Feb		Tinck?
Elizabeth Watts	53		Md	Mar		lungs
Catherine M.Strobel	2		Md	Apr		lung inflam.

MORTALITY SCHEDULE OF MARYLAND

persons who died during the year ending 1 June 18 50

COUNTY Baltimore   DISTRICT 13th Dist. Baltimore City

name	age	mar wid	birth place	mon. died	Occupation	cause of death
Ann Hulbert	42	M	Md	Nov		consumption
Joseph Hulbert	1		Md	Dec		brain inflam.
James McDevott	40	M	Irel	Dec	tavernKeep.	brain fever
Alexander R.Findlay	8mo		Md	Sep		dysentary
Sally Pearson	1mo		Md	Feb		catarah
Emma Z.Webster	8mo		Md	Jun		chola.infan.
Mary E. Webster	14		Va	Oct		typhoid
Richard Elliss	62	M	Md	Mar	farmer	pleurisy
William Adams	74	M	Md	Dec	farmer	typhoid
Eugene Gill	7		Md	Mar		pneumonia
Mary Ruff	32	M	Md	Dec		congest.fever
Charles Baltzell	63	W	Md	May	drygoodStore	nervous
George L. Addison	37	M	Md	Aug	carpenter	consumption
Mary Ann Condon	4mO		Md	Mar		water on brain
Emily T.Meredith	1		Md	May		water on brain
Janus R. Leehe	19		Md	May	none	consumption
Mana L.Shriver	29	M	Md	May		childbed
Mary Ann Bowen	2		Md	Nov		complication
Washington Reid	33	M	N.Y.	Feb	U.S.Navy	Bilious fever
14th E. Dist.Ward						
Mark Butler	48		Irel.	none	laborer	typhoid
Mike Fahy	20		Irel.	"	laborer	typhoid
Isaac Cox	35		Md			typhoid
Catherine Rusenberger	40		Ger	"		dysentary
Margaret Dednick	36		Ger.			consumption
Hugh McGee	50		Irel			manna Port.
Cathanne McGuick	36		Irel			bronchitis
Waller Belle	30		Md			consumption
Margaret Barrett	40		Irel.		remittant	fever
Edward Bamall	-		none			dysentary
Rosa Rosenberg	-		Ger.			none
Mike McElroy	-		Ger.			remitt.fever
Ellen Brady	-		Irel			typhoid
Esel Bramberger	-		none			dysentary
George Neston						dysentary
Mary Ann Cole	26		Baltimore	(	from Butler	heart
Owin Riley					all persons	typhus
Dan Egon				died at the		manus Port.
Owen Syms	30		Irel.	Baltimore		syphilus
George Snyder	35		Ger	infirmary -to		typhoid
Mr. Finn	30		Irel.	bottom of page)		typhoid
C.Frazier	40					remitt.fever
Patrick Donohue	32		Irel			pneumonia
Mrs. Hetritt	45		Ger.			dropsy
Catharine Gleeson	26		Irel			typhoid
Thomas Cauley	50		Irel		laborer	consumption
Patrick Kennedy	46		Irel			pleuirsy
Mrs. Cunningham	40		Irel			pneumonia
Mrs. Adreson	38		Md			consumption
Mary Faskey	38		Irel.			bronchitis
John Sangnor	56		Irel		laborer	heart
14th Ward						
			44			

persons who died during the year ending 1 June 18_50_

COUNTY Baltimore   DISTRICT 14th Ward-Baltimore City

name	age	mar wid	birth place	mon. died	Occupation	cause of death
Catharine Simpson	26	M	Irel.	Nov		unknown
Margaret Simpson	1		Md	Jul		consumption
Francis M. Ginn	4		Md	Apr		scarlet fever
John T. Ginn	4		Md	Jul		scarlet fever
Francis M. Green	8		Md	Apr		droplsey
George Carson	84	W	Pa	Aug	blacksmith	paralysis
Thomas Atkins	69	M	Md	Sep	shoemaker	consumption
Mary Ann Gates	6mo		Md	Aug		dysentary
Samuel H. Gates	20		Md	Sep	clerk	yellow fever
J.Pinto(fem)	1		Md	Aug		not named
Charles John Hart	56	M	Eng.	Feb	merchant	" "
John Gwinn	2		Md	Feb		croup
William Mitchell	35	M	Irel.	Dec	stonecutter	consumption
Henry Baker	28		Md	Aug	glasscutter	consumption
Christian Hinton	24	W	Germ.	Apr		none
Rebecca Maginder	39	m	Md	Mar		lungs
Julius T.Ducatel	54	M	Md	Apr	physician	none
Elizabeth Daws	50	M	N.J.	Nov		consumption
Barbara E. Monte	14		Md	Apr		none
Dillwyn P. Graham	14		Md	Jun		dysentary
George Birch	35	M	Md	Jun	shoemaker	consumption
John A. Dwyer	15		Md	Feb		gastric fever
Nicholas D. Forks	6		Md	Apr		accident
Alice Bertha Cainer	3		N.Y.	Apr		consumption
Franklin Sherttze	5mo		Md	Feb		catarrh
John Thomas Penley	3		Md	Oct		scarlet fever
Matilda Elmo	4mo		Md	Jun		consumption
George Derr	42		Germ.	Nov	tailor	dropsey
Rachael Metzell	22		Md	Dec		scarlet fever
William Metzele	1		Md	Dec		scarlet fever
Perry Anderson	9mo		Md	Jul		none
Laura b. Hayman	4		Md	Feb		none
William Hayman	6		Md	Oct		summer compl.
Thomas H.G.Wharten	5		Md	Mar		none
Charles A. Deminger	45		Md	Jan	bookbinder	heart
Catherine S. Munch	8mo		Md	Sep		fits
Mary Munch	9mo		Md	Feb		catarrh
M.M.Chambers(fem)	1		Md	Aug		none
Wm.Taylor	1		Md	Mar		none
Jane C. Sweeney	14		Md	Sep		dropsy
Epps Ellery	69		Mass	Jul	Jeweller	cholora
Robert Callen	11		Md	May		dropsy
Julius Goldsbon	25		Md	Nov	merchant	typhoid
Eugene Goldsbon	11mo		Md	Jul		cholera
Elizabeth Geddess	3mo		Md	Aug		thrush
Sarah L. Griffith	3da.		Md	Mar		none
James P.Small	11mo		Md	Oct		dysentary
Frank Medlart	2mo		Md	Oct		bowel conges.
Mana Lee	50		Md	May		c.rheumatism
Benjamin F. Hamilton	6		Md	Feb		typhoid

persons who died during the year ending 1 June 18<u>50</u>

COUNTY Baltimore   DISTRICT 14th Ward, Baltimore City

name	age	mar wid	birth place	mon. died	Occupation	cause of death
Isiah Gordon	15		Md	Dec		sonsumption
Mary T. Honan	2		Md	Aug		dysentary
Henry Melchon	44		Ger.	Feb	cabinetmaker	dyropsy
Charles Will	18		Md	Jun		consumption
Mary A. Javen	33		Md	Oct		dropsey
Biddy Curley	9		Irel.	Dec		collic
Margaret Caffey	--		Md	Aug		convulsion
William O'Brien	48		none	Feb	labouer	consumption
Hennrietta Effeline	2mo		Md	Feb		none
Susannah Effeline	4mo		Md	Feb		none
Laura D. Hartzell	10mo		Md	Oct		scarlet fever
James Marshall	32		Md	Apr	shoemaker	consumption
Easter Smith	38		Md	Dec		child bed
Hester Smith	5		Md	May		teething
Charles A. Mettee	64	W	Ger.	Mar	blacksmith	consumption
John Madena	3		Baltim.	Feb		thrush
Emily D. Carter	33		Md	Sep		typhoid
Amanda Clifton	2da		Md	Jan		typhoid
RochsAnna Dorsey	44		Md	Apr		lung congest.
John Page Dutton	3		Md	May		scarlet fever
Mana Ryan	34		Va.	May		consumption
Phillip Henry Ryan	6		Md	Oct		consumption
Kate Stine	3		Md	Mar		typhoid
Barbara Stant	49	M	Ger.	Jul		none
William M.Fuller	4mo		Md	Jun		bowel inflam.
Isabella Rieman	20		Md	Jun		gastric fever
Daniel McCauly	64	M	Md	Jul	cooper	appolplexy
Louisa Forney	74	W	Pa	Nov		dropsey
Deborah Kemper	59	W	Md	Feb		heart
Emma Ball	5mo		Md	Feb		catarrh
Ann E. McIntosh	2mo		Md	Jul		catarrh
Charles B. M. Hook	14		Md	Jul		brain
Margaret Wallace	64	W	Pa.	Feb		typhoid
Margaret Gounce	40	W	Pa	Mar		consumption
Joseph Burns	17		Md	Mar		none
Mary C. McGlennan	3		Md	Jun		scarlet fever
Fredericha Willithan	67		Ger.	Apr		typhoid
Thomas Inloes	31		Md	none		none
Rosina M. Cauley	1		Md	May		accident
Sarah Nicholson	1		Md	May		lungs
Emma Risa Reiss	2		Md	May		brain congest.
William Cox	22		Md	none	laborer	pneumonia
James Kelly	39		Ire.	none	confectioneer	cancer
George DeCoursey	40		Ire.	none	tailor	pneumonia
Alexander Smith	36		Md	none	coachman	mania Aort.
George Langhley	40		Ire.	none	laborer	remitt.fever
Casin Cox (male)	24		Md	none	laborer	brain congest.
Jerry Burke	19		Ire.	none	cooper	erysipulus
Robert Tenison	none		Ire.	none	sailor	consumption
Samuel Baker	none		Md	none	sailor	remitt.fever
Bennett Lader	50		Md	none	sailor	dropsey

46

MORTALITY SCHEDULE OF MARYLAND

persons who died during the year ending 1 June 1850

COUNTY Baltimore   DISTRICT 14th Ward-Baltimore City
                                                           15th Ward

name	age	mar wid	birth place	mon. died	Occupation	cause of death
Samuel Fountain	36		Md	none	sailor	consumption
Matthew Anderson	--		Sweden	none	sailor	diarrhea
S.Hughes (male)	34		Md	none	sailor	dropsy
J.F.Millar	48		Ger.	none	sailor	diarrhea
William McGuire	25		Md	none	sailor	erysipulus
			15th Ward			
Mary A. Martin	3da		Md	May		unknown
John Brice	80	W	Md	Jan	none	old age
Isabella Kyle	30		Md	Jun		typhoid
Martha Adams	15		Va	unkn.		small pox
Elizabeth Marfield	78	W	Ger.	Oct		paralytic
Lawrence Furlong	34	M	Mass.	Jul	auctioneer	cholora
Emma O. Weems	8mo		Md	Aug		brain inflam.
Ellen V. Fales	1		Md	Jan		brain fever
William Dobbins	73	M	N.J.	Sep	carpenter	unknown
Richard L.Wallace	10		Md	Aug		dysentary
Elizabeth Travers	60	M	Md	Aug		complicated
Elizabeth Riggin	40		Md	Apr		breast inflam.
Ernest H. Meyer	36	M	Ger.	Aug	grocer	typhoid
John Reynolds	42		Ire.	May	painter	unknown
Margaret A. Brady	2		Md	Jun		spasms
Isabel Everet	1		Md	Aug		dysentary
Margaret Nicholi	76	W	Ger.	Apr		old age
Thomas Fitzer	5		N.J.	Feb		lung dis.
Noah Gassaway	49	M	Md	Aug	merchant	dysentary
Andrew Bopp	37	M	Ger.	Jun	grocer	typhoid
Francis Bopp	1		Md	Aug		lung disease
Margaret E.R.Salgues	19		WestInd.	Aug		dysentary
Frederick A. Glatzell	39	M	Ger.	Dec	hatter	typhoid
John Morran Jr.	1da		Md	Aug		unknown
Daniel Ricketts	48	M	Md	Aug	machinest	consumption
Gotleib Deiterich	1		Md	May		unknown
Jacob Kessler	37	M	Ger	Jun	tailor	small pox
Charles Candee	37	M	N.Y.	Mar	boilermaker	pleurisy
Samuel Hopkins	43	M	Pa.	Aug	stonecutter	dropsey
Margaret A. Hirsh	6		Md	Jul		brain inflam.
Thomas E. Heffner	8mo		Md	Aug		summer compl.
William Raeling	2		Md	May		water on brain
Robert Tatam	39	M	Md	Apr	none	lung disease
James Thompson	6		Md	May		brain fever
Mary Murphy	40	M	Md	Apr		consumption
Hugh Gelley	56	M	Ire.	Mar	laborer	consumption
Mary Bersick	26	M	France	Dec		consumption
Elizabeth E. Grindall	5		Md	Nov		lung disease
James Jeffries	38		Pa.	Nov	huckster	consumption
Mary A. Evans	1		Md	Jul		whooping cough
Richard Batee	29	M	Md	Feb	ploughmaker	consumption
Ann M. Batee	6mo		Md	Feb		consumption
William P. Stewart	8mo		Md	Aug		summer compl.
William H, White	2		Md	Jul		dysentary
Ann E. Fulk	18		Md	Apr		small pox

persons who died during the year ending 1 June 18<u>50</u>

COUNTY Baltimore   DISTRICT 15th Ward-Baltimore City

name	age	mar wid	birth place	mon. died	Occupation	cause of death
Alice A.A. Quirk	1		Md	Aug		summer compl.
William W. Flanigan	44	M	N.C.	Jun	sailor	inflam.breast
Gada Dare	40	M	Md	Dec		quinsy
Mary E.Collins	10mo		Md	Oct		summer compl.
George T. Townsend	3		Md	Aug		diarhea
Frederick Mans	47	M	Ger.	Mar	locksmith	brain inflam.
Thomas L. Dowling	49	M	Md	Jan	blacksmith	diarrhea
Susan Jones	15		Md	Aug		cholera Morrb.
Ellen Ewing	1		Md	Nov		teething
Thomas H. Maning	1		Md	Sep		teething
Mary E. Graham	2		Md	Jul		fits
Benjamin E. McLane	7mo		Md	Jul		cholera inf.
Henry C. Stumpf	1mo		Md	Nov		unknown
Susan E. Willing	1		Md	Aug		summer compl.
Elizabeth Gerlinghurst	26	M	Ger.	Mar		consumption
Elisabeth Girvin	3		Pa.	Dec		croup
Mary Parker	1		Md	Apr		bowel inflam.
Thomas Collins	29	M	Ire.	Jun	laborer	consumption
Margaret Collins	25		Ire.	Jun		consumption
Joseph McNeal	10mo		Md	Jul		summer compl.
Leonidas Levering	40		Md	Oct	merchant	unknown
Mary F. Boston	1		Md	Aug		summer compl.
Catharine Harig	62	M	Ger	Sep		consumption
Andrew P. Dicks	2		Md	Feb		catarrah fever
Andrew P.Dicks	2		Md	Feb		cattarah fever
Edward L. Kavn	3		Switz.	Dec		small pox
Simon Martin Jr.	2		Md	Jan		cattarah fever
Worthington R. Dickey	3		Md	Mar		cronic croup
James Milroy	10		Md	Feb		typhoid
Joseph Hutchinson	1mo		Md	Jan		premat.birth
Susannah Robinson	2		Md	Jul		cholera infan.
Arnold H. Ballard	14		Md	Jun		drowned
Emma J. Butler	22	M	Md	Apr		bowel inflam.
James H. Patten	58	W	Md	Jan	cabinetmaker	consumption
Daniel Smith	39	M	Md	Jun	grocer	bronchitis
Henry H. Mortimer Jr.	1		Md	Jul		dysentary
Eleanor Scott (Mul)	25		Md	Aug		childbirth
Ludwig H. W. Nicolai	44	M	Ger.	Nov	grocer	cancer
Hester M. Nichols	4mo		Md	Jul		water on brain
William W. Robinson	1		Md	Jul		summer compl.
James T. Robinson	7mo		Md	Mar		teething
Charles W. Elton	61	M	Eng.	Apr	grocer	heart disease
Martha A. Davis	33	M	Md	Sep		consumption
Frances Queen	12		Md	Aug		consumption
Louisa Woldmann	1		Md	Jun		consumption
Mary Stinchcomb	77		Md	Mar		old age
Mary Sanner	51	W	Md	Jun		heart
Alexander Russell	84	M	Ire.	Jul	bricklayer	diarrhea
Alicia L.L. Tear	1		Md	Aug		diarrhea
Gerhard Hunichenn	3		Md	Jan		catarrah fever
Sarah E. Corkran	1		Md	Jul		cholera infan.

MORTALITY SCHEDULE OF MARYLAND

persons who died during the year ending 1 June 18_50_

COUNTY   Baltimore   DISTRICT 15th Ward, Baltimore City

name	age	mar wid	birth place	mon. died	Occupation	cause of death
Jefferson Schults	48	M	Md	Oct	merchant	unknown
John Ball	30	M	Md	Jan	tailor	stomach inflam.
Moses Joseph	52	W	Holland	Jan	jeweller	bilious pleur.
Emma L. Reese	3		Md	Jan		croup
Mary Kimmell	30	M	Ger.	Mar		consumption
Joseph L. Moreland	35	M	Md	Aug	merchant	consumption
Mary McDowell	40	M	Md	Nov		consumption
Henry H. Arthur	6mo		Md	Jul		consumption
Thomas Kennedy	29		Eng.	Sep	clergyman	dysentary
Rebecca Willard	29	M	Md	Apr		consumption
Mary V. Taylor	2mo		Md	Aug		summer compl.
Martha H. Briding	38	M	Md	Aug		gastric fever
Benjamin F. Cannon	1		Md	Aug		summer compl.
Amelia B. Woodcock	49	M	Md	Jun		heart
Mary Hittmeyer	23	M	Ger.	Dec		cholora morb.
Henry Hittmeyer	7mo		Pa	May		varialoid
John Waite	1hour		Md	Nov		weakness
Adella Rose	3		Md	Mar		scarlet fever
Solomon Lauer	25		Ger.	Oct	clerk	typhoid
Margaret McNelly	42		Pa.	Aug		typhoid
James McNamara	40	M	Ire.	Jun	laborer	sunstruck
Clara B. Causey	1		Md	Aug		teething
Joseph Brown	43		Md	Nov	shoemaker	dropsy
Mary P. Hanson	62	W	Pa.	Jul		heart
James Harris	40	M	Eng.	Feb	servant	consumption
William Meusel	49	M	Ger	Jan	tinner	cramp stomach
Fanny Stewart	2hrs.		Md	Sep		premature birth
Charles L. Snyder	5		Md	Jun		scarlet fever
Serena Snyder	3		Md	Jun		scarlet fever
Phillip E. Richardson	2		Md	Nov		scald
Aravilla A. Osborne	45		Md	Nov		consumption
Wiegand F. Reese	11mo		Md	Apr		summer compl.
Wilhelmina Eilbecker	2		Md	Nov		bowel comp.
William Johnson	62	M	Md	Dec	sailor	gravel
William J. Stephens	1		Md	Jul		accident
Sarah Pridgen	40	M	Ire.	Sep		cancer
Laura Peirsen	1		Md	Jun		brain fever
Jehu Cruser	13		Md	Jul		hemmorage
Isaac Cruser	9mo		Md	Dec		consumption
Elizabeth Neepier	4		Md	Nov		dysentary
Hugh & Ann E. Graham	3da.		Md	Nov		premature birth
Ella Farmer	7mo		Md	unkn.		cholera inf.
Joseph A. Stevens	2mo		Md	May		dysentary
Catharine Gerlagh	1mo		Md	Jul		summer compl.
Levin Dashields	41	M	Md	Dec	blacksmith	bilious pleurisy
Margaret Gissel	33	M	Ger.	Aug		consumption
James L. Stevenson	3		Md	Jun		scarlet fever
Robert V. Skinner	11mo		Md	Jul		teething
George W. Manning	3		Md	Aug		scarlet fever
James W. Maddox	8mo		Md	Aug		summer compl.
Rachel Simpson	4		Md	Apr		scarlet fever

name	age	mar wid	birth place	mon. died	Occupation	cause of death
Edward Read	3		Va.	Jan		typhoid
Joseph Turner	59	M	Md	Aug	merchant	paralysis
Emmanuel Holshart	4mo		Md	Mar		bowel inflam.
Charles F. Hogendorf	3mo		Md	Oct		catarrah fever
Mary Baltsell	9mo		Md	Jul		bowel inflam.
			16th Ward			
Margaret O'neil	9mo		Md	Jul		summer compl.
Sarah Taylor	28	M	Md	Jul		consumption
James McGrath	11mo		N.Y.	Nov		teething
Clara Wright	1		Md	Dec		interm. fever
Catharine Freale	88	W	Irel.	Aug		old age
Sarah E. Riggin	16		Md	Mar		typhoid
Joseph S. Barrow	1mo		Md	Dec		spine
Joseph G. Waters Jr.	5mo		Md	Mar		erysipelas
Martha A. Lyons	1		Md	Sep		bilius dysentary
Maria L. Wagner	1		Md	Sep		bilius dysentary
Mary E. Watts	3		Md	Jul		spine
George A. Rawlings Jr.	1mo		Md	Mar		bowel inflam.
Edwin Gorton	1		Md	Oct		dysentary
Hannah Lewisson	2mo		Md	Jan		cattarah fever
Lawrence Marple	7		Pa.	Dec		brain inflam.
Susanna Chase	30		Md	Jan		typhoid
Frances M. Johnson	22	M	Pa.	Aug		childbed
Sewall J. Milnor	14		Md	Sep		accident
John Hoffman	2		Va.	Oct		croup
Charles E. Lusby	5mo		Md	Mar		croup
William Wode Jr.	7mo		Md	Jun		summer compl.
John Kornman	3wks		Md	Oct		premature birth
William Kornman	2mo		Md	Oct		premature birth
William H. Sheckells	6mo		Md	Sep		unknown
Charles T. Rogers	6		Md	Nov		croup
Elizabeth A. High	22		Md	Sep		diarrhea
Elisa Albers	74	W	Pa.	Mar		heart
Catharine Kerns	72		Md	Mar		appoplexy
William W. Blaher	6mo		Pa.	Nov		whooping cough
Elizabeth Shane	62	M	Md	Oct		appoplexy
John Schneider	2da.		Md	Feb		cold.
Sophia Schneider	2		Md	Feb		cattarah Fever
Catharine Cross	39	M	Md	Nov		childbed
Elisa Cross	5mo		Md	Apr		interm. fever
Thomas Keegan	2		Md	May		scarlet fever
Hugh Keegan	5		D. C.	May		scarlet fever
Ann Codey	9mo		Md	May		scarlet fever
Sarah Humphreys	68	W	Pa.	Nov		appoplexy
Julia A. Dunn	4		Md	Dec		brain fever
Alexander Levy	22		Md	Jan	clerk	cold
Joseph O'Brien	7mo		Md	Sep		teething
Catharine T. Gallup	52	W	Md	Jul		dysentary
Thomas Parsons	64	M	Md	Oct	shoemaker	heart
Baby Boyce	28hrs		Md	Dec		unknown
Benjamin F. McClellan	1		Md	Jun		scrofula

persons who died during the year ending 1 June 18 50

COUNTY Baltimore   DISTRICT 16th Ward,Baltimore City

name	age	mar wid	birth place	mon. died	Occupation	cause of death
Mary R. Stewart	1		Md	Oct		brain fever
Winfield Scott Deems	1		Md	Oct		unknown
Mary T. Fennell	3		Md	Jun		hemorahage
Mary E. Lindsey	13		Md	Jun		rheumatism
George Hoover	52	M	Md	Apr	butcher	unknown
Martha Scanlan	19		Md	Nov		fits
Catharine R. Gatch	18		Md	Oct		typhoid
Conduce Gatch Jr.	15		Md	Jan		typhoid
Goerge R. Bourne	5		Md	Jan		typhoid
Mary Oursler	27		Md	Jan		consumption
John Smith	80	W	Ger.	Jul	baker	old age
Mary E. Love	6mo		Md	Aug		cholera
Catharine E. Ullrich	2		Md	Nov		scalded
Ann Disney	67		Md	Dec		typhoid
Sarah L. Redgrave	53	M	Md	Mar		typhoid
George E.Rodney	6mo		Md	Sep		dysentary
Jacob Houck	59	M	Alexandria Va.		PanaceaMaker	bil.pleurisy
Catharine Stahl	5mo		Md	Mar		catarrah fever
Mary A. Kemper	5mo		Md	Feb		catarrah fever
Joseph Wehage	2		Md	Apr		white swelling
William J. Crangle	3		Md	Sep		croup
Mary E. Logue	7mo		Md	Mar		brain
Augusta Lants	2mo		Md	Jul		unknown
Eunetta Shumacher	53	M	Ger.	Jun		cholera
Martha J. Robb	7mo		Md	Jul		croup
Susannah Pampillion	68	W	Md	Apr		consumption
Charles A. Vinzant	5da.		Md	Sep		unknown
Elizabeth R. McCauley	1		Md	Apr		unknown
Laura J. Vinzant	4		Md	Nov		fall
Elizabeth M. M.Wells	3		Md	Dec		unknown
Elizabeth M.M. Wells	23	M	Md	Dec		rheumatism
Rachel A. Simms	2wks		Md	Jul		unknown
Thomas Snyder	54		Pa.	Aug	laborer	unknown
Jeremiah & Richard Seth	1da		Md	Jun		unknown-twins
Anna M. Hooper	8mo		Md	Jul		summercomplaint.
Pauline E. Hollingsworth	2		Md	Jan		water on brain
Margaret Francke	4mo		Md	Jun		dysenterry
John Dobbin	55	M	N.Y.	Aug	bootmaker	heart
John T. Golden	3wks		Md	Aug		heart
Catharine McAvoy	45	W	Ire.	Sep		dysenterry
Jarret Della	1		Md	Aug		bowel inflam.
Sarah R. Lee	1		Md	Aug		unknown
John Lee	41	M	Md	Feb	huckster	consumption
William J.Bertsch	2mo		Md	Dec		unknown
John Peters	32	M	Md	May	brickmaker	sudden
Caroline Warfield	26	M	Md	Apr		consumption
Susan Cromwell	4mo		Md	Sep		unknown
Jeremiah Brooks	4		Md	Nov		scarlet fever
Margaret E. Brooks	7mo		Md	Nov		scarlet fever
Ann E. Dunn	11		Md	Mar		St.Vitus Dance
John P. Knox	8mo		Md	May		teething
Joseph Milburn	45	M	Eng.	Oct		consumption

51

MORTALITY SCHEDULE OF MARYLAND

persons who died during the year ending 1 June 1850

COUNTY Baltimore   DISTRICT 17th Ward, Baltimore City

name	age	mar wid	birth place	mon. died	Occupation	cause of death
Emma Reichert	10mo	'	Md	Jul		summer comp.
Amelia Croder	50	M	Ger.	Feb		dropsey
John Eshem	39	M	D.C.	Sep	brickmaker	shot
John Cavalier	1		Md	Aug		throat
Bernard Wilk	41	M	Ger.	Mar	laborer	consumption
Alverda Lathe	8mo		Md	Jan		cattar.fever
James Leman	6mo		Md	Jul		summer compl.
Joseph T. Hanlin	1		Md	Jan		teething
Levinia Statlin	47	M	Ger.	Apr		small pox
Mary E. Mauly	4		Md	Nov		burnt
Hannah Ayard	45	M	N.J.	Jul		diarrah
Elizabeth J.Taylor	4		Md	Sep		burnt
Eliza Visher	1mo		Md	May		erasilalis
Amelia Lohrman	2		Md	Mar		small pox
John Thomas	19		Md	Nov	marines	unknown
Margaret Brian	46	M	Eng.	May		consumption
Robert Bowen	1		Md	Aug		consumption
William Colt	24		Md	Apr	shinglemaker	fits
Mary Colt	21		Md	Apr		consumption
Susan Snyder	28	M	Va.	Aug		consumption
Elizabeth Buckley	2		Md	Jul		dysentary
Rebecca Greenly	50	W	Del.	Jan		pllerisy
William Ward	46	M	Md	May	shipcarpenter	hung self
Mary McFarland	99	W	Irel	May		old age
Emma S. Bruce	1		Md	Jun		dysentary
Sophia Morelston	49	W	Md	May		diareah
William H. North	11		Md	May		liver disease
Sarah C. Warick	1		Md	Jun		summer compl.
Jonas Maddens (Mul)	43	W		Md	Fireman	lung inflam.
Christian Tyburn	50	M	Md	Mar	fisherman	pleurisy
John H. Nickel	6mo		Md	Jul		cholera
Joseph Hooper	2		Md	Sep		diarreah
Mary Ann Bursick	23	M	Ger.	Oct		consumption
Benjamin James	35	M	Md	Feb	glassBlower	mania Portia
Hannah Page	37	M	Md	May		unknown
Sobella Lee	67	W	Pa.	Aug		old age
Francis Wyatt	1		Md	Jul		lung infect.
James E. Trainer	9mo		Md	Aug		water on brain
Wm. H. Wrixham	11mo		Md	Aug		head complain.
Cahtarine Closkey	9mo		Md	May		croup
Sarah Sherlock	28	M	Md	Jun		consumption
Sarah Norfold	1		Md	Dec		teething
Mary Fulberg	2mo		Md	May		irasiphilus
Mary Cullins	84	W	Va	Sep		old age
Jzmes B. Pyre	11mo		Md	Aug		measles
Sylvester Wheeler	3		Md	Oct		pleurisy
Jane Horney	25	M	Md	Aug		typhoid
Edward McKimmons	1		Md	Jul		summer complain.
Joshua S. Bush	29		Md	Aug	cabinetmaker	consumption
Clara Ann Bush	1		Md	Jul		teething
Mrs. Eckard	40	M	Md	Aug		typhoid

52

MORTALITY SCHEDULE OF MARYLAND

persons who died during the year ending 1 June 1850

COUNTY Baltimore   DISTRICT 17th Ward, Balitmore Cty

name	age	mar wid	birth place	mon. died	Occupation	cause of death
James B.M.Tyler	1		Md	Aug		summercomplaint.
Robert A. Bassett	1		Md	Jul		teething
Alexander Tuell	1		Md	Jul		teething
R. H. Tuell(male)	2		Md	Sep		unknown
William C. Harris	55	W	Mass	Oct	trader	dysentary
Catharine Baker	71	M	Ger.	Jul		dysentary
George Rankin	43	M	Ger.	Aug	cooper	dysentary
Caroline Fisher	1		Md	Dec		croup
William Roberts	5mo		Md	Feb		cholera
Charles Bridenstein	2		Md	Sep		unknown
William Youst	22		Ger.	Jul	carter	drowned
Mary Ruhl	10		Ger.	Aug		dysentary
Christoph Herbert	21		Ger.	Jul	shoemaker	diarreah
Joseph Knight	13		Md	Jun		shot
Catharine Phillip	60	W	Ire.	Aug		diarreah
Alexander McLaine	9		Md	Nov		unknown
Sarah McCall	6		Md	Dec		cold
Margaret Miller	54	M	Ger.	Jun		unknown
Joseph Conway	26		Md	Oct	fisherman	drowned
Betsy Conway	30	M	Md	Dec		consumption
Sarah E. Dempster	14		Md	Aug		dysentary
Sophia Knolein	11mo		Md	Aug		unknown
Bridget McGrath	1		Md	Jul		brain inflam.
Mrs. Hensworth	79	W	Ger.	Feb		old age
Charles O.Wittley	3		Md	Jan		croup
Barbary Wigart	66	W	Ger.	Feb		unknown
Hannah Burger	66	W	Ger.	Aug		dropsey
Joseph Sharp	51	M	Eng.	Jan	laborer	consumption
Elisha Osborn	40	M	Md	Nov	potter	consumption
Sophia Morsie	28		Md	Sep		dysentary
Samuel Morgan	26		Md	Sep	laborer	unknown
Alexander Towsen	14		Md	Jul		consumption
Ellin Moss	7		Md	Oct		croup
Amanda Hampton	2		Pa.	Jul		dysentary
Christopher Ryan	10		Ger.	Jul		summer compl.
Joseph Pferff	1		Md	Feb		small pox
Jacob Aikler	5		Md	Apr		small pox
Margaret Eaton	45	M	Irel	Aug		heart disease
John Merritt	42	M	Md	Seo	stonecutter	consumptoin
Robert Cooley	9		Md	Sep		consumption
Rebbecca Cummings(black)	62	W	Md	Nov		dropsey
Catherine Upperman	1		Md	Jul		summer compl.
Henrietta Retta	38	M	Md	Jan		dropsey
Elizabeth Hasbaugh	2mo		Md	Jan		croup
Elizabeth C. Cordes	11mo		Md	Apr		croup
Sarah Parker	4		Md	Apr		dysentary
Samuel Ed. Mitchell	11mo		Md	Mar		diarreah
William R. Webster	8		Md	Sep		fall
Charles Shytt	4		Md	Jul		measles
Thomas Boclay	40	M	Md	May		consumption
Sarah Ann Solgee	33	M	Md	Nov		consumption
Samuel Taylor	46	M	Eng.	Dec	weaver	dysentary

53

persons who died during the year ending 1 June 18<u>50</u>

COUNTY   Baltimore   DISTRICT   17th Ward, Baltimore City
                                                    18th Ward,

name	age	mar wid	birth place	mon. died	Occupation	cause of death
Edward A. Ruark	1		Md	Aug		dysentary
			18th Ward			
Jacob Shyrock	3		Md	Aug		Typhoid
Joseph Shyrock	1		Md	Aug		typhoid
John Yost	59	M	Pa.	Mar	teacher	consumption
Mary E. Staggers	24		Md	Feb	millner	consumption
William Y. Moore	1		Md	Aug		dysentary
Charles Guinn	1		Md	Jun		still born
Henry Rackford	2mo		Md	Dec		cold
Martha Summers	21		Md	Mar		lungs
William Rothrock	1		Md	Aug		diareah
Isaac Forsyth	97		Pa	Oct	farmer	dropsey
Benjamin Owings	39	M	Md	Nov	car driver	consumption
Elizabeth Tyland	2mo		Md	Aug		dysentary
John Clark	42		Md	Jul	clerk	dropsey
Joseph Stall	3days		Md	Feb		premature
Sarah McBride	62	W	Ire.	May		dropsey
Ellen S. Cacher	1		Md	Mar		whooping cough
Thomas Buckler	36	M	N.Y.	Apr	bootmaker	consumption
Julia M. Buckler	2		Md	Jun		W. brash
John B. Collins	2mo		Md	Jun		consumption
William Dean	56	M	N.Y.	Apr	shoemaker	consumption
William Jenkins	46		Eng.	Sep	collector	artery disease
Ann Allen	28	M	Md	Jun		none
Atrerda?Marks	3		Md	Aug		measles
Joseph Litchfield	8mo		Md	Aug		dysentary
Elnora Kinsaled	4		Md	Dec		croup
Ada Richard	1day		Md	Jul		still born
Lett. Spence(fem)	7mo		Md	Jul		measles
Ellen Ellenbrook	2		Ger.	Jul		catarrah fever
Julia P. Briggs	29		Ohio	Apr		heart dis.
Emily Albert	1		Md	Oct		scarlet fever
Jacob Unbrist	7		Md	Dec		scarlet fever
Charlotte Mansfield	17		Md	May		dysentary
Josh Galaway	33		Md	Feb		consumption
Martin Fogel	8mo		Md	Apr		heart dis.
George Hagner	63		Md	May		apoplexy
Joseph Philpot	11mo		Md	Feb		brain inflam.
Nathan Vinton	50	M	Md	Jul		drowned
Charles Jeinour	70	M	Pa	Aug	farmer	dropsy
Margaret Jeinour	75	W	Md	Mar		none
George W. Baker	19		Md	Aug	cabinetmaker	typhoid
Mary E. Hooper	41	M	Md	Jul		dysentary
David Hartman	9day		Md	Sep		croup
Ellen Shankles	1mo		Md	May		unknown
Richard Shankles	1mo		Md	Jul		unknown
Elizabeth Warns	2mo		Md	Jul		colic
David Gray	3		Md	Apr		sudden
William Handy	2		Md	Aug		dysentary
Susan Wilson	60	W	Md	Nov		gravel
William C. Brown	3		Md	Nov		lung inflam.

MORTALITY SCHEDULE OF MARYLAND

persons who died during the year ending 1 June 18<u>50</u>

COUNTY   Baltimore   DISTRICT   18th Ward, Baltimore City

name	age	mar wid	birth place	mon. died	Occupation	cause of death
George Ruth	5		Md	Jan		scarlet fever
John Debel	4		Md	Jan		scarlet fever
Caroline Debel	2		Md	Feb		croup
Rebecca J. McCurley	1		Md	Nov		whooping cough
Rebecca Connelly	40	M	S.C.	Jun		consumption
A. Airman (fem)	34	M	Ger.	May		consumption
George Stuart	45		Md	Mar	clerk	consumption
C.W.Glanding (male)	3mo		Md	Feb		whooping cough
Elizabeth Emick	21	M	Md	Feb	mantiamaker	consumption
Laura V. Shields	1		Md	Jan		none
Garnet Austin	43	M	Md	Mar	clerk	typhoid
Sarah C. McGirch	2		Md	Jan		scarlet fever
James McGirch	1		Md	Jan		scarlet fever
Mary A. McGirch	4		Md	Feb		scarlet fever
Grafton Downing	4		Md	Aug		bowel compl.
John C. Harvey	3mo		Md	Aug		dysentary
Mary Hoffman	80	W	Pa.	Dec		old age
Elizabeth Hissig	7		Md	Nov		scarlet fever
Mary Heney	1		Pa.	Aug		dysentary
John A. McHeald	7		Pa.	Dec		croup
Thomas Wentford	24	M	Pa.	Dec		consumption
Elizabeth Bidings	41	W	Md	Apr		childbirth
Bridget Hids	1		Ire.	Aug		dysentary
William J. Young	11mo		Md	Jul		dysentary
George W. Price	1mo		Md	Mar		head Dis.
Mary Shay	8mo		Ire.	Dec		cold
Thomas R. Kelly	1		Md	Mar		catarrah fever.
Emily A Cheny	1		Md	Sep		drowned
Mary Barnhart	6mo		Md	Aug		dysentary
Mary Harrwood	77	W	Md	Jun		consumption
John Harwood	48		Md	Nov	clerk	consumption
Sarah McGilton	27		Md	Dec		dysentary
Mary V.Bowers	1		Md	May		eursipilus
Sarah Williams	4		Md	Apr		scarlet fever
William P. Webster	1		Md	Jan		consumption
William Ringold	3mo		Md	May		ftis
Ed G.Beeker	7mo		Md	Aug		typhoid
Beal Dusall	35	M	Md	Sep		typhoid
Raybold Mane	25	M	Md	Oct	merchant	cong.brain
Clara C. Kenman	5		Md	Nov		freasets?
R.M.Nairn (male)	11mo		Md	Sep		dysentary
Rosina Mung	31		Ire.	Dec		consumption
Andrew Botts	41	M	Ger	Apr	butcher	scarlet fever
William Cary	1		Md	Jun		worms
Shadrack R. Fowler	2		Md	Jan		croup
Gertrude M. Fowler	3mo		Md	Mar		brain inflam.
Godfrey Hafner	9mo		Md	Mar		fits
L.B.Gisendaffer(fem)	2da.		Md	May		unknown
Joseph Carson	6mo		Md	Dec		brain
Eliza Brown	28	M	Va.	May		childbed
Lewis Gosnek	1		Md	Jan		Gat.fever
Samuel Mealy	19		Va	feb	carpenter	typhoid

55

MORTALITY SCHEDULE OF MARYLAND

persons who died during the year ending 1 June 18<u>50</u>

COUNTY Baltimore   DISTRICT 18th Ward, Baltimore City

name	age	mar wid	birth place	mon. died	Occupation	cause of death
David Belt	1		Md	Apr		fever
William Street	15		Md	Jan	bricklayer	typhoid
William Black	51		Md	Jan	farmer	killed
Joseph Brady	1day		Md	Apr		childbed
Alice Kennedy	2		Md	Sep		scarlet fever
Elizabeth Hoffman	74		Md	Sep		rheumatism
Oliver H. Grimm	2		Md	Oct		croup
Mary M. Smith	29		Md	Dec		consumption
Clara M.Smith	2		Md	May		spine dis.
Julia Wiseman	48	M	N.J.	Aug		consumption
Eliza Kephart	30		Md	Aug		kidney dis.
Goseta Hunt	33	M	Md	Sep		child bed
Emma Fahensteck	7mo		Md	Apr		consul.
Charles A. Davidson	2		Md	Mar		"
Matilda F. Hill	2da.		Md	sep		croup
Rudolph S. Poulson	1		Md	Oct		dysentary
Joseta F. Hunt	1mo		Md	Sep		asthma
Phillip Hartman	8mo		Md	Nov		croup
William Cuney	47	M	Md	Oct	carpenter	heart dis.
Margaret Waters	7		Md	Dec		typhoid
Joseph L. Dyatt	8		Md	Jan		catarrah
William Ratcliffe	45	W	Del.	sep	merchant	consumption
Josephine Field	1		Md	Jun		bil.?
? McMillan(fem)	37		Md	Jun		consumption
Roclin? Alex	41		Md	Nov	wheelright	typhoid
John D. Hosner	1		Md	Sep		whooping cough
George E. Lowrey	2mo		Md	Dec		whooping cough
Martha Baxter	80	W	Md	Dec		old age
John Duncan	5		Md	Mar		measles
Emily Duncan	2		Md	May		consumption
Mary Cooper	36		N.Y.	Apr		consumption
Virginia Bentley	16		Md	Apr		consumption
Rose Murray	34	M	Ire.	Dec		consumption
Henry W. Rose	1		Md	Dec		whooping cough
Mary S. Crow	2		Md	Dec		scarlet fever
Louisa Binnerman	41	M	Ger	Jul		cholera
Frederick Binnerman	24		Ger.	Jul		cholera
Louisa Y. Fefle	2		Md	Dec		catarah
Sarah E. Grimes	2		Md	Mar		catarrah
Sarah Norris	77	W	Md	Jan		old age
Lorenzo Hobbs	2		Md	Dec		heart dis.
John Neehard	22		Ger.	Feb		cold
Emma Conner	1		Md	Mar		whooping cough
James Allen	48	M	Md	Dec	carpenter	diarreah
Margaret Sheriff	87	W	Md	Aug		old age
John H. Wagner	3da		Md	Oct		head disease
Louis S.Reynolds	3		Md	Mar		whooping cough
Ellen C.Reynolds	3mo		Md	Mar		whooping cough
Mary T. Reynolds	3mo		Md	Mar		whooping cough
Mary E. Price	42	W	Md	Apr		lung inflam.
Joseph Ried	3		Md	Nov		typhoid
Sarah C. Harper	17	M	Md	Oct		child bed

persons who died during the year ending 1 June 18_50_

COUNTY Baltimore   DISTRICT 18th Ward, Baltimore City

name	age	mar wid	birth place	mon. died	Occupation	cause of death
Ann B. Stevens	28	M	Md	Nov		paraletic
James M. Haskins	4mo		Md	Jul		heart disease
Elizabeth Johnson	32	M	Md	Aug		consumption
Isaac Wentz	39	M	Pa.	Apr	Agent	consumption
Isaac Wentz Jr.	2		Md	Sep		croup
Alsinda Mitchell	4		Md	Sep		dysentary
John Roy	19		Md	May	sailor	heart disease
Sarah Arnold	25	M	Md	Jul		liver Compl.
William Hammondtree	2mo		Md	Jul		diareah
Charles E. Perry	1		Md	Jul		croup
Ann Gwinn	45	M	Md	Oct		consumption
Walter Gwinn	1		Md	May		croup
Eliza Tilist?	76	W	Ire.	Apr		old age
Mary S. Blissard	1		Md	Dec		dysentary
George A. Blackstone	1		Md	Jun		brain inflam.
Andrew W. Pascoe	1		Pa.	Jul		dysentary
Joseph Hiskey	67	W	Ger.	Apr	pianomaker	consumption
Lawrence Dolan	29	M	Md	Nov	hatter	consumption
George Hindlehouse	1mo		Md	Sep		croup
John H. Moore	45	W	Md	Apr	machinest	consumption
Sarah N. Ogle	1		Md	Aug		dysentary
John W. Freeburger	37		Md	Mar	waterman	burnt
Mary A. Enson	29	M	Md	Apr		dyofrefisia
Elizabeth Allen	20		Md	Sep		confimat?
Emily Banks	4		Md	Aug		cancer
Caroline M. Arnig	26	M	Md	Dec		dysentary
James Atwell	33	M	Md	Aug	brickmaker	consumption
Hester A. Atwell	1		Md	Mar		heart disease
Elizabeth Galoway	45		Md	Nov		consumption
Abraham Ferrell	26		Md	Aug	engineer	typhoid
Frederick Ennis	23	M	Pa.	feb	bootmaker	consumption
John Pasler	35	M	Ger	Apr	tailor	consumption
Susan Shillenberger	39	M	Md	Jul		heart disease
Mary L. Lammerick	7		Md	Dec		head disease
Margaret Thornton	5		Md	Aug		whooping cough
Hannah Hensil	60	W	Ger	Dec		consumption
Phillip J. Wild	80	W	Ger	Jan	laborer	old age
William Griffin	23	M	Md	Nov	cooper	typhoid
Emma Thompson	2		Md	May		scalded
Mary A. Mulligan	42	M	Md	Mar		heart disease
William E. Henery	3mo		Md	Jun		dysentary
Henry Voltz	6mo		Md	Jul		inflamation
Margaret Feinons	75	W	Md	Mar		lung inflam.
Mary Hoffman	80	W	Ger	Dec		old age
Ann M. Stoddard	15		Md	May		consumption
Michael Owings	19		Md	Feb		consumption
William Dunjan	77	W	Pa	Jun	cityBailiff	old age
Elizabeth Runner	1		Md	Sep		dysentary
Othesate Reef	2		Md	Aug		dysentary
Frank Rossman	10		Md	Oct		scarlet fever

name	age	mar wid	birth place	mon. died	Occupation	cause of death
Thomas Patterson	32		Eng.	Feb	glasscutter	cramps
Robert Acker	58	W	Md	Jul	druggist	paralysis
Henry Riply	46	M	Ger	Dec	laborer	pleurisy
Sarah A. Poulton	1mo		Md	Aug		Whooping cough
David Lainbright	1		Md	Aug		brain disease
Alfred A. Woodall	12		Md	Aug		drowned
Phillip Hannigan	1		Md	Aug		consumption
Catherine Presly	75	W	Ire.	Sep		dysentary
John Brown	30	M	Ger.	Nov	engineer	killed on RR
Rufus Griffith	2mo		Md	Apr		unknown
John Berry	5		Md	Jan		scarlet fever
John Drier	1		Md	Aug		unknown
Pelick Bosworth	39	M	Va.	Dec		paralysis
George Rey	34	M	Md	Dec	brickmaker	cholera
Mary S. Lauer	19	M	M	Jan		confinement
Mary E. Debilus	3		Md	Sep		sudden
Lanehart Ruper	1		Md	Aug		dysentary
Robert Turner	20		Md	Jul	fireman	diareah
Laura Stallings	1		Md	Oct		dysentary
Conrad H. Seymour	7mo		Md	Aug		brain congest.
Joseph Merket	48	M	Canada	Apr	laborer	bowels
Henry Farmer	11mo		Md	Apr		dysentary
Ferdinand Myers	25		Md	May	hatter	consumption
Henrietta Gist	6mo		Md	May		cold
Sarah E. Gadd	4		Md	Apr		scarlet fever
John H. Gadd	2		Md	Apr		scarlet fever
Sophia Weiland	1mo		Md	May		cramps
Susan Stamp	28	M	Md	Jul		consumption
Mary E. Carson	10mo		Md	Mar		diarreah
Elizabeth Bentley	71		Eng.	Dec		scarlet fever
Mary A. Shaw	17		Pa.	Nov		fever
Alberta L. Lyeth	3		Md	Jan		dysentary
William Holton	24	M	Md	Oct	OmnibusDriv.	consumption
Mary W. Holton	7mo		Md	Oct		unknown
Matilda Thomas	2		Md	Dec		spasms
			19th Ward			
Achial Carmichael	61	W	Md	Jul		consumption
William Boyd	67	M	Md	Sep	rasiermaker	consumption
Sarah Zimmerman	43	M	Md	Aug		consumption
Mary Katenkamp	11mo		Md	Aug		summer compl.
Mich Merklant	39	M	Ger	Oct	carpenter	lockjaw
Mary Clapp	3mo		Md	Aug		summer compl.
William McElroy	43	M	Irel.	Oct	weaver	sudden
James Reid	11mo		Md	Aug		unknown
John Lambert	1mo		Md	Mar		unknown
Mary Lambert	2		Md	Mar		unknown
Elizabeth Childs	78	W	Md	Mar		cold
Robert Alexander	24		Md	May		unknown
Sarah D. Simpson	20		Md	Jun		brain inflam.
Ann Spicer	59	W	Md	Mar		typhoid
Eliz.Smith	19	M	Ger.	May		child bed

58.

persons who died during the year ending 1 June 1850

COUNTY BALTIMORE   DISTRICT   18th Ward, Baltimore City
                                                19th Ward, Baltimore City

name	age	mar wid	birth place	mon. died	Occupation	cause of death
Isabel Williams	65	M	Scot.	Aug		diareah
Margaret Young	11		Md	Sep		cholera
RobertaGoodman	1		Md	Apr		spasms
Charles Rise	35	M	Ger.	May	shoemaker	Expl. sudden
Peter Bitzler	25	M	Ger	Aug		cholera
George T. Bishop	1mo		Md	Jun		consumption
Eliza Dinges	84	W	Ger.	Jul		old age
Barbara Brown	1mo		Md	Jun		fits
Julia A. Todd	50	M	Md	Apr		Rhematism
Eva Smith	32		Md	Sep		consumption
Sarah McIntosh	56	W	Md	Apr		pleurisy
DavidDufalter	51	M	Ger	May	farmer	rup. blood ves.
Ginney Clark	46	M	Md	mar		heart
Jeanett Duncan	16		Md	Sep		consumption
Ann Laviller	63	W		Mar		old age
Josephine Madden	1		Md	Sep		water on brain
William Trenkle	39	M	Md	Jan	wheelright	consumption
Mary Trenkle	71	W	Md	Jan		paralysis
Adam Lerner	47	M	Ger	Jul		lung abs.
Adeline Phillips	20		Md	Jun		consumption
Levin C. Shields	20		Md	Apr		lung abcess
Louisa Shipley	7		Md	Nov		spasms
Sarah Ochter	83	W	Pa.	Dec		old age
Thomas McHale	26		Md	Dec		consumption
Margaret Pfeiffer	49	M	Ger.	Sep		consumption
Ann Hancock	76	W	Md	Feb		consumption
Nancy Allen	28	M	Md	Jun		liver compl.
Joanna Taner	29	M	Ger	Sep		fits
Lewis James	6mo		Md	Mar		scarlet fever
Rachel V. Marriott	6		Md	Oct		small pox
George Hugh	2		Md	Jun		dropsy
Margaret Gist	4		Md	Dec		scarlet fever
John R. Kemp	58	M	Pa.	Dec	auctioneer	spasms
George Benninger	70	W	Pa	May		old age
Robert Aiken	9mo		Md	Nov		whooping cough
John Lerner	44	M	Ger	Jul	laborer	consumption
Henry Anthony	68	M	Pa.	Jul	iron dealer	dyspessia
Mary A. Glen	4mo		Md	Jul		summer compl.
James Warrington	81	•W	Irel	Jan	none	old age
Mary Webster	20		Ger.	Apr		decline
Henry Schultz	24	M	Ger	Mar	butcher	typhoid
Rachel Murray	76	W	Md	Nov		lung inflam.
W. Whittington(male)	4mo		Md	Apr		decline
John R. Bell	1mo		Md	Jun		unknown
Emily E. Benson	7mo		Md	Aug		dysentary
James McCuenn	18		Irel.	Aug		brain dis.
Eliz Schonberger	40	M	Ger.	May		consumption
Mary Simpson	42	M	Va	Apr		consumption
Sarah Turner	36		Irel	Nov		child bed

MORTALITY SCHEDULE OF MARYLAND

persons who died during the year ending 1 June 18<u>50</u>

COUNTY   Baltimore   DISTRICT   20th Ward, Baltimore City

name	age	mar wid	birth place	mon. died	Occupation	cause of death
Cordelia Trater	15		Md	Mar		consumption
Andrew Sperka	2		Md	Jun		scarlet fever
David Seckel	50		Ger.	Feb	carpenter	fever
William Crowe	51	M	Irel	Jul		unknown
Casandra Smith	16		Md	Oct		cholera
Jesse Shultz	37	M	Md	Apr	driver	unknown
Mary Griffith	26		Md	Jul		interm. fever
Patrick McGirk	28	M	Irel.	Dec	grocer	consumption
John W. Findele	1		Md	Sep		croup
James Jackson	3mo		Md	Jun		summer compl.
William Gibson	3		Md	Sep		dropsy
Laura Lovejoy	24		Md	N v		diarhea
Henry Jacobs	4		Md	Jul		croup
Catherine Kulb	24	M	Ger	Jun		child bed
Mary Kulb	1mo		Md	Jun		sudden
John Kulb	27	W	Germ	Apr		consumption
William McKinnell	38	M	Ohio	Jan	merchant	murdered
Charlotte Spalding	22		Md	Jan		typhoid
Mary E. Dushane	4		Md	Jun		water on brain
Catherine Ernst	1mo		Md	Mar		cramps
John Ernst	7		Ger	Oct		cramps
Ann Campbell	26		Irel.	Jan		sudden
Margaret Campbell	30		Irel.	Jul		sudden
Ellen Maguire	43	W	Irel	Jun		breast inflam.
C. Liberkomp (fem)	36	M	Ger	Jul		yellow fever
Charley O'Farrell	23		Md	Mar	carter	typhoid
Mary Shaeffer	4mo		Md	May		summer compl.
Samuel Waneicker	56		Ger	May	shoemaker	Sin?
Martin Fisher	44		Ger	Jun	tanner	sunstroke
James McLaughlin	45	M	Irel	Jul	candlemaker	liver compl.
John Weist	7mo		Md	Jul		brain fever
J. Gerlach (male)	46	M	Ger	Jan	grocer	dropsy
George Wall	38	M	Ger	Mar	L. Maker	unknown
James Gaston	48		Irel	Jan	b. founder	ulcer
Prudence Bennett	60	W	Md	Jan		tremors
John Bower	39	M	Ger	Mar	shoemaker	small pox
Caroline Norris	7mo		Md	Jul		brain fever
Jane Merchant	2mo		Md	Oct		unknown
James Bayly	4		Md	Nov		dropsy
Susan Bayly	4		Md	Apr		brain fever
John F. Burbank	3		Md	Mar		interm. fever
Peter Rider	1		Md	Jun		influ.
William S. Colwell	2mo		Md	Nov		dropsy
George Maccubbin	11mo		Md	Feb		spasms
Patrick McGlennan	52	M	Irel	Jul	weaver	unknown
John Biers	56		Irel	Jun	weaver	bilious fever
Mary Perejoy	23	M	Md	Apr		consumption
Lydia Williams	2		Md	Dec		consumption
Ann H. Zimmerman	1mo		Md	Jul		fall
William T. Russell	4		Md	Aug		scarlet fever

MORTALITY SCHEDULE OF MARYLAND

persons who died during the year ending 1 June 1850

COUNTY Baltimore   DISTRICT   20th Ward, Baltimore City

name	age	mar wid	birth place	mon. died	Occupation	cause of death
Mary Russell	6		Md	Aug		scarlet fever
David Burke	1mo		Md	Jun		Summer compl.
Ann Quinlan	1		Md	Oct		fall
Robert W. Hart	28		Md	Oct	merchant	bowel infl.
Mary J. Brown	1mo		Md	Jul		deckube
Thomas Wright	47		Md	Feb	merchant	erryespelas
Edward Small	29		Md	Aug	clerk	dysentery
Sophia Crook	1		Md	Jul		cholera
Edward Crook	1		Md	Jul		cholera
Susan Deal	76	W	Md	Nov		old age
Caroline Godman	3mo		Md	Nov		decline
Lewis Seltzer	32		Md	Nov	butcher	cholera
James Marshall	40		Md	Nov	shoemaker	consumption
John Fester	6mo		Md	Nov		teething
S. Clarke (male)	55	M	Mass	Nov	teacher	typhoid
Frederick Wilman	2		Md	Jul		croup
Samuel Keplinger	62	M	Md	Feb	silversmith	appoplexy
John McKeever	47	M	Ire.	Feb	stonemason	unknown
Mary Horner	34		Pa.	Dec		weakness
Samuel Brumley	1		Md	Aug		brain fever
Lucy E. Clark	2		Md	Mar		brain inflam.
Helen R. Clark	1		Md	Mar		scarlet fever
B. Sanlin (fem)	27		Md	Sep		consumption
Sophia Neumier	31		Md	Jul		consumption
Mary E. Gaston	2		Md	Mar		fever
Samuel Masters	1		Md	Jul		summer compl.
Edwin Dorsey	6mo		Md	Aug		diareah
Alex Draper	71		Del.	Feb	none	unknown
Eliza Wright	23	W	Md	Jul		cholera
Nathan Clarke	74	W	Md	Jun		consumption
Robert H. Leslie	26	M	Md	Nov	merchant	typhoid
A. W. Clarke (male)	8		Va	Nov		infant.Rheum.
Lemuel Hawkins	13		Md	Oct		brain inflam.
Eliza Fowler	1		Md	Jul		dysentary
Joshua Stapleton	5		Md	Apr		scarlet fever
Ruth Howell	30		Md	May		consumption
Elizabeth Davidson	87	W	Md	Jul		old age
Mary Cole	70		Md	Jun		heart disease
Eliza Williams	7mo		Md	Apr		catarrah fever
Columbus Irwin	1		Md	Aug		dysentary
Andrew Carman	2mo		Md	Dec		decline
			Mt. Hope Hospital			
James Hechum	25	M	Md	Apr	clerk	brain fever
Henry Hawkins	70	M	Md	Jun	unknown	unknown
Matthew Saivley	60		Ire.	Jun	merchant	heart disease
Ester Bracelam	32		Pa	Jul		consumption
John Vincente	70	M	Md	Jul	seacaptain	appoplexy
Eliz. Freeland	80	M	Md	Jul		debility
Sister Rufina Ware	36		Pa	Aug		consumption
Eliza Drashnid?	85	M	Md	Aug		debility
William Bruck	2		La.	Jul		dysentary

61

MORTALITY SCHEDULE OF MARYLAND

persons who died during the year ending 1 June 1850

COUNTY   Baltimore   DISTRICT   20th Ward, Baltimore City

name	age	mar wid	birth place	mon. died	Occupation	cause of death
			Mt. Hope Hospital			
Cath. Wiseman	18		Ger	Aug		typhoid
James Kerr	39		Ire.	Aug	merchant	consumption
James Carey	25		Ire.	Sep	clerk	consumption
Charles Ross	30		Md	Sep		intern. Fl.
R. Kerly (male)	30		Ire.	Sep	laborer	dysentary
William Kinny	45		Ire.	Oct	clerk	unknown
James Thomas	25	M	Md	Dec	physician	brain fever
Francis Thorne	35	M	Md	Dec	physician	inter. fever
Jacob Penn	40	M	Md	Jan	mechanic	interm. fev.
Susanna Long	80	M	Md	Feb		debility
Richard O'Dwyer	30		Ire.	May	clergyman	brain inflam.
Agnes Randolph	27	M	Md	May		consumption
Mary Saul	28		La.	Aug		consumption
Mary McKenna	85	M	Ire.	Aug		cancer
William Ashmun	35		Md	Jul		interim fever
Owin Donnely	50	M	Irel	Jul		consumption
Robert Brown	40		Md	Jan		brain inflam.
			1st. District			
Julia Burk	72		Ire.	Mar		not listed on
Lewis Collis (fem)	30		Ger	Jul		this pg.139
Maria Morison	25		Ger	Aug		
John Walton	65		Md	Aug	none	ALMS HOUSE
Stephen Farren	51		Ire.	Jun	peddler	from best infor-
Christian Tella	37		Ger	Aug	none	mation census
James McLean	46		Irel.	Jun	plumber	taker could
William Taylor	55		Md	May	laborer	obtain.
Elizabeth Ash	52		Md	Jul		
Cornealius Griscum	51		Irel	Jun	shoemaker	
Peter Doyle	66		Irel.	Jul	laborer	
John Kinsey	68		Ger	Jul	laborer	
Francis Lewis (black)	37		Md	Jun	none	
John Frederick	39		Ger	Jan	sailor	
George Harden	47		Ger	Jul	none	
Everitt Dwyer	61		Irel	Jul	shoemaker	
Sarah Elsey	47		Md	Jul		
Patrick Martin	40		Irel	Jul	none	
Euphemia Hane	47		Md	Jun		
John F. Miller	49		Ger	Jul	none	
Vincent G. Johnson	30		Md	Jun	none	
Letitia Cambell	78		Ire.	Jul		
Peter Agler	1		Ger	Sep		
Rebecca Scott	39		Unkn.	Jun		
Lafayet Cook	1		Md	Jun		
Elizabeth Brown	19		Md	Jul		
David Conway	19		Ire.	Aug	laborer	
John Taylor	30		unkn.	Jul		
Peter Sweedenbury	37		Md	Jul		
Eliza Whittington(black)	45		N.J.	Jul		

62

MORTALITY SCHEDULE OF MARYLAND

persons who died during the year ending 1 June 18<u>50</u>

COUNTY Baltimore   DISTRICT 1st District

name	age	mar wid	birth place	mon. died	Occupation	cause of death
Cathrine Vestling	38	M	Ger	Aug		dysentary
Lizza Vestling	8mo		Md	Aug		dysentary
Mercy A. Musgrave	6mo		Md	Jul		whooping cough
Thomas Gill	23		Md	Sep	laborer	accident
John Gill	51	M	Eng.	Mar	shoemaker	unknown
Elizabeth Baltzell	73		Va	Feb		unknown
Susan Clemens	31		Md	Oct		consumption
Hughey Bone	1mo		Md	Apr		unknown
Gelson Thomson	59	M	Md	Nov	laborer	dropsey
John Hinebaugh	6mo		Md	Aug		diarrhea
Nancy Siryer?	46	W	Irel	Nov		gastric fever
John W. Rigley	12		Md	Aug		diareha
Francis Lot Armatage	24		Eng	Mar	cabinetmaker	cramps
Elizabeth Robison	2mo		Md	May		dropsey
Ephraim Gallagher	2		Md	Oct		croup
Mary A. Buckingham	52	M	Eng	Mar		heart disease
Alevia McClain	1mo		Md	Oct		rash
Elizabeth Griffith	66		Ire.	Jul		dropsy
Samuel H. Ware	11mo		Md	Aug		inflamation
Mary J. Ware	8		Md	Aug		bowel cos.
Conrad Faster	1		Md	Apr		small pox
Nathaniel Gruin	49	M	Md	Apr	farmer	unknown
George Hiller	1		Md	May		unknown
William Myers	1mo		Md	May		unknown
Harriet Steel	42	M	Eng	Feb		pleurisy
Alice A. McMann	4		Md	Jul		cholaria
Eliza Thomas	51	M	Md	Aug		bronchitis
Eldin Appleby	3mo		Md	Mar		scarlet feever
Elizabeth Barton	4		Md	Mar		scarlet fever
Mary Barton	2		Md	Feb		scarlet fever
Abarilla Cooper	42	M	Md	Jan		child bed
Charles H. Lindle	1mo		Md	Feb		chatrrah fever
Ann Young	59	W	Md	Jul		unknown
Elizabeth Carroll	82	W	Gcr	Feb		old age
George Schibeline	46	M	Ger	Jan	weaver	scroffola
Ann Slager	43	M	Ger	Apr		unknown
Harriet Scipper	48	M	Md	Nov		unknown
William H. German	28	M	Md	Nov	laborer	cholic
Henry Swartz	49	M	Md	Mar	farmer	paralises
Dr. A.J. Swartz	78	W	Ger	Apr	physician	unknown
Mary Henderson (black)	30	M	Md	Mar		childbed
Robin Vaughn	19		Md	Feb	shoemaker	consumption
James Bosley	27	M	Md	Dec	machinist	small pox
John Ward	74	M	Md	Sep	laborer	unknown
Ann Earp	44	W	Md	Apr		palsey
Louis Earp	14		Md	Jul		plurisy
Joel Greenfield	27	M	unkn.	Dec	merchant	consumption
Caroline B. Warfield	32	M	Md	Jun		inflamation
Amanda Dicas	18		Md	Sep		consumption
Phillip McNuty	56	M	Ire.	Sep	stonemason	bilious fever
Caroline Butler	11mo		Md	Mar		pleurisy

MORTALITY SCHEDULE OF MARYLAND

persons who died during the year ending 1 June 18<u>50</u>

COUNTY Baltimore   DISTRICT 1st.District

name	age	mar wid	birth place	mon. died	Occupation	cause of death
Hannah J. Hughes	11mo		Md	Jun		brain fever
Elihu Smith	50	M	Md	Jul	cooper	dispepsia
John Mullenex	23		Va	Mar	laborer	unknown
Matilda Mullenex	19		Va	Mar		unknown
Hannah Mullenex	44	M	Va	Mar		consumption
Samuel Mullenex	4		Va	Mar		unknown
Christina Mullenex	3		Va	Mar		unknown
Louisa Mullenex	9		Va	Mar		unknown
Amelia Mullenex	17		Va	Mar		unknown
Edward Brashaw	1		Md	Feb		grastric fever
William Hartwell	40	M	Ire.	Aug	laborer	unknown
Mary E. Schanogts	32	M	Ger	Mar		child bed
James H. Garman	1mo		Md	Jul		Iresipatis
Elizabeth Hitchcock	34	M	Md	Feb		consumption
John T. Bags	8mo		Md	Sep		Disintary
Elizabeth Hoges	56	W	Md	Sep		disintary
Joseph Smith	81	M	Eng	Apr	farmer	old age
Elizabeth A.Merryman	1		Md	Aug		whooping cough
Benjamin Wheeler	65	M	Md	Oct	farmer	dropsy
Mary P. Matthews	3		Md	Feb		scarlet fever
Olover Matthews	5		Md	Feb		scarlet fever
Sarah Matthews	11mb		Md	Feb		scarlet fever
Caleb Lowe	21		Md	Apr	sailor	yellow fever
Rada Price	80	M	Pa	May		plurisy
Mordic Price of M.	80	M	Md	May	farmer	Nomania
Elijah R. Ensor	3		Md	May		scarlet fever
Josephen Greacy	1		Md	Nov		quincy
William Wooden	40	M	Md	Oct	laborer	paretitic
Willian T. Anderson	2		Md	Apr		croup
Sedikiah Masemer	1		Md	Aug		diarrhea
Mary J. Armacort	7		Md	Aug		gastric fever
Grafton Bowen	3mo		Md	Jul		typhoid
Henry Levenline	59		Ger	Aug	none	
John Huggins	76		Md	Feb		no causes on this page
Dedrick Hickman	41		Ger	Jul		
Benjamin Green(black)	61		Md	Oct	laborer	
John Upton	67		Md	Jul	blacksmith	
William Porter	52		Eng	Jun	cooper	
William Doake	70		Scot.	Jul	weaver	
Francis Treacy	5		Md	Jul		
Martha Morrison	26		Md	Jul		
Jethro Dunkan	90		N.J.	Jul		
John Shoder	50		Ger	Aug	laborer	
Elias Jones	62		Md	Sep	laborer	
Thomas Benson	63		Wales	Nov	blacksmith	
William Morgan	49		Pa.	Nov	laborer	
Zacharia Taylor	2mo		Md	Dec		
Rode Kelty (male)	55		Ire.	Jan	tanner	
D.Stumpenhouse	45		Ger	Feb	laborer	
Samuel Morgan	1mo		Md	Jan		
Benjamin Coe	42		Md	Mar	none	
Felix Logan	40		Irel.	Jan	laborer	

64

MORTALITY SCHEDULE OF MARYLAND

persons who died during the year ending 1 June 18<u>50</u>

COUNTY Baltimore   DISTRICT 1st District

name	age	mar wid	birth place	mon. died	Occupation	cause of death
James Gallager	55		Ire.	Mar	laborer	Alms house
John Gerst	49		Ger	Apr		
James Baker	21		Ger.	Feb		
John Millet	1mo		Md	May		
John T.Whittington(black)	5		Md	Jun		
Louis Robinson	51		Md	Jul		
Risden Harrison	53		Md	Jul	shipcarpenter	
Nicholas Gallager	61		Md	Jul		
Eveline Smith	31		Md	Jul		
Ann Smith	2mo		Md	Aug		
William Edwards	41		Md	Jul	laborer	
Briget Higans	48		Ire	Aug'		
John A. Killady	20		Ire.	Jul	none	
Andrew Welsh	60		Ire.	Jun	carpenter	
Sophia Creswell	23		Md	Jun		
Rose Bush	80		WestInd.	Jul		
Charles Hansen	82		Md	Jul	none	
Elizabeth McKeoan	75		Md	Jul		
Charles Digan	25		Irel.	Jul	none	
E.M.D. Raine	50		D.C.	Jul	teacher	
Stewart A. Cornick	60		Md	Jul		
John Hubert	54		France	Jul	laborer	
Christing Masner(black)	33		Ger.	Jul	mariner	
Barbara Hearter	3		Md	Oct		diarrhea
Lawrence W. Mitzler	6mo		Md	May		brain fever
Augustus Stump	3		Ger	Dec		croup
William Hannah	9		Md	Nov		disentary
Eveline S. Post	3mo		Pa	Apr		lung inflam.
Maria Smith	33	M	Md	May		consumption
Benjamin Griffith	77	M	Md	May	farmer	eresepolas
Susan Penny	25		Md	Mar		consumption
Eliza Baker	37	M	Md	Apr		consumption
Edward C.Shelly	7		Md	Nov		unknown
Isaac VanBebber	66	W	Md	Jan		paraletic
Henry Walter	11mo		Md	Apr		unknown
John Groff	28		Ger	Jan		unknown
Catherine Sides	10		Pa	Feb		unknown
William L. Gibson	67	M	Ga.	Sep	clergyman	unknown
Jane Light	36	M	Md	Feb		unknown
Charles R. Loyd	2		Md	Mar		disentary
Alfred Worrell	6		Md	Aug		diarrhea
William Lori	3mo		Md	Jul		unknown
Urith E. Myers	4		Md	Aug		scarlet fever
Mary E. Wilson	6		Md	Aug		scarlet fever
Clementine Wilson	2		Md	Jul		lung inflam.
John Hamilton	1		Md	Jul		scarlet fever
John L. Lee	1		Md	Jun		scald
George Richardson	55	M	Md	Aug		sucide
Margaret Harbeson	12		Irel.	Jul		small pox
Mary A. Harbeson	5		Irel	Jul		small pox
Jane Harbeson	1		Irel	Jul		small pox

65

MORTALITY SCHEDULE OF MARYLAND

persons who died during the year ending 1 June 18<u>50</u>

COUNTY   Balitmore   DISTRICT   1st District

name	age	mar wid	birth place	mon. died	Occupation	cause of death
Robert E. Wilson	4		Md	Jul		scarlet fever
Henrietta L. Ray	1		Md	May		unknown
Ellen Carmichel	1		Md	May		dropsy
Ann S. Switzer	15		Md	Aug		congest.fever
Jacob B. Uppercos	35	M	Md	May	carpenter	sorethroat
Rebecca Starr	38	M	Md	Jul		consumption
Rheuben Hammond	41		Md	Jan	none	Manupta?
John Younger	49	M	Md	Mar		typhoid
John Waltemeyer	33	M	Md	Apr	engineer	congistien
Mariah L. Cunningham	6		Md	Oct		bronchitas
John McManus	23		Irel.	Oct	miner	unknown
John Smith	30	M	Irel.	Feb	laborer	disentary
Thomas Clanan	43	M	Irel	Jan		bilious fever
Christian Ourspring	25	M	Ger.	Mar	miner	unknown
Catharine A. Ourspring	4		Md	May		chickenpox
John Schmidt	37	M	Ger	Jun	laborer	accident
Mary Lurman	4mo		Md	Apr		unknown
Christian Schibe	1mo		Md	Apr		unknown
William Garner	9mo		Md	Nov		scarlet fever
George Barr	4mo		Md	Apr		unknown
Frances Scharer	1		Md	Aug		summer compl.
Charles Miller	6		Ger	Dec		measles
William Byden	60	M	Eng	Nov	stonemason	dropsy
George Lemmer	34	M	Ger	Mar	tailor	consumption
Theresa Horman	1		Md	May		fits
Joseph Strank	1mo		Md	Jan		unknown
Joseph Starr	6mo		Md	Aug		consumption
Joshua Lee	45	M	Md	May	farmer	unknown
William Parks	26	M	Md	Sep	farmer	unknown
Susan Beers	60		Md	Jul		
Mary Monrow	49		Md	Jul		Alms house
Alice Conelly	46		Irel	Jul		none on this page
John Dempsey	49		Md	Jan	chairmaker	
JamesBarkley	41		Scot.	Sep	weaver	
Mary Montgue	46		Eng	Nov		
Susan Jeffries	42		Md	Jul		
John Garren	68		N.Y.	Jul	carpenter	
Joseph Stewars	26		Md	Aug	cooper	
Dortha Bilsen	44		Ger	Jul		
Adam Arnold	43		Ger	Jul	none	
Charles Brown	10		Md	Aug		
Michael Papto	64		Ger	Jul	none	
John Moles	50		Md	Jul	coopersmith	
James Hughs	30		Irel.	Aug	laborer	
Arena Hagard	33		Md	Jul		
Martha Wirters	15		Md	Jun		
William Meseke	62		Ger	Jul	none	
James O'Brian	10		Va.	Mar		
John Miller	65		Ger	Jul	shoemaker	
James Hickey	70		Irel.	Jul	laborer	
John Ormsby	78		Irel	Jul	laborer	
Thomas Elliott	73		Md	Jul	plasterer	

66

MORTALITY SCHEDULE OF MARYLAND

persons who died during the year ending 1 June 18_50_

COUNTY Baltimore   DISTRICT 1st District
                                   2nd District

name	age	mar wid	birth place	mon. died	Occupation	cause of death
Margaret Kenly	76		Irel.	Nov		
Hannah Herring	44		N.Y.	Jul		
? Lungran (male)	63		Swed.	Jul	mariner	
		2nd District				
Benjamin F. Green	33	M	Md	Apr	farmer	pleurisy
Vincent Green	38	W	Md	Jan	farmer	pleurisy
John Langwell	50	M	Md	May	laborer	heart disease
Ann R. Cole	9mo		Md	Feb		croup
Susan Murphy	2		Md	Apr		scarlet fever
Jane Plavin	9mo		Eng.	Nov		quincy
Ellen Grant	1mo		Md	Jul		unknown
Mary Comegges	3mo		Md	Sep		bilious fever
Christopher Jones	10mo		Md	Oct		teething
George W. Bailey	37	M	Md	Oct		unknown
John Hayden	40	M	Irel.	Sep	manager	dysentary
Ellen Knight	4		Md	Jan		scarlet fever
Joseph Bennett	32		Md	Dec	farmer	unknown
David Wilson	29		Md	Mar	blacksmith	poleurisy
Charles York	10mo		Md	Jun		pleurisy
Edward D. Hughes	3		Md	Sep		scarlet fever
Elisth Bidelison	62	W	Md	May		unknown
Edward Eagleston	10		Md	Dec		dysentery
Susan Eagleston	7mo		Md	Aug		biloius
Stephen Grimes	78	M	Md	Jan	farmer	pleurisey
Eliza Lackey	1		Va.	Jul		dropsy
Margaret Tereon	70	W	France	May		unknown
Elizabeth Binner	63	W	Md	Dec		consumption
Julia Kelly	2		Md	Sep		dysentary
Sussannah Collins	3mo		Md	Jun		dysentary
Mary E. Havener	8mo		D.C.	Jul		water on brain
Elizabeth Black	2		Md	Aug		croup
Caroline Anhart	37		Ger	Aug		consumption
Florence G. Brainard	1		Md	Jun		dysentary
Joseph Burgan	20		Md	Sep	farmer	typhoid
John E. Shanklin	1		Md	Apr		scarlet fever
Susannah Shanklin	21	M	Md	Sep		consumption
William H. Mitchell	9		Md	May		scarlet fever
Nancy Lagg	60		Eng	Nov		unknown
Samuel Peterson	25		Md	Nov		small pox
Susan Brown	2		Md	Nov		croup
Ellen Carter	80		Md	Jun		old age
Lewis Wicks	6mo		Md	Jul		dropsy
Jonas Shertz	14		Pa	May		typhoid
William Willingham	36	M	Md	Feb	farmer	consumption
David Keep	9mo		Md	Aug		unknown
Ellen Herbert	70	W	Md	Feb		unknown
Frederick Grosscufs	70	M	Pa.	May	farmer	bowel inflam.
Mary Meads	82		Md	Apr	farmer	old age
Thomas Moore	16		Md	Sep	farmer	dysentary
Zeno Chalk	72	M	Md	Feb	farmer	biloius
Isabel Wells	5		Md	Aug		unknown
Mary Francis	5mo		Md	Aug		dyesentary
			67			

MORTALITY SCHEDULE OF MARYLAND

persons who died during the year ending 1 June 18<u>50</u>

COUNTY BALTIMORE   DISTRICT 2nd District

name	age	mar wid	birth place	mon. died	Occupation	cause of death
Amanda Brognard	40		Verm.	Mar		dropsey
Rebecca Carter	70		Md	Dec		old age
William Carter	83		Md	Jan	shoemaker	pleurisy
John Merryman	84		Md	Nov	farmer	old age
Mary Morton	80		Irel.	Jul		old age
James Bosley	82		Md	May	farmer	palsy
John Wier	33		Md	Nov	farmer	tumor
Balinda Housman	23		Md	Aug		dropsey
Elizabeth Plournan	24		Md	Oct		fever
Cassandra Williams	60	M	Md	Feb		pleurisy
Hannah Slade	30		Md	Oct		unknown
Ruth Collet	73		Md	Apr		unknown
Barbara McDonald	3mo		Md	Aug		dysentery
Mary McDonald	3mo		Md	Aug		dysentery
John Bockhotel	18		Md	Nov	farmer	gastric fever
Thomas Gorsuch	12		Md	Oct		scarlet fever
Hannah Gorsuch	12		Md	Aug		dysentery
Rebecca Griffin	89		Md	Apr		old age
George Canoles	10		Md	Aug		scarlet fever
Sarah Stansbury	5		Md	Jan		scarlet fever
John Buck	82		Md	Oct	farmer	old age
Joseph Black	1		Md	Jul		pulmonary
Sophia Mace	55		Md	Nov		unknown
Catherine, Emily, Charlotte Alfred, Josephine, Olenia, Phillip, Mary McCubbin	all under 10		Md	Dec		scarlet fever
Louisa Thompson	17		Md	Sep		bilious fever
James Thomas	60	W	Md	Oct	farmer	dropsy
Andrew Doyle	23		Irel.	Mar	laborer	accident
Eliza Gupton	4		Md	Jul		dysentary
Cath. Burns	7		Md	Apr		catarah
Enneanor Shaffer	1		Md	Mar		croup
Nancy Alexander	87	W	Pa	Oct		old age
Maria Banks	29		Md	Apr		consumption
John Bowlin	11mo		Md	Dec		bilious
Phillip Deane	21		Md	Oct	laborer	bilious
George Ensor	41	M	Md	Aug	rolling mill	consumption
Richard Hawkins	5		Md	May		accident
Robert McCauley	55	M	Irel	Sep	farmer	pleurisy
Ruth Parks	76	W	Md	Jul		old age
Samuel Wilson	99	M	Md	Aug	farmer	liver compl.
Mary Hitch	80	W	Md	Aug		brain inflam.
Sarah Hardy	60		Md	Aug		lung inflam.
Mary Wallers	1		Md	Aug		water on brain
Sarah Harryman	4		Md	Nov		dysentery
Laura Ford	1		Md	Oct		unknown
Ellen Knight	4		Md	Jan		scarlet fever
Joseph Bennett	32		Md	Dec	farmer	unknown
John Biddle	66	M	Md	May	farmer	dysentery
William Lewis	1		Md	Jul		none
Patrick Moriarity	28	M	Irel.	Jul	laborer	sun stroke
Mary Butler	21	M	Md	Apr		scarlet fever

MORTALITY SCHEDULE OF MARYLAND

persons who died during the year ending 1 June 1850

COUNTY   BALTIMORE   DISTRICT   2nd.Dist.

name	age	mar wid	birth place	mon. died	Occupation	cause of death
John Deal	74	W	Eng	Mar	shoemaker	paralytic
Henry Bides	62	M	Ger.	Aug	carpenter	unknown
Deborah Burgan	8mo		Md	Aug		dysentary
Eli Gammon	2		Md	Oct		bronchitis
Margaret Lustatz	46	M	Ger	Mar		unknown
Mary Fanastell	62	M	Ger	Aug		typhoid
James Siddon	69		Md	Feb		bowel inflam.
Phillip Pearce	78		Md	Oct		dropsey
Thomas Parlette	1mo		Md	May		small pox
Francis Gruss	89	W	Ger	Sep		old age
Charles J. Bullins	35	M	N.Y.	Feb	merchant	stomach inflam.
Augustus Plowman	17		Md	Jan	cottonspinner	Rhemutism
William Curry	43	M	Md	Sep	cottonpacker	consumption
Mary Madden	76		Md	Apr		brain inflam.
Mary Gillingham	66	W	Md	Feb		consumption
William Carmine	1		Md	Mar		fits
Drucilla Ford	67	W	Md	Jan		old age
James Bravard	9mo		Md	Dec		unknown
James Macubbin	10		Md	Jan		scarlet fever
Elizabeth Macubbin	14		Md	Dec		scarlet fever
Charles Macubbin	12		Md	Dec		scarlet fever
Valentine Cross	6		Md	Jan		scarlet fever
Charles Cross	2		Md	Jan		scarlet fever
Ann Strickland	76		Md	Jun		consumption
Mary Chambers	1		Md	Jun		dysentary
Nathan Daniels	90		Md	Dec	laborer	consumption
Edwin Holt	10		Md	Feb		unknown
James Bowen	20		N.J.	Apr	farmer	consumption
Timothy Murtagh	60		Irel	Jul	laborer	ship fever
Francis Hunt	1		Md	Aug		bowel inflam.
Melchizedick Green	70		Md	Apr		intoxication
Mary Green	103		Md	Dec		cancer
Joseph Murray	61		Pa	Apr		catarrah
Eliza Pearce	48	M	Md	Aug		gastric fever
William Slade	75	M	Md	Jun	farmer	palsy
James Hunter	74		Md	Sep	farmer	dysentery
Elizabeth Hutchins	62	W	Md	Dec		paralysis
Carter Hutchins	8		Md	Apr		unknown
Walter Perdue	48		Md	Mar	farmer	dropsy
Richard Kemp	74	W	Eng.	Oct	manufacturer	appoplexy
Margaret Hartman	14		Md	Sep		dysentery
Mary Ballard	11mo		Md	Oct		teething
Nancy Stevenson	42	M	Irel	May		unknown
Andra Smith	27		Md	Dec		consumption
Anna S.James	5		Md	Sep		dysentery
Christian Bartol	65	M	Ger	Jul	blacksmith	unknown
Elizabeth Harris	27		Md	May		consumption
John Shields	58	M	Irel.	Aug	gardener	dysentary
Georgiann Waters	6		Md	Apr		unknown
John Norris	50		Irel	Jun	laborer	sun stroke
Elizabeth Ross	20	M	Md	May		spasms

MORTALITY SCHEDULE OF MARYLAND

persons who died during the year ending 1 June 18 50

COUNTY Baltimore   DISTRICT 2nd.Dist.& 5th Dist.

name	age	mar wid	birth place	mon. died	Occupation	cause of death
Susan Bradley	1		Md	Jan		dysentary
Ann Nolan	29	M	Irel	Apr		typhoid
Elizabeth Amos	67		Md	Mar		consumption
Charles Amos	7mo		Md	Aug		brain dropsy
Charles Brinber	37		Eng	Sep		unknown
Rebecca Hedrick	45	M	Md	May		consumption
Benajamin Culver	72		Md	Mar	carpenter	cancer
Susan Martin	13		Md	Aug		dysentery
Ann Henneman	1		Md	Aug		dysentery
James Gray	19		Md	Aug	laborer	brain congest.
Charles Hurst	1mo		Md	Apr		pneumonia
Mary Hammond	50		Md	Apr		unknown
Edward Hughes	3		Md	Sep		scarlet fever
Mary Miller	4		Md	Aug		cholera
Isiah Ennis	1		Md	Aug		brain fever
Augustus Winter	7mo		Md	Jun		dysentery
George Dunning	60	M	Md	Mar	trunkkeeper	heart disease
Jacob Gunter	2		Md	Apr		unknown
Achsah Gott	70	W	Md	Aug		dysentery
John Hopkins	72	M	Md	Mar	farmer	erisipelas
Rebecca Hopkins	60	M	Md	Mar		erisipelas
Thomas Riley	6mo		Md	May		dysentery
Emily R. Cole	1		Md	Jul		dysentery
Isaiah Beooks	37	M	Md	Jun	laborer	bilious fever
Samuel Williams	1mo		Md	Oct		catarah
5th District						
Charlotte Rainbow (mul)	50		Md	Oct		swelling
Daniel Wisner	10mo		Md	Oct		eresypilius
Frances Shaul	23		Md	Oct		dysentary
John T. Cole	8		Md	Aug		dysentary
Kinsey Naylor	59		Md	Jan	farmer	asthma
Charles Poleman	50		Ger.	Mar	laborer	sudden
Melchor Thompson	20		Md	Feb	farmer	lock jaw
Joshua Green	18		Md	May		pleurisy
Robert Harper	50		Md	Dec	laborer	palsy
Jacob Wheeler	2		Md	Aug		dysentary
J.T.Wilhelm	10mo		Md	Aug		dysentery
Mary Duffy	2		Md	Apr		burnt
John Martin	7		Md	Sep		dysentery
Margaret Crother	2		Md	Jun		jaundice
Linda Peregoy	19		Md	Oct		typhoid
Mary A. Peregory	17		Md	Feb		typhoid
Samuel Bond	3		Md	Feb		Bas.fever
Elizabeth Cox	27		Md	Mar		consumption
Amos Cox	50	M	Md	Dec	farmer	consumption
Jane Cullison	1		Md	Aug		dysentery
George Louck	57		Md	Apr		paulsey
Ellen Clother	14		Md	Feb		catar.fever
Louis Ports	4mo		Md	Jan		brain inflam.
Joshua Marshall	6		Pa	Oct		dysentary
Michael Hair	70		Md	Mar	farmer	consumption
Elizabeth Wisner	1		Md	Mar		scarlet fever

70

MORTALITY SCHEDULE OF MARYLAND

persons who died during the year ending 1 June 18 <u>50</u>

COUNTY BALTIMORE - CALVERT   DISTRICT 5th District & 6th Dist.

name	age	mar wid	birth place	mon. died	Occupation	cause of death
James Crow	21		Md	Mar	teacher	fits
Belinda Armacost	1		Md	Mar		dropsy
			6th District			
Thomas Albin	3		Md	May		scarlet fever
Mary Vanderslice	40	M	Md	Jul		consumption
Polly Gist	65		Md	Mar		paulsey
John Sanchard	40		Pa	Nov	farmer	liver compl.
Catharine Bolinger	22		Md	Mar		typhoid
Alice Ann Rhule	2		Md	May		inflamation
James Palmer	10		Md	Sep		dysentary
Frances Palmer	3		Md	Sep		dysentary
Elizabeth Williams	5		Md	Jul		inflamation
Ann Morris	10		Md	Sep		dysentary
Hy Marsh	2		Md	Mar		bil.fever
William Tracy	7		Md	Sep		fits
Hugh Keasy	42	M	Md	Apr		fever
Casander Williams	56	M	Md	Feb		bil.pleurisy
William Bull	7mo		Md	Feb		cathar.fever
			CALVERT COUNTY -Dist.1			
William S. Sangston	47	M	Carol.Co.	Jun	merchant	unknown
James E. Sellors	40	M	Calvert	Jan	farmer	brain inflam.
Samuel A. Jenson	25		"	May	manager	brain inflam.
Ann Pardoe	70	W	"	Mar		old age
James J.Pardoe	34	M	"	Oct	farmer	congest.fever
Benson Pardoe	4		"	Jun		dropsy
Susan Young	30	M	"	Aug		spasms
Rebecca Taylor	60	W	"	Feb		old age
Elizabeth King	25		"	Jul		congestion
Benjamin Johnson	5		"	May		unknown
Everat T. Pardoe	7mo		"	Feb		unknown
Thomas Simmons	5		"	Sep		fever
William Simmons	30	M	"	Oct	farmer	consumption
Edwin Hungerford	30	M	"	Mar	machanic	pleurisy
Joseph Stewart	57	M	A.A.Co.	Nov	farmer	consumption
John B. Joy	49	M	St.MaryCo.	Dec	farmer	consumption
William A. Tolley	34	M	Som.Co.	Sep	farmer	bowel inflam.
Teresa Wheeler	3mo		Calvert	Sep		brain inflam.
Angaline Wheeler	3		"	Sep		brain inflam.
William J.Jones	1		"	Jan		unknown
Mary Allen	1		"	Aug		bilious
David Allen	2mo		"	Oct		bilious
Hannah Gray	17		"	Sep		throat inflam.
Ruth Cockran	25	M	"	Sep		fever
Joseph T.Wilson	45	M	"	Sep	farmer	typhoid
Jane Sollars	50	W	"	Sep		rheutism
Elizabeth Reynolds	70	W	Md	Dec		heart disease
Margaret Allnutt	68		Md	Mar		paralytic
Mary A. Turner	8		Md	Oct		worms
Elizabeth Hodgkins	31	M	Md	Jul		child birth
Henry M. Spicknell	22		Md	May		dysentary

71

MORTALITY SCHEDULE OF MARYLAND

persons who died during the year ending 1 June 1850

COUNTY -CALVERT-CAROLINE   DISTRICT

name	age	mar wid	birth place	mon. died	Occupation	cause of death
Amelia Leitch	60	W	Md	Jan		dropsy
Sarah A. Soper	13		Md	Aug		bowel comp.
Rebecca Soper	3		Md	Jul		bowel comp.
Druscilla Norfolk	30		Md	May		dropsey
Rebecca Taylor	26	M	Md	Apr		pleurisy
Priscilla E. Norfolk	6		Md	Sep		stomach dis.
Walter Crawford	6		Md	Oct		croup
Martha Crawford	4		Md	Oct		croup
Martha Brightly	32	W	Md	Aug		palsy
Mary Jane Brightly	4		Md	Oct		billious
Rebecca D. Dowell	27	M	Md	Jun		consumption
Cornelia Dowell	2		Md	Oct		consumption
James W. Ross	6		Md	Jan		dropsey
Walter B.Williams	2		Md	Jan		scarlet fever
Priscilla Bowen	75	W	Md	Jan		not known
Zachariah Hance	18		Md	Aug	planter	unknown
Benjamin F. Ward	3		Md	May		dropsey
John Beckett	55	M	Md	May		appoplexy
Drusilla Gray	40	M	Md	Feb		consumption
		CAROLINE COUNTY				
Mary Spurry	4mo		Md	Nov		none
Saray Spurry	3mo		Md	Aug		none
Mary Bishop	30	M	Md	Mar		consumption
George Milby	1		Md	Sep		unknown
Frances Roe (male)	11		Md	Aug		none
William Howley	69	M	Md	none	farmer	heart dis.
Sarah Baggs	5		Md	Sep		heart disease
Margaret A. Thomas	37		Md	Aug		consumption
William E. Straughan	29		Md	Mar	farmer	typhoid
Joseph Manering	45	M	Md	Aug		disentary
Mary E. Morgan	22	M	Md	Mar		pleurisy
John Whitby	35		Md	Dec		throat inflam.
Rebecca Wheeler	75	M	Md	Oct		old age
James Satterfield	60	W	Md	May		none
Mary Rathele	39	M	Md	Feb		none
James Cooper	43	M	Md	Nov	carpenter	arisyplisis
Ann James	80	W	Md	Jun		old age
James Harris	1mo		Md	Oct		none
Margaret Thorp	53	W	Md	Jul		none
Mary Mathews	83	W	Md	Jul		cholora
Thomas Roe	63	M	Md	Apr	farmer	consumption
Joseph Pearson	2mo		Md	Sep		unknown
Willie Cockran	5		Md	Jul		dyeriah
Davy E. Harriss	1		Md	Aug		dysentary
Sarah Garretson	40	M	Md	Jan		unknown
Thomas Garner	26		Md	Oct	merchant	not known
??elle Turner (fem)	31		Md	Mar		consumption
Mary Davis	2mo		Md	Jan		consumption
James Saulsbury	38	M	Md	May	farmer	sudden
John Parris	40	M	Del.	Jun	farmer	unknown
John W. Andrew	20		Md	May	laborer	none

72

MORTALITY SCHEDULE OF MARYLAND

persons who died during the year ending 1 June 18 50

COUNTY-CAROLINE - CARROLL DISTRICT

name	age	mar wid	birth place	mon. died	Occupation	cause of death
Lucinda Christopher	35	M	Md	Mar		consumption
Benjamin Atwile	86	W	Md	May		dysentary
Thomas Willis	18		Md	May	laborer	typhoid
Mary Eaton	6mo		Md	Jul		dysentary
Jane Chaffnick	20	M	Md	Apr		bilious
Margaret Kenton	67	M	Md	May		consumption
Elizabeth Chesman	29	M	Md	May		consumption
Mary Rickets	45		Md	Aor		none
Ann W. Stewart	22	M	Md	Dec		conpurment
Elizabeth Welloughby	68	W	Md	Dec		consumption
Alexander Nicholson	2		Md	Dec		brain inflam.
Eliza Carey	40		Md	Nov		liver compl.
Mary Carey	26	M	Md	Sep		kick by horse
Samuel Stevens	31		Md	Feb	laborer	consumption
James Hicks	21		Md	Apr	laborer	pleurisy
Elizabeth A. Lester	2		Md	Sep		dysentary
			CARROLL COUNTY -Dist.4			
Daniel Elserode	9		Md	Jul		fever
William H. Jones	23		Md	Jul	farmer	bleeding
Margaret Bush	33	M	Md	Aug		typhoid
Dinah Bush	4mo		Md	Sep		typhoid
Ann Maria Bush	10		Md	Sep		typhoid
Francis M. Flater	2		Md	Jan		scarlet fever
Elisha H. Flater	3		Md	Feb		scarlet fever
Franklin M. Horner	7mo		Md	Jan		croup
Susanna Dennoss	7		Md	Apr		typhoid
Samuel Bond	2		Md	Jan		gastric fever
William E.T.Brown	2		Md	Jan		scarlet fever
Elias Blizzard	42	M	Md	Oct	farmer	pleurisy
Henry Clay Garner	1		Md	Sep		cholera
Benjamin F. Brothers	1mo		Md	Apr		scarlet fever
John Williams	80	W	Md	Nov	farmer	sudden
			District 8			
Richard Shultz	9		Md	Sep	farmer	dysentary
William Coltrider	20		Md	Feb	farmer	cat.fever
Mandelia Warehune	8		Md	Feb		epilepsy
Conrad Ebaugh	65	M	Md	Sep	farmer	typhoid
Andrew Ebaugh	49	M	Md	Dec	farmer	typhoid
Eve Nasse	72	M	Pa.	Jul		paralysis
Hiram Brown	3mo		Md	May		bowel inflam.
Elizabeth Ebaugh	88	W	Pa	Apr		old age
Michael Laner	1		Md	Nov		fever
Ann Mary Miller	5		Md	Jan		cat.fever
George Armacost	40	M	Md	Nov	stonemason	dropsy
Thomas B. Murray	40	M	Md	May	farmer	consumption
Jacob Rineman	1		Md	Aug		dysentary
Mary A. Coppersmith	5mo		Md	Jul		dysentary
Elizabeth A. Merryman	10		Md	Sep		typhoid
Eleanor A. Rote	7		Md	May		consumption
Ashton A. Marshall	14		Md	Jul		dropsey
Samuel T. Keller	7mo		Md	Aug		dysentary

persons who died during the year ending 1 June 18_50_

COUNTY - Carroll Co.   DISTRICT -8-5-2 -3

name	age	mar wid	birth place	mon. died	Occupation	cause of death
Margaret Hour	10mo		Md	Jul		dysentary
Elizabeth Fawble	68	M	Md	May		sudden
District 5						
Mary Lague	84	M	Md	Mar		pleurisy
JuliAnn Crooks	2		Md	Mar		scarlet fever
Hamutal T.Wilson	25		Md	Mar		consumption
Elizabeth Shineflow	83		Md	May		old age
George Shipley	75	M	Md	Oct	farmer	unknown
Ellin S.Bennett	13		Md	Jul		worms
Margaret Trott	6mo		Md	Jul		unknown
Nancy Brown	68	M	Md	Apr		sudden
George F. Warfield	80	M	Md	Dec	merchant	complicated
Oliver L. Ensor	9mo		Md	Feb		consumption
George Patterson Jr.	5		Md	Dec		scarlet fever
Lydia Gillis	4		Md	Jun		scarlet fever
Henry Hewitt	9mo		Md	Aug		bowel inflam.
Amos Gather	63		Md	May	none	lung disease
William C. Day	9day		Md	Apr		unknown
Elizabeth A. Buckingham	19		Md	Apr		pleurisy
Robert B. Shipley	6mo		Md	Jul		unknown
District 2						
Charles R. Alcock	2		Md	Jan		scarlet fever
William A. Shaw	1mo		Md	Jul		cholera
John T. Stonaker	4		Md	Dec		scarlet fever
Andrew Werble	65		Md	Apr	farmer	old age
Jesse Stem	3		Md	Dec		scarlet fever
William Taylor	14		Md	Aug		bowel inflam.
James H. McKinstry	4		Md	Dec		scarlet fever
George Pusey	74	W	Md	May	hatter	chronic
Joseph Englar	5		Md	May		scarlet fever
Catharine S. Wolf	4mo		Md	Jan		chronic
Elizabeth Englar	72	W	Pa	Nov		old age
Mary C. Norris	17		Md	Apr		typhoid
Phillip Greenwood	66	M	Md	Nov	farmer	heart disea.
Phillip Greenwood of Jno	38		Md	May	farmer	cholera
Francis M. Ecker	3mo		Md	Apr		burnt
Godfrey Piper	87	W	Germ.	Oct	weaver	diarrhea
Francis Mullinix	29	M	Md	Aug	blacksmith	inflamation
Esther Hibberd	34		Md	May		pleurisy
Elias Stutler	11		Md	Jun		fever
Jacob R. Hafely	1		Md	Aug		cholera
Mary C. Hesson	5		Md	Feb		croup
Susan Circle	7		Md	Apr		scarlet fever
Uriah Baust	27		Md	Dec	farmer	billios
Ezra D.Rinehart	12		Md	Apr		scarlet fever.
District 3						
Jacob F. Kump	10mo		Md	Nov		burnt
John Earhart	55	M	Md	Jul	farmer	scrofilia
Samuel Bankert	6		Md	May		catarah
Samuel Messinger	53	M	Ger.	Feb	farmer	consumption
George Notter	73	W	Md	Apr	farmer	nervous fever

COUNTY CARROLL   DISTRICT -3-6-7

name	age	mar wid	birth place	mon. died	Occupation	cause of death
Susana R. Farmwell	1		Md	Apr		cat.fever
Elizabeth Hahn	79	W	Md	Oct		accident
Hezekiah Flickinger	6mo		Md	Aug		fever
District 6						
David Whiteleather	39	W	Md	Sep	farmer	cat.fever
Susanna Masemer	27	M	Md	Sep		child bed
George Betchner	3mo		Md	Sep		cholera
Martha F. Little	2		Md	Jun		fever
James B. Houck	1mo		Md	Jan		cholera
Catharine Wentz	84	W	Md	Mar		old age
George Stone	32	M	Md	Sep	shoemaker	bronchitis
Jacob Warner	49	M	Md	Jul	farmer	appoplexy
Sarah C. Shaffer	2		Md	Oct		croup
Joshua Brown	79	M	Md	Jan	farmer	inflamation
District 7						
Charles E. Bowenson	10mo		Pa	Aug		disentary
Francis T. Wagoner	1mo		Md	Aug		disentary
James M. Sholman	1mo		Md	Jul		head dis.
George Shafer	1		Md	Oct		disentary
Catharine Durbin	57		Md	Dec		cancer
Martha A. Warner	4		Md	Jan		scarlet fever
Mary X. Stevenson	6mo		Md	Jul		disentary
Elizabeth Nichodemus	25	M	Md	Jul		consumption
Maria F. Shriver	30	M	Md	May		typhoid
Ruth Magee	70	W	Md	Jan		old age
Richard Brown	57	M	Md	Mar	trader	dropsy
Margaret A. Zahn	10mo		Md	May		brain dis.
Elizabeth Freet	13		Pa	Feb		scarlet fever
District 9						
Sarah Mentzer	31		Pa	Feb		consumption
Hannah Dayhoff	28		Md	Sep		consumption
Sarah Sellman	11		Md	Sep		disentary
Mary E. Murray	1		Md	Dec		croup
Elizabeth Drach	45	M	Md	May		appoplexy
Thomas W. Frizle	7		Md	Apr		brain inflam.
Lucy A. Hood	1		Md	Sep		cholera
Mary J. Little	8		Md	Mar		burnt
Barbara Nusbaum	11		Md	May		catarah
Priscilla Aldrige	33	M	Md	Mar		typhoid
Peter Horn	1		Md	Dec		scarlet fever
Alpheus Spurier	74	W	Md	May	farmer	lung inflam.
David Fisher	2		Md	Mar		scarlet fever
Benjamin S. Duvall	6		Md	Apr		typhoid
Robert T. Davis	11mo		Md	Mar		scarlet fever
Amelia Davis	70	W	Md	Mar		lung inflam.
Joseph T. Cushing	5		Md	Aug		diarreah
Adazella Dell	7mo		Md	Mar		unknown
Francis A. Cook	18		Md	May	laborer	consumption
William Z. Frizzle	11mo		Md	Apr		scarlet fever
Margaret A. Rudesill	2		Md	Feb		bronchitis
Martha Fleigle	1mo		Md	May		cholera
Mary C. Shaner	71	W	Md	May		broncitis
William Cornell	69	W	Md	Mar		palsy

MORTALITY SCHEDULE OF MARYLAND

persons who died during the year ending 1 June 18_50_

COUNTY   CARROLL- CECILCOUNTY DISTRICT -7-

name	age	mar wid	birth place	mon. died	Occupation	cause of death
John W. Null	8mo		Md	Apr		cat.fever
John Davis	1		Md	May		strangulation
Threresa Spalding	15		Md	Feb		heart dis.
Abraham Null	82	M	Md	Feb	farmer	phthysic
Jacob Snyder	81	W	Md	Jan	farmer	appoplexy
Margaret A. Lister	1		Md	Aug		cholera
Thomas Newcomer	4mo		Md	Aug		cholera
Elias G. Morrison	17		Md	Mar	farmer	typhoid
John H. Warner	11mo		Md	Oct		bronchitis
Lydia Beal	40	M	Pa.	Aug		consumption
John M. Null	20		Md	Jan	farmer	typhoid
William Pool	4mo		Md	Oct		inflamation
John Duttero	64	W	Md	Apr	farmer	inflamation
Barbara Slagenhaupt	64	W	Md	Apr		appoplsexy
CECIL COUNTY- 3rd Dis.1st.Sub.Div.						
John Howard	9mo		Md	Sep		bil.disentary
Rachel Casho	30	M	Md	Apr		confinement
Samuel Staples	45	M	Conn.	Jun	farmer	rheutism
Mary Moore	9mo		Md	May		brain inflam.
George McCullough	1		Md	May		not known
Richard Bradford	2		Md	Jan		croup
James Hemphill	65	M	Md	Apr	Miller	consumption
Nancy Badger	65		Md	Feb		drunkeness
Mrs.Sarah Atkinson	60	M	Md	mar		unknown
Sarah Hyland	28	M	Md	Nov		consumption
Caroline Crouch Sr.	36	M	Md	Feb		confinement
Caroline Crouch Jr.	5		Md	Nov		brain inflam.
Richard Mahan	63		Md	Feb		unknown
Vicinity of Elkton						
Hugh Davis	1mo		Md	Feb		cat.fever
Sarah McCliston	57		Md	Mar		bilious fever
Hannah Lee	5mo		Md	Jun		brain inflam.
Harriet Ingless	19		Md	Aug		unknown
William Barr	55	M	Md	Apr	farmer	scurvy
Margaret Woodrow	47	M	Md	May		unknown
Mary Gillaspie	41	M	Md	Jan		unknown
James Gillaspie	10		Md	Jan		unknown
Eliza A. Chancy	26		Md	Jun		dysentary
Josiah Woodrow	45	M	Md	Jan	farmer	suicide
John Harris	1		Md	Aug		urriss.
Mary Brown	53	M	Md	May		womb disease
Samuel Wilson	45	M	Md	Mar	farmer	liver compl.
Joseph W. McGregor	34		Md	Nov		sonsumption
Deborah Strickland	22	M	Md	May		consumption
Henry T. Grant	2mo		Md	Nov		whooping cough
Sarah A. Sutton	22		Md	Jan		brain fever
Mary A. Strickland	11mo		Md	Aug		consumption
Annabel Cowan	6		Md	Aug		consumption
John W. Murry	1		Md	Sep		scarlet fever
Jesse Dysart	25		Md	Aug	carpenter	cat.fever
Jesse Baldwin	46	M	Del.	Aug	farmer	typhoid
John M. Devine	21		Pa.	Aug	carpenter	consumption

persons who died during the year ending 1 June 18_50_

COUNTY -CECIL   DISTRICT 2nd.Subdivision

name	age	mar wid	birth place	mon. died	Occupation	cause of death
John W. Alexander	2		Md	Sep		dropsy
Margaret Richardson	86		Md	Oct		consumption
Harriet Wilson	50		Md	Dec		fits
John Boyd	75		Ire.	Dec	none	unknown
Sarah Jackson	1		Md	Mar		lung inflam.
Peter Elberte	83		Md	Mar		consumption
Lydia Spence	30		Pa	Apr		consumption
Allen Wilson	60		Md	Apr	none	fits
Jane Spence	3		Md	May		consumption
Mathias Tyson	54		Md	Jun	farmer	accident
Louisa Kinkard	50		Md	Jul		cholera
Catherine Hammond	70		Md	Jul		consumption
Mary E. Pierce	11mo		Pa	Jan		fits
Mary A. Canan	2mo		Md	Apr		unknown
Thomas H. Lamey	4		Md	Nov		unknown
Josiah Cruthers	50	M	Md	Jun	laborer	Drunkidness
Lemon Spence	12		Md	Feb		consumption
Sarah E. Coe	21		Eng	Mar		consumption
Robert Wright	5mo		Md	Sep		unknown
Henry Harvey	1		Md	Feb		scalded
James R. Moody	2wks		Md	May		croup
Eleanor Kimble	26	M	Pa	Dec		consumption
Clarence S. Kimble	5mo		Pa	Nov		consumption
Catherine Kimble	5mo		Pa	Nov		consumption
Thomas J. Jones	17		Md	Sep	carpenter	typhoid
Emma McCreary	6		Md	Aug		dysentary
Robert Hews	75	M	Ire.	Feb	weaver	stomach
Margaret Hews	35		Md	Feb		liver compl.
Jacob Cooper	75		Pa	Jun	wheelwright	lung inflam.
John Gill	79	M	Del.	Nov	farmer	consumption
John McCauly	27	M	Md	Apr	farmer	lung inflam.
William Lowery	75	W	Md	Feb	farmer	consumption
Charles Morris	3		Pa	Oct		worm fever
Clayton Carter	4		Md	Nov		brain inflam.
Joseph C. Carter	45	W	Md	Feb	paper manuf.	consumption
Margaret Mahoney	39	M	Md	Feb		dropsy
Eliza Terry	38	M	Pa	Oct		confinement
Slayton Terry	3mo		Md	Dec		unknown
John Hearns	25		Md	Sep	carpenter	dysentary
Mary E. Nowland	14		Md	Jan		typhoid
Richard Girvin	26		Ire.	Apr	ditcher	typhoid
Jeramiah Rodgers	72		Md	Dec	farmer	pyralitic
William H. Ruby	11		Pa	Sep		unknown
Eliza J. Lee	26		Md	Mar		lung inflam.
Eliza J. Newton	9		Pa	Aug		heart disease
David Wiley	60	M	Ire.	Aug	weaver	cancer
Jesse Lowe	35		Md	Dec	farmer	frozen
Rebecca A. Weaver	29		Md	Sep		fever
Richard E. Cruthers	3		Md	Oct		dysentary
John Cruthers	45	M	Md	Jun	farmer	consumption
Margaret S. Krauss	2		Md	Nov		burnt
Margaret Woodrow	44	M	Md	Feb		typhoid
Sarah McCullough	28		Md	Oct		consumption

persons who died during the year ending 1 June 18_50_

COUNTY -CECIL   DISTRICT   2nd Sub.Div.

name	age	mar wid	birth place	mon. died	Occupation	cause of death
Thomas Gillaspie	49	W	Md	Sep	cooper	eyrasipilas
Pheby Hill	11mo		Md	Feb		consumption
Ann H. Custer	29	M	Md	Feb		palsy
John Fulton	18		Md	Sep	farmer	dysentary
Ruth Richey	20	M	Md	Oct		bil.fever
Robert Dempsy	50	M	Pa	Aug	farmer	bowel inflam.
Emily Gurley	60	W	Md	Apr		unknown
Rebecca Webb	22		Md	Apr		consumption
Franklin Hasson	4mo		Md	Apr		consumption
James McCurry	3mo		Md	Aug		consumption
Rebecca Waddle	1mo		Md	Aug		sudden
Daniel Preston	89	W	Md	Jan		old age
Leonard Spencer	3mo		Md	Nov		sudden
Sarah Wilson	11	.	Md	May		lungs
Nathan Lackland	59	M	Md	Oct	farmer	consumption
Rebecca Ramsey	10		Md	Sep		dysentary
Peter Hammersmith	77	W	Md	Jul		unknown
John Richardson	1		Md	Apr		unknown
Ruth White	77	W	Ire.	Aug		unknown
Nevin McCormich	2		Md	Aug		unknown
Amanda Reynolds	36	M	Md	May		unknown
Mary Warring	87	W	Md	Aug		unknown
Amos C. Millender	27	M	Md	May	laborer	consumption
Mary Millender	1		Md	Jul		consumption
Ruth Anna Millender	3		Md	Jun		unknown
Jessy Ginna	53	M	Pa	Aug	farmer	pyralitic
George Brown	61	M	Md	Apr	carpenter	bronchitis
Jane Carr	40	W	Irel.	Oct		unknown
Elizabeth Stue	57		Md	Jul		cholera
John D. McCrutchen	75		Md	Mar	miller	sore leg
Rachel Boyer	44	M	Pa.	Feb		unknown
Ann A. Sweet	1		Md	Oct		dysentary
Eli W. Jamey	22		Md	Mar	schoolteacher	consumption
John Brooks	44	M	Eng.	Feb	weaver	unknown
Mary A. Steel	5		Pa.	Dec		scrofola
William Marshall	69	M	Eng.	Sep	farmer	liver compl.
Margaret Davis	25	M	Md	May		consumption
Samuel McClenahan	4		Md	Nov		brain inflam.
Sarah A. McMullen	5mo		Md	Mar		lung inflam.
Mary J. Kidd	27	M	Md	Sep		unknown
Sophia Wilson	27	M	Md	Feb		confinement
Mary E. Wilson	2wks		Md	Feb		unknown
Samuel Walker	35		Md	Jul	quaryWorker	crushed
Rachel Cora	70		Md	Mar		palsy
Allen Brown	51	M	Md	Aug	farmer	cholera
Rachel Brown	45	W	Md	Aug		cholera
David Brown	68	M	Pa.	Jan	farmer	palsy
James R. Kirk	34		Md	Feb	farmer	consumption
William A. Kirk	23		Md	Jan		dyseopsia
Cecillia Kelly	75	W	Md	Aug		dysentary
Elizabeth Pierce	28	M	Pa.	Mar		sudden
Charles H. Reynolds	28		Md	Jan	machinist	bronchitis

MORTALITY SCHEDULE OF MARYLAND

persons who died during the year ending 1 June 1850

COUNTY -CECIL -CHARLES   DISTRICT 2nd.sub.-1st sub.

name	age	mar wid	birth place	mon. died	Occupation	cause of death
Taylor Reynolds	58	M	Md	Apr	farmer	consumption
Jeramiah Jackson	50		Md	Aug	none	bil.fever
Ann Jackson	70	W	Md	Feb		unknown
Hester Reynolds	27		Md	Oct		consumption
Charles Foard	--	M	Md	Sep	Meth.Minister	typhoid
Eliza Foard	73		Md	Oct		dysentary
George Baker	19		Md	Aug	cabinetmaker	none
Rebecca Graham	64	M	Md	Oct		billious
Samuel Phillips	35	W	Md	Mar	blacksmith	unknown
Catherine Smith	53		Md	Jun		consumption
Martha Murphy	8		Md	Mar		unknown
Robert Emmond	39	M	Md	Nov	blacksmith	unknown
Rebecca Biddle	11		Md	Sep		consumption
Leona D. Biddle	23		Md	Sep		consumption
Ann Wareham	35		Md	none		none
Henry A. Scanlin	11mo		Md	Aug		dysentary
Rebecca Crow	73		Md	Aug		fever
William Sterlan	70	M	Md	Jul	farmer	dropsy
William Birch	3mo		Md	Feb		unknown
George Rhode	70	W	Md	Feb		unknown
Jacob Price	1		Md	Feb		unknown
Julia Byard	75		Md	Mar		rhemat.
Benedict Jones	54	M	Md	Jun	farmer	unknown
John Foard	53		Md	Jan		heart
Justice Burges	1		Md	Aug		bil.fever
Sarah E. Howard	5		Md	Jan		unknown
Uphere? Cope	45	M	Md	Dec	farmer	typhoid
Sarah Biggs	5		Md	Jun		unknown
5th Dist.						
Isaac Lost	60	M	Md	Jul	farmer	unknown
Alexander Thackery	1		Md	Oct		unknown
Nicholas George	44	M	Md	Sep	farmer	dysentary
Samuel George	8		Md	Sep		dysentary
CHARLES COUNTY						
William Morris	3mo		Md	Sep		unknown
Mary Brent	30	M	Md	Sep		dysentary
Richard Stewart	2		Md	Feb		dysentary
Caroline Long	27		Md	Feb		dysentary
George M. Freeman	22		Md	Dec	farmer	fever
Eliza E. Perry	28	M	Md	Jun		unknown
Edwin Jones	22		Md	Sep	none	cong.fever
John M. Carpenter	3mo		Md	Jul		unknown
Catherin Millar	13		Md	Nov		unknown
Amelia Alen	42		Md	Dec		dysentary
Elizabeth Alen	2		Md	Jan		dysentary
Wheeler Richards	38		Md	Feb	farmer	unknown
Ann Murdock	2		Md	Jan		consumption
Penelope Owen	38		Md	Sep		dropsy
Elizabeth S. Mattingly	42	M	Md	Oct		child bed
Nathan E. Dent	3		Md	May		consumption
Eliza Keich	43	M	Md	Nov		Nuralia
William Lyon	62	W	Md	Apr	farmer	pleurisy
Eleanor Herbert	80	W	Md	Mar		old age

persons who died during the year ending 1 June 18<u>50</u>

COUNTY -CHARLES   DISTRICT Boyantown

name	age	mar wid	birth place	mon. died	Occupation	cause of death
John N. Lamar	45	M	Md	May		consumption
Uz Goldsmith (male)	40	M	Md	Apr		unknown
Trusia Roby	8		Md	May		unknown
Nilson Roby	42	M	Md	Mar		unknown
Eliza Dent	2		Md	Aug		unknown
Ann Shaw	73	W	Md	Mar		old age
Edward Murphy	8		Md	Feb		bilious pleurisy
Hugh Cox	73	M	Md	Dec	farmer	apoplexy
Sara Mathew	73	W	Md	Oct		Oppexsia?
Jonas Smith	29		Md	May	farmer	unknown
Elizabeth Cook	30	W	Md	May		unknown
Nathan S. Dent	50	M	Md	Jan		consumption
Ann A. Johnson	55	M	Md	Jan		unknown
			Allens Neck Dist.			
Hawkins Handcock	37	M	Md	Jul,	farmer	unknown
Thomas Brookland	53	M	Md	Mar	garmer	dypetsia
Josephin Sevann	4		Md	Jun		unknown
Harriet Sevann	55		Md	Feb		cold
Margaret C. Barnes	11mo		Md	Sep		teething
Sydna Flowers	8		Md	Jul		dysentary
James Handcock	65	W	Md	Nov	farmer	unknown
Rebecca Whittle	25	M	Md	Jan		consumption
William Holmes	40	M	Md	Mar	farmer	unknown
Ann P. Posey	2		Md	Mar		inflamation
Thomas Posey	21		Md	Sep	farmer	consumption
Elizabeth Lloyd	2mo		Md	Mar		summer comp.
J. Rond (male)	48	M	Md	May	farmer	pleurisy
Jane Bailie	35		Md	Mar		unknown
John Dyer	11		Md	Aug		dysentary
Charles Lancaster	65	W	Md	Nov	farmer	dyspesia
Alonzo Hollis	55		Md	Jan	none	Cout
Henry Hemsly	4		Md	Sep		brain conges.
Elizabeth Roby	26		Md	Jul		conges. fever
Lucind Clemens	22		Md	Jan		consumption
Hezekiah Padget	48		Md	Jan	farmer	consumption
Susan Roly	66	M	Md	Aug		consumption
George Harris	1		Md	Dec		dysentary
Michael Farell	50	M	Md	Feb	farmer	small pox
Thomas Latimore	73		Md	Jul		erysipelis
Ann Roby	57	W	Md	Jul		dysentary
Thomas Gedelings	85	W	Md	Dec	farmer	old age
Judson Padget	42	M	Md	Oct	agent	cold
Jane C. Covington	23	M	Md	Apr		cold
Henry B. Cooksey	2		Md	Apr		unknown
Ann Padget	84		Md	Feb		old age
Julia Jameson	5		Md	Oct		bil. fever
Lothern Ford (fem)	38	M	Md	Aug		unknown
Martha A. Padget	32	M	Md	Jul		consumption
Walter R. Simmes	4		Md	Sep		unknown
Thomas Shute	15		Md	Mar		pleuirsy
Elizabeth J. Lucas	23		Md	Jul		fever
Elizabeth Hutchens	49	M	Md	Jun		consumption
Thomas McPherson	64	W	Md	Aug	farmer	apoplexy

MORTALITY SCHEDULE OF MARYLAND

persons who died during the year ending 1 June 18_50_

COUNTY - CHARLES- DORCHESTER DISTRICT -Allens

name	age	mar wid	birth place	mon. died	Occupation	cause of death
Amelia Newman	60		Md	May		old age
William Newman	22		Md	Dec	journeyman	pleurisy
Joseph Ratcliff	37		Md	Nov	farmer	consumption
Sarah Ratcliff	37		Md	Mar		consumption
Adelade Ratcliff	5mo		Md	Jan		unknown
James W. Linkins	5		Md	Sep		dropsy
Ann Maria Wedding	18		Md	May		pleuirsy
Catharine Roberson	70		Md	Jul		cold
George H. Barns	5		Md	Aug		dysentary
Mary E. Kildrick	20	M	Md	Mar		cold
James Kildrick	6mo		Md	Jul		inflamation
Isabella C. Den	48		Md	Feb		unknown
Eglantine Brown	21		Md	Nov		unknown
Thomas G. Williams	54		Md	Sep	farmer	bil.fever
			DORCHESTER COUNTY-Dist.1 (poor handwriting)			
Joseph Hopkins	33		Md	Feb	hater	consumption
Mary Whisnit	48		CecilCo.	Sep		dropsy
Samuel Lefonte	75		Caro.Co	Sep	farmer	unknown
Julia Cook	65		Md	Sep		unknown
Ann Winterbottom	48		Md	May		unknown
W. Dail(male)	22		Md	May		unknown
Thomas Jenkins	6		Md	Oct		unknown
William Skinner	66		Md	Mar	farmer	unknown
Mary Woolford	19		Md	Jun		small pox
James Warfield	35		Md	Jul	mariner	unknown
Mary Warfield	1		Md	Jul		unknown
William Thomas	66		Md	Jan	farmer	unknown
Thomas Hubbard	76		Md	Apr	farmer	unknown
Levin Fooks	45		Md	Apr	farmer	unknown
Sarah Phillips	55		Md	May		unknown
Mary North	40		Md	Dec		unknown
Josiah Marshall	47		Md	Jan	farmer	unknown
Eliza Colston	22		Md	May		unknown
James Fluharty	27		Md	Apr	farmer	unknown
Mary Fluharty	40		Md	Aug		unknown
Sarah Vane	30		Md	Dec		unknown
Mary Twiley	25		Md	Oct		chronik
John Stone	16		Md	Feb		unknown
M.Colison(male)	42		Md	Nov	farmer	unknown
Margaret Mears	50		Md	Sep		unknown
Mary Short	70		Md	Mar		unknown
W.J.Thompson(male)	23		Md	Jul	farmer	pleurisy
John Crosby	60		Md	Jan	farmer	unknown
Eliza Hicks	40		Md	Oct		unknown
Martin M. Dean	45		Md	Aug	farmer	unknown
Sarah Wilcox	65		Md	Feb		unknown
Mary Marshall	9		Md	Sep		unknown
John Mcguire	23		Md	Aug	mariner	unknown
Sarah Coleson	17		Md	Aug		unknown
Thomas Jones	19		Md	Sep	farmer	disentary
S. Green(male)	70		Md	Jul	laborer	unknown

MORTALITY SCHEDULE OF MARYLAND

persons who died during the year ending 1 June 18 50

COUNTY -DORCHESTER   DISTRICT -Dist.1 & 2

name	age	mar wid	birth place	mon. died	Occupation	cause of death
David Brion	37	M	Del.	May	farmer	billious
Margaret A. White	11		Md	Sep		unknown
Edwan White	1		Md	Oct		teething
Byard E.J.Mooney	2		Md	Aug		bil.fever
Sally E. Mooney	12		Md	Aug		bilious fev.
Mary A. Bell	1		Md	Jul		col.inf.
Mary Bell	70		Bermoda	Feb		old age
Molley Jones	32		Del.	Apr		bil.fever
William Thomas	1		Md	Apr		measels
Elizabeth Hurtock	48	M	Md	Jun		consumption
Isaac Wright	88	M	Md	Jan	farmer	old age
Elizabeth Smith	76	W	Md	Oct		consumption
Edward Wheatley	49	M	Md	Jul	drover	coleramos
Lovey Thompson	72	M	Del.	Feb		"
Luke Mezzick	60	M	Md	May	teacher	pleuricy
Amelia Price	41	M	Md	Oct		consumption
William Franton	70	W	Md	Jan	farmer	pleurisy
Mary Lewis	23		Md	Sep		dropsey
Mariah Lewis	21		Md	Jul		dropsey
Celia Kinnamon	1		Md	Dec		inflam.
Margaret A. Henry	10		Md	Feb		inflam.
John H. Benden	4mo		Md	Sep		diareah
James Lucas	49		Md	Jun		disapation
Stephen Andrews	3		Md	Feb		measles
Elizabeth White	50	W	Md	Nov		diareah
Abraham Collins	75	W	Md	Jul		coleramos
Martha Jacobs	10		Md	Nov		croup
Priscilla Lane	37	M	Md	Dec		inflamation
George W. Noble	3mo		Md	May		jandiz
Division 3						
Sarah J. Haywood	1mo		Md	Mar		eracipulus
Charles H. Creighton	12		Md	Sep		consumption
John Troth	19		Md	Feb	sailor	unknown
Ann Travers	40		Md	Mar		pleurisy
Major Travers	24		Md	May	sailor	consumption
Levin W. Fisher	1		Md	Jun		bil.fever
Henrietta J. Lake	22	M	Md	Apr		consumption
Jacob W.J.Jones	20		Md	Apr	sailor	measels
Eliza E.Robinson	2		Md	May		unknown
George Pritchett	55	M	Md	Apr	oysterman	pleuricy
Secila Dean	52	W	Md	Aug		consumption
Elizabeth Dean	24		Md	Aug		consumption
George Dean	20		Md	Dec		consumption
Levin Wroten	17		Md	Jul	farmhand	cholera
George Timmons	38		Md	Dec	sailor	influenza
Sarah Bramble	55		Md	Jan		pleuisy
John E. Kirvan	40		Md	Feb	oysterman	unknown
Julian Elliott	18		Md	Mar		unknown
George Langrell	38		Md	Feb	sailor	consumption
Abraham Elliott	6mo		Md	unkn.		unknown
Slighter S. Dean	1		Md	Mar		pleurisy
Mary G. Weatherly	2		Md	Jul		billious

82

MORTALITY SCHEDULE OF MARYLAND

persons who died during the year ending 1 June 18_50_

COUNTY -DORCHESTER -FREDERICK DISTRICT -3

name	age	mar wid	birth place	mon. died	Occupation	cause of death
Margaret E. Cooper	3		Md	Jun		unknown
Edwin F. Cooper	10		Md	Aug		bilious
Casander Tylor	20	M	Md	Dec		unknown
Mary E. Bibby	8mo		Md	Feb		unknown
Mathias Arnol	12		Md	Oct		unknown
William S. Burton	3		Md	Aug		infirmat.
Uiriah Todd	35		Md	Feb	merchant	unknown
Sarah A. Neal	25		Md	Aug		consumption
Mary A. Parker	25	M	Md	Jun		unknown
			FREDERICK	COUNTY-Jefferson		Dist.
Fanny E. Hoffman	9mo		Md	Jul		hydroceplis
Catharine Gittings	35	W	Md	Sep		apoplext
Ann E. Ray	6mo		Md	Jan		convulsions
Charles A. Keller	3		Md	Aug		accident
George J. Fester	22		Md	Nov	clerk	congest.fever
Mary J. Mahoney	4		Md	Aug		croup
America Sparrow	3		Md	Jan		scarlet fever
Ruth Ridgeley	94	W	Md	May		old age
Elizabeth Wise	55		Md	Mar		dropsy
Lucretia R. Hale	3mo		Md	Aug		diahreah
James Wm.Turner	27	M	Md	Dec	shoemaker	typhoid
Joseph H. Dixon	1		Md	Jun		accident
Wm. Ridenbough	10		Md	Oct		drowned
George Willard	79	M	Md	Dec		old age
			Petersville District			
Charles S. Reid	2mo		Md	Apr		pneumonia
Daniel Cochren	46	M	Md	Jan	blacksmith	liver disease
Mary Paget	57	M	Md	Dec		bilious
George B. Kay	1mo		Md	Aug		unknown
Robert C. Biser	2		Md	Mar		scarlet fever
Clara Clagett	4		Md	Jun		pneumonia
Charles M. Lohrman	3mo		Md	Jul		brain fever
Stephen Staley	55	W	Va.	Apr	minister	consumption
James Hurley	5mo		Md	Jun		thrush
Joseph H. Knot	6mo		Md	Mar		spasms
Eliza Marlow	55		Md	Dec		apoplexy
William W. Hilleary	1mo		Md	Mar		catarrah
Delana Ennis	44	M	Md	Dec		cancer
Edward Yates	55	M	Md	Aug	carpenter	cancer
Ellen V. Richards	2mo		Md	Jan		croup
John C. Wilson	40	M	Md	May	merchant	cholera
Eleanor Johnson	56	M	Md	May		pneumonia
Elizabeth Hilleary	76		Md	May		pneumonia
Henry Buckley	4		Va.	May		whooping cough
Thomas Johnson	69	M	Md	Aug	miller	disentary
Harriett A. Smeltzer	26	M	Md	May		child bed
Georgianna Hayes	4mo		Md	Jul		catarrah
William H.Walker	2mo		Md	Oct		cough
Susanna Fisher	19		Md	Apr		consumption
Ann Clark	3		Pa.	Jan		brain inflam.
George Rhodes	67	M	Md	Mar	farmer	dropsy

persons who died during the year ending 1 June 18_50_

COUNTY -Frederick   DISTRICT -Petersville

name	age	mar wid	birth place	mon. died	Occupation	cause of death
Elizabeth Fox	5		Va.	Dec		dropsy
Hester S.Pearce	2		Md	Jul		accident
William Wagner	34	M	Md	Jul	cooper	bronchitis
Frederick A. Shank	33	M	Md	Oct	farmer	cong.fever
			Woodsboro Dist.No.11			
Joseph Pler	49	M	Md	Mar	labor.	hurt
James Hannretton	8		Md	Feb		none
John Carmack	66	M	Md	Apr	farmer	none
Isaac Lynn	78	M	Md	Apr	none	apoplexy
Isabella Hogle	2		Md	Feb		teething
Michalel Wachter	50	M	Md	none	clergyman	lung congest.
Phillip F. Fogle	1		Md	none		croup
Henry Beck	27		Md	Mar	carpenter	iryspepsia
Margaret E. Mort	11mo		Md	May		none
Catherine Warner	43		Pa.	Jul		consumption
Abraham Welker	7mo		Md	Oct		none
John Fine	56	W	Md	Apr	laborer	dropsey
David Hope	26	M	Md	Jul	laborer	sudden
Gideon E. Harnrus	8mo		Md	Jul		diarrhea
Willie A. Bidler	8		Md	Jun		scarlet fever
Phillip F.T.Wilson	9mo		Md	Mar		cat.fever
Susan M. Kemp	40	M	Md	May		cong.fever
Peter Young	76	W	Ger.	Feb	none	old age
Aire V. Crancer	19		Md	Jan		scarlet fever
Ann Agusta Vanfossen	1		Md	Jul		dysentary
Casandra Summers (Mul.)	17		Md	Jul		child bed
Cornelia A. Shrine	1		Md	Aug		spasms
Elizabeth Holtzapple	68	W	Md	Jul		consumption
Susannah Gedullins	62	W	Md	Mar		consumption
Catharine Holler	4mo		Md	Apr		pleurisy
John Ledgewood	83	W	Md	Mar	none	dropsey
Catherine Barrick	58	W	Md	Apr		pleurisy
George Zimmerman	53	M	Md	Feb	farmer	pleurisy
Mary E. Bidles	3		Md	Jul		scarlet fever
			Barkeys Town			
Elizabeth Thomas	20		Va.	May		erysipelas
Robert G. Dixon	22		Md	Oct	farmer	bil.fever
James L. Wilson	46	M	Md	Apr	blacksmith	pleuisy
Mary A. Kephart	68	W	Md	May		unknown
Mary E. Tingstrom	3mo		Md	Apr		croup
Charles T. Trundle	1		Md	May		cat.fever
Mary A. Jones	37	M	Va.	May		consumption
Hugh Larkins	42	M	Ire.	Sep	stonemason	bowel inflam.
Susan T. Lewis	11mo		Md	Sep		bil.fever
Catherine Davis	62	W	Md	Feb		pneumonia
Jane B.Anderson	22	M	Md	Jan		consumption
Tabitha Swarengin	99	W	Md	Aug		old age
Josiah D. Trundle	61	M	Md	Dec	farmer	pleurisy
Martha Milone	33		Md	Mar		unknown
Charles Herstons	85	W	Spain	Oct	none	sudden
Charlotte E. Kephart	1		Md	Jul		consumption
Daniel J. Baker	2mo		Md	Feb		croup

persons who died during the year ending 1 June 18_50_

COUNTY -FREDERICK   DISTRICT-Hackeys Town

name	age	mar wid	birth place	mon. died	Occupation	cause of death
			Creagirstown E.Dist.			
Jacob Cramer	80	M	Md	Jul	none	E.morbus
Adam Clem	60	M	Md	Mar	none	c.
Catherine Morningstar	36	M	Md	Nov		pleurisy
James P. Blair	2		Md	Mar		cat.fever
Martin N. Valentine	4		Md	Dec		scarlet fever
John L. Rodensen	7		Md	Oct		scarlet fever
Elizabeth Harman	34	M	Md	Aug		child bed
Joseph Walton	33	M	Md	Sep	merchant	C.
Henry C. Meed	5mo		Md	Oct		croup
George Six	55	M	Md	Jan	stonemason	C.
Julia T. Frys	8mo		Md	Mar		brain
Mary A.E. Hoffner	17		Md	Apr		fits
Levi Creager	39	M	Md	Apr	stonemason	diahheah
George Wilhite	87	W	Pa.	Apr	none	old age
Jacob Creager	50	W	Md	Sep	none	diarreah
Milton G. Carmack	1		Md	Apr		scarlet fever
Phebe Slusser	64	M	Md	Jul		C.
Magdalene Hulton	81	W	Md	Apr		palsy
Mary Barrick	52	M	Md	Apr		unknown
John Sweeney	50		Ire.	Jun	none	cong.fever
Mary Boone	70	W	Md	Aug		paralysis
John Hacking	70		Ire.	Aug	none	C.
Mrs. Alnor	70	W	Ger.	Jun		C.
Mary Vanhorn	60	W	Md	Jun		cancer
Thomas Craine	95	W	Md	Nov	none	paralysis
George Hoffman	75	W	Md	Nov	none	paralysis
John Yellers	75	W	Md	Jan	none	pluritis
Jacob Misener	70		Md	Mar	none	scropila
			Frederickstown			
Dianna Myerley	10		Md	Mar		scarlet fever
Catherine Teliniard	62	M	Md	May		C.
Adam Getzendenner	63	M	Md	Mar	carpenter	C.
Peter Ogle	71	M	N.J.	Apr	blacksmith	C.
Mary E. Hiteshere	81	W	Md	May		unknown
Charlotte Barnes	1		Md	Jun		measels
Charles E. Mantz	7mo		Md	Feb		inflamation
John C. Fritchee	69	M	Md	Nov	skindresser	C.
Thaddeus T. Tucker	1mo		Md	Jul		diarreah
Cornelia C. Cromwell	15		Md	Mar		s.fever
Caroline M.B.Woodward	4		Md	Oct		dropsy
Michael Gamon	47	M	D.C.	Oct	innkeeper	dropsy
John F. Miller	6		Md	Jul		measels
Martha E. Mix	5		Md	Jan		Cat.fever
Rosanna McCaffrey	3mo		Md	Sep		diahheah
Em.M.Eichelberger(male)	6mo		Md	Apr		inflamation
Lucy Pendleton	15		Va.	Sep		dysentary
Sarah C. Dofler	6		Md	Feb		croup
Eliza McSchley	25		Md	Jan		C.
Barbara McSchely	37	M	Md	Jan		C.
Ann Elbert	66	M	Md	Mar		C.
George A. Cole	17		Md	Feb	carpenter	Eurisipilus

MORTALITY SCHEDULE OF MARYLAND

persons who died during the year ending 1 June 1850

COUNTY -FREDERCIK   DISTRICT -Fredericktown

name	age	mar wid	birth place	mon. died	Occupation	cause of death
William W. Woodward	1		Md	Oct		measels
Catherine Nichols	4		Md	Feb		scarlet fever
John Ross	15		Md	Feb		eurisiplus
John S. Miller	73	M	Md	Mar	apothocary	paralisis
Wiliam Adams	3		Md	Apr		spasms
Julian Noys	26		Md	Sep		C.
Mary Fout	69	W	Md	Mar		appoplexy
William Tice	43		Md	Jun	none	unknown
Joshua Haller	72	M	Md	Mar	pumpmaker	nerves
Mary A. Pettit	13		Ind.	Aug		congestion
Charles B.Bennet	14		Md	Apr.		B.fever
Louisa Brushears	40	W	Md	Jan		cancer
Mary T. Etchison	1		Md	Mar		S.Fever
Mary E. Mason	1		Md	Sep		dysentary
William E. W. Lease	1		Md	Nov		C.morbus
Catherine Fogler	66	W	Md	Feb		C.
Joshua Doub	44	M	Md	Mar	merchant	diabetus
John C. Rhoads	8		Md	Jun		unknown
William R. Thomas	39		Md	Feb	none	heart disease
Mary Nast	8mo		Md	Jul		diarreah
John W. Miller	19		Md	Aug	butcher	Epelepsey
Clara E. Mantz	2		Md	Jan		C.
Richard Webster	23		Md	Nov	clerk	C.
Eliza Bringle	1mo		Md	Jul		diherreah
Mathias E. Bartgis	55	M	Md	Aug	Lawyer	Janders
Mary A. Doub	36	M	Md	Feb		C.
George Dartzbaugh	4		Md	Mar		S.Fever
Frances Caines	4		Md	Feb		S.Fever
George Leather	88	W	Md	Jan	blacksmith	bil.fever
Annie C. Howard	8		Md	May		S.fever
Nicholas Turbutt	68	W	Md	Feb	none	C.
Wm.H. McCannon	53	M	Md	Sep	farmer	rheumatism
James W. Reynolds	36	M	Md	Jul		spasms
Susan G. Young	40	M	Md	Jul		C.
Eliza Flick (mul)	50	M	Md	Jul		C.
Catherine Licks	73	M	Md	Aug		diharreah
Mary Dill	24	M	Md	Sep		C.
Barbara Haufman	69	W	Md	Oct		cancer
Milton Mantz	25	M	Md	Nov	druggist	spasms
Barbara Fite	48	M	Ger.	Nov		dropsy
Elizabeth Peake	70	W	Md	Dec		C.
Jacob Heller	63	M	Pa.	Mar	ropemaker	heart disease
John Ryon	66	W	Ire.	Mar	peddler	C.
Clara Bishop	51	M	Md	Mar		C.
Mark Bishop	46	W	Eng.	May	blacksmith	spasms
James S. McPherson	65		Md	Apr	none	mania
Margaret Young	71	W	Md	Apr		C.
John Hett	8		Ger.	Jan		unknown
Peter Hagan	66	W	Ire.	Feb	farmer	accidental
Joseph G. Mahn	9mo		Md	Apr		unknown
Catherine Rhoads	56	M	Ger.	Oct		unknown
Jonathan Haufman	55	M	Md	Mar	carpenter	pleuisy
Susan Simon	61	M	Md	Oct		pleurisy

86

persons who died during the year ending 1 June 18_50

COUNTY Frederick   DISTRICT

name	age	mar wid	birth place	mon. died	Occupation	cause of death
Elizabeth Shaeffer	80	W	Md	Jan		old age
Elizabeth Fox	2		Md	Aug		diareah
John Dunlap	5		Md	Oct		Sc.fever
Josephene Staub	9		Md	Oct		sc.fever
Emly Morgan	1		Md	Mar		fits
Clasa E. Hager	1		Md	Feb		C.fever
Daniel Staley	38	M	Md	Oct	farmer	S.Fever
Amelia Staley	25	W	Md	Oct		S.fever
Annedius L. Ramoburg	20		Md	Oct		S.fever
Nicholus Holtz	87	W	Md	Aug	farmer	old age
Margaret Gottinger	73	W	Md	Apr		pleurisy
Edward Howard	28		Md	Mar	none	dysentary
Wesly Pool	50		Md	Mar	none	dysentary
George Myers	50	W	Md	Mar	none	paralysis
Robert Thompson	60		Ire.	Mar	none	C.
John McCahan	50	M	Md	Jun	laborer	unknown
Michael Hibbert	18		Ger.	Jul	none	unknown
Catoctin E.Dist.						
Eve M. Geltzinger	78	W	Pa.	May		dropsy
Silas L. Marker	1mo		Md	Jun		unknown
Hannah Stottlemyer	22	M	Md	Apr		child bed
Susan Warner	33	M	Md	Aug		consumption
Catherine A. Hays	31	M	Md	Mar		unknown
Elizabeth Duple	72	W	Md	Feb		dropsy
Cornelius Kline	6mo		Md	Dec		croup
Barbara A. C. Raysner	11mo		Md	Jun		croup
Francis Neff (fem)	40	W	Md	Mar		cancer
Middletown E.Dist						
Martha A.D. Rice	3		Md	Aug		scarlet fever
Mary M. Smeltzer	69	M	Md	May		paralysis
John Kepler	76	W	Pa.	Jul	none	dysentary
Dawson Bell	9		Md	Aug		scarlet fever
Catharine Mullendore	76	W	Va	Nov		dropsy
Martha E. Ramsbury	3		Md	Oct		scarlet fever
Calvin F. Rudy	2mo		Md	Apr		cat.fever
Joshua N. Wise	1mo		Md	Oct		unknown
John H.S.Smith	1		Md	Mar		cat.fever
Helen R. Bear	1mo		Md	Jun		convulsion
Mary McCartney	51	M	Md	Mar		dropsy
Soppia Miller	1mo		Md	Apr		unknown
Solomon Brown	27		Md	Apr	laborer	consumption
John H. Gross	1		Md	Nov		brain infec.
Andrew J. Kailer	2		Md	May		lung infect.
John T. Poffenbeyer	7mo		Md	Sep		brain afflect.
Elizabeth Schindle	64	W	Md	Oct		lung infl.
Sarah Petinjall	63	W	Md	Mar		heart dis.
Rebecca Keller	30	M	Md	Aug		consumption
Ann A. C. Kissinger	40	M	Md	Apr		consumption
John H. Carpenter	16		Md	Feb	laborer	pleurisy
William H. O'Neal	4		Md	Aug		accident
Ann C. Sharer	5mo		Md	Dec		scarlet fever
Jacob Lorentz	29		Md	Jul	shoemaker	consumption
Joanna Swearingen	26		Md	Mar		consumption

MORTALITY SCHEDULE OF MARYLAND

persons who died during the year ending 1 June 1850

COUNTY FREDERICK-   DISTRICT Middletown E.Dist.

name	age	mar wid	birth place	mon. died	Occupation	cause of death
John W. Bowlen	1		Ind.	May		brain infl.
Joseph Rhodrick	1mo		Md	Feb		unknown
Rebecca Beckwith	56		Md	Aug		unknown
William Brant	43	M	Ger	Feb	weaver	pneumonia
Mary Weaver	5mo		Md	Jun		measles
Cornelius D. Easterday	3		Md	Mar		croup
Oliver E. Collentz	1		Md	May		unknown
Catharine Ramsbury	41	M	Md	Apr		consumption
Matilda C. Alexander	2		Md	Apr		croup
Elizabeth Delander	62	W	Md	Sep		dysentary
Harlan Keller	6		Ohio	Feb		typhoid
George W. Beckenbough	8		Md	Sep		scarlet fever
Daniel House	25		Md	Jun	laborer	lockjaw
Daniel Selsam	53	M	Md	May	carpenter	eresipilus
Sarah E. Ward	1mo		Md	Jan		convulsions
Julia A.C. Flook	7		Md	Sep		scarlet fever
John Bowlus	76	W	Md	Feb	none	unknown
Ruth A. Hilberg	27		Md	Jul		dropsy
Lydia Whip	29	M	Md	Oct		consumption
John Zeigler	32	M	Md	Aug	laborer	dysentary
William O.Flook	6		Md	Aug		scarlet fever
Sarah E. Flook	5		Md	Aug		scarlet fever
Charles E. Warfield	6mo		Md	Sep		lockjaw
Cornelia Collenburger	6		Md	Jul		throat inf.
Martha Ligget	5		Md	Dec		inf.throat
Marilda B. Warfield	54	M	Md	Jun		dropsy
Election Dist.#8						
Esther Albaugh	64	M	Pa.	Mar		b.cholic
Elizabeth Fose	74	W	Md	Nov		dropsy
Warren W. Kinzer	9mo		Md	May		paralysis
Christianna Boght	92	W	Md	Mar		old age
Henry Poole	54		Md	Jan	farmer	consumption
Jesse Clary	67	M	Md	Nov	clerk	dropsy
Anna Condon	50	M	Md	Feb		lung inflam.
Jesse Ker Myers	10mo		Md	Sep		brain infl.
Rosanna Fose	54		Md	Oct		consumption
Jesse Grabill	1		Md	Apr		s.fever
Margaret Diedderan	62	W	Md	Nov		paralytic
Emeline V. Nichodemus	2		Md	Sep		dysentary
Phillip Nusbaum	3		Md	Aug		dysentary
Anna Nusbaum	42	M	Md	Sep		dysentary
Barbara A. Nichodemus	42	M	MD	Mar		childbed
Susanna Dudderan	76	W	Md	Jul		iresipilus
Susan Kiler	24		Md	Jul		iresipilus
Martha Gaither	53		Md	Oct		consumption
Mary A. Moshen	24	M	Md	Apr		unknown
Cass Goshage	55		Md	Oct		unknown
Michael Danner	73	M	Md	Aug		ulcer
Lydia M. Wilson	24	M	Md	Apr		b.pleuirsy
Acsha Watts	70		Md	Apr		pleuisy
Ann Williams	65	W	Md	May		lung inflam.
NEWMARKET DISTRICT						
Mary M. Davis	17		Md	Jan		spine afflec.

88

MORTALITY SCHEDULE OF MARYLAND

persons who died during the year ending 1 June 1850

COUNTY   FREDERICK   DISTRICT =NewMarket Dist.

name	age	mar wid	birth place	mon. died	Occupation	cause of death
Thomas C. Shipley	49	M	Md	Jul	farmer	debility
EliasW. Botoler	43	M	Md	Jun	farmer	consumption
Manah Farquaha	35	M	Md	Jul		paralysis
Mary C. Ramsbury	4		Md	Aug		flux
Ann S. Watenbaker	42	W	Md	Aug		asthma
Thomas Mount	33	M	Md	Apr	wheelright	pleurisy
Lucien Falconer	5		Md	Feb		consumption
John Thomas Sr.	70	M	Md	Jul	tailor	papalysis
George W. Cook	33		N.Y.	Nov	teacher	sudden
Deaton Hammond	5		Md	Feb		scarlet fever
Joseph Rusinger	25	M	Ojio	Nov	blacksmith	hemmorage
John H.M.Smith	57	M	Md	Dec	physician	C.
Peter E. Rhodes	1		Md	Jan		pleurisy
Charles A. Naylor	8		Md	Oct		sorethroat
George W.Naylor	4		Md	Oct		sorethroat
Ebe Hyall	51	M	Md	Feb	distiller	dropsy
Elizabeth Mobberly	79		Va	Apr		paralysis
Rachel Holland	48		Md	Jun 1st		dropsey
Sidney J. Todd (fem)	16		Md	Jun		pneumonia
Amelia Hollway	2mo		Md	Jul		dysentary
Baker Ward	23		Md	Mar	laborer	C.
Frances L. Nichols	10		Md	Mar		consumption
Thomas H.S.Wood	1		Md	Oct		penumonia
James Smith	51	M	Apr		blacksmith	b.pleurisy
George Davis	78	M	Pa.	May	farmer	palsy
Henry Riggs	77	M	Md	Jan	carpenter	C.
John Jacob Sponselle	11mo		Md	Jun		spasms
Ann Frazer	24		Md	Jun		sore throat
Nathan Hammond	6		Md	Feb		scarlet fever
Catherine Sheets	39	M	Md	Jun		dropsy
George Dunawin	16		Md	Dec	laborer	spinal infl.
Jacob Buchy	44	M	Md	May	shoemaker	pleurisy
Benjamin Deicth	60	M	Md	Jul	farmer	cholera
Wilson Baker	14		Md	Feb		scarlet fever
Mary Davis	47	W	Md	Apr		palsy
Barbara A. Baker	3		Md	Feb		scarlet fever
Mary Klass	1		Md	Jan		mumps
Ann Purdy	48	M	Md	Sep		cancer
Plummer Janis	49	W	Md	Jun	farmer	lung conges.
John Rine	63	M	Md	Nov	farmer	dropsy
Cinderela Thompson	1		Md	Jul		diareah
Sarah E. Rine	1		Md	Mar		scarlet fever
Margaret Leaser	49	M	Md	Nov		dropsey
Ann R. Myers	19		Md	Aug		s.Fever
Elizabeth Myers	16		Md	Aug		S.fever
Martin Myers	10		Md	Aug		s.fever
Ann Harbaugh	62	W	Balt.Co.	Feb		dropsy
Mary Ridenour	27	M	Pa.	Sep		consumption
Conrad Hamburgh	59	M	Pa.	Sep	farmer	y.jaundice
Aaron Willian	59	W	Md	Mar		consumption
Abigail Seiss	34	M	Md	Feb		cramp
			5th E. Dist.			
Mary B. Elder	50	M	Md	Mar		consumption

MORTALITY SCHEDULE OF MARYLAND

persons who died during the year ending 1 June 18_50_

COUNTY FREDERICK - Hartford   DISTRICT 5th Elect.Dist.

name	age	mar wid	birth place	mon. died	Occupation	cause of death
Mary Muller	64	W	Pa.	May		pleurisy
Magdaline Troxel	68	W	Pa	May		consumption
Margaret Agnew	no	W	Md	none		none
George A. Mentzer	1mo		Md	Sep		unknown
George Winter	67	M	Pa	Feb	wagonmaker	consumption
Michael E. Zimmerman	27		Md	Aug	tailor	consumption
Belinda Dorsey	22		Md	Oct		consumption
Frederick Black	1		Md	Apr		bowel infl/
William Lininger	19		Cam.Co.Pa.	Jun		consumption
Peter Feezer	58		Md	Oct	laborer	fever
Mathias Zacharias	59	M	Md	Jul	farmer	fever
Elizabeth Biggs	37	M	Md	Dec		consumption
George Hershide	57		Ger.	Feb	farmer	palsy
John Berk	54	M	Md	May	carpenter	fever
Mary Lind	80	,W	Md	Aug		old age
John A. Keepers	1		Md	Mar		unknown
Henry Zumbruin	65	W	Ger	Jan	laborer	unknown
Greenbury Pedicord	74	W	Md	Mar	laborer	cholic
Amanda C. Pedicord	3		Md	Aug		dropsy
William Wetly	56	M	Md	Sep	butcher	unknown
Rachael Eyler	90	W	Md	Oct		old age
Sister Sally Thompson	71		Md	Dec	Sis.Charity	old age
Mary Galice	17		NewOrleans	Dec	orphan)	consumption
Phillip H. Barrick	3mo		Md	Feb		none
Henry J. Septer	14		Md	Jun		none
Peter Rider	60	M	Md	Jun		fever
Nancy Smallwood	50		Md	Jan		accident
Maria Welty	23		Md	Jan		fever
Margaret Willet	16		Md	Jan		fever
Elizabeth Waite	50	M	Md	Sep		sudden
Mary Canan	70		Md	Sep		old age
Mary Hayden	73	W	Md	Jul		apoplexy
Henry Soubrink	75	W	Ger	Dec		old age
Elizabeth Hobbs	85	W	Md	Apr		old age
HARTFORD- 2nd & 3rd Dist.						
William R. Smith	15		Md	Jul		bilious
James A. Williams	30	M	Md	Mar	garmer	sucide
William L. Nilson	23		Md	May	farmer	consumption
Margaret Ruff	36		Md	Dec		consumption
Mary Daugherty	37	M	Pa.	Aug		drowned
John W. Daugherty	7		Pa.	Aug		dysentary
Ellen Bayless	35	M	Md	Dec		sudden
Eleanor Barnes	72	W	Md	Aug		sudden
John J.W. Tignor	3		Md	Aug		bil.dysentary
Robert Cantlin	14		Md	Apr		scarlet fever
Henry Parker	6		Md	Feb		scarlet fever
William F. McCandless	14		Md	Sep		C.
Mary F. Williams	2		Md	Jul		dysentary
Thomas Williams	2mo		Md	Sep		bil.fever
Sarah Alice Roby	1		Md	Jan		sorethroat
Martha T. Norris	9mo		Md	Sep		bil.fever
Reverdy J. McNabb	9mo		Md	Aug		dysentary

MORTALITY SCHEDULE OF MARYLAND

persons who died during the year ending 1 June 1850

COUNTY   HARTFORD   DISTRICT   2nd.& 3rd E.Dist.

name	age	mar wid	birth place	mon. died	Occupation	cause of death
(family all under 9yrs. Frances,Merriman,Rebecca Sarah,Arnold MAGNISS	9		Md	Aug		dysentary
Mary Maddon	77	W	Md	Apr		pleuricy
Thomas B. Walker	70	W	Eng	Oct		none
William Deaver	50		none	Dec		none
Charlotte Gillbert	40		none	Nov		none
M. McGlilean	48		none	Nov		none
Charles Ferrill	30		none	Jan		none
Adam Wright	35		none	Sep		none
Henry Hardin	70		Md	Jul		none
John Sniders	60		none	Nov		none
J. Hartley(male)	82		Pa.	Sep		old age
Thomas Slade	50		none	Jan		none
Samuel Bradford	50		none	Sep		none
Henry Moore	55		none	May		none
Frank Clark	58		none	Jul		none
Charlotte Grunn	40		none	Jun		none
Elizabeth Fall	40		none	Aug		none
Charlotte Flenk	30		none	Nov		none
S. Davis (male)	50		none	Jan		none
Thomas Clark	60		none	Jun		none
Benjamin Richardson	78	W	Md	Dec	farmer	old age
Moses S. Lancaster	2		Md	Feb		gas.fever
Isaac Scott	50		Md	Feb		pleurisy
Deborah Nogle	26	M	Md	Jul		dysentary
Mary Nogle	1		Md	Aug		dysentary
Samuel Holland	64	W	Md	Oct	farmer	bil.dysentary
E. West(male)	73	M	Md	Mar	farmer	paralities
Elizabeth A. Macklin	30		Md	Aug		dysentary
Eliza Cunningham	22		Md	Oct		consumption
Jane Cunningham	55	M	Md	Nov		consumption
William Hollingsworth	1		Md	Jul		Col.inf.
Mary E. Hanway	3mo		Md	Jun		fast fever
Joshua Clark	30	M	Md	Aug	farmer	bil.dysentary
Ann Tradway	84	W	Md	May		old age
Samuel Holbrooks	50		Md	Oct	cooper	consumption
Holland McCormich	1		Md	Dec		teething
Benjamin Standford	30		Md	Feb	carpenter	consumption
Thomas Green	10		Md	Jul		dysentary
Henrietta Boarman	3		Md	Sep		dysentary
John B. Cheyneywith	10mo		Md	Aug		dysentary
Mary O'Donnell	22		Md	Dec		consumption
Sarah Robinson	26		Md	Mar		consumption
Rachel Brill	35	M	Md	Aug		col.mort.
Isaac Pyles	55	M	Md	Dec	farmer	sudden
Sarah Jourdan	82		Ire.	Jan		old age
John Jourdan	75	W	Ire.	Dec	farmer	cong.fev.
Ann Jones	95	W	N.J.	Jan		cong.fever
Mary P.Webster	4		Md	May		scarlet fever
Johanna Webster	2		Md	Apr		scarlet fever
George A. Silvers	4		Md	Nov		scarlet fever
Elizabeth Hoops	1mo		Md	Apr		pleurisy

91

MORTALITY SCHEDULE OF MARYLAND

persons who died during the year ending 1 June 18_50

COUNTY HARFORD   DISTRICT 3rd Census Dist.

name	age	mar wid	birth place	mon. died	Occupation	cause of death
Mary Ward	76	W	Md	Jun		old age
Hanna Brown	40		Md	Sep		unknown
Gayver?Hoforinz	39	M	Md	Apr	farmer	unknown
James A. Knight	10		Md	Sep		lock jaw
Charlott F. Knight	3		Md	Oct		scarlet fever
Sarah E. Murphy	1		Md	Jun		colra.Inf.
James Hughs	73	M	Md	Jan	farmer	consumption
Charles Webster	28		Md	Jun	laborer	consumption
Virginia Turner	8		Md	Aug		b.fever
William W. Lister	1mo		Md	May		unknown
Joshaway F. Numbis	2		Md	Sep		dysentary
Anna M. Bolton	10		Md	Aug		dysentary
Titus T. Knight	57		Md	Jan	laborer	consumption
Daniel Stockham	4		Md	Jul		dysentary
Sarah Frigger	70		Md	May		unknown
Samuel Shanin	53	M	Md	Mar		unknown
Mary Rinard	76	W	Md	Nov		unknown
William C. Hase	19		Md	Apr	none	pleurisy
John R. Cunningham	7mo		Md	Aug	none	corl.inf.
Thomas N. Garrison	33		Md	Aug	none	apoplexy
Patrick Riley	2		Md	Feb		fits
Christina Weber	28	M	Ger.	May		consumption
James Wilson	46	M	Ire.	Jan	teacher	dropsy
Joseph C. Baker	3mo		Md	Feb		unknown
John S. Camrun	42	M	Md	Jan	Ins.Rep.	consumption
Long Forthys	2		Md	Feb		fever
Was.P.Chud?	51	M	Md	Apr	farmer	unknown
Marthy Singleton	26	M	Md	Jan		consumption
Edward Jackson	48	M	Md	Oct	Capt.	consumption
Charles Gilbert	65		Md	Sep		diarreah
Malin Thompson	77	W	Md	Jul	laborer	consumption
July A. Mitchell	43	M	Md	Dec		palsy
Kent Mitchell	60	W	Md	Mar	farmer	consumption
Richard Barns	44	M	Md.	Sep		sudden
George Osborn	1		Md	Oct		unknown
Mary Gilbert	35		Md	Mar		conusmption
Jane Gilbert	70	W	Md	Dec		S.Fever
Thomas Evins	28		Md	Jun	cooper	sudden
Robert Miller	17		Md	May	laborer	consumption
John Pritner	44	M	Pa.	Feb	laborer	b.fever
Samuel Cunningham	72	W	Pa	Sep	farmer	S.Fever
Thomas Mitchell	66		Md	Apr		unknown
William Sappington	61	W	Md	Dec	Dor.	appoplexy
Elizabeth Gillaspy	36	M	Md	Dec		unknown
Richard Robinson	66	W	Md	Dec	farmer	infra.B.
Sarah Rouse	73	W	Md	Jan		unknown
George M.D.Bramble	5		Md	Aug		disentary
Elizabech Ptecek	55	M	Md	May		b.Pleurisy
Waltin F. Hiddy	2		Md	Aug		disentary
Mary A. Sendes?	55	W	Md	Feb		pleurisy
Ellin Deverix	66		Ire.	Aug		disentary
Francis A.Nelson	7		Md.	Sep		b.Fever

92

persons who died during the year ending 1 June 1850

CC   DISTRICT 1st.Census Dist.

name	e	mar wid	birth place	mon. died	Occupation	cause of death
Isaac J. E.		M	Md	Jun	merchant	cancer
James A. P.			Md	Dec	carpenter	typhus
George E. I			Md	Aug		disentary
Martha J. E			Md	Aug		disentary
Rebecca A.			Md	Jun		lung dis.
Samuel Rigd.		W	Md	Oct	laborer	consumption
Baker Rigdo.		M	Md	Oct	farmer	consumption
Eliza Allin	11mo		Md	Jul		disentary
Lidia Carr	44	M	Md	Jun		unknown
Margaret Scarborough	89	W	Md	May		old age
Walter F. Forwood	7		Md	May		scarlet fever
John Roberts	20		Eng.	Jul	farmer	gastric fever
Deberrow Nagle	25	M	Md	Jul		disentary
Sarah F. Nagle	1		Md	Aug		disentary
Elizabeth J.Adams	25		Md	Aug		typhoid
William Whiteford	80		Md	Nov	farmer	bowel infla.
Margaret Slemons	79	M	Md	Jul		gastric fever
Joseph Warner	91	W	Md	Jul	watchmaker	unknown
Ruth E. Healy	22		Md	Dec		unknown
William H. Davis	8mo		Md	May		unknown
Mary Hensil	57	M	Md	Feb		unknown
Robert H. Geams	27		Md	May	laborer	unknown
John C. Hutchison	16		Pa.	Dec		fall
Daniel Kenly	64	M	Md	Dec	blacksmith	unknown
Mary Strour	89	W	Md	Jul		unknown
Mary J. Ostler	1		Pa.	Jul		disentary
George W. Cunningham	12		Md	Oct		unknown
Cooper L. Boyd	58	M	Md	May	farmer	lung inflam.
Sylvester Boyd	7		Pa.	May		drowned
Mary Henry	19		Md	Mar		brain infl.
Jesse Reece	75		Md	Feb	farmer	unknown
Jane Demos	36		Md	May		disentary
John Demos	15		Md	Mar		consumption
Zachariah McFaddan	9mo		Md	Nov		scarlet fever
Julia A. Day	11		Md	Sep		scarlet fev.
George Tearel	42		Md	Jun	laborer	small pox
Mary Hughes	16		Wales	Mar		unknown
Ellen Chalk	56	W	Md	Feb		unknown
Elizabeth Whitaker	63	M	Md	Jan		pleurisy
Roger Street	76	M	Md	Mar	farmer	unknown
Lewis Thompson	4mo		Md	Jul		coliz Morb.
Ann Boyd	11		Md	Oct		Scarlet fever
James Anderson (black)	31		Md	Jan	laborer	unknown
William Durham	1mo		Md	Oct		unknown
James Wood	72	W	Md	Jul	farmer	heart disease
John Wood	45	M	Md	Jan	farmer	heart disease
John Stretehoof	88	W	Pa	Dec		old age
Oliver Evans	43		Del.	Jul	carpenter	consumption
Charlotte A. Wiley	2mo		Md	Apr		small pox
Elizabeth Nelson	58	M	Md	Jul		gast.fever
Mary E. Heaps	6		Md	Sep		dysentary
Robert Glenn	13		Md	Aug		dysentary

persons who died during the year ending 1 June 18__50__

COUNTY KENT   DISTRICT -2nd.& 1st.

name	age	mar wid	birth place	mon. died	Occupation	cause of death
Mary E. Clark	5		Md	Jun		brain infl.
Ann Shay	35		Md	Aug		H.cough
Virginia A. Shay	3		Md	Aug		scarlet fever
Mary A. Quimby	5		Md	Sep		dropsey
George B. Usilton	30		Md	Sep		brain fever
Burtis Usilton	1		Md	Sep		sum.compl.
William J. Rowley	3		Md	Oct		scarlet fever
Eliza Crawford	12		Md	Oct		scarlet fever
Eda Crawford	11		Md	Jul		scarlet fever
Charles W. Dugan	1		Md	Aug		billious
			1st.Election Dist.			
Mary Greenwood	1		Md	Aug		scrofula
Susan Everett	10		Md	Sep		S.Fever
John Elisen	4		Md	Oct		s.fever
William Quimby	4		Md	Oct		bil.fever
Elin Shay	33	M	Md	Nov		bowel congest.
Benjamin Greenwood	19		Md	Jan		consumption
John Comegys	10		Md	Feb		throat dis.
charles B. Tilden	42		Md	Feb	tavernkeeper	Erisepelus
N.A.Hollingsworth(male)	44		Md	Feb	farmer	neumonia
Mary S. Thomas	63	W	Md	Mar		old age
Elizabeth Tilden	40	W	Md	Mar		throat dis.
Mrs. Griswould	40	W	Md	Mar		consumption
Mrs. Elbrun	35	W	Md	Apr		bowel inflam.
Samuel German	45	M	Md	Apr	sailer	pleurisy
Elizabeth Weeks	75	W	Md	May		parylisis
Solomon Gauff	38		Pa.	Sep	laborer	bil.fever
Henry Caleb	6		Md	Feb		inflam.
Lyangus Jones	8		Md	Mar		bil.fever
Margaret Hines	11		Md	Apr		euysipilis
William Hines	16		Md	Sep		dropsy
Mary R. Wells	1mo		Md	Sep		sum.comp.
Sarah Hulbert	16	M	Md	Jun		sum.comp.
Henry Eisenbury	21		Md	Jun	laborer	consumption
Martha A. Boyd	15		Md	Aug		unknown
Jane Hodges	20		Md	Sep		bil.fever
Aeorgannia Adkinson	16		Md	Aug		pleurisy
Margaret Skaggs	29	M	Md	Sep		consumption
Mrs. M. Burns	45		Md	Sep		billious
			3rd E.Dist.			
Charles S. Osborn	24		Md	Jun	farmer	chronic
Rebecca M. Stewart	4		Md	May		Wormfev.
Ann Meekins	50	W	Md	Jan		chronic
James Houston	4		Md	Sep		bowel inflam.
John Biddle	2		Md	dec		typhus
Edward Lain	55		Md	May	farmer	bil.fever
Samuel Kennard	73	M	Md	May		chronic
Margaret A. Herrick	16		Del	Apr		brain fever
Christianna Newman	70		Md	Oct		chronic
Levenia Garvin	50		Md	aug		cholera
Amelia a.E.Baiscin	33	M	Md	Apr		unknown

94

MORTALITY SCHEDULE OF MARYLAND

persons who died during the year ending 1 June 18_50_

COUNTY   KENT- MONTGOMERY   DISTRICT -3rd.E.Dist.

name	age	mar wid	birth place	mon. died	Occupation	cause of death
Emily Minez	40	M	Md	Sep		Lung Dis.
Eliza Minez	2mo		Md	Mar		lung dis.
Araminta Spear	32	M	Del.	Jun		liver comp.
Susan Mann	38		Md	Aug		chronic
William P. Parks	3		Md	Jul		brain cong.
MONTGOMERY COUNTY 1st.or Craelin Dist.						
Phineas Paxson	73	M	Pa	Apr	farmer	gradual decl.
Samuel White	61	M	Md	Feb	farmer	dyspepsy
Matilda Case	34	W	Md	Sep		consumption
male Stabler	5d.		Md	Aug		unknown
Mary Reed	14		Md	Aug		bil.fever
Juliana Smith	36	M	Md	Jun		puerperal fever
John & Mary Hall	1mo		Md	Jul		chol.infant.
Anne Waters	89	w	Md	Apr		old age
Jesse Allnutt	56		Md	Apr	farmer	typhoid
Ann Harding	74	W	Md	Mar		pleurisy
John M. Stewart	40		Md	Nov	farmer	consumption
Charles Craddick	88		Md	May	farmer	old age
Ann R. Groomes	2		Md	Mar		croup
George Stricker	40		Md	Mar	farmer	bowel inflam.
Verlinda Merrick	75		Md	Aug		unknown
Phillip Holland	43		Md	May	farmer	lung congest.
Casandra Wilcoxen	66	W	Md	Sep		dysentary
John Leamon	53	M	Md	Jan	carpenter	bil.cramp
Henry T. Leamon	3		Md	Jan		scarlet fever
George Evely	75		Md	May	farmer	killed
Robert Miles	45		Irel.	Sep	laborer	unknown
2nd.or Clarksburg Dist.						
Mary E. Crawford	1		Md	Mar		scarlet fever
Eliza J. Benson	10mo		Md	Feb		scarlet fever
Rachel A. Howes	2		Md	Apr		scarlet fever
Ninian Read	39		Md	Dec	blacksmith	kidney dis.
William M. Woodfield	2mo		Md	Jul		summer comp.
Marian White	40		Va.	Aug		consumption
Richard Young	85	M	Md	Apr	farmer	apoplexy
John W. Duball	25		Md	Apr	farmer	consumption
Otho Duvall	29		Md	May		unknown
Elvira Duvall	6		Md	May		croup
Francis T. D.Molineaux	1mo		Md	Mar		croup
5th or Berrys Dist.						
Charles Wm. Farquhar	1mo		Md	Nov		unknown
W. Henry Farquhar	3		Md	May		scarlet fever
Elisha G. Johnson	2		Md	Mar		scarlet fever
Mary Annis Bond	11		Md	Mar		scarlet fever
Maria Peirce	45	M	Pa	Nov		epilepexy
Richard G. Fawcett	6mo		Md	Mar		heart dis.
William Valdenar	45	M	Md	Sep	farmer	heart dis.
John Rabbitt	1		Md	Apr		scarlet fever
William Raunie	9		Md	Apr		sczrlet fever
Mary E. Wilson	19		Md	Sep		consumption
Anna Hardy	11mo		Md	May		croup
Kate Gentle	3		Md	Dec		scarlet fever
Mary Horner	52		Va.	Nov		consumption

MORTALITY SCHEDULE OF MARYLAND

persons who died during the year ending 1 June 1850

COUNTY -MONTGOMERY   DISTRICT 5th or Berrys

name	age	mar wid	birth place	mon. died	Occupation	cause of death
Barutha Mullican	60	M	Md	May		apoplexy
Ann E. Bready	38	M	Md	Dec		apoplexy
Polly Gates	40	W	Md	Feb		dropsy
Henry C. Gates	5		Md	Apr		scarlet fever
Comfort Sullivan	60	M	Md	Jul		consumption
Massy Mason	79		Md	Jun		cong.fever
Martha Jane Palmer	13		Md	Apr		scarlet fever
John W. Moore	4		Md	Mar		scarlet fever
			4th Dist. Rockabe Dist.			
John Poole	45	M	Md	Sep	innkeeper	unknown
Samuel Leake	53	W	Md	Sep	pumpmaker	fever
Mary Lyddane	6mo		Md	Aug		uknown
James P. Atwood	4		Md	Mar		scarlet fever
Anna Miller	7		Md	Mar		scarlet fever
William Gray	30		Md	Aug	ditcher	pain?
Eliza Case	32	M	Md	Apr		child bed
Frederick Watts	33	M	Va.	Sep	lockeeper	diarrhea
James W. Henderson	9mo		Md	Aug		diarrhea
Susan Offatt	30	M	Md	Aug		diarrhea
Rene A. Boswell	84	W	Md	Jan		old age
John Herter	67	W	Md	Sep	farmer	unknown
Cephas Nichols	76		Md	Nov	farmer	consumption
Samuel Nichols	77	M	Md	Mar	farmer	consumption
Amanda Magruder	11		Md	Apr		diarrhea
Eveline Harrison	33	M	Md	Apr		consumption
Lewis Hill	2mo		Md	Oct		chills
Elizabeth Bayless	59	W	Md	Dec		plurisy
Tyson Weight	19		Md	Nov	laborer	unknown
Florentina Lideke	49	M	Prussia	Sep		consumption
William Dalzier	26	M	Irel.	Jan	boatman	fever
William Ray	37	M	Md	Aug	blacksmith	diarrhea
Henry Fraser	27	M	Md	Jul	farmer	diarrhea
Sarah Paxton	62		Pa.	Mar		pneumonia
Peter Hawkins	76	M	Md	Aug	farmer	paralytic
Axia Gatton	84		Md	Nov		unknown
John Hurley	79	M	Md	May	farmer	rheumatism
Catherine White	73	W	Md	Jul		unknown
George Buskirk	89	W	Md	Jul		cancer
John Mines D.D.	75	M	Va	Jun	clergyman	none
Harrice Litton	67	M	Md	May		none
Minor Anderson	5		Md	Dec		scarlet fever
			2nd or Clarksburg E. Dist.			
Walter F. Hedley	7		Md	Sep		none on this page
Ellen R. Hedley	1		Md	Oct		
Caroline Sheckels	4		Md	Apr		
Hezekiah Beale	63	M	Md	Dec	farmer	
Ellen Poole	60	M	Md	Aug		
Richard H. Lawson	4		Md	Dec		
Nancy Browning	78	W	Md	Jun		
Thomas Gibbons	62	M	Md	May	farmer	
Dorothy H. Harmon	36	M	Germ.	Nov		
George W. Tabler	1		Md	Jul		
Keziah Layton	84	W	Md	Feb		

MORTALITY SCHEDULE OF MARYLAND

persons who died during the year ending 1 June 18<u>50</u>

COUNTY MONTGOMERY- Pr.George DISTRICT - 2nd.Clarksburg E.Dist.

name	age	mar wid	birth place	mon. died	Occupation	cause of death
Emily L. Corbin	1		Md	Dec		none on this page
Maria Rhodes	61	W	Md	Jul		
Sarah J. Taylor	5		Md	Sep		
James W. Taylor	1		Md	Oct		
Elizabeth Reid	9		Md	Sep		
William M. Nicholson	10		Md	Aug		
4th Rockirbe Dist.						
John Lowe	49	M	Md	Sep	none	apoplexy
Richard Bean	85	W	Md	Jan	none	old age
Ellen Ferguson	6		D.C.	Dec		scarlet fever
Jane N. Beale	56	W	Md	Aug		apoplexy
3rd Medleys E.Dist.						
Sophia C. Jones	22	M	Md	Jul		unknown
Henry Smith	20		Md	Dec	laborer	consumption
Emily Poole	4mo		Md	Apr		scarlet fever
James Cocklin	35		Ire.	Apr	laborer	pleurisy
Jacob H. Eldridge	4		Md	Mar		scarlet fever
Edgar N. Eldridge	3		Md	Mar		scarlet fever
Robert Soper	81	W	Md	Apr	none	erysipelas
Blanche Poole	2		Md	Mar		scarlet fever
Mary F. Tuttle	8		Md	May		scarlet fever
Levi Veirs	75	W	Md	Sep	farmer	fever
Mary E. Caldwell	6mo		Md	Jun		brain infl.
Sophia Johnson	60		Md	Jun		paralysis
Mortimer Williams	3		Md	Mar		scarlet fever
Nathan B. Clay?	29	M	Md	Jul	laborer	knee dis.
James E. Williams	8mo		Md	May		scarlet fever
Joseph F. Lowe	8		Md	Jan		scarlet fever
Margaret Connelley	6mo		Md	May		unknown
John T. Benson	3		Md	Dec		scarlet fever
Napoleon Fisher	13		Md	Sep		fever
Mary Alinda Fechtig	2mo		Md	Mar		pneumonia
Mary E.Eichelberger	3d.		Md	Feb		unknown
Josephine Pumphris	1		Md	Jan		unknown
Sarah M. King	4		Md	Dec		scarlet fever
James E. Hopkinson	24		Md	Sep	carpenter	diarrhea
Nathan T. Hempston	49		Md	Mar	farme r	unknown
PRINCE GEORGES CO.-Bladensburgh & Vansville D.						
James Williams	1		Md	Jan		scarlet fever
Sarah A. Tenley	1		Md	Nov		bowel inflam.
Jule Calvert	1		Md	Oct		worms
William S.Fowler	3		D.C.	Feb		dropsy
William Messinger	74		Md	Sep	teacher	old age
Levi Hayse	34		Md	May	farmer	pleuirisy
James A. Simpson	1mo		Md	May		unknown
Amelia C. Carter	19		Md	Apr		scarlet fever
Dorinda Brashears	25		Md	May		child bed
DorindaMarquer	24		Md	May		child bed
Mary R. Soper	2		Md	Jul		measles
Harrison S. Wallace	2mo		Md	Jul		hydrocephlis
Julia A. Lowe	36		Md	Jul		peur.fever

97

persons who died during the year ending 1 June 18 50

COUNTY -PRINCE GEORGE   DISTRICT Bladensburg & Vansville

name	age	mar wid	birth place	mon. died	Occupation	cause of death
William T. Brown	29		Md	Mar	merchant	consumption
Sarah M. Parson	1		Md	Jul		measles
Robert Hayward	45		Md	Aug	tailor	unknown
Harriet Wright	76	W	Md	Jun		erysipelxy
Ruben M. Hyatt	9mo		Md	Jul		measles
Florence Middleton	1		Md	Jul		measles
William H. Burgess	8mo		Md	May		unknown
George E. Lowe	3		Md	Jul		measles
Adeline Linn	10		Md	May		measles
Elizabeth Francis	45		Md	Jul		brain cong.
Columbus D. Francis	3		Md	Jul		croup
Ann L. Lowndy?	46		Md	May		debility
Susan Norton	1		Md	Sep		cho.infant.
Laura V. Carlton	2		Md	Sep		Gast.fever
Henry Carlton	4mo		Md	ep		cho.infant.
Elizabeth Wright	43		Md	May		congestion
William A. King	1mo		Md	Oct		fits
Martha Harvey	34		Md	Aug		brain inf.
Elizabeth Bartley	5mo		Md	Sep		unknown
Taylor Wood	3		Md	Sep		scarlet fever
Sarah Wilson	78	M	Md	Mar		old age
James Richrdson	64	M	Md	Jan		consumption
John Davis	1		Md	Dec		brain inf.
Rufus Warfield	1mo		Md	Jan		cho.infant.
Mary Warfield	3		Md	Apr		dysentary
Caroline Kirby	11		Md	Sep		bowel.Infl.
Thomas Wiggins	39	W	Md	Jul		unknown
Eleanor Darby	38	M	Va.	Apr		brain infl.
Elizabeth Chaulk	34		Md	Mar		consumption
James E. Stephenson	24		Md	Sep	soldier in Mexico-dysentary	
Tobias Anderson	30	M	Md	Dec	grocer	lung.inflam.
Mary Riddle	50	W	Md	Sep		consumption
George Chaulk	1mo		Md	Mar		fits
Sarah E. Darby	7mo		Md	Aug		unknown
Eliza Ridgeway	16		Md	Jun		brain infl.
William Miles	45	M	Md	Aug	laborer	unknown
Thomas Miles	13		Md	Jun		brain inflm.
Daniel Kernan	24		Md	Jun	farmer	dropsy
James Ryan	6		Md	Feb		suffocation
Caleb Clarke	76	M	Md	Dec	planter	insanity
Sarah Baker	52	W	Md	Feb		measles
Sarah J. Baker	23		Md	Feb		measles
Josiah Beale	75	W	Md	Oct	farmer	consumption
Margaret Larner	73	W	Ire.	Apr		consumption
Ann Beall	45		Md	Jul		consumption
Margaret Larner	73	W	Ire.	Apr		consumption
Smith Dugan	6mo		Md	Sep		Worms
Biddy Larner	32		Md	Dec		consumption
James A. Baker	4		Md	Aug		scarlet fever
Mary C. Shaw	7		Md	Jul		scarlet fever
James E. Shaw	5		Md	Jul		scarlet fever
John H.Murphy	7		Md	Jun		scarlet fever
Peter Jordan	26		Ire.	Jan	laborer	bil.pleuricy
George Hoffnagle	75	M	Md	Jan		pleurisy

98

persons who died during the year ending 1 June 18_50_

COUNTY -PRINCE GEORGE   DISTRICT -Blandensburg

name	age	mar wid	birth place	mon. died	Occupation	cause of death
Mary Riddle	12		Md	Jul		scarlet fever
Richard Riddle	4		Md	Jul		scarlet fever
William C. Brashears	35		Md	Oct	Texan Const.	small pox
AQUAScO Dist.						
Margaret Turner	24	M	Md	Apr		stomach
Benjamin B. Gray	30	M	Md	Sep	physician	unknown
Leonard T. Pearce	23		Md	Feb		consumption
Elizabeth Naylor	70	W	Md	Apr		dropsy
Martha Arme	50		Md	May		C.
Augustus M. Bowling	7mo		Md	Jul		teething
Elizabeth Adams	32	W	Md	Sep		dysentary
Mary ᵃ. Adams	12		Md	Sep		dysentary
Sarah Garner	50		Md	Oct		diarrhea
Sally Boswell	55	W	Md	Dec		C.
William T. Grimes	3		Md	Apr		scarlet fever
MARLBOROUGH DISTRICT						
Jessee Talbot	87	W	Md	Apr	planter	dropsey
Martha E. Stocket	7		Md	Oct		sudden
Samuel Harris	40		Md	Feb	Innkeeper	C.
Mrs. Beall	41?		Md	none		none
Mrs. Hodges	69	M	Md	Dec		C.
Mary Adams	20		Md	Sep		diarreah
Edward Dement	21		Md	Sep		L.compl.
William Gunton	3mo		Md	Sep		dysentary
John Ring	40		Md	Oct	farmer	accident
George Dorsey	2		Md	Feb		C.
Sarah Naylor	52		Md	Oct		diarreah
William Piles	6mo		Md	Aug		none
Elizabeth Windle	33		Md	Sep		C.
Margaret Ryan	23		Md	May		typhus
William Mitchell	82		Md	Jul		old age
Mrs. E. Wood	28	M	Md	Apr		C.
Patrick Carroll	23		Ire.	Jan	Soldier	PHisis?
Elizabeth Everett	37		N.Y.	Jun		same
SPAULDINGS DIST.						
Thomas Pearce	1		Md	Jul		w.cough
Mary Lyles	17		Md	unkn		unknown
NOTTINGHAM DISTRICT						
JohnA. Talbot	8mo		Md	Jul		S.compl.
William Crook	1		Md	Oct		worms
A.R.A.Mackall(fem)	35		Md	Mar		C.
John Warring	1		Md	Mar		C.
E.Haldenback(fem)	19	M	Md	Aug		cold
Robert Richards	36		Md	Sep	manager	consumption
PISCATAWAY DISTRICT						
John Boswell	40	M	Md	Feb	farmer	C.
Phebe Lambert	83	W	Md	Nov		old age
John H.T. Marshall	25	M	Md	Dec	physician	C.
Eleanor J. Marshall	8mo		Md	Apr		water on brain
Jane Davis	62		Md	Feb		paralysis
Edith Adams	66		Md	Sep		C.
E. Claggett(fem)	74	W	Md	Apr		paralysis
George Underwood	40		Md	unkn.	farmer	C.

MORTALITY SCHEDULE OF MARYLAND

persons who died during the year ending 1 June 18_50_

COUNTY PRINCE GEORGE   DISTRICT   Piscataway Dist.

name	age	mar wid	birth place	mon. died	Occupation	cause of death
Henry Locker	40	M	Md	Jul		fever
John W. French	8		Md	unkn		brain fever
Lloyd M. Lowe	37	M	Md	Aug	farmer	cholera
Mary E. Ashley	30	M	Md	Jun		consumption
QUEEN ANNES DIST						
Col.Wm.T. Wooton	55	M	Md	Jan		sudden
Catherine Sprigg	3		Md	Mar		scarlet fever
John Wells	10		Md	May		typhoid
Jerry Wells	53		Md	Jan		typhoid
QUEEN ANNES COUNTY-1st dist.						
Samuel W. Cole	6mo		Md	Oct		unknown
Mary E. Hazel	32		Md	Jun		consumption
Benjamin Levrage	75	M	Md	Jul	farmer	unknown
Nancy Levrage	73	W	Md	Jul		unknown
Benjamin Seward	1		Md	Aug		cho.infant.
Lucy G. Clow	8		Md	Oct		dysentary
Margaret C. McAllister	1		Md	Sep		brain inflam.
Charlotte A. Rouse	1		Md	Apr		unknown
Christopher Baxter	26		Md	Dec		typhoid
Isaac Leverett	2		Md	Jul		unknown
Indiana Leverett	16		Md	Nov		unknown
James T. Neal	2		Md	Jul		measles
Susanna Rash	70	W	Md	Aug		old age
Kitty Raisin (black)	1mo		Md	Apr		unknown
Jessee Clark	8mo		Md	Aug		unknown
Mary A. Patrick	1mo		Md	May		unknown
Mary E. Fields	6		Md	May		unknown
Risden Sparkes	1mo		Md	Aug		unknown
Fletcher Perkins	1mo		Md	Jul		unknown
Elizabeth Jarrell	1mo		Md	Aug		unknown
2nd Election Dist.						
Fansela Wooddall	1		Md	Mar		unknown
John Tucker	60	M	Md	May	farmer	unknown
Mary M. Boyer	6		Md	Oct		unknown
Charles Betton	38		Md	Dec	laborer	unknown
Ann P. Merridith	8		Md	Nov		bil.dys.
David Merridith	2		Md	Nov		bil.dys.
Ara A.E.Hurlock(fem)	3mo		Md	Oct		dysentary
William Finley	6mo		Md	Oct		none
Samuel Sparks	2		Md	Sep		unknown
Thomas Dating	35		Md	Oct	tailor	epilepsy
William Townes	4mo		Md	Oct		bilious
Mary H. Green	33		Md	Dec		congestion
Lemuel Dunbacco	35		Md	Jul	merchant	consumption
Adaline Harrington	35		Md	May		unknown
Sarah E. Betton	20		Md	Feb		unknown
Hester A. Spiney	40		Md	Jul		consumption
Harriett Griffin	3mo		Md	Jul		sum.compl.
Ellen Price	35		Md	Mar		consumption
John Rolph	30	M	Md	Oct	merchant	consumption
David L. Sparkes	25		Md	Mar	teacher	typhoid
Eugene Crane	18		Md	May		typhoid

100

persons who died during the year ending 1 June 1850

COUNTY -QUEEN ANNES Co.   DISTRICT-2nd E.Dist.

name	age	mar wid	birth place	mon. died	Occupation	cause of death
William Coursey	4mo		Md	Oct		unknown
Mary Hackett	30	W	Md	Aug		decline
Francis Hackett	9		Md	Jul		unknown
Daniel Hall	1		Md	Sep		unknown
Ann Elliott	39	M	Md	May		unknown
William lliott	1mo		Md	May		unknown
Henry Hendrix	75	M	Md	May	farmer	old age
Nathan Longfellow	50		Md	May	farmer	unknown
Sarah E. Smith	6		Md	Sep		cholera
Mary M. Rochester	1mo		Md	Dec		unknown
Wesley Rolph	26		Md	Jun	farmer	cholera
William Primrose	67	M	Md	Feb	tavernkeeper	sorethroat
Samuel Weekly	1		Md	Sep		jaundice
George W. Cook	2mo		Md	Jul		inflam.
Helen T. Ruth	10		Md	May		scarlet fever
William R. Ruth	1		Md	Sep		sum.dis.
1st Election Dist.						
Reese Walls	40		Md	Jun		bil.fev.
Sarah E. Tolson	3mo		Md	Oct		unknown
Robert S. Welch	35	M	Md	Sep	carpenter	unknown
William Beck	22		Md	Jun	farmer	unknown
William Alley	59		Md	Jul	farmer	C.Rheumatis
Mary A. Alley	2		Md	Jul		bowel inflam.
William Kirby	47	M	Md	Nov	sailor	unknown
3rd Election Dist.						
Joseph E. Foster	1		Md	Jul		chol.inf.
Mary Smith	36	M	Md	Nov		dyspepsia
Samuel J. Brown	9		Md	Mar		scarlet fever
Mary Legg	55		Md	Jun		unknown
James H. Covington			Md	Jun		unknown-Alms House
Sarah Price	60		Md	Dec		unknown- "
Solomon Horney	2mo		Md	Nov		unknown-"
Ann E. Lucas	1mo		Md	Jun		accident
Sarah A. Whittington	31		Md	Aug		Con.
Susan Reese	1mo		Md	Aug		unknown
Anna Roberts	1mo		Md	Dec		unknown
James V. Newman	8		Md	Dec		typhoid
James Ussleton	38		Md	Dec	farmer	cons.
Susan Holliday	79	W	Md	Jul		gangrene
Nancy R. Holliday	16		Md	Dec		hemmorage
Robert Sparks	1mo		Md	May		unknown
Mary E. Bostick	1mo		Md	Jul		W.cough
Mary Jane Class	30		Md	Mar		consumption
James Hadley	2		Md	Jul		unknown
Joseph Thompson	37		Md	Jun	laborer	consumption
William L. George	2		Md	Mar		bil.remit.
Nathan Carmean	38		Md	May	farmer	typhoid
John Nabb	59		Md	Oct	carpenter	consumption
Mary A. Desage	25		Md	Sep		typhoid
Josiah Desage	1		Md	Sep		typhoid
Sarah E. Merridith	5		Md	Jan		scarlet fever
Elizabeth Nevill	68	W	Md	May		unknown
Anna Bradley	8mo		Md	Aug		unknown

MORTALITY SCHEDULE OF MARYLAND

persons who died during the year ending 1 June 1850

COUNTY -QUEEN ANNES CO.   DISTRICT -3rd E.Dist.

name	age	mar wid	birth place	mon. died	Occupation	cause of death
Thomas A. McFeely	15		Md	Jul	clerk	cholera
Edward & Mary Hamilton	3mo		Md	Jul		chol.Inf.
Kensay H. Thomas	1		Md	Feb		chol.
Robert Goldsborough	76		Md	Oct	physician	unknown
Edward F. Calloway	43		Md	Dec	farmer	bil.pleurisy
Stansbury Moffitt	41		Md	Jul	butcher	unknown
Samuel Goldsmith	47		Md	Jul	laborer	bil.pleurisy
Samuel Vickers	11		Md	Nov		unknown
Mary E. Rowlenson	23		Md	Dec		Con.
Ann Haslett	24		Md	Sep		Con.
Philomon L. Gilder	1mo		Md	Sep		unknown
Susan Conner	33		Md	May		pleurisy
Nathan Baynard	1		Md	Aug		bowels
Thomas Garey	20		Md	Aug	carpenter	Con.
William C. Duhamel	6mo		Md	Jul		dysentary
5th Election Dist.						
Sarah A. Chambers	37	M	Del.	Mar		unknown
Gerald Coursey	80		Md	Aug	gentleman	gout
Robert Brown	30		Md	Jan		congestion
Annanias Gossage	60		Md	Sep	farmer	dropsy
James Rimmer	4		Md	Oct		unknown
James P. Butler	9		Md	Apr		scarlet fever
Thomas Hughes	28	M	Md	Mar	farmer	dropsey
John McFeeley	3		Md	Mar		scarlet fever
Mary E. Allen	30	M	Md	Aug		child bed
William Kirby	60		Md	Sep	farmer	cons.
John D. Perkins	2		Md	Oct		unknown
4th Election Dist.						
Leah Sparkes	70		Md	Jan		cons.
Tabitha Hampton	28	M	Md	Oct		cons.
James A. Earle	1		Md	May		unknown
Susan Bright	38	M	Md	Nov		pleurisy
Elbert Gibson	40		Md	Jun	none	Mania Po.
Elizabeth Ringgold	75	W	Md	Aug		unknown
Reubinine Ringgold	10		Md	May		wor.Fever
Sarah E. Bryan	21		Md	Oct		diaharria
Sarah Bayley	8		Md	Oct		gastric fever
Tabitha Lewis	55		Md	Mar	laborer	Cons.
Mary J. Ringgold	21		Md	Mar		child bed
William Joiner	84		Md	Jan	none	unknown
5th Election Dist.						
William Wiggins	30	M	Md	Dec	farmer	typhoid
William Morgan	4mo		Md	Jul		chol.inf.
John R. Driver	43	M	Md	Feb	farmer	Parals.
Sarah Ewing	1		Md	Aug		bil.Cat.
Nancy Cooper	42	M	Md	Jun		typhoid
Josiah Bland	46	M	Md	Jul	farmer	cholera
Sarah E. Lewis	23		Md	Nov		Cons.
Margaret Ellers	30	M	Md	Sep		unknown
Samuel W. Jarman	2		Md	May		unknown
Samuel T. Wright	3		Md	Feb		scarlet fever
James Coursey	11		Md	Nov		scarlet fever
Nathaniel Coursey	5		Md	Nov		scarlet fever

MORTALITY SCHEDULE OF MARYLAND

persons who died during the year ending 1 June 18_50

COUNTY =QUEEN ANNES-ST MARYS DISTRICT 3rd E.Dist.

name	age	mar wid	birth place	mon. died	Occupation	cause of death
Mary E. Sullivan	30	W	Md	Aug		bil.fever
Henrietta O. Baynard	3		Md	Jul		bil.fever
Mary Jane Chambers	4mo		Md	Jul		chol.inf.
Henrietta Montigue	25	M	Md	Apr		child bed
Henrietta Montigue	1mo		Md	May		unknown
Joel Montigue	1mo		Md	Aug		unknown
Jonathan Knotts	45		Md	May	farmer	pleurisy
Mary M. Goodman	3mo		Md	Jul		unknown
William J. Reed	7mo		Md	Aug		cholera
John Lucas	26		Md	Mar	laborer	pleurisy
Ann Vickers	27		Md	Mar		unknown
Frances Dyott	38	W	Md	Apr		cons.
Ann Dyott	70	W	Md	Oct		cons.
Ann Cooper	37		Md	May		liver com.
Sarah Ann Richardson	18		Md	Jul		cons.
SAINT MARY'S CO.-3rd E.Dist.						
Peter Mugg	75	W	Md-St.M.	Mar	farmer	plleurisy
Amos Davis	46	M	Md	Mar	farmer	gravel
Hannah H. Abell	44	M	Md	Dec		unknown
George C. Peacock	2		Md	Jul		unknown
William F. Mills	4		Md	Feb		measles
Ann Russell	72	W	Md	Sep		consumption
Mary E. Stone	1		Md	Feb		teething
Edward H. Posey	27		Md	Nov	farmer	absess
James Hill	70	M	Md	Jan	farmer	unknown
Wm. F. Russell	5mo		Md	Aug		bil.fever
William F. Greenwell of	35	M	Md	Apr	laborer	unknown
Ann Raley Jas	35	M	Md	Jun		consumption
Catherine E. Watts	18		Md	Jun		consumption
Ann Peacock	83		Md	Apr		unknown
Joseph S. Thompson	10mo		Md	Jul		unknown
Benedict Guy	3da.		Md	Mar		unknown
George Dunbar	47		Md	May	laborer	dropsey
Jeremiah Haysil	54	M	Md	Apr	farmer	unknown
Frederick J. Greenwell	7		Md	Sep		unknown
Charles L. Durant	6mo		Md	Jul		summer c.
Ann M. Howard	1		Md	Sep		summer c.
Wm. F. Greenwell	63	W	Md	Dec	innkeeper	dropsey
Mary J. Russell	1		Md	Aug		summer c.
John A. Hayden	35	M	Md	Jan	farmer	consumption
Wm. M. Gilliams	26	W	Pa.	Aug	farmer	bilious
Francis Hayden	68	M	Md	May	farmer	consumption
Susan Greenwell	63	W	Va.	Jun		consumption
Charlotte Wheeler	10mo		Md	Jul		unknown
Nana Wheeler	3		Md	Aug		unknown
Mary M.Moore	52	W	Pr.GeoCo.	Mar		appoplexy
Joseph Jarboe	5mo		Md	Aug		summer C.
Mary E. Forrest	1mo		Md	May		accident
Virginia Hearne	6mo		Md	Sep		b.fever
John L. Hearne	45		Md	May	none	dropsey
Ignatius Goldsborough	75	M	Md	Dec	farmer	unknown
Ann P. Peacock	30		Md	Aug		unknown
Martha H.Goldsborough	15		Md	Sep		unknown

103

MORTALITY SCHEDULE OF MARYLAND

persons who died during the year ending 1 June 18_50_

COUNTY -St.Marys   DISTRICT -3rd E.Dist.

name	age	mar wid	birth place	mon. died	Occupation	cause of death
William Turner	40	W	Va.	Nov	laborer	unknown
Eliza Turner	36	M	Md	Nov		b.fever
Charles A. Greenwell	63	M	Md	Apr	farmer	unknown
John Goddard	22		Md	Dec	bootmaker	braininflam.
Sylvester Greenwell	45	W	Md	Mar	none	unknown
Hannah Clarke	2		Md	Oct		unknown
Caroline Price	25		Md	Nov		b.fever
Wm. H. Leach	4mo		Md	Jan		unknown
James D. Sutton	45	W	Calv.Co	Dec	physician	consumption
John F. Spencer	26		Md	May	farmer	typhoid
Mary E. Kirby	20		Md	Jun		unknown
Richard Thomas	48	M	Md	Oct	farmer	appopletic
John J. Wise	1		Md	Aug		unknown
Samuel D. Legrand	80	M	Eng.	Oct	none	typhoid
Joseph Dyer	6		Md	May		unknown
Morgan Crosier	68	W	Pa.	Jul	carpenter	unknown
Charles L. Durant	6mo		Md	Jul		summer compl.
Amelia Reintzel	52	M	Mont.Co	Mar		consumption
Benjamin McKay	3mo		Md	Dec		unknown
Jane E. Biscue	28		Md	Oct		dropsy
2nd District						
Robert Bean	25	M	Md	Jan		consumption
James E. Milbourn	17		Md	Jul	none	unknown
Elizabeth R. Crane	2		Md	Aug		croup
Elizabeth Warren	25	M	Md	Nov		consumption
R.A. Gibbons(male)	29		Md	Dec	tailor	consumption
Robert V. Edwards	9		Md	Dec		fits
Richard Adams	10mo		Md	Sep		unknown
Richard Watts	42	M	Md	Aug	carpenter	cont.fever
Mary Watts	54		Md	May		dispepsia
George W.C.Railey	28		Md	Mar	none	consumption
Mary Sanner	50	M	Md	Jan		unknown
Henry N. Kirk	44	M	Md	Jul	farmer	amputation
Charlott F. Kird	37	W	Md	Jan		effort of B.
James A. Spencer	11mo		Md	Apr		unknown
Mary B. Thompson	33	M	Md	Jan		dropsy
John Lorrence	99	M	Md	Dec	laborer	soreThroat
Thomas T. Tea	39	M	Md	Jan	carpenter	typhoid
Margaret Cortney	19		Md	Oct		consumption
Thomas Thompson	52	W	Md	Jan		parelitic
James F. Dailey	1		Md	Oct		worms
Rebecca Ford	61	W	Md	Jul		dispepsia
Lewis C. Cortney	1		Balt.Co	Mar		unknown
Mallinda Gill	75		Md	Feb		unknown
Elizabeth Armesworthy	73		Md	Jun		consumption
George Crane	52	W	Md	Aug	farmer	unknown
Lidia A. Penbrook	2		Md	Apr		summer comp.
John T.S. Thompson	1		Md	Aug		summer comp.
Violetta G. Hall	33		Md	Aug		unknown
Charles W. Williams	1day		Md	Jan		unknown
William H. Cullison	9da		Md	Nov		b.inflam.
Thomas Carren	54	M	Eng	Dec	shoemaker	b.pleuricy
Thomas H. Biscue	43	M	Md	Jun	farmer	unknown

104

MORTALITY SCHEDULE OF MARYLAND

persons who died during the year ending 1 June 18_50

COUNTY - St. Marys   DISTRICT -4.E.Dist.

name	age	mar wid	birth place	mon. died	Occupation	cause of death
John Blanagin	50	M	Va	Jul	laborer	b.inflam.
Randolph Ellice	43	M	Md	Nov	farmer	neumonia
Attaway Chiseldine (fem)	1mo		Md	Aug		hopping cough
Richard P.Blackstone	11mb		Md	Jul		measles
Elizabeth Bond	1mo		Md	Apr		fits
Sarah M. Bowls	18		Md	Mar		unknown
Elizabeth A. Thomas	1mo		Md	Oct		yellowJaundice
John B. Mattingly	43	M	Md	Dec	farmer	accident
Mary A. C. Chum	25	M	Md	Mar		unknown
Martha A. Chum	1		Md	Apr		unknown
Ellen N. Tippett	26		Md	May		consumption
Catherine Revell	33		Md	Nov		child bed
Jane C. Paine	7mo		Md	Jul		b.affect.
Mary E. Norris	3da		Md	Dec		fits
John Love	1da		Md	Apr		sudden
John H. Garner	4		Md	Oct		unknown
Robert H. Apuces	28		Md	Jan	tailor	dropsey
William Winsatt	40		Md	May	tailor	Tremens?
Mary E. Tracy	48	M	Md	Feb		unknown
Elizabeth Drury	65	M	Md	Jun		consumption
Ebenezer Brookbart	17		Md	Feb	laborer	typhoid
John H. Swan	4		Chas.Co.	Mar		dropsy
Allen T. Woodburn	8mo		Md	May		unknown
Ann Shomwell	58	M	D.C.	Feb		dispepsia
5th Election Dist.						
William Wood	62	M	Md	Nov	laborer	accident
Rosetta Wood	10		Md	Feb		pleuricy
William Thomas M.D.	60	M	Md	Sep	farmer	pleurisy
Benonia Garner(male)	5		Md	Sep		unknown
Mary J. Long	1		Md	Jun		unknown
Jane M. Harrison	10		Md	May		consumption
Alexander Lyon	70	M	Chas.Co.	Feb	farmer	consumption
SOMERSET COUNTY -2nd Division						
Otho Collier	2		Md	Jul		bil.dysentary
Elizabeth E. Rider	30		Md	Aug		bil.dysentary
Michael Murrell	5		Md	Jul		hooping cough
John W. Daily	8		Md	Jul		bil.dysentary
Emma F. Rider	2		Md	Jul		scarlet fever
Mary Hasting	7mo		Md	Nov		pleurisy
Alphius Ennis	3mo		Md	Jul		bil.dysentary
John P. Ennis	1		Md	Sep		Head Plurysa
Alevia Booth	7		Md	Aug		Head Plurysa
Eliza J. Humphreys	26		Md	Aug		bil.dysentary
Alvin Dickson	6		Md	Sep		unknown
Henry Evans	74	M	Md	Sep		unknown
Elizabeth Baker	42	M	Del.	Dec.		unknown
Calvin Venables	48	M	Md	Apr	farmer	unknown
Isaac Sulivan	56	M	Del.	Feb.	farmer	unknown
Rachael Waller	1		Md	Aug		Col.Morbus
Hetty Robinson	44		Md	Apr		brain inflam.
Samuel Hearn	11		Md	Jul		bil.dysentary
Mary Hull	38	W	Md	unkn.		unknown

MORTALITY SCHEDULE OF MARYLAND

persons who died during the year ending 1 June 1850

COUNTY -SOMERSET   DISTRICT -2nd.Division

name	age	mar wid	birth place	mon. died	Occupation	cause of death
Margaret Freeney	2mo		Md	Jul		bil.dysentary
Elizabeth E. Nichols	1		Md	Aug		brain inflam.
Mary A. Wilson	21		Md	Aug		unknown
Sarah G. Bradley	1		Md	Sep		bil.dysentary
Napoleon W. Hull	43	M	Md	Sep	farmer	bil.dysentary
Elizabeth A. Russell	25	M	Md	Sep		bil.dysentary
Mary Bennett	36	M	Md	May		bil.plurysa
Sally Gillis	60	W	Md	Oct		bil.dysentary
Charlotte Horsman	36		Md	Sep		bil.dysentary
James Horsman	45		Md	Jun	farmer	consumption
Severn Majors	38	M	Md	Oct	farmer	bil.dysentary
Mary E. S. Elsey	26	M	Md	Nov		unknown
Elizabeth H. Byrd	40	M	Md	May		bil.fever
Swain Bennett	56	W	Md	Jul	blacksmith	unknown
Rhoda English	60	W	Md	Dec		consumption
Virginia T. wallace	11mo		Md	Mar		bil.plurysa
Zepora Seebrese	10		Md	May		unknown
William James Nelson	10		Md	Aug		bil.dysentary
John T. O. Taylor	7		Md	aug		bil.fever
William James Hopkins	1mo		Md	Feb		unknown
Alpheus Collins	1		Md	Mar		unknown
Levi Hughes	1		Md	Jul		bil.dysentary
Sarah M. Evans	1		Md	Aug		Col.Morbus
Mary E. White	9mo		Md	Oct		bil.dysentary
James Denson	72	M	Md	Oct	farmer	bil.dysentary
Polly Denson	68	W	Md	Nov		dropsy
James Wainright	40	M	Md	Oct	farmer	dropsy
Rosanna Wainright	6		Md	Oct		bil.dysentary
George W. Wainright	2		Md	Dec		bil.dysentary
Joshua Wainright	67	W	Md	Sep	farmer	bil.dysentary
Albert T. Robinson	1		Md	Jul		unknown
Robert Catlin	30		Md	May	farmer	C.
Sarah E.B. Mezick	1		Md	Aug		bil.dysentary
Milly Horner	11		Md	Sep		dropsy
Caroline R. Turner	2		Md	Nov		whopping cough
Samuel J. Quinn	2		Md	Aug		bil.dysentary
John Larmore	36	M	Md	Oct	blacksmith	unknown
Mary F. Walter	2		Md	Dec		whopping cough
Hester Lewis	4		Md	Sep		bil.fever
Tubman Jackson	54	M	Md	Mar	shoemaker	sudden
Sarah E.Covington	23	M	Md	Oct		child birth
Robert Walter	11mo		Md	Feb		croup
John Daugherty	71	M	Md	Oct	farmer	unknown
Samuel Barkley	40	M	Md	Dec	farmer	unknown
Mary E.Dashiell	23	M	Md	Oct		nervous fever
Benjamin J. Dashiell	51	M	Md	May	farmer	consumption
Emily G. Covington	8mo		Md	Jun		bowel.inflam.
John W. Winsor	8mo		Md	Jul		bil.dysentary
Nancy Wainright	45	W	Md	unkn.		unknown
Christina Cooper	2		Md	Mar		hooping cough
James W.Wainright	1		Md	Jun		bil.dysentary
William James Elliott	14		Md	Feb		brain infl.
Daniel D. Kennerly	7mo		Md	Oct		unknown

MORTALITY SCHEDULE OF MARYLAND

persons who died during the year ending 1 June 18 50

COUNTY - SOMERSET   DISTRICT -2nd.Div.

name	age	mar wid	birth place	mon. died	Occupation	cause of death
William Jackson	2		Md	Dec		unknown
Mary A.E.Smith	4		Md	May		unknown
Charles R. Smith	5mo		Md	May		unknown
Charles M.W. Rhoades	11		Md	Oct		brain infl.
Mary A. Bounds	15		Md	Apr		consumption
Margaret A. Bradley	8		Md	Aug		brain inflam.
John V. Humphrise	44	M	Md	Aug	farmer	liver dis.
Levisa Lowery	50	W	Del.	Jul		unknown
Joshua T. Porter	14		Md	Dec		unknown
John E. Fletcher	7		Md	Mar		dropsy
Margaret Davis	4		Md	Mar		unknown
Robert Twilly	17		Md	Aug	none	brain infl.
Mary E. Waller	22		Md	Jul		bil.dysentary
Mary Dickerson	28	M	Md	Jun		unknown
Mary D. Willing	6mo		Md	Sep		unknown
John Q.A.Wainright	19		Md	Nov	sailor	cold
George Crockett	65	M	Md	May	laborer	unknown
Ann Mezick	8mo		Md	Jan		bil.dysentary
John Twilly	61	M	Md	Nov	farmer	dropsey
Wm.Augustus Donoho	10mo		Md	Oct		unknown
Mary E. Manders	9mo		Md	May		cold
Ataline White	9		Md	Feb		sudden
			1st.Division			
Jesse W. Colbert	3mo		Md	May		hooping cough
John E. Hall	2		Md	Jun		worms
Elsey Evans	30	M	Md	Oct	waterman	fever
Catharine Kelso	7mo		Md	Dec		scarlet fever
Nancy Davis	78		Md	Mar	housekeeper	influenza
Humphris Beachum	22		Md	Mar	spinner	consumption
Nancy Smith	80	W	Md	unkn		unknown
George W. Waters	20		Md	Jul	shoemaker	cholera
Sarah J. Tull	1		Md	May		hooping cough
William Fowler	35		Md	Dec	overseer	kidney dis.
Isaac Gillis	65	W	Md	unkn	oysterman	unknown
Lawrence M. Roberts	2		Md	Jun		dropsy
James Brinkley	70	M	Md	unkn	oysterman	consumption
Elliott Kersey	50	M	Md	Oct	farmer	rhumatism
Susan Lewis	45		Md	unkn	.	unknown
Jane Slocomb	32		Md	Feb		palsy
Isaac Hunt	45	M	Md	Mar	laborer	unknown
William Reddish	55		Md	Sep	teacher	consumption
Sarah Denson	50		Md	unkn		unknown
James Stewart	40		Md	Sep	shoemaker	intemperance
Nancy Wingate	52	W	Md	unkn		unknown
William Crouch	65		Md	Dec	mariner	consumption
John T. Jones	45	M	Md	Sep	farmer	consumption
Cordelia W. Chelton	3		Md	Dec		worms
Ann O. Chelton	3mo		Md	May		worms
Rachel Dorothy	25	M	Md	Nov		fever
Hyram Dise	1		Md	Sep		worms
John Riggin	68	M	Md	Mar	carpenter	lung inflam.
Jane Thomas	2		Md	Mar		drowned

persons who died during the year ending 1 June 1850

COUNTY - SOMERSET   DISTRICT 1st Div.

name	age	mar wid	birth place	mon. died	Occupation	cause of death
Mary Sterling	86	M	Md	Jul		unknown
Olevia Johnson	3mo		Md	May		fall
Elijah S. Lawson	50	M	Md	Jul	farmer	lung inflam.
Charles Cullen	32		Md	Sep	mariner	fever
William H. Johnson	26		Md	Mar	mariner	lung dis.
Aaron Langford	46	M	Md	Jan	farmer	killed by tree
Aaron Langford	7mo		Md	Jul		bowel inflam.
Thomas Coulborne	5mo		Md	Jul		bowel inflam.
Mary J. Bell	4		Md	Mar		croup
James D. Burnell	20	M	Md	Aug	none	dysentary
Ann Langford	60	W	Md	Jul	knitter	cancer
John Cluff	9mo		Md	May		unknown
Benjamin Langford	9		Md	Oct		fever
Samuel Tull	30	M	Md	Oct	farmer	bil.fever
Isaac Dryden	1		Md	Mar		measles
Tubman Dryden	55	M	Md	Jan	farmer	pleurisy
William Turpin	72	W	Md	May	farmer	dropsey
Ralph Turpin	20		Md	Apr	oysterman	consumption
Matilda Bosman	8		Md	Aug		bil.fever
Alfred Porter	1		Md	Mar		unknown
Mathew Marinder	53	M	Md	Feb	oyesterman	pleurisy
Nathaniel Dorothy	46	M	Md	Oct	farmer	bil.fever
Asariah Davis	35	M	Md	Mar	farmer	pleurisy
Samuel B. Dickerson	30		Md	Feb	tailor	consumption
Mary Miles	5mo		Md	Apr		lung inflam.
William Stewart	86	M	Md	May	farmer	old age
Stewart W. Jones	4		Md	Oct		bil.fever
Thomas Dorman	64	M	Md	Nov		pleuirsy
Stephen C. Dashiell	6mo		Md	Jan		unknown
Clanky Gardner	56	M	Va.	Oct	landlord	bil.fever
Lucinda McCrady	7		Md	Nov		lung infl.
Henry Carnell	47		Md	Jan	farmer	bil.fever
Catharine Riggen	4		Md	Oct		unknown
Adaline Riggin	8mo		Md	May		Col.infant.
Samuel smith	2mo		Md	Jul		hooping cough
Elizabeth Ward	70	M	Md	Aug		lung inflam.
Henry Powell	2		Md	Oct		dysentary
Thomas Henderson	1		Md	Jul		bil.fever
Margaret Ross	5		Md	Oct		fever
Thomas Bosman	1mo		Md	Mar		fall
Milly Austin	55		Md	Oct	housework	fever
Edward Bussells	6mo		Md	Oct		unknown
Charles Noble	6		Md	Aug		bil.fever
Albert Parsons	3		Md	Oct		bil.fever
Mary Jones	2		Md	Oct		bil.fever
Henry Matthews	55	M	Md	Mar	farmer	consumption
Edward Dryden	2		Md	aug		bil.fever
Siner Catling	49	W	Md	Aug		unknown
Levin Beach	60	W	Md	Aug	farmer	unknown
Ann Beach	70	M	Md	May		unknown
Mary Matthews	70	M	Md	Aug		dysentary
Elizabeth Miller	26	M	Md	Mar		consumption

persons who died during the year ending 1 June 1850

COUNTY -Somerset DISTRICT -1st Div.

name	age	mar wid	birth place	mon. died	Occupation	cause of death
Mary Milbourne	76	M	Md	Sep		unknown
Sarah Maddux	78	W	Md	Feb		old age
Thomas Shores	4		Md	Mar		hooping cough
Elizabeth Shores	27	W	Md	Feb		liver dis.
Sarah Shores	17		Md	Mar		liver dis.
Rachael Williams	63	M	Md	Sep		consumption
Elijah Williams	1		Md	Oct		hooping cough
Mary White	35	M	Md	Feb		liver dis.
Jesse McDorman	21		Md	Jan	farmer	consumption
William McDorman	20		Md	Oct	farmer	consumption
Bridget Shores	75	W	Md	Oct		old age
Sydney Shores	22		Md	Jan	sailor	liver dis.
Stephen J. Shores	1		Md	Jan		hooping cough
Milky A. Jones	34	M	Md	May		unknown
Nancy Jones	1		Md	Aug		fever
John T. Parks	1		Md	Sep		bil.fever
John Jones	70	M	Md	Sep	farmer	bil.fever
Marcellus Jones	25	M	Md	Sep	farmer	bil.fever
Jehu Tylor	5		Md	Jul		hooping cough
George Scott	45		Md	Aug	farmer	bil.fever
Elisha Forman	1		Md	Jul		hooping cough
Jane Webster	72	W	Md	Mar		old age
Priscilla Mace	59	W	Md	Mar		consumption
Nancy Rowe	60	W	Md	Mar		consumption
Nancy Winsor	80		Md	Jan		consumption
Bennett Mister	43	M	Md	Dec	farmer	unknown
Nancy Evans	80	M	Md	May		unknown
Mary Bradshaw	1		Md	Apr		hooping cough
Charles W. Marsh	12		Md	Sep		bil.fever
George Smith	5		Md	Jul		bil.fever
Alexander Jones	57	M	Md	Nov	farmer	pneumonia
Mary Waller	8		Md	Oct		fever
Leroy Waller	1		Md	Aug		fever
Mary E. Ballard	3mo		Md	Apr		hooping cough
James Winsor	78	W	Md	Mar	farmer	liver dis.
Polly Davis	70	W	Md	Mar		pleurisy
Anannias Wilkins	14		Md	Oct		fever
Mary Langford	22	M	Md	Aug		lung inflam.
William H. Langford	3		Md	Oct		brain inflam.
William King	80	W	Md	Apr	farmer	gravill
William H. Dorsey	2		Md	Jan		croup
James Powell	4		Md	Jun		head fall
Anna Marsh	8		Md	Sep		bil.fever
Joseph McIntyre	4		Md	Sep		bil.fever
Matilda Lard	2		Md	Sep		bil.fever
John Disharoon	73	W	Md	Oct	farmer	bil.fever
Hetty Turner	52	M	Md	Mar		consumption
Eliza Hayman	3		Md	Apr		worms
Alonzo Gunby	5		Md	Aug		scarfula
Adaline Dashiell	2		Md	Sep		dysentary
Frances S. Spence	8		Md	Jul		scarlet fever
Sameul Bedsworth	26		Md	Sep	farmer	bil.fever
Robert Foxwell	2		Md	Jul		hooping cough

MORTALITY SCHEDULE OF MARYLAND

persons who died during the year ending 1 June 1850

COUNTY -SOMERSET   DISTRICT -1st Div.

name	age	mar wid	birth place	mon. died	Occupation	cause of death
Laura Ann Harris	6		Md	Aug		bil.fever
John Harris	4		Md	Aug		unknown
Zadock Leatherbury	12		Md	Sep		bil.fever
Theobold Leatherbury	4		Md	Oct		bil.fever
George A. Gibbons	14		Md	Aug		dysentary
Nancy Harrington	78	M	Md	Oct		bil.fever
Asaraih Vetry	5		Md	Oct		bil.fever
James Dashiell	5		Md	Sep		bil.fever
Francis Dashiell	3		Md	Nov		bil.fever
Mary Tyler	102	W	Md	Mar		old age
Littleton B.Bradshaw	78	W	Md	Aug	mariner	bil.fever
Aaron Bradshaw	57		Md	Feb	farmer	consumption
Rebecca Winsor	40	M	Md	sep		palsy
Elizabeth Crockett	78	W	Md	Sep		consumption
Joseph Covington	8		Md	sep		typhoid
William Wright	22		Md	Feb	carpenter	pleurisy
Lovey Austin	45	M	Md	Sep		pleurisy
Infant Stone	1mo		Md	Apr		fall
Edwin Weatherly	38	M	Md	May	farmer	bil.fever
Hariett Cree	15		Md	Sep		bil.fever
Matilda Smith	8		Md	Sep		bil.fever
Angeline Hitch	20		Md	Mar		consumption
George Malone	67	M	Md	Jun	farmer	palsy
Thomas Murray	50	M	unkn.	Jul	mariner	dropsy
Samuel Marshall	45	M	Md	aug	hugher	bil.fever
Samuel F.Marshall	15		Md	Aug		bil.fever
Thadeus Disharoon	11mo		Md	Jul		unknown
Eugene Harkum	1		Md	May		scarlet fever
Eleanor Banks	30		Md	Dec		consumption
Ann Cooksey	3		Md	Feb		worms
Henry White	42	M	Md	Feb	farmer	E.fever
Dorcas Jones	79	W	Md	Nov		old age
Joshua Crouch	83	M	Md	Oct	fisherman	dropsey
Thomas Magrath	36	M	Md	Mar	mariner	drowned
Emily Magrath	9		Md	May		consumption
Hester Magrath	2		Md	Sep		worms
Henry Crouch	3		Md	Aug		dysentary
Samuel P. Valaningham	1		Md	Apr		hooping cough
George W.Jones	12		Md	Sep		bil.fever
John Baily	1		Md	Aug		bil.fever
Eleanor Linton	18		Md	Jun		bil.fever
Fanny Linton	60	M	Md	Jun		billfever
William Linton	18		Md	Jun	oysterman	bil.fever
Emily Linton	10		Md	Jun		bil.fever
Ann Harris	58	M	Md	Aug		bil.fever
Sarah E.Harris	4		Md	Aug		bil.fever
Perry Harris	2		Md	Aug		bil.fever
		TALBOT COUNTY				
Sharlott W. Everist	44	M	Frede.Co	Jan		heart
Nancy Faulkner	68	W	Carol.Co	Jan		old age
Mary E. Killman	20		Tal.Co	May		unknown

persons who died during the year ending 1 June 1850

COUNTY   TALBOT   DISTRICT

name	age	mar wid	birth place	mon. died	Occupation	cause of death
George F. Leonard	4mo		Tal.Co	May		unknown
Mary E. Leavis	11		"	May		typhoid
Mariah Banning	63	W	"	Jul		infirmity
Elizabeth Dawson	76	W	"	Sep		old age
James A. Blades	1		"	Nov		unknown
Harriet Miller	6mo		"	Jul		infant.
Susanna Lenard	6mo		"	Jul		croup
Ann Horner	87		"	Oct		old age
Edman P. Way	3		Dorc.Co	Jul		scarfula
George Henry	9		Tal.Co	Feb		typhoid
Robert H. Ozman	7		"	Feb		scarlet fever
Charles N. Satterfield	6		"	Sep		b.fever
Susan A. Smyth	27	M	"	Apr		consumption
Corneli Satterfield	19		"	Jun		consumption
Eliza Harrington	41	M	"	Jun		liver
Mary A. Hall	4		Md	Apr		croup
Perry G. Edmondson	2mo		"	Jul		infant.
Hiram Edmondson	14		"	Jun		scarlet fever
Mahala Leison?	28		"	Jun		child birth
Albert Gabs	1mo		"	Mar		fits
Martha Seymore	1mo		"	Jun		infant.
Daniel McFarland	18		"	Apr	machinest	consumption
Philemen Hemsley	9mo		"	May		indigestion
M.R.Hayward(fem)	14		"	Aug		S.fever
Elizabeth H. Blake	33		"	Jul		consumption
Elizabeth Nealy	11		M	Jul		scarlet fever
Rebecca Fidderman	73	W	"	Oct		cancer
Rebeca Fidderman Jr.	14		"	Jul		brain inflam.
Susan Hoxter	13		"	Jan		brain inflam.
Martha E. Satterfield	6mo		"	Jul		infant.
Mary T. Goldsborough	33		"	Oct		prarlysis
Hellen C. Collier	4mo		"	Jun		brain inflam.
Henry M. Clark	29		Del.	May	farmer	bilious
Benjamin F. Titzgerald	18		Del	Oct		liver D.
Mary F. Horney	2		Md	Feb		S.fever
Ivan F. Wrightson	1mo		Md	Jul		infant.
Mariah C. Chaplain	25	M	Md	Sep		P.Fever
Emily Callahan	6		Md	May		brain D.
Julia Millikin	63	M	Md	Aug		rumatist
Benjamin Homes	39	M	Md	Dec	farmer	brain inf.
Josiah Chaplain	49		Md	May	farmer	liver
Thomas S. Carter	60	W	Md	Jul	farmer	hernia
Mary Hughlett	1		Md	Jul		cold
Elizabeth Fushee	39	W	"	Jun		cancer
Sarah A. Stotner?	32	M	Md	Aug		child bed
James A. Stotner	5		Md	Oct		dropsy
William Clark	1		Md	Sep		Summer comp.
Mary R. Kary	4mo		Md	Feb		unknown
Alice Leonard	2		Md	Mar		dropsey
Elizabeth Neighbors	29	M	Md	May		cronic
William Richardson	1mo		Md	May		none
Eliza Clark	40	W	Md	Sep		inflamation
Matilda A. Shepard	33	M	Md	Jul		consumption

111

MORTALITY SCHEDULE OF MARYLAND

persons who died during the year ending 1 June 18_50_

COUNTY -TALBOT   DISTRICT

name	age	mar wid	birth place	mon. died	Occupation	cause of death
William H. Horney	1		Md	Sep		inflamation
John W. Parrott	1		Md	Sep		inflamation
Susan A.Hardin	11mo		Md	Aug		brain inflam.
Ann Eason	40		Md	Jan		inflamation
Elias Hopkins	56		Del	Jun	farmer	erisipilis
Thomas S.Porter	33	M	Md	Nov	wheelright	consumption
Samuel E.Buck	5		Md	Aug		typhoid
Richard Conden	60	M	Md	Feb	h.carpenter	pleuisy
Mary C McGinny	41	M	Md	Aug		consumption
Robert McGinny	2		Md	Sep		bil.fever
Mary A.Rose	2		Md	Jul		unknown
Sally Goldsborough	20		Md	May		consumption
Clement Fisher	5mo		Md	Oct		dirreah
William T. Warner	1mo		Md	Feb		fits
William E.Wilson	1mo		Md	Aug		fits
Louisa Frampton	8		Md	Apr		dropsey
Ann K. Hubbard	33	M	Del	Jun		measels
Westley W.Hubbard	15		Md	Jun		measels
Francis Hubbard	7mo		Md	Aug		disentary
Susan Hobbs	23	M	Md	Aug		unknown
Susan Harrison	28	M	Md	Jan		pleurisy
Ruther W.Ares	2		Md	May		Nerve fever
Sally Benson	36		Md	Sep		consumption
Martha Satchell	6		Md	Nov		worm fever
George Davis	5mo		Md	Jul		consumption
Andrew Dyott	53	M	Md	Apr	farmer	typhoid
Edward Carter	1		Md	Jul		bowel infl.
Hester M. Hopkins	20		Md	May		consumption
Richard Collison	76	W	Md	Oct		old age
Robert Kemp	5		Md	Jul		disentary
Peter D. Lamdin	61		Md	Jul	farmer	paralitis
Harriet Farmer	1		Md	Jan		sudden
Thomas Cooper	53	W	Md	Apr	farmer	sudden
Elizabeth Haddaway	34	M	Md	May		sudden
William Harris	81	W	Md	May	shipcarpenter	old age
James Haddaway	41	M	Md	Nov	carpenter	bil.fever
Catherine Lomin	40	M	Md	Jun	.	unknown
Ann Sewill	9		Md	Aug		disentary
Ellen Sewill	7		Md	Aug		disentary
George Sewill	2		Md	Aug		disentary
Mary L. Sewill	7		Md	Sep		s.fever
Theresa Sewill	17		Md	Sep		disentary
Margaret E. Wise	2		Md	Mar		s.fever
William P.Cooper	1mo		Md	Mar		fits
Emily Jackson	4		Md	Jun		worms
Ann R.Jackson	8		Md	Dec		s.fever
James Jackson	9mo		Md	Dec		s.fever
Oakley Cummings	57	M	Md	Sep	shipcarpenter	sudden
John Owen	70	W	Md	Apr	farmer	consumption
Thomas S. Porter	30	M	Md	Sep		consumption
Stephen Catrup	25		Md	Sep	teacher	diareah
George Wright	3mo		Md	Jun		unknown
John Chaffins	47	M	Md	Jun	farmer	inf.lungs

112

name	age	mar wid	birth place	mon. died	Occupation	cause of death
Catherine Elliott	18		Md	Apr		consumption
James B. Golt	58	W	Md	Apr	farmer	spine
Eliza M. Prior	5mo		Md	Jul		disentary
Charles A Franklin	1		Md	Jun		disentary
Henry Thomas	2mo		Md	Feb		sudden
Sarah E Neue	4mo		Md	Oct		disentary
Henrietta M. Lilghman	39	M	Md	Dec		consumption
Amelia Willis	3		Md	Jul		scar.fever
Henrietta Brown	63	W	Md	Aug		diarreah
Mary Bayne	3		Md	Jul		cold.
Oswold willis	3mo		Md	Sep		col.inf.
Edward?A.Smith	25		Md	Apr	carpenter	lung cong.
Julianna Mason	6		Md	Sep		infl.coli.
Susan R. Collins	2		Md	Oct		cong.brain
Lucretia Richardson(bla)	50		Md	Sep		heart
Martha J.Chaplin	4mo		Md	Jul		Inf. Sum.
Thomas E. Adams	2		Md	Sep		inf.sum.
B.F.Whirett(male)?	23	M	Md	Sep	cabinetmaker	pleurisy
Harriett Barret	35	M	Eng.	May		fever
John Roby	12		Md	May		fever
Sarah Harper	9mo		Md	Jun		fever
Jarramiah Sausman	46	M	Md	Nov	laborer	fever
Simon Arby	1mo		Md	Apr		fever
William Higgs	1		Md	Apr		fever
Susan Ramsay	70	W	Md	Aug		fever
Julia Blackford	30	M	Md	Oct		fever
Jacob Knock	4		Md	Feb		fever
Henry Rinehart	80		Pa.	May	none	C.
Frances Wolf	4mo		Md	Feb		fever
Elizabeth O'Brian	4		Md	Aug		fever
Elizabeth M. Candla	3		Md	Mar		fever
Andrew Morgan	5		Md	Aug		fever
Joseph Brown	10mo		Md	Jun		fever
WASHINGTON COUNTY-Dist.2						
Dixon R. Boyd	8		Md	Feb		winter fever
Samuel K. Boyd	2		Md	Mar		winter fever
Margaret Boyd	43	M	Md	Mar		none
Sarah L. Mann	9		Md	Mar		s.fever
Sarabella Ercer	16		Md	Jun		dropsy
William A. Arnold	11		Md	Mar		winter fever
Elizabeth Arnold	18		Md	Mar		winter fever
Mary E. Kay	21	M	Md	Mar		winter fever
Matthew McClannahan	44	M	Md	Jun	teacher	winter fever
Joseph Grosh	34	M	Md	Mar	farmer	none
John D. Grosh	1		Md	Mar		unknown
Charles Durney	6		Md	Jan		unknown
Joanna A. Myers	3		Md	Feb		winter f.
Jerimiah Mason	64	M	Md	Sep	minister	poisoned
Jeremiah Mason	33	M	Md	Nov	merchant	congist.f.
David Ridenour	45	M	Md	Dec	merchant	none
Roman Cahill	4mo		Md	May		croup
Martin Myley	26	M	Md	Apr	merchant	consumption

MORTALITY SCHEDULE OF MARYLAND

persons who died during the year ending 1 June 18<u>50</u>

COUNTY-WASHINGTON   DISTRICT No.2

name	age	mar wid	birth place	mon. died	Occupation	cause of death
Daniel Gaslinger	36	M	Pa	Dec	carpenter	congestion F.
William Beard	52	M	Md	Aug	farmer	none
Jane Houck	66	M	Pa.	Dec		none
Catherine Motter	57	M	Md	Jun		none
Franick Mille	52	M	Ger.	May	laborer	unknown
Gloria Stone	1		Md	Jan		croup
Denton McCoy	30	M	Md	May	carpenter	accident
Samuel Myers	44	M	Va	Jun	farmer	spasms
John J. mitz	13		Md	Jun		none
John A. Haley	10		Md	Jul		unknown
John Irwin	50	M	Md	Mar		none
Catherine Christ	5mo		Md	Nov		croup
Elizabeth Neucander	35	M	Md	Oct		unknown
Henry Herbert	2		Md	Aug		winter fever
Catherine Ankney	60	M	Md	Jan		consumption
Mary A Breuer	2mo		Md	Sep		unknown
Mary A. Nicodemas	45	M	Md	Aug		dropsy
Susan Masters	35	M	Md	Sep		consumption
Martin Erntz	19		Ger.	Nov	tailor	consumption
Matilda McClain	35	M	Md	Sep		rheumatism
Clara Alee	10mo		Md	Aug		s.fever
Daniel Fink	25		Md	Feb	laborer	consumption
Robert Shednick	58	M	Md	Jun	farmer	consumption
Margaret Higgs	25	M	Md	Feb		winter f.
Jeremiah Canable	9mo		Md	Dec		unknown
John Hawkings	41	M	Va	May	b.smith	sudden
Sarah Grey	22		Md	Mar		consumption
william Hodges	23		Md	Dec	farmer	none
Thomas M. Voy	60	M	Ind.	Mar	laborer	none
Catherine Congan	3		Md	Mar		sudden
John Hunter	60		Md	May		none
Elizabeth Prather	15		Md	Aug		cone
Josephine Hays	8		Md	Sep		sudden
Charles W.Piper	9mo		Md	Feb		fever
S.S.Cunningham(male)	10mo		Md	Apr		fever
Nancy Null	1		Md	Jan		fever
M.E.Shinabuck	2mo		Md	Mar		fever
Thomas Trice	1mo		Md	Apr		fever
Susan Chaney	1mo		Md	Apr		fever
Patrick McDonald	40	M	Ire.	May	laborer	fever
Lewis Rodgers	1		Md	Mar		croup
Sarah Robison	66	M	Md	Mar		fever
David Charlton	2		Md	Apr		C.
James Goldin	23		Md	Aug	laberer	C.
Henry C. Woltry	63	M	Md	Apr	farmer	C.
John Stonehaker	26	M	Md	Dec	farmer	C.
James Davis	12		Md	Jun		fever
M.C.Miller(fem)	17		Md	Dec		fever
Georeg Leferis?	72	W	Md	Apr	farmer	fever
Mary S. Towson	21		Md	Aug		fever
Hannah Mousley	27	M	Md	Mar		C.
Elizabeth Rishard	32	M	Md	Oct		fever

MORTALITY SCHEDULE OF MARYLAND

persons who died during the year ending 1 June 1850

COUNTY -WASHINGTON   DISTRICT No.2

name	age	mar wid	birth place	mon. died	Occupation	cause of death
Susan Booser	47	M	Md	Jun		fever
Susan Daugherty	25	M	Md	Apr		fever
Margaret Knoble	1		Md	Oct		fever
John W.West	7mo		Md	Jul		fever
Othella Marker	1		Md	Nov		fever
Jacob Footman	4		Md	May		fever
Tennison Rowe	50	W	Md	Jan		fever
John Rodinick	4		Md	Dec		fever
Michael Easlosker	43	M	Md	Feb	forgeman	accident
Susan Harris	4		Md	May		fever
June Bolinger	3mo		Md	Jul		fever
Elizabeth Gloss	79	W	Md	Jul		C.
John Gloss	49	M	Md	Nov	cooper	fever
Elizabeth Reid	6		Md	Dec		fever
Ann C.Bowers	7mo		Md	Jul		fever
Mary Shackelford	2		Md	Dec		croup
Margaret Hines	6		Md	Apr		fever
Julia Myers	7mo		Md	Dec		fever
Rodney Shaw	5		Md	Aug		fever
Urilla Palmer	5mo		Md	Apr		fever
Andrew Baker	1		Md	Apr		fever
Mary Crocket	3		Md	Jan		none
Jonathan Colbert	5		Md	Feb		sudden
Elizabeth McKinley	17		Md	Jun		winter f.
James H. Bowles	69	M	Md	Nov	farmer	sudden
Harriet Stephens	63	M	Md	Apr		congest.
Joseph Castle	19		Va.	Mar	tailor	none
Edward Dearburn	35		Va	Apr	tailor	none
John S. Kelly	60	W	Ire.	Mar	laborer	unknown
Samuel Miller	68	M	Md	Jun	farmer	none
Elizabeth Shank	7		Md	Jun		unknown
District #1						
Samuel Liday	53	W	Md	Dec	stagedriver	compl.
John Fouk	76		Va	Feb	carpenter	compl.
Delia Dorsey (mul)	80		Md	Mar		palsy
Patrick Prior	50		Ire.	Apr	laborer	palsy
Elizabeth Miller	16		Md	Apr		sudden
David Simmon	70		Ger.	Apr		consumption
William Patrick	80		Md	May		consumption
Rebecca Dewalt	16		Md	May		sudden
Julia Baker	75	W	Ger.	May		consumption
Catherine Penner	7		Md	Oct		scarlet fever
Ann R. Ridenhour	4		Md	Nov		scarlet fever
David Fessler	1		Md	Jun		scarlet fever
Lucinda Tigert	5		Md	Jun		scarlet fever
Catherine Hoffman	22	M	Ger	Mar		child bed
Anna Trout	3		Md	Oct		flux
Sarah McFarren	1		Pa.	Feb		scarlet fever
Hannah Smith	30		Md	Mar		consumption
Susan Miller	1		Md	Sep		scarlet fever
Sarah J. Simpson	7		Md	Jul		diarreah
Elizabeth Middlekauff	31		Md	Aug		lung Inflam.
Infant of Peter Specks	4mo		Md	Mar		spasms

115

persons who died during the year ending 1 June 18 50

COUNTY   WASHINGTON   DISTRICT   No.1

name	age	mar wid	birth place	mon. died	Occupation	cause of death
infant of Brinksman	1mo		Md	Apr		lung flem.
Alfred Bargdoll	1mo		Md	Sep		spasms
Lucinda Eakle	1mo		Md	Sep		flux
Amanda Miller	8mo		Md	Oct		diarreah
John McDowell	1		Md	Jun		dysentary
Ane Myers	46	M	Md	Mar		consumption
John P. Steffy	55		Md	Nov		consumption
Barabara Beard	3		Md	Dec		scarlet fever
Elizabeth Relph	85	w	Md	Dec		palsy
Henry Myers	56	W	Md	Jul		consumption
John H. Lohman	5		Md	Dec		scarlet fever
Anne e. Loury	12		Md	Feb		scarlet fever
Samuel Middlekauff	4		Md	Jun		bil.fever
Ann M. Zeigler	1		Md	aug		thrush
Catherine McCormac	9		Md	Mar		worms
infant ofMathias H.Oster	4mo		Md	Jul		spasms
Christopher Miller	71	W	Pa	Jul	blacksmith	consumption
Ann Witmer	19		Md	Jul		consumption
inf.ofJames Cunningham	11mo		Md	Mar		tumor
Catherine Baltz	26	M	Ger	Dec		child bed
inf.of Geo.Francis	1day		Md	Mar		none
Jacob Hopper	51	M	Pa.	Aug	farmer	consumption
Jacob Resh	6mo		Md	Aug		spasms
John Knodle	7		Md	Jul		brain infl.
Janett O. Knodle	2		Md	Sep		spasms
samuel E. Wealty	1mo		Md	Dec		spasms
Mary Fultz	87	W	Pa	Oct		old age
Susanna Stoufer	23	M	Md	Dec		dropsy
John Ryan	66	W	Ire.	Mar	physician	lung inflam.
Susan J. Lees	1		Md	Apr		scarlet fever
Susannah Osborn	13		Md	May		cold
Mary G. Winters	2		Md	Nov		scarlet fever
Andrew Houser	4mo		Md	apr		dropsey
Catherine Gilbert	23	M	Va	Feb		child bed
Agustus Bower	1mo		Md	Jul		fits
Preston Zeigler	3		Md	Mar		cat.fever
Reuben B Bikle	3mo		Md	feb		brain inf.
Jacob Floral	46	M	Md	Feb	laborer	pleurisy
Allice C. Lohrman	1		Md	aug		infant.
Andrew Mayhew	5		Md	May		unknown
George Beard	86	M	Md	Feb		palsy
Mrs. Houseman	80	W	Md	Dec		palsy
Charles McIntire	24		Ire.	Jul	laborer	mannasotia?
Henry Wiles	45		Ire.	Jul		consumption
Henry Preminger	65		Md	Jul	carpenter	consumption
John McLaughlin	80		Ire.	Jul	laborer	dysentary
William Strain	40		Ire.	Aug		unknown
William Shane	70	M	Md	Aug		consumption
Mary C.Brady	4		Va	Mar		cat.fever
Benjamin Smith	76		Md	Jun	none	old age
James Culler	26		Md	Jun	laborer	bowel inflam.
Lietitia Smith	75		Ire.	Mar		old age
William Carbit	3		Md	Sep		liver dis.

persons who died during the year ending 1 June 18 50

COUNTY WASHINGTON   DISTRICT No.1

name	age	mar wid	birth place	mon. died	Occupation	cause of death
Mary Y. Chambers	72	W	Pa	Mar		pleurisy
George W. Lynch	1		Md	Dec		brain inf.
Lucy Collins	2mo		Md	Feb		chronic
Margaret Lyons	79	W	Md	Dec		old age
Amanda Smith	3		Md	Sep		chronic
Susan Montebaugh	64	M	Md	Jun		consumption
Elias Snyder	36	M	Md	Jan	farmer	dropsy
Samuel H. Knodle	1		Md	Dec		scarlet fever
Susannah Shoats	82	W	Md	Feb		head affl.
Hiram Keplinger	5		Md	Jan		bowel inflam.
Catherine Gwinn	56	M	Md	Mar		chronic
Maryetta Easterday	1		Md	Sep		dropsy
Matilda E. Boteler	1		Md	Mar		appoplexy
Daniel Knadler	11		Md	May		scarlet fever
Lawson D. Knadler	3		Md	Apr		scarlet fever
Martha Hadle	75	W	Md	Apr		paraletic
William Shover	7		Pa.	Oct		fits
Nancy Emmert	36		Md	Jan		pulmanory
Lauretta Bomberger	8mo		Md	Jul		diarreah
Mary C. Lows	5mo		Md	Jul		head afflec.
Leander Snyder	8mo		Md	Dec		liver afflec.
Eliza Cox	35	M	Md	Apr		consumption
Catherine Stonebraker	66	M	Md	Dec		consumpti on
			Hagerstown	District		
John P. Grantz	40	M	Ger	Mar	farmer	hernia
George Martenye	85		Md	Feb	none	paraletic
James P. Kelly	1mo		Md	Apr		whooping cough
William May	43	M	Ger.	Apr	watchmaker	pleurisy
Mary C. Reid	2		Md	Mar		convulsions
Daniel A. Stonebreaker	4mo		Md	Mar		convulsions
Catherine Waller	72	M	Md	Apr		cancer
Elizabeth Yeakle	62	M	Md	apr		chro.R.
Charles W. Cook	1mo		Md	Aug		thrust
Susan Iseminger	35	M	Md	Jun		consumption
William P. Clark	3		Md	Jul		head dis.
Barbary L.Hearchner	5mo		Md	Jan		whooping c.
Elizabeth Ridernour	36	M	Md	Nov		consumption
Joseph Messmen	62	M	Ger.	May	none	mania P.
Elizabeth Weldone?	70		Md	Jul		cho.Morb.
William Rowland	1		Md	May		chronic
Barbary Shokeslager	75	M	Pa	Sep		paraletic
George Wilson	8mo		Md	Apr		cat.fever
Adelade M.Beasly	11mo		Md	Jul		chol.morb.
Barbara Griffith	64	W	Md	Jul		chronic
Elizabeth Myers	60		Md	May		consumption
Mary M. Cramer	9mo		Md	May		thrush
Frank Freaner	23		Md	Apr	printer	chronic
Nicholas Ross	46	M	N.J.	Jan	none	chronic
John H. Albert	1		Md	Sep		summer comp.
Henry Clay James	5		Md	May		consumption
George Wright	3		Md	Sep		scarfula
Sarah C. Heard	28	M	Pa	Oct		consumption

MORTALITY SCHEDULE OF MARYLAND

persons who died during the year ending 1 June 1850

COUNTY -WASHINGTON-WORCESTER DISTRICT -Hagerstown

name	age	mar wid	birth place	mon. died	Occupation	cause of death
Louisa Swartz	5		Md	Mar		fever
Polly Hase	54		Md	Mar		cancer
Alice Alexander	3		Md	Feb		cat.fever
Rebecca Fiegly	68		Md	Apr		phalsey
Mary E. Reynolds	1mo		Md	Apr		spasms
Mary A.E.Shank	17		Md	May		scrofula
Ann Rider	4?		Md	May		consumption
Helen J.Gelwicks	11mo		Md	Jul		chol.infan.
Charles c.Crist	11mo		Md	Mar		convulsions
Jacob Rowland	64		Md	Apr		dropsy
Lydia Hahn	51		Md	Nov		dysepsia
Margaret Hagerman	38	M	Pa	May		child bed
John Shafer	41	M	Pa.	Apr	shoemaker	consumption
William Scott Williamson	1		none	none		chol.inf.

WORCESTER COUNTY 1st.& 9th E.Dist.

name	age	mar wid	birth place	mon. died	Occupation	cause of death
William Tull	13		Md	Jul		disentary
Mahala Camell?	32	M	Md	Oct		unknown
Ann M. Ennis	23	M	Md	aug		unknown
Mary Guthry	3		Md	Feb		whooping cough
William Larmore	1		Md	Feb		whooping cough
Eveline Cropper	3		Md	Nov		whooping cough
Ellen Cropper	1		Md	Jun		tif.fever
Rachel Clarvoe	1		Md	Jun		fits
Thomas Gray	8mo		Md	Mar		unknown
James H. Tilman	24		Md	Feb		accident
Alias Tinde?	2mo		Md	Jun		worms
Leticia Holsten	1		Md	Jul		worms
James Lewis	70	M	Md	Apr	farmer	heart dis.
George Conner	62	M	Md	Nov	carpenter	manisolia
George Trehearn	58	M	Md	Apr	farmer	fever
Louisa J. Pool	4mo		Md	May		fever
Charles McNara	3		Md	Nov		worms
Edward F. Melson	5		Md	Jul		unknown
Catharine Burnett	60	W	Md	Aug		dropsy
Jessa Lekertt	40	M	Md	Aug	farmer	unknown
Susan Collins	40	M	Md	Jan		dropsy
Ellingen Hammond	3		Md	Sep		fever
Edwin R. Townsend	4		Md	Nov		inflamation
Samuel H. Townsend	1da		Md	Aug		sudden
William S. Nelson	15		Md	Sep		fever
Sarah M. Jones	3		Md	Sep		whooping cough
Jane Milborn	43	M	Md	Jun		unknown
George R. Smith	6mo		Md	Mar		unknown
Elijah Knox	28	M	Va	Mar	farmer	t.fever
Rachel Mitchell	60	M	unknow	May		unknown
Sally Dryden	35		Md	Feb		unknown
James Flemming	51		Md	Feb	none	consumption
John Blades	48		Md	Jun		dropsy
Margaret Wells	23		Md	Jul		unknown
William J. Divars	15		Md	Aug		unknown
Luther Blades	45	M	Md	Sep	farmer	fever
Mary E.Pruitt	3		Md	Mar		fits

MORTALITY SCHEDULE OF MARYLAND

persons who died during the year ending 1 June 18_50_

COUNTY -WORCESTER   DISTRICT 2nd & 1st.

name	age	mar wid	birth place	mon. died	Occupation	cause of death
Mary Powell	45	M	Md	Jul		unknown
Richard Scarbrough	53	W	Md	Dec		unknown
Hannah Jones	95		Md	Mar		old age
George J.D.Bishop	6mo		Md	Aug		disentary
Amanda J. Chapman	1mo		Md	Jun		unknown
Sarah F. Hudson	10mo		Md	Jun		unknown
			3rd Election Dist.			
Sarah Henman	56	M	Md	Aug		cancer
John Mumford	3		Md	Aug		disentary
Mary Gray	42		Md	Dec		unknown
Zadock Lynch	62	M	Md	Aug	farmer	unknown
Sally Baker	60	M	Md	Oct		unknown
Charles H. Jones	7		Md	Dec		unknown
Nancy C. Rodney	2		Md	Jul		disentary
Wrixham Lynch	70		Md	Aug	farmer	unknown
Isaac Tindal	7		Md	Dec		fever
Ann Jarman	69	W	Md	Apr		unknown
James Warren	58	M	Md	Dec	farmer	unknown
Edward Williams	71	W	Md	Jul	none	dropsy
Mary C Quillin	5mo		Md	Jan		whooping cough
Jane L.Evans	8mo		Md	Oct		croup
Joel Williams	43	M	Md	Sep	farmer	typhoid
Thomas Riley	54		Md	Aug	shipcarpenter	heart dis.
William Gault	2		Md	Mar		disentary
John Collings	4		Md	Dec		disentary
Sarah Timmons	7		Md	May		accident
Rachel Bradford	30	M	Md	Jun		dropsy
Josiah Davis	6mo		Md	sep		unknown
Polly Holloway	71	W	Md	Feb		unknown
Elizabeth Lathberry	35	M	Md	Aug		unknown
James S. Williams	7mo		Del.	Jul		summer compl.
Ann C. Baynum	27	M	Md	Jul		consumption
James Baynum	1		Md	Aug		unknown
William Calhoon	3		Md	Oct		consumption
Hancy Hall	68	W	Md	Mar		consumption
James King	45	M	Md	Dec	none	unknown
James Collins	6mo		Md	Sep		thrash
Ann Bolds	55	W	Md	Jul		consumption
George L. Bowen	9mo		Md	Jun		consumption
Elana Bowen	9mo		Md	Jun		brain inflam.
C.H.Davis (male)	9mo		Md	Jul		teething
William E. Hudson	11		Md	Jun		consumption
Laura A. Smith	30		Md	Jan		fits
William H. Griffin	9		Md	Dec		typhoid
Evaline Evans	2		Md	Oct		disentary
Mary Mumford	38		Md	Oct		unknown
Isaac T. Jarman	11		Md	Jan		unknown
Rachel Jarman	6		Md	Jul		unknown
Epelita Cooper	31	M	Md	Sep		unknown
Elya H. Brimer	39	M	Md	Sep		unknown
Charles Showell	35		Md	Jul		disentary
Eleanor J. McAllen	4		Md	Jan		measles

119

persons who died during the year ending 1 June 18__

COUNTY -Worcester County   DISTRICT 4th E.Dist.

name	age	mar wid	birth place	mon. died	Occupation	cause of death
Samuel J.Wilkerson	1		Md	Jul		diareah
William J. Fooks	7mo		Md	Aug		diareah
Nancy Wyatt	78	M	Md	Sep		bilious
William S. Evans	29		Md	Apr	farmer	C.
William J.S.Davis	2		Md	Aug		brain infla.
Robert Downs	70	W	Md	Feb	farmer	C.
Martha Sneed	63	M	Md	May		C.
Polly West	46	M	Del.	May		consumption
Margaret Dale	2		Md	Mar		C.
Robert J.F. Richardson	21		Md	Apr	laborer	unknown
Hiram J. Powell	3		Md	Mar		C.
Thomas H. Smack	7		Md	Mar		unknown
Matilda Quillen	25		Md	Jan		pleuiisy
Matilda Littleton	22		Md	Apr		C.
Gatty E. Middleton	4mo		Md	May		dysentary
Mary ⊥. Brittingham	3		Md	Oct		b.fever
Thomas Adkins	25		Md	Jan	brickmason	C.
8th Election Dist.						
James W. Morris	23		Md	May		dysentary
Susan Dykes	56	W	Md	Mar		unknown
James R. Fooks	16		Md	aug	laborer	bilious fever
Margaret C. Fooks	1		Md	sep		bilious fever
John Carry	44		Md	Feb	farmer	C.
Georeg W. Bussels	3		Md	Jun		dysentary
William P.McGrath	1		Md	Oct		dysentary
Matilda Barnes	33	M	Md	Feb		con.
Latitia A. Toadvine	27	M	Md	May		bil.fever
Mary C. Hayman	66	m	Md	Mar		dropsy
Isaac Dryden	53	M	Md	May	farmer	C.
Sarah A. Hearn	23		Md	Aug		bil.dys.
Ambrose Dixon	60	W	Md	May	farmer	C.
Nancy Dykes	37		Md	Aug		bil.dys.
Nathan P. Parsons	44	M	Md	Nov	shoemaker	unknown
George R. Parsons	19		Md	Apr	farmer	diabetis
5th Election District						
Henry C.Wailes	9mo		Md	Aug		C.
Alfred C. Jordan	6mo		Md	Sep		brain inf.
Hester E.Brittingham	11mo		Md	Sep		dys.
Levin Thomas Parsons	8mo		Md	Aug		dyst.
Mary C.Parsons	2mo		Md	Feb		croup
Harriet H.Hayman	8mo		Md	Dec		burn
Mary F. Dixon	2		Md	Sep		unknown
George W. Dixon	5mo		Md	Sep		unknown
Anthony G.Parsons	1		Md	Aug		dropsy
Elizabeth Hammond	71	M	Md	Apr		unknown
Gattura Parker	57	W	Del.	Sep		unknown
7th Election District						
Theophilus White	70		N.Y.	Mar	teacher	unknown
William Smith	50	M	Md	May	tailor	dropsy
Thomas H. Dryden	37	M	Md	Nov	farmer	unknown
Roland Bevans	60	M	Md	Oct	farmer	bil.fever
Sally Hayman	43	M	Md	Oct		unknown
Mary A. Ruark	73		Md	Aug		unknown

persons who died during the year ending 1 June 18<u>50</u>

COUNTY -WORCESTER COUNTY   DISTRICT -7th E.Dist.

name	age	mar wid	birth place	mon. died	Occupation	cause of death
Margaret E. Clogg	2mo		Md	Apr		croup
Dabid H. Powell	42	M	Md	Apr	farmer	infl.lungs
William H.A. Pope	2		Md	Mar		croup
Rufus F. Powell	12		Md	Jun		dys.
Elizabeth M. Stuart	1		Md	Aug		h.cough
Grace Cottingham	79	W	Md	Apr		C.
James W. Bishop	26	M	Md	Dec	farmer	Erasip.
Mary Holland	79		Md	Dec		brain infl.
Stephen Bounds	52	M	Md	Sep	farmer	con.
Mary J.E. Townsend	5		Md	May		unknown
Sarah A.Richardson	22	M	Md	May		C.

persons who died during the year ending 1 June 18_60

COUNTY   ALLEHGANY CO.   DISTRICT

name	age	mar wid	birth place	mon. died	Occupation	cause of death
Jane Caton	1		Md	Mar		cat.fever
Ann E.Smith	41		Md	Aug		unknown
Nannie D. Bruce	28	M	Md	Jul		childbed
Benjamin Fritch	1mo		Md	Jan		unknown
George Fisher	25		Md	Jul	farmer	bil.fever
John Conner	23		Md	Jul	laborer	byrailroad
Mary Howard	17	M	Md	Jul		child bed
John S.Winters	1		Md	Jul		bowel inflam.
William Judy	1mo		Md	Jun		unknown
Samuel Taylor	21		Md	May	laborer	consumption
William C. Nantling	29	M	Pa.	Mar	farmer	lung fever
John Spade	35		Irel.	Jan		dropsey
Laura R. Haller	4mo		Md	Feb		unknown
Eliza S. McKinze	25		Md	May		dropsey
Phillip Sissel	50	M	Md	May	farmer	pleurisy
Charles Hilly	33	M	Md	Oct	farmer	by lightning
Catherine Sweeney	66	W	Va.	Apr.		old age
Charles Grant	43	M	Md	Oct	hotelkeeper	unknown
Margaret Bannan	37		Irel.	Apr		unknown
Moses T.Grummade	44	M	Md	Oct	farmer	dropsy
Henry Miller	49	M	Va.	Aug	merchant	liver compl.
Mary A.Sexton	7		Md	Jun		asthma
George W. Knight	1mo		Md	Jul		unknown
James Hammell	51	M	Md	Nov		consumption
Margaret P. Evans	25	M	Eng.	Nov		consumption
Famma V. Holbaugh	1mo		Md	Aug		unknown
Mary Halsted	10		Pa.	Dec		typhoid
Samuel Halsted	7		Pa	Dec		typhoid
Bridget McDonnel	1		Pa.	May		unknown
William Holiday	28		Md	Jan	carpenter	by railroad
H.S. Butts(male)	65	M	Md	Feb	RR agent	kidney dis.
Henry Mattingly	22		Md	Jul	merchant	typhoid
William Sigler	6		Md	Oct		croup
Mary A. Butler	25	M	Md	Feb		consumption
Mary Walsh	6mo		Md	Aug		unknown
Deborah Scott	79	W	Md	Dec		old age
May Kolb	11		Md	Dec		unknown
Catherine Blake	31	M	Md	Feb		consumption
Susannah Clippinger	2		Md	Apr		brain inflam.
Catherine Dicken	52	W	Ger	May		consumption
Ellen Taylor	2		Md	May		croup
S.M.Kellick	30	W	Ger.	Mar	merchant	consumption
Henry Karns	93	W	Pa.	May	cabinet maker	unknown
H. B. Burton (male)	19		Md	Mar	printer	consumption
Edmond Fitzmire	1		Md	Jun		unknown
James A.Fisher	14		Va	May		drowning
Mary Knost	1		Md	May		unknown
Catharine Rabold	58		Pa.	May		hanged herself
Mary L. Lyers	1		Md	Jul		unknown
Mary E. Grunfeld	2		Md	Dec		croup
Ann E. Taylor	1		Md	Oct		unknown
Henry Brinher	1		Md	Jul		unknown
Lucy Cragg	3		Md	Aug		consumption

122

persons who died during the year ending 1 June 1860

COUNTY -ALLEGHANY   DISTRICT

name	age	mar wid	birth place	mon. died	Occupation	cause of death
Julia M. Bowns	1		Md	Feb		unknown
Annie Jordan	2		Md	Apr		unknown
John Valentine	76	M	Md	Apr	farmer	old age
Goerge House	14		Md	Jun		dorwned
Charistopher Quance	1		Md	Sep		bowel inflam.
Katherine Bushey	9		Md	Nov		bruning
Frederick Shipley	48	M	Md	Apr	hotelkeeper	consumption
Frederick Butler	59	M	Eng.	May	laborer	unknown
Parker Pennington	50		Pa.	May	shoemaker	consumption
Burgess Magruder	66	M	Md	Apr	hatter	consumption
Francis Abrael	1		Md	none		unknown
Patrick Brady	40		Irel.	Jun	laborer	consumption
William Crisap	43		Md	Dec	laborer	killed
James Morgan	50		Irel.	Oct		consumption
Timothy Carton	60		Irel.	Oct		consumption
Charles Magnus	73		Ger.	Jul		unknown
James Migalen	22		Irel.	Oct		unknown
Virginia Jones	25		Md	Dec	domestic	child bed
Sarah Denson	39	M	Md	Oct		consumption
Mary A.Winfield	1		Md	Apr		unknown
Henry Steel	1		Md	Feb		unknown
John Valentine	77	M	Md	Apr	farmer	old age
William H. Hinkle	32	M	Md	Jul	farmer	consumption
Jesse Chapman	59	M	Md	Jun		consumption
Mary Chapman	64	M	Md	Feb		consumption
Ruth A. Eastman	23	M	Pa.	Aug		child bed
Joseph Neal	70	M	Md	May		old age
Thomas Gordon	79	W	Ger.	Dec		old age
David Lynn Jr.	21		Md	Nov	civilEngeneer	consumption
Thomas H. Healy	8mo		Md	Aug		unknown
Joseph Wolfe	1mo		Md	Feb		unknown
John Moore	62		Irel.	Dec	laborer	consumption
Mary Bates	34		Md	Mar		unknown
Samuel T. McEvay	1		Md	Sep		unknown
John Mark	53	M	Ger.	Feb		droppsy
Henry Kulp	4mo		Md	Sep		unknown
Ann Holbeck	16		Ger	May		bil.fever
Charistopher Buckly	30		Md	Jan		unknown
Alfred Lewis	1		Md	Apr		unknown
John Cowan	1		Md	Sep		unknown
Mary Gotten	35	M	Ire.	Jul		consumption
John Goodwin	33		Scot.	May	tailor	consumption
Mary Canold	28		Irel.	Jun	domestic	child bed
Henry BBarns	38	M	Md	Mar	farmer	bowel inflam.
Ellen Shaw	14		Md	Jul		unknown
Thomas Travish	26	M	Eng.	Nov	miner	mine fall
Elizabeth Kelmer	53	M	Md	Apr		consumption
George Carter	64	M	Va	Sep	farmer	typhoid
Sophia Diffenbaugh	14	M	Md	May		consumption
Joseph Dean	87	M	Eng.	Jul	carpenter	old age
Charles M. Riel	17		Md	Jan	farmer	typhoid
Francis V. Ross	22		Md	Jun		unknown

123

persons who died during the year ending 1 June 18_60_

COUNTY -ALLEGHANY   DISTRICT

name	age	mar wid	birth place	mon. died	Occupation	cause of death
Patrick Fassenbacker	16		Md	Feb		unknown
George Michael	61	M	Md	Aug	farmer	dropsy
Mary Jacobs	82	W	Md	May		old age
Lewis Davidson	78	W	Md	Mar		consumption
Mary Smith	21	M	Md	Mar		consumption
Edmond Bucy	90	W	Md	Mar	farmer	old age
Sarah Piper	52		Md	Dec		consumption
David Smith	40	M	Md	Apr	carpenter	whiskey
Thomas Twigg	2mo		Md	Apr		unknown
Maria Walford	3		Md	Aug		unknown
Mary Fletcher	82	W	Md	Feb		old age
Joseph M. Dean	18		Md	Jun		consumption
Elizabeth Sellers	75	W	Pa.	Apr		old age
Susan Ward	66	W	Md	May		old age
Millie Roley	50	M	Va.	Sep		drowning
Sarah P. Roley	16		Md	Sep		drowning
Henry Hager	30	M	Md	Sep		drowning
Lemuel Shipley	62	M	Md	Apr	laborer	old age
James H. Bevans	42	M	Md	Dec	lawyer	hemorage
Mary Shoaff	6mo		Md	Mar		lung conges.
Emeline Fouch	19	M	Md	Apr		child bed
Massey Beall	63	M	Va.	Jan		unknown
Michael O'Tool	1mo		Md	Aug		summer d.
Louis Race	3mo		Md	Mar		lung cong.
Catherine Stanp	86	W	Md	Nov		old age
Thomas McCann	33	M	Irel.	Sep	miner	sudden
Sarah Reese	4mo		Md	Mar		convulsion
Patrick Maloney	2		Md	Sep		summer comp.
Mary Atkinson	37	M	Scot.	Jun		heart dis.
Margaret Condon	40	M	Irel.	Aug		dropsy
Hugh Timkle	46	M	Irel.	Dec	miner	lung infl.
James Breidy	11		NovaSc.	May		typhoid
Michael Kelly	40	M	Irel.	May	laborer	brain dis.
Daniel McKinsey	14		NovaSc.	Jul	miner	sudden
Henrietta Pagenhardt	67	M	Ger.	Jun		lung dis.
William James	9mo		Md	Jul		brain fever
Leonard Moore	46	M	Md	Nov	butcher	consumption
Mary Malone	2		Md	Feb		convulsion
John Dalbon	25		Pa.	Jul	laborer	consumption
Esther James	64	M	Wales	Aug		unknown
John Evans	68	M	Eng.	Jul	laborer	D.
Elizabeth Finegan	4		Pa.	Apr		burnt
Henry Specht	50		Germ.	Jun	miner	sudden in mine
Anthony Horner	50	M	Ger.	Jul	miner	sudden in mine
Margorie Fatkin	3mo		Md	Jun		teething
William Anderson	50		Md	Aug	laborer	dropsy
William Limon	30	M	Eng.	Apr	miner	consumption
Fanny McMullen	5mo		Md	Jun		brain fever
Sarah Winter	68	M	Md	Sep		nerve afflect.
Nancy Workman	2		Md	Mar		croup
Rachel Porter	73	M	Md	Oct		apoplexy
Ann Porter	1mo		Md	Jan		convulsion
John Kelly	43	M	Ire.	Jan	carpenter	chronic

MORTALITY SCHEDULE OF MARYLAND

persons who died during the year ending 1 June 1860

COUNTY -ALLEGHANY-ANNE ARUNDEL DISTRICT

name	age	mar wid	birth place	mon. died	Occupation	cause of death
Hannah McGonder	75	M	Ire.	Jan		consumption
John Blocker	68	M	Md	Jun	farmper	dropsy
William Massette	3		Md	Jan		pneumonia
John Gasti	30	M	Md	Apr	laborer	apoplexy
Evan Sloan	23		Pa	Jun	laborer	consumption
William Keagher	4		Md	Jan		lung fever
Caroline Campbell	40	M	Pa.	Oct		carbuncle
George Potter	28	M	Md	Jun	farmer	cholera
Catherine Dusel	20	M	Md	May		child bed
Samuel Raily	40	M	Irel.	Jan	farmer	heart dis.
Henry Peck	78	W	none	Sep		bronchitis
Harrison Johnson	1		Md	Feb		cat.fever
Sarah Speilman	67	M	Md	Sep		cholera
Nancy Fite	68	M	Md	Oct		cancer
Helen Fraaitly	48	M	Md	Nov		consumption
Marcus Cisler	6		Md	Sep		croup
John Balster	39	M	Ger	Oct	laborer	consumption
John Peters	1		Md	May		summer dis.
George Soar	69	M	Md	May	farmer	gravel
Mary Brag	45	M	Md	Apr		child bed
Matilda Wardwall	40	M	Md	Apr		dropsy
Mary Kemmell	24	M	Irel.	Jan		none
Daniel Ganer	18		Md	Oct	laborer	brain fever
James Halfner	1		Md	Dec		fever
John Ligge	51	M	Eng.	May	merchant	cholera
Sarah King	2		Md	Jan		croup
Jacob Gingney	6mo		Md	Sep		fever
George Moon	11		Md	Aug		scarlet fever
			ANNE ARUNDEL CO.-Annapolis Dist.			
Elizabeth Somerline	1mo		Md	Nov		dysentary
Henry Kollman	5		Md	Sep		brain fever
John Snooks	27		Bavaria	Nov	laborer	cholera
Gilbert Murdock	7mo		Md	Sep		brain des.
Richard Jones	40		Md	Mar		consumption
Anson Thorpe	40		Mass	Feb	teacher	suicide
G. S. Stilghman	6mo		Md	Jan		eysepilas
John Hammond	70		Md	Jan	printer	heart dis.
Sally A. Coldazer	30	M	Md	Jul		cholera
Anna Capron	15		Md	Jan		consumption
T.Wiggins (male)	26	M	Md	Mar		consumption
			THIRD. District			
Robert Moss	63		Md	Aug	farmer	dropsy
John Stansbury	43	M	Md	Feb	farmer	consumption
John Ross	2		Md	Sep		typhoid
Samuel Spriggs	1mo		Md	Apr		scarlet fever
Thomas Linthicomb	19		Md	Jan	farmer	pleurisy
Ann Jones	1		Md	Mar		pleurisy
Sally Mounce	1mo		Md	Feb		typhoid
			2nd. E. Dist.			
Sarah A. Duvall	43	W	Md	Sep		stomach inflam.
Caroline Higgins	22		Md	Apr		consumption
Barton Duvall	60	M	Md	Jul	farmper	dropsy

125

persons who died during the year ending 1 June 18 60

COUNTY -ANNE ARUNDEL   DISTRICT 2nd.E.Dist.& 1st.E.Dist.

name	age	mar wid	birth place	mon. died	Occupation	cause of death
Richard Cooksey	28		Md	Dec	farmer	diabetes
Matilda Chaney	72	M	Md	Apr		old age
Stephen Beard Sr.	78	M	Md	Jul	farmer	Calculus
Kitty Duvall	64		Md	Feb		stomach tumor
Marcus Crandall	46	M	Md	Apr	manager	pneumonia
Thomas Keckett	24		Md	Sep	farmer	consumption
Thomas Holliday	72	M	Md	Jun	farmer	congestive
John Cummings	25		Md	Mar		congestive
Wilks Welch	9mo		Md	Jul		whooping cough
Samuel Carr	52	W	Md	Jun	farmer	poison
Jemima Richardson	93	W	Md	May		old age
Peter O'Toole	28		Irel.	Feb		consumption
5th Election Dist.						
John Benson	75	M	Md	Jan	farmer	paralysis
Solin Benson	2		Md	Aug		typhoid
Charles Benson	6mo		Md	Oct		typhoid
Joseph Hankins	80		Md	Feb	farmer	consumption
Nancy Smith	87	M	Md	May		old age
Meania Gailer	56	M	Md	Nov		pneumonia
8th Election Dist.						
Margaret Hall	22		Md	May		heart dis.
Charlotte Trott	28	M	Md	Mar		measles
B. Leitch(male)	46	M	Md	May		stomach inflam.
Thomas Armiger	67		Md	Dec	farmer	pneumonia
Benajmin Armiger	2		Md	May		croup
Dorcas Howard	40	M	Md	Jul		convulsions
Lucy A. Gibbs	1		Md	Jun		dysentary
Ann Darnall	66		Md	Feb		pneumonia
4th Election Dist.						
Margaret Humphreys	23		Ire.	Jan		consumption
Elizabeth Anderson	75	W	Md	Aug		jaundice
Charles Linthicum	18		Md	Apr		consumption
Jane Chase	46		Md	May		consumption
Charles Kirby	4		Md	Aug		dysentary
1st Election Dist.						
James R. McCloud	10mo		Md	Aug		whooping cough
Linda Foster	33	M	Md	Oct		consumption
Peter Nelson	44	M	Denmark	Aug	mariner	yellow fever
John J. Porter	42		Eng.	Apr	mariner	drowned
George Jubb	16		Md	Oct		consumption
Jane Jubb	5mo		Md	Jul		teething
James E. Knowles	1		Md	Aug		bil.dysentary
William Dawson	20		Md	Aug		heart dis.
Thomas H. Lambden	78	M	Md	Jun		dropsy
Barbary Schmidt	87	W	Baden	May		consumption
Robert C. Grey	2		Md	Mar		throat dis.
Edwin H. Barnes	1		Md	Jun		teething
William Farlan	1		Md	May		measles
Richard Booze	35	M	Md	Jan		consumption
Henry Lever	39	M	Baden	Jul	mariner	on ship
Joseph White	86		Portugal	Feb	boatbuilder	old age
Hugh Dougherty	65	M	Md	May	carpenter	pneumonia
George McLaughlin	4mo		Md	Mar		spasms

126

MORTALITY SCHEDULE OF MARYLAND

persons who died during the year ending 1 June 18_60_

COUNTY -   1st. ward   DISTRICT city of Baltimore

name	age	mar wid	birth place	mon. died	Occupation	cause of death
John T. Patterson	7		Md	Mar		measles
Joseph Crimmon	46	M	France	Jul		heart dis.
Theresa Crimmon	5		Md	Jan		heart dis.
Jemima Allen	48	M	Md	Jun		bil.fever
Edward Burke	40	M	Ire.	Mar	laborer	consumption
Mary A. Burke	3		Md	Mar		small pox
James E. Burke	2		Md	Jun		spasms
John W. Welch	17		Md	Oct		yellow fever
Thomas Foley	89	M	Eng.	Sep		old age
Sibella Anderson	69		Md	Aug		old age
Ann R. Chaney	29		Md	Oct		consumption
Patrick McKenny	22		Ire.	Feb	carter	consumption
Joshua Evans	28	M	Md	Apr	laborer	consumption
Isabella Cullen	30		Md	Jul		consumption
William Marks	2		Md	Dec		croup
Maggie D. Janney	4		Md	Mar		scarlet fever
John White	62		Md	Mar	laborer	bronchitis
William Bradford	1		Md	Nov		teething
James Sannders	42		Hamburg	Jun	laborer	typhoid
Isabella Bellinger	25		Pa.	Jul	seamstress	yellow fever
Mary Klinefelter	9mo		Md	May		cholera
Margaret Booze	23	M	Md	May		heart dis.
William J. Evling	4mo		Md	sep		brain fever
Charles Evling	1		Md	Sep		teething
Adam Hurst	4		Md	Dec		spasms
George Keriman	4		Md	Sep		scarlet fever
Emily Bottimore	1		Md	Jul		Summer compl.
Lewes Frank	10		Baden	Oct		brain fever
Walter B.Miller	9		Md	Jan		typhoid
Mary A. Hulsuma	6		Md	Mar		spasma
Henry Seester	5		Md	Mar		scarlet fever
William G.A.Rogers	2mo		Md	Sep		brain fever
William Brock	3mo		Md	Aug		summer comp.
Caroline Hanson	36	M	Hanover	Nov		yellow fever
Charles Hanson	10		Md	Nov		yellow fever
Frederick Hanson	3mo		Md	Nov		yellow fever
Henry Miller	8mo		Md	Spr		catarph
Eliza Wilkenson	42		Md	Aug		bowel infl.
Mena Thompson	35	M	Baden	Mar		consumption
Hugh J. Doyle	19		Md	Dec		killed
Charles Jacks	19		Saxon	Sep	baker	consumption
John R. Hartly	11		Md	Aug		typhoid
Margaret Scales	59	W	Canada	Mar		ulcer
Frederick Krotter	19		Prussia	Dec	laborer	lockjaw
Lucy Mahoon	8mo		Md	Aug		teething
Mary O'Donnell	30	M	Ire.	Aug	seamstress	spasms
William Brown	58		D.C.	Jan	shoemaker	insane
Martha Henry	11mo		Md	Aug		teething
Gorege P. Moreland	1		Md	Nov		croup
Adam Engle	5		Md	Jun		drowned
Thomas P.McCluske	1		Md	Dec		catarhh
Emma C.Miller	11mo		Md	May		whooping cough
Rosa Johnson	22		Md	Jun		heart dis.

127

name	age	mar wid	birth place	mon. died	Occupation	cause of death
James White	7mo		Md	Jun		cholera
Mary E. Biscoe	1		Md	May		teething
Samuel McGlinn	26	M	Md	Apr	tobacconist	consumption
Elizabeth Ritter	3		Md	Feb		scarlet fever
Conrad Burgan	2		Md	Mar		scarlet fever
Margaret Yoe	38	M	Copenhaven	Oct		bil.fever
Sarah Searley	29		Md	Nov		heart dis.
Henry Dundore	54	M	Pa.	Sep	shoemaker	yellow fever
Henrietta Heisner	54	M	Saxony	Dec		consumption
Catharine Heisner	1		Md	Apr		teething
William Kalputh	30		Prussia	Oct	mariner	rheumatism
Catharine Kalputh	31		Prussia	Oct		typhoid
Charles Ugenhautz	9		Md	Sep		yellow fever
Margaret Henry	4		Md	Feb		croup
John Seller	4		Md	Apr		scarlet fever
Barbary Brown	1		Md	Feb		croup
Mary A. Detenberg	39	M	Darmstadd	May		dropsy
William Sterling	9mo		Md	Jul		teething
Sarah A. Sterling	3		Md	Jan		hemorhage
Sophia Kepler	2		Md	Mar		croup
Rosa Baltzell	3		Md	Apr		croup
Bernard Hamill	32	M	Hanover	Apr		spasms
Elizabeth McGrath	27		Ire.	Oct		consumption
Margaret Schuh	54		Baden	Mar		consumption
Frank Schaffer	9mo		Md	Apr		summer comp.
George Gaik	10mo		Md	Aug		summer comp.
James McGaw	54	M	Ire.	Jul	trader	drowned
Isabella Belloin	26		Pa.	Oct		yellow fever
George Wm.Herman	10		Bavaria	Aug		throat dis.
Mary F. Jones	1		Md	Dec		teething
Deborah Conoway	46	M	Md	feb		consumption
Marian H. Townsend	11mo		Md	Jul		whooping cough
Matilda Holland	2mo		Md	Jan		unknown
Margaret Hammond	69	M	Darmstadd	Oct		paralysis
Susan Bartlett	77	M	Md	Jun		old age
Susan Price	79	W	Md	Apr		parylytic
Joseph Gosman	5mo		Md	Jul		whooping cough
Catharine Peterson	53	M	Sweden	Apr	seamstress	heart dis.
Solomon Marshall	60	M	Md	Dec	laborer	drowned
WilliamJ. Bradehouse	14		Md	Oct		lock jaw
Wesley Badehouse	4mo		Md	Aug		summer comp.
Jos.L.Stansbury	14		Md	Jun		scrofula
William N. Fisher	1		Md	Jan		croup
Daniel Powell	11mo		Md	Jun		brain fever
Rebecca Berliner	4		Md	Oct		croup
Ann A. Lewis	3		Md	Apr		measles
Lavena Brooks	7		Md	Oct		dropsey
John Hany	76	M	Md	May	pilot	debility
Ann Wayland	21		Md	Feb	stamstress	cholera
Mary E. Cosgrove	9mo		Md	May		dyesentary
Sarah Cullen	26		Mass.	Mar		consumption
Elijah R. Sinners	55	M	Md	Dec	mariner	yellow fever
William McDonald	26		Md	Mar	carpenter	consumption

128

name	age	mar wid	birth place	mon. died	Occupation	cause of death
Charles Shane	2mo		Md	Aug		summer comp.
Conrad Stubenger	1		Md	Jul		summer cmp.
Emily Dennis	9		Md	Nov		typhoid
Charles A.Dorrittee	1		Md	Aug		teething
Neily Rauch	7mo		Md	Jun		summer comp.
Eve M. Greeves	29	M	Md	Dec		child bed
David Greeves	5		Md	Jun		measles
Rose Taltorn	2		Md	Mar		measles
Jacob K. Dietz	2		Md	Jul		whooping cough
Amanda Dietz	4		Md	Jul		whooping cough
Elizabeth Lewis	67	W	Md	Aug		paralytic
William J. Philips	21		Md	Jul		throat tumor
Howard L. Rusk	4mo		Md	Aug		summer comp
Augustus Brown	40	M	Md	Jan		consumption
Archibald Cook	32	M	Md	Oct		consumption
Mena Schillenberg	1		Md	Feb		croup
Sarah Welch	15		Ire.	May		measles
Robert Clary	22		Md	Dec		typhoid
Susanna Spariner	27		Eng.	Jul		consumption
Mary Gephart	28		Wertenburg	Dec		bil.fever
Sarah Bradly	5mo		Md	May		brain fever
Willie Files	10mo		Md	May		scalded
Samuel McPherson	1		Md	Aug		whooping cough
John Davis	30		N.C.	Aug	merchant	bil.fever
Caroline Ragnas	2		Md	Sep		teething
George Robb	6		Bavaria	Jul		dropsy
John Robb	2		Md	May		measles
Annie M. Moll	24		Cohessen	Mar		consumption
William H. Munroe	5		Md	Dec		small pox
James C. Munroe	9		Md	Dec		small pox
Thomas B. Kerny	1		Md	Aug		teething
Mary Grout	10mo		Md	Sep		scarlet fever
Christopher Wining	3		Md	Aug		scarlet fever
Charles Hyde	1		Md	aug		summer comp.
Caroline Hyde	4mo		Md	Jan		spasms
Elizabeth Breting	36		Md	Aug		cholera
Mary A. Webb	17		Md	Dec		consumption
Thomas Glover	11mo		Md	Aug		sonsumption
Frank Weble	10mo		Md	Jul		teething
Barbara Deitzer	11		Baden	Aug		scarlet fever
Alice A.Christopher	1		Md	Sep		consumption
John Gardiner	3mo		Md	Sep		consumption
Mary A. Wentworth	2		Md	Mar		scarlet fever
Timothy Felvin	1		Md	Feb		spasms
Mary White	3		Md	Apr		measles
John Cummings	1		Md	Jan		lung congest.
			2nd Ward			
Anna M. Cadel	2		Md	Sep		croup
William K. Kirland	5		Md	Dec		brain fever
Margaret Berry	33	M	Md	Sep		consumption
Lewis Berry	3		Md	Sep		water on brain
Martha J. Stephenson	1		Md	Oct		croup
Louisa Hoofnagle	3		Md	Jul		measles

MORTALITY SCHEDULE OF MARYLAND

persons who died during the year ending 1 June 18 60

COUNTY City of Baltimore   DISTRICT 2nd Ward

name	age	mar wid	birth place	mon. died	Occupation	cause of death
John F. Dill	6mo		Md	May		croup
Alice C. McMunz	1		Pa	Jun		measles
Mary A. Bower	1		Md	Jan		croup
Margaret Green	2		Md	Nov		heart dis.
Sarah Bukenwald	1		Md	Jun		brain cong.
Ursula Schon	20		Bavaria	Oct		yellow fever
Elizabeth Seabust	1mo		Md	Jun		croup
Mary Peterson	80	W	Md	Jul		heart dis.
Mary Bevins	70	W	Md	Jul		heart dis.
Maria Whelters	50	W	Md	Mar		brain dis.
Henry Killog	22		Md	Nov	laborer	stabbed
Clara Deitz	1mo		Md	Sep		unknown
Margaret Kitman	1mo		Md	Dec		sudden
Andrew Barth	2		Md	Mar		unknown
Louisa Brochel	1		Md	Dec		unknown
Caroline Gethes	1		Md	Feb		scarlet fever
Margaret Kanicy	1mo		Md	Jun		croup
Mary Pfaff	1		Md	Nov		dysentary
Caroline Taylor	1		Md	Sep		dysentary
Margaret Foabz	1		Md	Oct		dysentary
Michel Pfelzer	29		France	Jan	laborer	consumption
Dora Gous	42	M	Middlefrank	May		dropsy
Thomas Maxley	23		Md	Jun		consumption
Henry Gellensbury	11mo		Md	Jan		croup
August Feinhard	16		Hessen	May		consumption
Charles Witz	2		Md	Feb		brain fever
Henry Rost	1		Md	Oct		brain fever
Lydia Wright	13		Md	Jan		heart dis.
John Marriott	1		Md	Feb		heart dis.
Isaac Eisfield	70	M	Bavaria	May		gravil
Joseph Finkel	57	M	Saxony	Dec	laborer	dropsy
Barbet Finkel	54	M	Saxony	Apr		dropsy
Mary Ringler	4		Md	Aug		dysentary
James Walsh	23		Eng.	Apr	clerk	consumption
Mary Baley	1		Md	Jun		brain fever
Adaline New	8mo		Md	Jun		dysentary
Mary Barerburg	33		Pa	Oct		measles
John Hitz	2mo		Md	Feb		dysentary
John Kopp	17		Saxony	May		consumption
Elizabeth Coughts	7mo		Md	Nov		brain fever
Charles Fisher	1		Md	Aug		dysentary
Maria Johnson (mul)	43		Md	May		gravil
Samuel Schenter	79	M	Prussia	Sep	storekeeper	heart dis.
Columbus Therunick	19		Md	May	laborer	typhoid
Catharine Schon	63	M	Hessen	Oct		dysentary
Charles Burcket	33	M	Bavaria	Nov	cooper	shooting
Joseph Arras	6		Md	Feb		bil.fever
Joseph Swibzler	58	M	Prussia	Nov	musician	consumption
Catherine Lippy	27	M	Bavaria	Oct		intemperance
Samuel Dargener	60	M	Va.	May		consumption
Caroline Fox	29	M	Hanover	apr		consumption
Frank A.Taylor	11mo		Md	Jan		cramps
Casper Stever	40	M	Saxony	aug	shoemaker	liver comp.

130

persons who died during the year ending 1 June 1860

COUNTY city of Baltimore   DISTRICT 2nd.Ward

name	age	mar wid	birth place	mon. died	Occupation	cause of death
Louisa Thorward	50	M	Hessen	Feb		debility
John Hallows	4		Md	Dec		spine dis.
Patrick Burnes	32	M	Irel.	May	laborer	dysentary
Sarah Ketler	10mo		Md	Jul		teething
William Ludwick	1		Md	Apr		measles
Henry Miller	5		Md	Apr		typhoid
Robert H. Bantmon	2mo		Md	Apr		typhoid
George Topkins	2		Md	Dec		teething
Mary Doughlous	6mo		Md	Oct		consumption
Fannie Wallis	26	M	Md	Aug		yellow fever
Samuel Mullen	25	M	Md	Sep	carpenter	yellow fever
Louisa H. Glady	33	M	France	Oct		yellow fever
Peter Beaver	36	M	Brunswick	Oct	laborer	sucide
John W. Helbz	6		Md	Jul		drowning
William Gravel	2mo		Md	Mar		spasms
William H.White	11mo		Md	Oct		teething
Jane Devina	73	W	Md	Jun		consumption
Henry Devina	38	M	Md	Jun		consumption
Eleanor Schone	9mo		Md	Aug		teething
Anna Lamberg	1		Md	Aug		croup
William Painter	42	M	Maine	Aug	tailor	yellow fever
John Cummings	33	M	Md	Mar	tailor	heart dis.
Hester Carroll	8		Md	Apr		consumption
Martha T. Hamell	2		Md	Oct		spasms
Goerge H. Muller	1mo		Md	Sep		measles
Margaret Menn	2		Md	Apr		scarlet fever
Lewis Boatwell	1		Md	Apr		scarlet fever
John Gigher	11mo		Md	Jun		dysentary
Conrad Louder	68	M	Pa.	Aug	collector	heart dis.
Edward Derbin	75	M	Mass.	Jan		spoplexy
Emma Schammel	2		Md	Apr		cat.fever
Elizabeth Lowman	2		Md	May		dropsy
Immanuel Sheatler	48	M	Bavaria	Jun	laborer	consumption
Thomas Abbott	53	W	Md	Feb	shoemaker	paralysis
Margaret Erghenbord	23		Hessen	Jan		croup
John Burns	5		Md	Dec		consumption
Frank Bean	3		Md	Apr		brain fever
Elizabeth Lewis	14		Ire.	May		dropsy
John Woods	67	W	Ire.	Mar		consumption
Owen Haggan	39	M	Ire.	May		lockjaw
Hugh Galleger	1		Ire.	Jan		brain fever
Jacob F.Crist	1		Ire.	Jan		cat.fever
Margaret McMahon	1		Md	Sep		dysentary
August Oberdick	49	M	Hanover	Apr	laborer	sudden
Julia Welsh	8mo		Md	Jun		water on brain
Edmond Wickens	44	M	Eng	Sep	carpenter	paralytic
Phaddendine Rees	2		Md	Nov		croup
Andrew Slatter	3		Md	Apr		croup
Margaret Better	34	M	Hanover	Feb		tumor
Sarah Gallager	4mo		Md	Mar		measles
Lawrence Byrne	22		Ire.	Nov		consumption
Elizabeth Hess	45	M	Hessen	Feb		drowned
Joseph Stuard	1mo		Md	Jun		dysentary

131

name	age	mar wid	birth place	mon. died	Occupation	cause of death
Budget Noonen	6mo		Md	Feb		Whooping cough
Lewis Krapp	1		Md	Sep		teething
Conrad Thughbright	4		Md	Apr		sudden
Frances H. Coath	45	W	Md	Oct		consumption
Cordelia Wiskey	69	W	Md	Jul		consumption
Carolien Brown	40	M	Md	Jul		consumption
Alice Beatty	3		Md	Jun		scarlet fever
Margaret O'Leary	29	M	Md	May		consumption
Martha A. Bunting	32	M	Md	Dec		consumption
Robert T. Wilkinson	39	M	Va	May	hatter	consumption
Thomas H. Landers	4		Md	Apr		spinal dis.
Margaret Babcock	21	M	Irel.	Apr		heart dis.
Francis Reed	40	M	Prussia	Apr		heart dis.
Andrew Slatter	3		Md	Apr		croup
			3rd Ward			
Ann Granby	90	W	Hamburg	Apr		rheumatism
Sally Slage	66		Eng.	Sep		rheumatism
Nancy Luke	74		Eng.	Jan		old age
James Isaacs	19		Eng	Jan		consumption
Mary Fulton	34	M	Eng.	Jan		consumption
Margaret Currins	26		Eng.	Feb		consumption
Jonah Eckert	22		Ger.	Jan		none
Mary Chamberlain	29	M	Md	May		consumption
Francis Tigler	16		Md	Feb		none
Sarah Collond	24		Md	Aug	seamstress	consumption
William Alcock	88	M	Md	May		old age
George Slater	30		Eng.	aug	Butcher	pheumonia
Mary Powell	32	W	Pa.	Oct	seamstress	dropsy
Edward Fieldman	17		N.Y.	Oct	clerk	hemorage
Mary Matthews	19		Md	May		consumption
Julia Harrison	13		Eng.	Nov		consumption
Laura Evans	40	M	Md	Apr		consumption
Hugh Williams	2		Md	Dec		diariahia
William Campbell	73	M	Md	Dec	machinist	diariahia
William Orr	40	M	Ire.	Jan	grocer	dropsey
George Johnson	9		Md	Aug		drowned
Ann Johnson	9		Md	Dec		water on brain
William Nicholas	1		Md	Aug		summer comp.
Mary Nicholas	3		Md	Sep		brain fever
Mary Morron	2mo		Md	Sep		summer comp.
Emma Beal	1mo		Md	Mar		summer comp.
John Och	24		Ger.	Apr	cigarmaker	consumption
Sarah Coleman	60	M	Md	Jan		dropsy
Ann Cullisnore	6mo		Md	Jun		consumption
Edward Whurry	64	M	Md	May	customOfficer	brain fever
William Scott	34	M	Md	May	shoemaker	consumption
Martin Clark	1mo		Md	Nov		teething
Frank Johnson	63		Md	Nov	laborer	consumption
Ann King	67		Ire.	Feb		consumption
David Johnson	2mo		Md	Jun		summer comp.
Sarah Kirby	23		Md	Feb		consumption
William Johnson	28		Md	Sep	carpenter	yellow fever
Richard Bowden	1		Md	Feb		measles

persons who died during the year ending 1 June 18_60_

COUNTY city of BALTIMORE   DISTRICT 3rd Ward

name	age	mar wid	birth place	mon. died	Occupation	cause of death
John Marshall	44	M	Md	Jun	carpenter	consumption
Mary Bates	2		Md	Apr		measles
Fanny Williams	59		Md	Jul		dropsey
William Robinson	1mo		Md	Apr		cold
James Kelly	33	M	Ire.	May	laborer	heart dis.
Rachel Botingham	1		Md	May		measles
Lewis Vicks	4		Md	Mar		scarlet fever
Ann Williams	15		Md	Nov		croup
George Clem	11		Md	Mar		scarlet fever
Robert Benny	44		Scot.	Jan	machinist	consumption
Mary McLinday	2		Md	Jun		brain fever
Ellen Birkhouse	6mo		Md	Dec		whooping cough
Julia Bush	6mo		Md	Dec		whooping cough
Sarah Ellis	24		Md	May		liver comp.
Samuel Printer	2mo		Md	Aug		summer comp.
Logan Conner	2		Md	Jul		summer comp.
Charles Pister	15		Md	May		consumption
Thomas Armstrong	40	M	Ire.	Dec	laborer	heart dis.
Thomas Ashton	21		Md	Dec	machinest	consumption
William Prunster	22		Md	Mar	clerk	consumption
James Cunningham	42	M	Md	Mar	merchant	consumption
Patrick Butler	2mo		Md	Aug		teething
John Gray	45	M	Md	Jul	sailmaker	bowel inflam.
Robert Wilson	66	M	Md	Mar	moulder	consumption
Thomas Hall	44	W	Md	Feb	tanner	consumption
4th Ward						
John Williams	40	M	Md	Feb	laborer	consumption
Turner West	3mo		Md	Sep		brain cong.
Nicholas Stark	55	M	Irel.	Oct		heart dis.
Edward Stewart	7mo		Md	Jul		brain fever
John Lycoff	45	M	Ger.	Feb	brewer	consumption
Dorry Lassing	60	W	Holland	May		ashma
Rebecca Hankey	77	M	Md	Jan		cancer
William Proctor	80	W	Eng.	Jan		old age
Margaret Wyble	50	M	Md	Mar		heart dis.
Charles Lancaster	17		Md	Nov		pheumonia
Francis Hyman	71	M	Eng.	Jun		consumption
John Cordrey	19		Maine	Sep		lockjaw
Peter Deirst	28		Md	Mar	paperhanger	consumption
William Raymond	2		Md	Apr		scarlet fever
Ann Neslin	15		Eng	May		sore throat
John Gates	29	M	Md	Apr	tanner	consumption
Henrietta Forbes	93	W	Md	Feb		old age
John Weekes	56	M	Md	Feb	blacksmith	consumption
James Weekes	15		Md	Apr		scrofafals
William Roney	86	W	Md	Mar		old age
Henrietta Instine	1		Md	Feb		spasms
Tobias Hands	60		Md	Mar		consumption
Nicholas Boyle	68	M	Md	Nov	flourmerchant	consumption
Willie Main	4mo		Md	Jun		teething
George Eckart	1		Md	Jan		whooping cough
Mary Sanders	33	M	Md	Jul		consumption

MORTALITY SCHEDULE OF MARYLAND

persons who died during the year ending 1 June 18 60

COUNTY city of BALTIMORE DISTRICT 4th Ward

name	age	mar wid	birth place	mon. died	Occupation	cause of death
Cathrine Yeager	34	M	Ger.	Aug		heart dis.
Moses Josephs	22		Ger.	Sep	clark	fever
Patrick Joyce	24		Irel.	Nov		consumption
Thomas Spellman	1mo		Md	Dec		scarlet fever
Charlotte Hautsman	2		Md	Jan		scarlet fever
Sophia Simpson	10		Md	Apr		liver dis.
George Simpson	5		Md	Oct		dropsey
Franklin Fannen	5		Md	Oct		consumption
Cathrine Shannon	27	W	Ire.	Nov		consulsions
Robert Register	4		Md	Jan		whooping cough
Mary Scotti	71	M	Mexico	May		cancer
Charles Schunk	8mo		Md	Feb		cold
George Hall	1		Md	Mar		cat.fever
Priscilla Comegys	87	M	Md	Jul		decay of Mature
Adelphia Graflin	3		Md	Sep		bràin cong.
Cathrine Jenkins	2		Md	Sep		consumption
Ella Claggett	6mo		Md	Jun		head dis.
Mary James	70	M	Md	Feb		old age
Mary Fisher	1		Md	Mar		heart dis.
Ann Powers	68	W	Ire.	Jan		old age
George Goneby	38	M	Ire.	Apr	blacksmith	pneumonia
Thomas Johns	39	M	Eng	Aug	mariner	yellow fever
Henry Hester	3mo		Md	Jun		scarlet fever
Laura Hester	9mo		Md	Jun		scarlet fever
Henry Clay	3		Md	Feb		scald
Thomas Lanigan	2		Md	Dec		small pox
Lewis Roheter	2		Md	Apr		scarlet fever
Mary Powell	1mo		Md	Sep		scarlet fever
John Cook	1mo		Md	Feb		spasms
Adam Barney	2		Md	Mar		cramp
Emma Perry	25		Md	Apr		heart dis.
Charlotte McCard	25	M	Md	Oct		consumption
Joseph Banister	78	M	Eng.	Jun		old age
Catherine Burris	18		Md	Feb		consumption
Sarah Thomas	9mo		Md	Mar		teething
Isabelle Hoobs	4		Md	Nov		sore throat
John Phillip	23		Md	Sep	surveyor	consumption
Jane Thomas	1		Md	Aug		consumption
Henry Honer	18		Md	Apr		disentary
5th & 6th Ward						
Joseph Riley	18		Irel.	Jul	blacksmith	consumption
James Gilmore	57	M	Ire.	Sep	trader	cancer
Alexander Cathell	38		Md	Sep		consumption
Ellen Kingston	35		Md	Feb		brain cong.
Willoughby Lewis	82	M	Ire.	Dec		neuraligia
Christiana Coffner	48	W	France	Mar		dropsy
Abiagail McCoy	57		Md	Jun		consumption
Maria Herzberg	64	W	Ger.	Mar		cramps
John Downs	44	M	N.Y.	Apr	store	consumption
Babbett Bentzinger	24	M	Wurtemberg	May		confinement
Mary Evans	35	M	Md	Apr		child bed
Maria Jane Evans	21	M	Md	Mar		consumption
Louisa Smith	79	M	Ger.	Feb		cholera

134

name	age	mar wid	birth place	mon. died	Occupation	cause of death
Mary A. Garvey	20	M	Irel.	Oct		cat.fever
Augusta Fisher	29	M	Hessen	Aug		consumption
Mary Dougherty	30	M	Irel.	Aug		confinement
Margaret Doud	4		Md	Feb		bil.dysentary
Eve Maria Maier	29	M	Md	May		confinement
Robert Perlius	1		Md	Jul		brain fever
Robert Harker	21		Del.	Jan	printer	consumption
Mary E. Allison	31	M	Md	Feb		consumption
George Flautt	64		Pa.	Jun	minister	bilious
Martin Roach	2		Md	Apr		consumption
John Reynolds	30	M	Ire.	Apr	laborer	consumption
Michael Pamart	74	W	France	Feb	liquordealer	paralysis
Mary Holliway	2		Md	Jan		consumption
John Tye	1		Md	Jan		scarlet fever
Nancy Sanders	31	M	Md	Jan	seamstress	consumption
John Sapfel	46	M	Baden	Aug	tailor	pleurisy
Ann Keyes	39		Md	Oct	seamstress	consummption
Olivia Bolton	3		Md	Apr		whooping cough
Maria May	63	W	Pa.	May	painter	paralysis
Iva P. Howard	9		Md	Dec		burnt
Eliza forsythe	33		Ire.	Jan		typhoid
William McKenny	1mo		Md	Jan		unknown
Ann McCann	38		Md	Dec		consumption
Mary Walters	92	W	Md	Jun	grocer	paralysis
Eliza Crocker	1mo		Md	Aug		brain fever
Francis Cassidy	39		Irel.	Jan		heart dis.
Edward McCormick	1mo		Md	Feb		unknown
Frederick B. Ring	35		Md	Mar		heart dis.
George P. Steck	2		Md	Dec		fever brain
Daniel Dobler	55	M	Md	Dec	boxmaker	apoplexy
John Burlander	37		Md	sep	cooper	spine dis.
Mary Jane Blades	35	M	Pa.	Jul	taileriss	consumption
Elizabeth Bing	2		Md	Oct		whooping cough
Ellen Selvage	30	M	Va	Mar		child bed
Vanhorn Feldt	5		Md	Aug		croup
Thomas Bransly	21		Md	Jan	biliardSalon	consumption
Adela Graham	47	M	D.C.	Jan		kidneys
Violet Rickets	81	M	Irel.	May		cancer
Jane McDowell	84	W	Irel.	Jan		old age
Marbella McClaine	55	W	Md	Feb		consumption
Benjamin Mills	14		Md	Feb		scrofula
Elizabeth G. Lowes	23		Wales	Apr	mantillamaker	consumption
William Chanceaulme	75	M	France	Mar	jeweler	heart disease
John H. Allen	4		Md	Sep		crofula
Lewis Hoopes	45	M	Bun.Ger.	Dec		dysentary
Elizabeth Spring	34	M	Darmstadt	Jan		child bed
Louisa Keisler	24	M	BunGer.	Apr		consumption
George James	18		Md	Jul	printer	consumption
Henry Clay Jarvis	17		Md	Jun		spine dis.
Margaret Jones	40		Md	Jan		consumption
Amos Brodbeck	48	M	Pa.	Apr	potter	consumption
William H. Hill	32	M	Md	Sep	moulder	consumption
Margaret Gault	57	M	Irel.	Jun		dysentary

135

MORTALITY SCHEDULE OF MARYLAND

persons who died during the year ending 1 June 18<u>60</u>

COUNTY   city of Baltimore   DISTRICT   5th & 6th Wards

name	age	mar wid	birth place	mon. died	Occupation	cause of death
John Godfrey	34	M	Md	Jan	tailor	consumption
James Godfrey	29	M	Md	Jan	tinner	brain fever
Julia Godfrey	31	M	Md	Feb	shirtbinder	consumption
Sarah Godfrey	9mo		Md	Jul		consumption
Solomon Sutten	31	M	Md	Jul	signmaker	consumption
James Randall	2		Md	Apr		brain dis.
Heorge T. Nuttall	20		Md	May		consumption
Elizabeth Porter	84	W	Irel.	Jul		old age
John Badinoff	37	M	Baden	Jun	machinest	accident
Mary Jane Sturgeon	15		Pa	Feb		brain cong.
Oscar H. Bright	2		Md	Sep		whooping cough
Clara Pifferling	1mo		Md	Sep		cholera
Ella B. Harrison	5mo		Md	Feb		consumption
Rachel Rose	40	W	Del.	Jul		consumption
Marcelus Vincente	1mo		Md	Oct		unknown
Ruth Darling	70	M	Md	May		old age
Ida Brown	1		Md	Feb		cat.fever
John H. Hooper	9		Md	Dec		fell
Joseph Miller	52	M	Hanover	Jul	shoemaker	brain fever
John Drissel	35	M	Bun.Ger	May	baker	accident
Caroline Dallam	42		Md	Feb		consumption
James Kane	19		Md	Feb	barkeeper	consumption
John Caley	3		Md	Feb		croup
William Hoffman	9mo		Md	Mar		croup
Sarah Ellender	46		Md	Jan		fell
Richard M. Warner	35	M	Va.	Nov	mariner	drowned
Alice Fritsch	4mo		Md	Sep		whooping cough
Richard Hall	53	M	Va.	Dec	shoemaker	pneumonia
John T. Horney	18		Md	Aug	brassfinisher	consumption
Catherine Boyle	83	W	Md	Feb		old age
Mary Ann Pindell	41	M	Md	Nov		consumpton
Joseph Ball	2		Md	Jun		brain fever
Mary Fletcher	72	W	Md	Feb		old age
Laura Boland	3mo		Md	Apr		consumption
Francis Halleck	2		Md	Mar		pneumonia
Bridget Grant	38	W	Ire.	Aug		consumption
William Rutledge	37	M	Md	Nov	bookeeper	consumption
Harriet Snyder	74	W	Md	May	baker	consumption
Agnes Colton	2		Md	Mar		consumption
David Logue	34	M	Md	Apr	wheelright	consumption
Frederick Lind	4mo		Md	Mar		brain inflam.
Morris Behrens	49	M	Prussia	feb	jeweler	liver inflam.
Ann Logue	80	M	Irel.	Jan		old age
Henry c. Allard	8mo		Md	Jul		brain fever
Mary F. Willis	18		Md	May		consumption
Sarah A. Craighton	35	W	Va.	Feb		concer
Priscilla Girdmanson	42	W	Md	Mar		consumption
Mary Williams	50	W	Md	Sep		paralysis
Lydia Taylor	10mo		Md	Aug		croup
Rosanna McGarry	8mo		Md	Oct		teething
Stephen McGarry	32		Ire.	Nov	huckster	lung hemmorage
Ann Clark	52	M	Md	Sep		paralysis
Lucy Stewart	10mo		Md	Dec		water on brain

name	age	mar wid	birth place	mon. died	Occupation	cause of death
George Colton	18		Md	Sep	seaman	cholera
Mary J. Steer	39	M	Md	Jan		inflamation
Mary K. Law	4		Md	Jul		croup
Ann E. Dowling	6mo		Md	Jul		cholera
Mary Stevens	77	W	Md	Mar		debility
John B. Banks	83	M	Md	May		apoplexy
Alfred J. Tunis	75		Md	Feb		consumption
John Steck	1		Md	Jul		dysentary
James Tucker	76	M	Md	Oct		old age
Jacob Dorsey	55		Md	Nov		liver compl.
Mary Ward	67	W	Md	Mar		cancer
Olevia Davis	6mo		Md	Jul		cholera
John R. Hand	3mo		Md	Apr		spasms
Edward J. Christopher	8mo		Md	Apr		dropsy
Alice A. Folks	1		Md	Sep		water onbrain
Nicholas Folks	60	M	Md	Jun	laborer	consumption
George S. Briget	20		Md	May	paperhanger	consumption
Richard Masters	58	M	Pa.	Feb	tailor	consumption
Brazilla Crawford	1		Md	Jan		brain fever
Robert Chase	11mo		Md	May		teething
Joshua Sheppard	4		Md	May		consumption
Fanny Smith	79	M	Md	May		debility
Jacob Rhumwalt	1mo		Md	May		unknown
Agatha Donovan	31	M	Eng.	Oct		heart distease
			7th Ward			
Thomas Bond	71	W	Md	Apr	laborer	consumption
Timothy Simes	52	M	Ver.	Aug	clerk	typhoid
Clark P. Heiser	2		Md	Jan		croup
John McCourt	10		Md	Sep		brain fever
Theodore Salter	7		Md	Oct		croup
Eliza T. Brady	30		Md	May		consumption
Lewis Winborg	11mo		Md	Oct		scarlet fever
Margaret Higgenbotom	80		Md	Mar		old age
Hezekiah Bush	1mo		Md	Nov		spasms
Sarah J. Pedercord	4mo		Md	Jun		fits
Hannah C. Haslett	30	M	Md	Apr		dropsy
Charles A. Hamil	2		Md	Jun		dysentary
Johy W. Hertz	1mo		Md	Jan		brain dis.
John Winternight	1		Md	Feb		croup
George Wells	6mo		Md	Aug		cholera
Willemenia Winternight	35		Hesses	Apr		consumption
Mary Rebensnider	7		Md	Aug		croup
Mary R. Digg	1		Md	Jun		consumption
Aaron R. Scheckels	49	M	N.J.	Dec		consumption
Emma Erhardt	2		Md	Jan		spasms
Sophia Wemburgh	10		Md	Apr		dropsy
Deborah Eden	26		Eng.	Oct		dysentary
Dorede Wise	17		Md	Nov		burnt
Catherine Wever	9mo		Md	Aug		dysentary
Henry D. Weaver	75	M	Hesses	May		dropsy
Margaret Nippard	21	M	Md	May		fever
Jeremiah Miller	48	W	Md	Jul	mason	consumption
Hannah Cable	37	M	Md	Feb		consumption

137

persons who died during the year ending 1 June 18 60

COUNTY city of Baltimore   DISTRICT 7th Ward

name	age	mar wid	birth place	mon. died	Occupation	cause of death
David Barbour	28	M	Md	Aug	copperworker	typhoid
Barbet Golstes	3		Md	Jul		dysentary
Priscilla Brown	24		Md	Sep		consumption
John Lattan	1mo		Md	May		dropsy
Susan Rahclift	35	M	Md	Sep		dysentary
Nathan Mansfield	2		Md	Mar		typhoid
Joseph D. Tennett	2mo		Md	Jan		paralysis
William Schafler	2		Md	May		typhoid
Leonard P. Lyons	1		Md	Aug		dysentary
Frederick e. Love	1		Md	Jul		cysentary
Robert Wilson	29	M	Md	Mar	moulder	consumption
Martin Dogged	48	M	Va.	May	clerk	consumption
Charles W. Knott	1mo		Md	Jan		consumption
Adaline Millsock	58	W	Md	Apr		paralytic
Charles E. Weathers	4		Md	Aug		croup
John Nicholson	5		Md	Feb		whooping cough
Ellen R. Brannon	17		Md	Dec		heart dis.
Nancy Griggren	74	W	Md	Apr		consumption
Callender Patterson	21		Md	Nov		murdered
Mary Bolman	6		Md	Mar		consumption
Henrietta Spandower	3		Md	Apr		dysentary
Henrietta LeRay	2		Md	Jan		scarletfever
Catherine Shaverline	1		Md	Aug		measles
Edwin Meyer	1		Md	Jul		croup
Mary Groves	85		Md	Sep		old age
Willamenia Bright	70		Md	Nov		lung abscess
Ida Graham	11mo		Md	Feb		unknown
Kate Solomon	10		Md	Feb		unknown
Ann Carr	1		Md	Jan		dysentary
Richard R. Marsh	34		Md	Jun	storekeeper	consumption
Eleanor Frelente	9		Md	Nov		brain fever
Rose H. Maywald	39	M	Prussia	Apr		suicide
Rebecca Hamell	59		Md	Dec		scarlet fever
Elenora Wilkins	5		Md	Feb		consumption
James Wilkins	5		Md	Feb		consumption
Anna E. Thompson	30	M	Md	Oct		brain fever
Charles Watts	7		Md	Aug		stomach inflam.
William L. Williams	25		Md	Mar	clerk	bil.dysentary
Laura F. Lynch	5		Md	Jun		unknown
Henry Washington	24		Md	May	barber	heart dis.
Mary E. Marsh	26		Md	Sep		consumption
Elizabeth Newman	3		Md	Aug		scarlet fever
Francis Bobman	15		Md	Nov		dropsy
John W. Bumbarger	76	W	Md	Mar	shoemaker	asthma
Sarah A. Glack	34	M	Va.	Mar		unknown
Joseph H. Garrett	48		Md	Dec	shoemaker	kydneys inflam.
David Sessel	38	M	Irel.	Apr	storekeeper	consumption
Henry B. Kidd	9mo		Md	Apr		cat.fever
Rosina Merryman	68	M	Wutemburg	Aug		lung inflam.
Mary D. Lanster	16		Md	Feb		typhoid
Fannie V. Elliott	4		Md	Aug		croup
Elizabeth F. Kirby	11mo		Md	Apr		teething
David Maccubins	39	M	Md	Jun	painter	consumption

persons who died during the year ending 1 June 1860

COUNTY city of Baltimore   DISTRICT 7th Ward

name	age	mar wid	birth place	mon. died	Occupation	cause of death
William F. Lightner	1		Md	Jun		brain fever
John O. Scheckels	4		Md	Jul		brain cong.
William Wagner	11mo		Md	Jun		dysentary
Catharine F. Vanner	11		Md	Nov		typhoid
Margaret Medinger	2		Md	Jul		whooping cough
Anna E. Carroll	1		Md	Aug		liver dis.
Hugh Chambers	3		Md	Apr		scalded
George E. Wesley	4		Md	Jan		cat.fever
Enos Mitchel	1		Hanover	Aug		dysentary
Ann Mullen	42		Md	Sep		consumption
Sarah Weaver	4		Md	Nov		croup
Frederick G. Leary	1		Md	Sep		dysentary
Mary J. Pratt	2		Md	Mar		croup
Gracey A. Gross	4mo		Md	Jul		cholera
Mary F. Harrison	1		Md	Jul		dysentary
William T. Wheeler	4		Md	Apr		stomach inflam.
Margaret Harper	58		Md	Dec		sonsumption
Ann P. Pond	2		Md	Jan		croup
Edwin Mace	1		Md	Nov		scrofula
Sylvester Shanks	7mo		Md	Aug		dysentary
Lucy Taylor	40		Irel.	Sep		consumption
Hezekiah Jolley	9		Md	Oct		dropsy
Wesley Blackstone	12		Md	Feb		consumption
Lewis T. Parker	1		Md	Nov		brain cong.
James L. Cox	10		Md	May		measles
Margaret Donohue	2		Md	May		measles
Anna Fonist	9		Md	Dec		rheumatism
James LeBuner	37		Md	Sep	Mason	accident-fall
James W. Elliott	4		Md	May		brain cong.
Elizabeth Pollard	60	W	Md	Feb		heart dis.
John Rice	43		Irel.	Feb	laborer	consumption
William F. Bryan	1		Md	Mar		consumption
Anna Parr	2		Md	Mar		croup
Margaret E. Henderson	18		Md	Nov		consumpton
Richard Downey	21		Md	Dec	shoemaker	consumption
Charles Cooper	34		Eng.	Jun	carpenter	rheumatism
James A. Church	3		Md	Aug		dropsy
William Etel	17		Md	Mar	barber	typhoid
Amelia Miller	5mo		Md	Aug		cramp
Daniel McDevitt	24		Md	Dec	painter	consumption
Fannie McKenna	2mo		Md	Sep		heart dis.
George W. Grover	11		Md	May		scarlet fever
Mary M. Kelmyer	7		Md	Mar		brain dis.
Elizabeth Egleton	4		Md	May		spine dis.
John Martin	53	M	Md	Dec	laborer	apoplexy
Hellen Martin	57	M	Md	Dec		apoplexy
Hester J. Hall	29		Va.	Jul		dispepsia
Mary E.T.T. Dutton	9mo		Md	May		mumps
samuel White	1		Md	Aug		dysentary
Elias Thompson	64	W	Md	Jan	shoemaker	heart dis.
Catherine Brusman	35		Md	Sep		neuralgia
Catherine Charles	15		Bavaria	Jan		small pox

persons who died during the year ending 1 June 18_60_

COUNTY city of Baltimore   DISTRICT 7th Ward

name	age	mar wid	birth place	mon. died	Occupation	cause of death
Frances E. Fowley	3mo		Md	Jun		lung inflam.
Eurich Spencer	39		France	Jul	machinist	consumption
Joseph Nader	1		Md	Aug		dysentary
Joseph Schlilt	52	M	Hesses	Jul	prop.agent	dyspepsia
Errick C. Quandt	67	M	Saxony	Jun	shoemaker	cholera
James Woods	17		Irel.	Jul	clerk	drowned
Jane T. Gorsuch	50	W	Md	Jul		consumption
Haiman C. Conner	59	M	Bavaria	Feb	cabinetmaker	dropsy
Mary A. Rogers	7		Md	Sep		croup
Godfrey Aman	53	W	Baden	Jun	butcher	fall
Barbet Freagenhain	27		Saxony	Jan		childbirth
Seth Danes	59	M	Md	Jan	shoemaker	paralysis
Richard Nelson	36		Md	Mar	mason	consumption
8th Ward						
Joseph Crough	9mo		Md	Sep		summer compl.
Andrew Smith	57	M	Darmsted	May	painter	heart dis.
Julius Muklenmeyer	1		Md	Jul		measles
Ann Owens	1		Md	Jul		spasms
Simon Schiminger	2		Md	Mar		consumption
Augusta Forsyth	2mo		Md	Apr		scurvy
Charles B. Mesner	3mo		Md	Aug		summer compl.
Joseph King	1mo		Md	Sep		small pox
Catherine Oehrig	53		W.H.Darmst.	Dec		heart dis.
John Schnider	7mo		Md	Jul		summer comp.
John Metz	5		Md	Sep		bowel inflam.
Adam Bidner	4		Md	Dec		scrofula
Louis Weaver	1		Md	Feb		spasms
Catherine Epple	5		Md	Aug		whooping cough
Ann Pogue	68	W	Md	Jan		brunt
Mary Creamer	4		Md	Aug		gastric fever
Ann O'Neal	55	M	Irel.	Aug		consumption
Charles Ambrose	6		Ger.	Nov		fits
Peter Empken	50	M	Bavaria	Jan	blacksmith	erysipelas
Elizabeth Radiger	2		Md	Oct		measles
Andrew Hook	1		Md	Aug		teething
Lillie Reinaker	1		Md	Nov		croup
Walben Leach	75	M	N.J.	Aug	paternmaker	consumption
Alexander Levering	6		Md	Feb		pneumonia
Estelle H. Mitchell	6		Md	Mar		measles
David Baker	74	M	Md	Mar	sumacDealer	paralysed
Mary Tidings	90	W	Md	Dec		erysipelas
Samuel T. Carvill	3mo		Md	Jul		summer comp.
John Webster	81	W	Eng	Jan	weaver	old age
George W. Hamilton	4mo		Md	Nov		whooping cough
Ida A. Bunce	2		Md	Jul		bil.dysentary
William W. Campbell	10mo		Md	Dec		croup
Mary J. Fletcher	16		Md	Sep		dysentary
William G. Craft	24		Md	Jan	butcher	lockjaw
Stewart B. Burke	17		Md	Sep	butcherApp.	typhoid
Abbie M. McKenna	20	M	Mass.	Nov		consumption
Eva Weaver	9mo		Md	Apr		teething
James Pentland	1		Md	Oct		teething
John Kuhnman	41	M	Oldenberg	Nov	shoemaker	consumption
Ann Eckell	45	M	Md	Apr		brain fever
			140			

name	age	mar wid	birth place	mon. died	Occupation	cause of death
John McElhaney	23		Irel.	Jan	tailor	heart dis.
Sarah McElhaney	25		Irel.	Mar		consumption
Isabella Lackey	69		Md	Mar	teacher	heart dis.
Catherine Moore	1mo		Md	Feb		unknown
Emily Forrestor	1		Md	Jul		summer comp.
Valentine Lenn	61	M	Bavaria	Apr	ragPicker	consumption
Amelia Lenn	60	M	Bavaria	Mar		consumption
Winifred May	7		Md	Oct		consumption
Patrick Canan	1		Md	Jul		summer comp.
Owen McCabe	30	M	Irel.	Aug		sun stroke
Mary Campbell	1		Md	Feb		cat.fever
Mary Flannigan	55	M	Irel.	Dec		cholera
Steven Kilfuff	3mo		Md	Jul		spasms
Francis Farrell	35	M	Irel.	Aug	laborer	run over
Isaac Miller	24		Md	Apr		consumption
Catherine Flaherty	3		Md	May		kings evil
Richard Mooney	1mo		Md	Jan		croup
Mary Tidings	80	W	Md	Jan		old age
Ann Cassiday	23		Irel.	Apr	dressmaker	consumption
Mary F. Lyons	3		Md	May		croup
James Henry	3mo		Md	Nov		scarletfever
William Wooden	37	M	Md	Dec	policeOfficer	dropsey
James Moore	48	M	Md	Aug	cabinetmaker	consumption
Mary Dowling	35	M	Irel.	Apr		consumption
Ann Masterman	4		Md	Jan		brain fever
Mary McLaughlin	6		Md	Oct		water on brain
Mary Taylor	66	W	Md	Mar		heart disease
Mary Houck	24		Bavaria	Sep		consumption
Conrad Houck	4mo		Md	Sep		cramp
Adam Herbert	1		Md	Dec		unknown
Clara Rober	7mo		Md	Apr		cat.fever
Ann Walsh	1		Md	Aug		summer compl.
William Ashton	52		Md	Jan	hatter	consumption
Mary L. Pennington	7mo		Md	Dec		water on brain
Francis Pasterford	73	W	Md	Mar		consumption
Cecelia Ruster	2		Md	May		brain fever
Robert Woodward	17		Md	May		consumption
Mary Cutherenger	59	M	Md	Oct		consumption
Wilhemena Reese	2mo		Md	Feb		fits
Dock Tracy	35		Md	Aug	loafer	intemperance
Felix Francolia	45		Italy	Sep	loafer	intemperance
Charles Antoni	35		Italy	Sep		intemperance
George Downs	25		Md	Nov	laborer	intemperance
Godfrey Winters	40		Ger.	Jan	carpenter	suicide
Agnes Stewart	73	W	Irel.	Oct		old age
Susan Diggs	25	W	Md	Sep		consumption
Mary E. Minnock	1		Md	Sep		teething
Emma Schroeder	1		Md	Sep		whoping cough
William E. Bayley	23		Va.	Feb		consumption
Ellen McKeever	5mo		Md	Aug		debility
Mary Morris	19		Md	Dec		cold
Frederick Hesse	49	M	Hanover	Jan	currier	heart dis.

141

persons who died during the year ending 1 June 18_60_

COUNTY city of Baltimore   DISTRICT   8th Ward

name	age	mar wid	birth place	mon. died	Occupation	cause of death
Joseph Priller	2		Md	Jul		cat.fever
John Bokel	6		Md	Aug		brain fever
Catherine Collison	1		Md	Oct		whooping cough
Lena Brackmeiner	1mo		Md	Jan		unknown
Ann E. McQuay	27		Md	Feb		cancer
Ann E. Zimmerman	1		Md	Apr		dysentary
Fredrkeka Zimmerman	20	M	Md	Mar		lung inflam.
Thomas W. Turner	28		Md	Dec		consumption
John T. Onion	3mo		Md	Jan		cat.fever
Thomas Towson	50	M	Md	Apr	tailor	burnt
Julia A. Morgan	24		Md	Apr		consumption
Eliza L. Ashpool	21		Md	May	teacher	consumption
Mary C. Kerr	6		Md	Jun		gastric fever
Barbara Baltzell	67	W	Bavaria	Jan		dropsy
Elizabeth Hebner	69	M	Bavaria	Aug		dropsy
Thomas Elliott	47	M	Md	Aug	painter	typhoid
Mary Eisenbauer	4		Md	Aug		summer comp.
Louisa Smeiser	26		Pa.	May	tailoress	consumption
Joseph Schuster	3		Md	Mar		croup
Henry W. Kirk	1mo		Md	Apr		pneumonia
John Knotts	8		Wertenb	Aug		fall
William O'Keefe	1		Md	Aug		summer cmp.
James A. Donahue	26		Irel.	Mar	tailor	consumption
Ellen Taylor	60	M	Md	Sep		kidney dis.
William Boyd	4		Md	Aug		pleurisy
Mary S. Street	22	M	Md	Dec		typhoid
John B. Wisner	30	M	Md	Jul	farmer	bronchetus
Mary Maloy	47	M	Irel.	Oct		consumption
Eliza J. Mullen	10mo		Md	Jul		summer comp.
Johanna Ingraham	36	M	Scot.	Jan		consumption
Fredereka Hercher	19	M	Md	Mar		confinement
John Hayes	68	M	Md	Dec	painter	bladder inflam.
Charles Smith	33		Md	Jun	hatter	dysentary
Margaret A. Bregel	59	W	Werten.	Mar		cancer
Catherine Butler	38	M	Md	Jan		cancer
Louis Donovan	10mo		Md	Jan		water on brain
Edward Carroll	1		Md	Aug		summer comp.
Eliza J. Gray	32	M	Irel.	Sep		consumption
Mary E. Dailey	28	M	Irel.	Oct		consumption
Catherine Emison	22		Md	May		typhoid
Mary Wilkins	1		Md	Dec		scarlet fever
Mary Klopsoth	4		Md	Dec		brain fever
Edwared Quigley	1		Md	Aug		summer comp.
Howard Gardner	8mo		Md	Apr		scarlet fever
Jane Russell	56		Irel.	Mar		heart dis.
Robert Gault	59=		Irel.	May	foundery	rheumatism
George F. Imhoff	29		Bavaria	Dec	shoemaker	yellow jaundice
Frances Martin	79		Md	Jan		old age
John Bain	42		Ger.	Oct	saloonkeeper	consumption
Charles Matthews	15		Cuba	Jan		dysentary
Lanna Kepperwill	2mo		Md	Sep		summer comp.
John Conoway	1mo		Md	Mar		unknown

name	age	mar wid	birth place	mon. died	Occupation	cause of death
Mary Ellen Ludman	11mo		Md	May		consumption
James Halpin	45		Irel.	Oct		unknown
Thomas Dabney	31		Irel.	Dec	laborer	liver compl.
Thomas Cassidy	3		Md	Sep		measles
Mary A. Buckate	2		Md	Dec		brain inflam.
John Wicker	35		Ger.	May	upholsterer	unknown
Isaac Monroe	74		Mass.	Dec	editor	appoplexy
Emily W. Monroe	70		N. H.	Jul		old age
10th Ward						
Ann E. Nicham	16		Pa.	Mar		burnt
Richard Sexton	8mo		Md	Jan		croup
Charles Young	1		Md	Nov		summer comp.
Andrew McCaffney	5		Md	Nov		croup
Mary German	16		Md	Oct		bil.fever
John W. Myer	49	M	Bavaria	May	tavernKeeper	paralysis
John Duberry	77	M	Pa.	Mar	hackman	dropsey
Sarah Brenan	52	M	Pa.	May		consumption
Josiah Davies	26	M	Md	Jan	policeOfficer	consumption
Walter Perkins	1		Md	Jun		cat.fever
Mary McPhall	79	W	Md	Sep		apoplexy
Elizabeth A.Hall	74	W	Ger.	Jul		old age
George Merryman	17		Md	Nov		rheumatism
Rositta Brundidge	59	M	Md	Aug		pneumonia
Susan P. Evans	60	M	Md	Sep		apoplexy
Hamitt Dawson	25		Md	Jan		consumption
Elisha Brown	76	M	Md	Apr		softing ofBrain
Charles Evans	4		Md	Mar		pneumonia
11th Ward						
Fannie C. Norman	60	M	Conn.	Apr		sonsumption
Francis E. Bettondorf	1		Md	Aug		scarlet fever
James B. Logsden	3		Md	Dec		Brain fever
Margaret Deal	84	W	Md	Apr		old age
Aletha Boswell	56	M	Md	Apr		consumption
John Hinds	2		Md	May		water on brain
Abbe L. Martin	2		Md	Feb		croup
Julian May	34		D.C.	Nov	U.S.Army	brain cong.
George May	44	M	D.C.	Oct	gentleman	heart dis.
Margaret Dorsey	39		Md	Nov		consumption
William VonKapff	7mo		Md	Dec		pneumonia
John P. Cockey	63	M	Md	Nov	physician	cancer
George Chase	21		N.Y.	Mar		consumption
John H. Crane	31		N.Y.	Sep	merchant	consumption
Ida Farley	5mo		Md	Jan		unknown
James Baker	50		Irel.	Jul	laborer	fall
Ellen Howard	40		Irel.	Apr	servant	dropsy
John McC. Cinnamond	4		Md	none		typhoid
Thomas N. Nelson	77	M	Irel.	none		lung inflam.
Andrew Williamson	74	W	Scot	none	manufacturer	heart dis.
Frances C. Pendergast	1		Md	none		water on brain
Mark A. Duke	36	M	Va.	none	stoveDealer	dropsy
Francis Riley	45	W	Irel.	none	shopkeeper	consumption
Charles Frick	36	M	Md	none	physician	depptheria

persons who died during the year ending 1 June 18_60_

COUNTY   city of Baltimore   DISTRICT   -11th Ward

name	age	mar wid	birth place	mon. died	Occupation	cause of death
Lamden C. Moale	17		Md	none		bowel inflam.
Mary Stickney	80	W	Mass	"		old age
Laura S. Maginnes	40	M	Md	"		consumption
Hester A. Howard	35		Md	"		consumption
John Nelson	64	M	Md	"	lawyer	unknown
Ann McNally	66	W	Eng.	"		heart dis.
Charles C. Spence	1		Md	"		teething
Ann Harwood	38		Md	"		consumption
Z.Collins Lee	59	M	Ca.	"	Judge	paralysis
L. Tiernan Chatard	26		Md	"	lawyer	consumption
Jacob Carmin	72	M	N.Y.	"	distiller	consumption
George Brown	72	M	Irel.	"	banker	heart dis.
John Manning	2mo		Md	Nov		debility
Bridget Clark	8mo		Md	Aug		brain fever
Mary Smith	23		Irel.	Jun	servant	consumption
Mary E. Harrington	1		Md	Aug		teething
Catherine Starr	79	W	Pa.	May		old age
Henry Jourdon	60	M	Eng.	Nov	seaman	appoplexy
Maria A. Hayden	81	W	Pa.	Mar		stomach inflam.
Lorenzo O'Cone	3		Md	Aug		spasms
Sarah McMullen	75	W	Md	Sep		old age
Theresa McMullen	25		Md	May	dressmaker	heart dis.
Henry Englehausen	52	M	Hanover	May	tavernkeeper	prarlytic
John Coolahan	5		Md	Jan		croup
John McCarney	44	M	Irel.	May	junkshop	bronchitis
S.Joshua Watson	68	W	Pa.	Mar	couchsmith	dropsy
William King(black)	18		Md	May	woolpacker	pneumonia
Wilhemenia Ewig	37	M	Ger.	Feb		consumption
Catherine McGee	42	W	Md	Mar		consumption
John P. Piper	61	M	Bavaria	Oct	shopkeeper	brain softning
Ann Harvey	66	W	Irel.	Feb		old age
James C. Hyland	50	M	Md	Jun		consumption
Chalres A. Boggs	19		Md	Aug	clerk	typhoid
Henry Shillinger	1		Md	Dec		croup
Henry J. Popp	5		Md	Nov		run over
William T. Murray	12		Md	May		typhoid
Allien S. Barnum	9mo		Md	Jan		cholic
Anthony Keenan	72	M	Irel.	Jul	hotelkeeper	old age
Frances V. Moale(male)	31		Md	Aug	lawyer	epileptick
Elizabeth A. Sterling	53	M	Md	Sep		cancer
Susanna McDowell	57		Md	Mar		paralysis
Elizabeth Fonderon	87	W	Md	Sep		old age
Margaret Read	10		Md	Dec		consumption
Mary Joice	12		Irel.	Dec	orphan	consumption
Mary Lafferty	7		Md	May	orphan	consumption
Catherine Dunn	11		Md	Sep	orphan	consumption
Ann McNamee	15		unkn.	Aug	orphan	consumpton
Mary Luby	14		"	Apr	orphan	scrofula
John Patterson	16		Md	Mar		heart dis.
Matilda Wright	76	W	Conn.	Nov		old age
James H. Mullan	18		Md	Apr	architects App.	consumption
Daniel P. Hays	32		Md	Dec	lawyer	brain cong.
Elisa Tiffany	34		Md	Oct		lung dis.

144

MORTALITY SCHEDULE OF MARYLAND

persons who died during the year ending 1 June 1860

COUNTY city of Baltimore   DISTRICT 8th Ward

name	age	mar wid	birth place	mon. died	Occupation	cause of death
Mary Reynolds	21	M	Irel.	Sep		typhoid
Mary McAvory	16		Md	Aug		expolosion
Dennis McColgan	36	M	Md	Jan	storekeeper	pistol shot
John E. McDonald	3		Md	Nov		croup
Catherine Toner	46	W	Irel.	Nov		brain infla.
Henry McKernan	4		Md	Mar		cat.fever
John McKenna	66	M	Irel.	Jul	wheelright	consumption
James McGarrity	33	M	Md	Nov	porter	brain fever
Patrick Monahan	59	M	Irel.	Aug	laborer	sun stroke
John M. Dorsey	1mo		Md	Oct		throat dis.
William P. Vansant	3		Md	Jan		pneumonia
Margaret Griffan	72	W	Md	Sep		consumption
John Doft	28	M	Md	Oct	blacksmith	consumption
John Casey	87	W	Irel.	Feb		old age
Catherine A. Scanlon	6wks		Md	Mar		unknown
Thomas Maguire	25		Md	Jul	coachtrimmer	consumption
Mary Toner	76	W	Irel.	Apr		old age
Aloysius Hanlon	2		Md	May		unknown
Susan Upton	73	W	Md	Nov		heart dis.
Louisa Ash	22	M	Md	Jan		hysterics
Peter Hanley	40	M	Irel.	Jan	shoemaker	intemperance
Margaret McCubbin	60	M	Pa.	Sep		heart dis.
William Slagen	9mo		Md	Apr		teething
William Hollis Kellar	3		Md	Nov		measles
Harman Kellar	8mo		Md	Dec		measles
Stewart B Burke	17		Md	Sep	butchershop	typhoid
Gertrude Weaver	1		Md	Jun		teething
Hugh McCarthy	40		Irel.	Feb	laborer	unknown
Mary A. Ratigan	7		Md	Jan		typhoid
Alice Edmondson	44	M	Md	Aug	laborer	sun stroke
Milton N. Roberts	3		Md	Apr		accident
Henrietta Mitchell	11		Md	Sep		typhoid
Adeliade Woltbaker	68	M	Hanover	Dec		fall
John P. S. Huble	19		Md	Oct		shot
Laura J. Schuck	18		Md	Feb		brain abcess
11th Dist. County of Baltimore						
Joseph F. Jerman	30		Md	Apr	farmer	sudden
Nancy Jerman	28		Md	May		consumption
Ann Reynolds	65		Md	May		paulsey
Jacob Dimuth	69		Md	Apr	farmer	pnumonia
Mary Williams	90	W	Md	Mar		old age
Hetty Hale	5mo		Md	Aug		summer comp.
Casey Brookhart	68	W	Md	Jun		old age
Sarah Brenton	5		Md	Sep		whooping cough
Elijah Carman	52	M	Md	Nov		none
Lucretia Carman	24		Md	Mar		consumption
William Wonn	54	M	Md	Feb	farmer	consumption
Laura Preston	6		Md	Sep		head
Robert Cadden	22	M	Irel.	Jun	preacher	dropsey
Louis Byerley	32		Ger.	Feb		consumption
Louis Allen	48		Md	Aug		cilious
Moses Rich	45	M	Ger.	Mar		consumptoin

145

MORTALITY SCHEDULE OF MARYLAND

persons who died during the year ending 1 June 18<u>60</u>

COUNTY -Baltimore   DISTRICT 11th Dist.

name	age	mar wid	birth place	mon. died	Occupation	cause of death
Elizabeth Shanklin	83	W	Md	Aug	farmer	dropsey
Andrew Dolinger	64	M	Ger.	May	farmer	consumption
			12th Dist.			
Clemmen Lemmon	23	M	Md	Mar		liver comp.
Other French	29	M	Md	Mar	farmer	pleuricy
Ann Harryman	40		Md	Jun		consumption
Mary A. Miller	43		Md	Mar		consumption
Daniel Steever	81		Md	Jun	gentleman	old age
Ann Coleman	8mo		Md	Dec		cat.fever
August Dager	35		Ger.	Sep		typhoid
Edward Cleary	52	M	Irel.	Jun	farmer	appoplexy
Margaret Creamer	1mo		Md	Mar		brain fever
Margaret Martell	24	M	Ger	Jan		lung dis.
Joseph Baker	8		Md	Sep		accident
Charles Hartman	1mo		Md	Nov		cramps
Rachel Davies	43	M.	S.Wales	Sep		consumption
Sarah Evans	3		Md	Sep		consumption
John Davies	30	M	Wales	May	coppersmelter	consumption
Michael Wise	1		Md	Jul		head dis.
Joseph Malone	4mo		Md	Jul		head dis.
Georgeanna Graves	1		Md	Mar		head dis.
Augustus Adams	2		Md	May		consumption
Leonard Brown	22		Md	Feb		cronic
Henry Grubber	65	M	Ger.	Jan	laborer	cold
Columbus Leugen	11mo		Md	Sep		spine dis.
William Poland	1		Md	Jun		head dis.
Franklin Fenby	1mo		Md	Feb		whooping cough
Lewis Ouls	1		Md	May		croup
Agerty Krastell	5		Md	Oct		scarlet fever
James Tucker	76	W	Md	Oct	farmer	old age
Henry Sippley	5		Md	Feb		croup
Robert Fitch	76	W	Md	Nov	farmer	old age
Samuel McCuller	40	M	Md	Sep	farmer	consumption
Sophia Rosengarth	2		Md	May		fits
Charles Zane	3		Md	Nov		croup
Cerlean Aheart	1mo		Md	Nov		head dis.
Louis Frakenberg	42	M	Ger.	Feb	farmer	bil.pleuirisy
Mary Kaler	52	M	Ger.	Mar		consumption
Mary Spear	65	M	Md	Apr		consumption
Margaret Hoffstrider	2mo		Md	Mar		head dis.
Caroline Claggett	42	M	Md	Jun		heart dis.
Charlott Green	29	M	N.J.	Mar		unknown
Elizabeth Unick	5		Md	Sep		croup
Richard Wilson	45	M	Md	Jun	laborer	unknown
Harrison Thompson	25	M	Irel.	Feb	farmer	pnuemonia
Margaret Senson	1mo		Md	May		summer comp.
Ida Button	1		Md	Oct		croup
Gustavus Lusby	4		Md	Nov		scarlet fever
			13th District			
Adam Waltemyer	89		Pa.	May	magistrate	old age
Phillip Brane	6mo		Md	Feb		teething
Ida Randell	1mo		Md	Dec		scarlet fever

146

name	age	mar wid	birth place	mon. died	Occupation	cause of death
Emmanuel Wade	1		Md	Dec		scarlet fever
Mary Sutton	60	M	Eng.	Dec		consumption
Mary Sleisenger	2		Md	Jul		croup
Elizabeth Forkison	70		Md	Feb		old age
Allen Holtz	5		Md	Nov		scarlet fever
Thomas F. Grainger	1		Md	Jan		croup
Charles Mandelbaum	1		Md	Mar		measles
Charles Martin	1		Md	Jul		chol.infant.
Charles Satz	3mo		Md	Apr		consumption
Anna Santz	11mo		Md	Apr		fever
AugustaKeil	5mo		Md	May		fever
Phillip Eulon	65		Md	Nov	watchmaker	head disease
Andrew Bower	1mo		Md	May		head disease
John C. Brown	18		Md	Feb	watchmaker	consumption
Annie S. Wilson	83		Md	Jan		old age
Amelia DeMarre	26		Md	Dec		child bed
Bertha Rosentuik	1		Md	Jul		whooping cough
James Lange	66		Irel.	Jan		consumption
Isabella Younger	2mo		Md	Feb		whooping cough
Charles F.Reinter	2		Md	Dec		cough
George Jette Galb	2		Md	Aug		whooping cough
John G. Deabring	41		Oldenberg	Oct		consumption
Mary A. Deabring	2		Md	Jan		fever
John Waring	70		Bavaria	Sep	carpenter	accident
Annie C. Dalyrumple	7		Md	Nov		scarlet fever
William Gilder	6		Md	Jun		scarlet fever
James Wrvin	1		Md	Jun		whooping cough
Julia Kehune	9mo		Md	May		cold
Emma Black	11		Md	Jan		scarletfever
Ferdinand Masyner	15		Md	May	cigarmaker	drowned
Bridget Dougherty	43		Irel.	Jun		typhoid
Edward Schird	11mo		Md	Aug		summer compl.
George Wygart	81		Md	Dec	gentleman	stroke
Thomas Flame	45		Irel.	Jun		maniapotua
Caroline Schaumteffel	10mo		Md	Aug		summer comp.
Martin Butler	42		Irel.	Mar	stonecutter	consumption
James Galligher	75		Irel.	Nov		old age
Anna Johns	1		Irel.	Jul		summer comp.
George W. Eckert	43		Pa.	Jul	bookbinder	brain fever
Archabel Maloney	42		Md	May	carpenter	Rheumatism
Charles Simon	1		Md	May		measles
Luther Ratcliff	30		Md	Jan	farmer	consumption
Laura A. Ratcliff	4mo		Md	Jan		cold
Daniel Kaufman	64		Md	Apr	painter	old age
Henry J. Gervin	21		Md	Jul		scarlet fever
Elizabeth Mariner	59		Md	Feb		pneumonia
Henry March	3		Md	Mar		croup
Mary White	16		Md	Dec		consumption
George Hausenvald	5		Md	Oct		croup
Mary E. Fisher	25		Md	Jan		consumption
Charles R.Norrie	1mo		Md	Aug		fits
Gotleib Meyer	79		SaxeWiemar	Feb.		old age

147

MORTALITY SCHEDULE OF MARYLAND

persons who died during the year ending 1 June 1860

COUNTY BALTIMORE   DISTRICT 12th Ward

name	age	mar wid	birth place	mon. died	Occupation	cause of death
Christina North	11		HesseWiemar	Feb		burned
Laura Getty	22		Md	May		lung inflam.
Henry Schmetz	2		Md	Jan		scarlet fever
James McCormick	48		Irel.	Dec	tavernkeeper	pleuricy
David Carovalle	76		Eng.	Feb		ashma
Perry Harried	7mo		Md	Aug		whooping cough
Levi Gross	35		Md	Dec	waiter	consumption
Harriet Heiner	33		Md	Jun		stomach inflam.
Louisa Buck	9mo		Md	Jun		cramps
James McCluckarty	60		Md	Jan	miller	rheumatism
Julius Wiffirth	2		Md	Jan		fever
Uriah Johns	72		Md	Feb	cigarmaker	old age
Nelson B. Werm	17		Md	Jul		drowned
Julia Goade	1		Md .	Jan		head dis.
Samuel Howart	5mo		Md	Jun		dysentary
Adeline Barlow	50		Md	Dec		consumption
Sarah Jones	34		Md	Sep		typhoid
Mary Wambler	40		Md	Aug		child bed
William Eastman	11		Md	Mar		accident
Elizabeth Henry	42		Md	Jan		consumption
Elizabeth C. Wilson	5mo		Md	Feb		fever
John Schiefer	2		Md	Feb		head disease
Mary C. Lambert	61		Md	Feb		consumption
William Goade	4da		Md	Oct		head disease
Bernart Landstreet	28		Md	Mar	clerk	consumption
Robert Pritt	1		Md	Aug		whooping cough
Sarah Paterson	8		Md	Jan		fever
Rosana Glinger	1		Md	Sep		consumption
Daniel Rockensberg	51		HesseDarmstadt		shoemaker	consumption(d.Ja
Emma Hunt	7mo		Md	Apr		fever
William Dorsey	3		Md	Jan		burnt
Alexander Valentine	4mo		Md	Jan		spasms
Margaret Washington	16		Md	Apr		consumption
Jacob Deckart	3		Md	Feb		consumption
Matilda Fisher	51		Md	Jan	washerwoman	lungs
Anna R. Thomas	29		Md	Jul		consumption
Martha LeSounard	16		Md	Oct		consumption
Mary Auriels	5		Md	Jul		consumption
William H. Nevines	16		Md	Nov		consumption
Rofean Johns	77		Md	Aug	farmer	old age
David James	33		Md	Nov	laborer	head disease
Charles H. Harvey	7mo		Md	Aug		cholera
William McCullison	1		Md	Jul		cholera
Stephen Black	33		N.Y.	Nov	clerk	accident
George Flienblin	21		D.C.	Mar		pneumonia
Bernard Lowenkamp	4mo		Md	Nov		head disease
Thomas H. Barret	1		Md	Aug		water on brain
Barbara Taylor	86		Md	Dec		old age
Amelia Farman	3		Md	Jul		brain disease
John B. Sherrity	5		D.C.	Jan		croup
Kruse Zimmerman	9mo		Md	Jan		brain dis.
James Wilson	72		Scot.	May	cook	heart dis.

148

MORTALITY SCHEDULE OF MARYLAND

persons who died during the year ending 1 June 1860

COUNTY BALTIMORE   DISTRICT 12th Ward

name	age	mar wid	birth place	mon. died	Occupation	cause of death
Mary Waliston	25		Md	Jun		consumption
Albert L. Johnson	59		Md	Mar	manufact.	pneumonia
David Houck	23		Md	Jan		accident
Margaret Holliday	50	M	Md	Dec		dropsy
Ella Roysten	2		Md.	Jun		ftis
Anna Beatty	3		Md	Jun		typhoid
Eliza Lange	1		Md	Jun		lung dis.
William T. Riddler	1mo		Md	May		unknown
Thomas McGuire	50	M	Irel.	Aug		consumption
Lewis Bower	1		Md	May		cat.fever
			14th Ward			
Lewis Wise	64	M	Baden	Feb	butcher	paralitic
Mary Field	55	M	Mass.	Mar		consumption
John Drost	3		Md	Mar		croup
Mary Waugh	52	W	Va.	Dec		consumption
Phelia Slack	45	M	Md	Dec		dyspepsia
George Webster	1		Md	Feb		whooping cough
Frederick Rogers	46		Mass	Jan	printer	kidney affect.
Anna E. Rawlings	70	W	Md	Mar		general deb.
Jesse Lippencott	37		Md	Nov	merchant	none
James Scholfield	19		Eng.	Jul	printer	bowel inflam.
Edwin Jenkins	4		Md	Jan		scarl t fever
William Fisher	14		Md	Apr		unknown
Joseph Long	10mo		Md	Apr		summer comp.
Anna M. Lewis	62	W	Md	Jul		spine dis.
Sallie Kahler	5		Mm	Apr		coup
Charles Richards	6mo		Md	Jul		dysentary
John Ryan	8mo		Md	Mar		brain dis.
Frank Kornman	1		Md	Jul		cold
Christian Kornman	26	M	Bavaria	Aug		typhoid
Henry Kornman	20		Md	Sep		typhoid
Theodore Cummer	1mo		Md	Jan		unknown
Caroline Koke	11mo		Md	May		Cat.fever
Henry Dietrich	82	W	HesseDarm.	Oct		old age
Charles S. Geddes	2		Md	Aug		bowel infl.
John F. Mullin	4mo		Md	Jan		unknown
Rebecca Cook	50	W	Md	Jan		dropsy
Mary Crockett	9mo		Md	Apr		measles
Bridget Madden	30	M	Irel.	Oct		child bed
Jacob Summer	79	W	Pa.	Apr	coachmaker	paralitic
Elizabeth Hopkinson	35	M	Md	Mar		heart dis.
Ann L. Ober	12		Md	Apr		bowel inflam.
Mary E. Motler	29	M	N.J.	Jan		consumption
Anna R. Williams	42	M	Va.	Jan		typhoid
Thomas Adams	3		Md	Jan		measles
			15th Ward			
Wilhemena Lanheim	7mo		Md	May		cat.fe ver
Susan Bowen	60		Pa.	Jul		jaundice
Mary Byer	3mo		Md	Mar		disentary
William B. Sawner	4		Md	Jan		scarlet fever
Hugh O'Neill	59		Irel.	Nov	huckster	lung inflam.
Margaret Schafer	72		Prussia	Jan		paralitic

149

MORTALITY SCHEDULE OF MARYLAND

persons who died during the year ending 1 June 1860

COUNTY BALTIMORE   DISTRICT 15th Ward

name	age	mar wid	birth place	mon. died	Occupation	cause of death
Frank Troll	41		Prussia	Jan	cabinet maker	liver dis.
Henrietta Rosenthall	10		Md	Sep		scarlet fever
Edward Rosenthall	6		Md	Sep		scarlet fever
Isabella Mitchell	1		Md	Jan		spinal dis.
Anna Nichols	6		Ger.	Sep		bilious fever
Bodd Smith	18		Md	Sep		consumption
Elizabeth Steiner	26		Md	Jul		consumption
Thomas Diggs	33		Va.	Apr	seaman	bil.fever
William B. Hodges	2		Md	Oct		measles
Sarah T. Wooters	2mo		Md	Jul		cholera
William D. Stevens	52		Md	Jul		consumption
Joseph Hick	1		Md	.Sep		croup
William Willett	20		Md	Mar	seaman	consumption
Samuel Wilson	38		Md	Feb	seaman	consumption
Mathew Reilly	43		Irel.	Dec	laborer	consumption
Albert Allen	48		N.J.	Jan	shoemaker	consumption
Conrad Reid	50		Ger.	Apr	locksmith	dropsey
Lydia G. Pumphry	6mo		Md	Aug		brain fever
Charles Hammershar	1		Md	Apr		burned
Elizabeth Schopp	2		Md	Apr		typhoid
Amelia Stone	1		Md	Aug		summer comp.
Matilda Lockerman	15		Md	Sep		dysentary
John H. Sewell	2		Md	Jul		brain fever
Emma K.Applegard	2		Md	May		spasms
Ann Thomas	6		Md	Feb		pleurisy
Amanda Butts	5		Md	Apr		scarlet fever
Mary Jenkins	5		Md	Dec		burned
Anna Pennington	5mo		Md	Jul		cholera
Mary Stone	43		Ger.	Aug		consumption
Fred Mettsolem	4		Md	Aug		cholera
Mary Lord	27		Md	Jan		sore throat
James Skinner	5mo		Md	Aug		cholera
John H. Travers	40		Md	Oct	merchant	consumption
Mary V.Berry	25	M	Md	Nov.		dropsey
Benjamin Berry	8		Md	Apr		scarlet fever
Julia Freelocker	7mo		Md	Jan		scarlet fever
John Union	19		Md	Oct		bilious
Margaret Wier	73	W	Pa	Feb		none
Alexander D. Reese	18		Md	Oct		brain fever
George Kilgore	24		Eng	Dec		consumption
William Woodside	60		Eng.	Jul	clerk	bronkitus
Maggie R. Gorgia	6mo		Md	May		croup
John Brooks	32		Md	Jun	machanic	consumption
Thomas Wilson	1		Md	Mar		brain fever
Georgana Sumall	1mo		Md	Sep		jaundice
Mary Fisher	2mo		Md	Apr		cold
John Thomas	24		Md	Jan	currier	disentary
James Dorsey	9		Md	Sep		rhumatism
Adam Feltner	22		Ger.	Dec	baker	consumption
James Morton	7		Md	Jun		scarlet fever
Hannah Casey	16		Pa.	Sep		brain dis.
James Ferlong	15		Md	Aug		Ansiputa?

150

MORTALITY SCHEDULE OF MARYLAND

persons who died during the year ending 1 June 1860

COUNTY BALTIMORE   DISTRICT -15th Ward

name	age	mar wid	birth place	mon. died	Occupation	cause of death
Mary E. Smith	20		Md	Jul		dispessia
Joseph Keyser	56		Ger.	May	grocer	liver dis.
Edward Umpton	31		Ger.	Sep	clerk	bowel cong.
Martha Stevens	17		Md	May		cramp colia
Louisa Carr	28		Md	Apr		consumption
Harriett Amey	15		Md	May		dropsy
Henry Storm	13		Md	Nov		liver comp.
Adam B.Kylis	27		Md	Nov	merchant	murdered
Sarah V. Cote	16		Md	Jul		sore throat
			16th Ward			
William Rode	2mo		Md	Dec		spasms
Annie Baker	11md		Md	Jul		summer comp.
Helen Barlige	2mo		Md	Oct		brainfever
Anna Pistol	8mo		Md	Jul		summer comp.
Mary Bell	62	M	Irel.	May		consumption
SamuelSchock	7mo		Md	Jul		thrush
Harriet Ferry	17		Va.	Aug	embroiderer	consumption
John Gallagher	40	M	Irel.	May	laborer	cancer
George Cummins	42		Md	Jul	bricklayer	heart dis.
Charloette Cummins	66	W	Md	Sep		consumption
Mary McGlaughlin	37	M	Irel.	May		child bed
Mary Forrest	1		Md	Jun		stroke
Harmon Wheeler	23		Md	Sep	paperstainer	consumption
Julia Legue	26	M	Md	Aug		consumption
Allen Taylor	32	M	Irel.	Dec	tinner	consumption
Mary Deise	3		Md	Jun		scarlet fever
Christian Bukman	6		Md	Sep		croup
John Hofstider	3		Md	May		summer compl.
Hannah Horn	35		Md	Oct		heart dis.
Mary Horn	6mo		Md	Dec		scarlet fever
Jacob Weller	7mo		Md	Jul		whooping cough
John Weller	4		Md	Jan		typhoid
Emma Redgrave	3		Md	Sep		scarlet fever
Frederick Stenwitz	64		Bavaria	Jun	baker	dropsy
Susanna Jones	16		Md	Aug		dysentary
Flora Rickets	21		D.C.	Apr		consumption
Margaret Marston	22	M	Md	Jul		child bed
Robert Merriman	2		Md	Jun		whooping cough
Mary Boehl	1mo		Md	Sep		unknown
Catherine Ring	71	W	Ger.	Sep		tumor
Elizabeth Jeys?	63	W	Md	Apr		consumption
George Recter	45		Md	Jul	sailor	yellow fever
James Toner	42		Md	Feb	clerk	consumption
Catharine Gross	4mo		Md	Jun		summer comp
Emma Rea	5mo		Md	Jun		head dis.
Harriett Sprigg	62		Md	Jun		cancer
George Butler	35	M	D.C.	Mar	carpenter	consumption
Susan Gorsuch	45	M	Md	Mar		stroke
Roda Claminge	85	W	Md	Jun		old age
George Hedrick	1		Md	Jun		summer compl.
John Reiss	79		Ger.	Mar		stroke
John Lawrence	2		Md	Apr		measles
Elizabeth Vickers	6mo		Md	Jun		bowel inflam.

151

name	age	mar wid	birth place	mon. died	Occupation	cause of death
Anna Perrin	2		Md	May		whooping cough
Edwin Bowers	6		Md	Apr		bowel inflam.
William Horris	80		Eng.	Jun		stroke
Susanna High	50		Md	Apr		consumption
Eliza Bines	20		Md	Apr		brain fever
Robert Strobel	3mo		Md	Apr		lung inflam.
Mary McClung	1		Md	Jun		brain cong.
John McGraw	11		Pa.	Dec		consumption
Ida Romney	1		Md	Apr		measles
Mary Leipe	19		Md	Jan		typhoid
Hestele High	1		Md	Apr		brain dis.
Ellen Watkins	3		Md	Sep		croup
Florence Bryan	1		Md	Feb		croup
John Smith	61		Md	Mar	baker	consumption
Harriett Ashman	4		Md	Dec		bowel inflam.
John Chamberlain	20		Md	Apr	shoemaker	consumption
John Able	1		Md	Aug		brain fever
Chrostiopher Raport	4		Md	Dec		consumption
George Ambolt	45	M	Ger.	Jan	carter	appoplexy
Emily Walage	2mo		Md	Mar		unknown
George Trumbor	22		Md	Feb	balcksmith	consumption
Charles Sarnoski	1		Md	Jun		dysentary
Catherine Owens	3		Md	Sep		scarlet fever
Jacob Adams	5		Md	Aug		scarlet fever
Mary Ayett	4mo		Md	Feb		spasms
Henry C. Rich	11mo		Md	Jul		pneumonia
Louisa Rushmeyer	3		Md	Feb		consumption
Emma Disney	1		Md	Feb		whooping cough
Leonard Disney	29		Md	Apr	R.R.Enginer	consumption
Francis Dunn	46		N.Y.	Jun	produce	abcess liver
Hugh Ruddy	2		Va.	Jul		scarlet fever
Caroline Enick	1		Md	Jul		head inflam.
William Wortlemeyer	1		Md	Aug		brain fever
Mary E. Brandy	9mo		Md	Jun		cholic infan.
Alexander Hollingshead	36		Md	Nov	papermanuf.	consumption
Elizabeth Faunchud	34		Ger.	Jul		water on chest
Eliza Meeks	10mo		Md	Aug		croup
Samuel Rosenburg	36		Md	Jul	brushmaker	unknown
Elijah Allen	79		Md	Jun	cooper	paralysis
Hiram Woods	4		Md	Aug		scarlet fever
Mary Miller	4		Md	Aug		scarlet fever
William Martin	11		Md	Mar		pleuricy
Shipley Liston	69		Md	Mar	carpenter	pneumonia
Caroline Bernard	48		Hanover	Jul		consumption
James White	2		Md	Aug		summer comp.
George Lloyd	1mo		Md	Mar		brain dis.
John Fraiser	75		Scot.	Jan	merchant	ruptured vessel
Georgana Whaly	2		Md	Sep		croup
Sarah Sanks	10mo		Md	May		teething
McHenry Bell	48		Md	Mar	engineer	head disease
George Bell	1		Md	Jan		catarrah
Mary Hoffman	71		Ger..	Feb		old age

152

name	age	mar wid	birth place	mon. died	Occupation	cause of death
Ellenor Erwin	8		Md	Dec		throat inflam.
John W. Riley	5		Md	Dec		croup
William D. Grubb	4		Md	Apr		heart dis.
Louisa Madden	18		Md	Jan		consumption
William Cecil	85		Md	Jun	farmer	stroke
Rebecca Dlessner	65		Pa.	Jun		old age
Francis Barker	79		Md	Jan		pneumonia
Jacob Washerman	11mo		Md	Sep		spasms
			17th Ward			
Thos. Shad	40	M	Ger.	May		consumption
Christian Winder	5		Md	Jul		rickets
Mary Barlage	1mo		Md	Oct		liver dis.
John Balstrum	3		Boston	Dec		scarlet fever
Catherine Balstrum	2		Boston	Dec		scarlet fever
Peter Hartman	4mo		Md	Aug		dysentary
Harman Sax	25		Ger.	Dec	cigarmaker	drowned
Louise Frank	24	M	Ger.	Dec		sonsumption
George Long	45	M	Md	Sep	painter	heart
Frederick Gunther	9mo		Md	May		teething
Levin Craig	1mo		Md	Aug		ericaplisis
M.Eichlager(male)	72	M	Ger.	Jun	tailor	consumption
Thomas Alworth	35		Va.	May	laborer	consumption
Eliza Grimm	1mo		Md	Jul		croup
Mary Jackson	51		Va.	Apr		consumption
James Burgan	33	M	Pittsburg	Jul	sterotype	inflamation
Jennetta Parsons	44	W	Jersey	Apr		consumption
Stephen Wright	23	M	N.Y.	Feb		consumption
Henry Daneker?	52	M	Md	Oct	tinner	fever
Joseph Wyatt	38	M	Va.	Dec	sailmaker	consumption
Ann Perry	47	W	Md	Jan		consumption
Thomas Perry	37	M	Md	Jan	engineer	drowned
Louis Krietz	54	M	Ger.	May	glassblower	heart dis
Ada Harris	9mo		Md	Feb		cold
Wlliam Fisher	18		Md	Sep	aprentice	heart dis.
William Parker	9		Md	Mar		measles
James Dudley	22		Md	Jan		consumption
Mary A. Fisher	23	M	Md	Feb		lung dis.
Elizabeth Brien	14		Md	Sep		consumption
John Ruark	2		Md	Jul		dysentary
Samuel Hawkins	28	M	Md	Aug		consumption
Cyrus Cochran	59	M	Md	Apr	laborer	consumption
Elizabeth Ward	82	W	Md	Apr		spine dis.
Henry Briscoe	4mo		Md	Jul		fits
Thomas Polan	30	M	Md	Nov	tailor	drowned
Susan Mae	27	M	Md	Aug	seamstress	liver comp.
Joseph Lilley	1		Md	Apr		measles
Louiza Fowler	55	M	Md	Jun		pleurisy
Frederick Brademeyer	33	M	Ger.	Jun	carpenter	unknown
Dorothy Filchmer	46	M	Ger.	Nov		unknown
Frederick Eckett	1		Md	Jul		unknown
Peter Lidecker	42	M	Ger.	Aug	painter	fever
Minerva Lukes	1		Md	Feb		teething
Mary Graham	28	M	Md	Oct		fever

persons who died during the year ending 1 June 1860

COUNTY BALTIMORE   DISTRICT -17th Ward (faded pages)

name	age	mar wid	birth place	mon. died	Occupation	cause of death
Louisa Fowler	54	M	Md	Jun		cholera
James Labaran	15		Md	Sep		typhoid
Sarah Ellis	57	M	Irel.	Jul		dropsy
William Merine	21	M	Md	Sep	sailor	yellow fever
Malkier Dixon	26		Va.	May	sailor	typhoid
Joseph Sharp	10mo		Md	Aug		teething
James Turner	33	M	Md	Jan	laborer	unknown
Samuel Granger	12		Md	Oct		typhoid
Isaac Meekins	49	M	Md	Feb	sailor	typhoid
Catherine Harman	46	M	Ger.	Mar		dropsy
Conrad Everhart	56	M	Pa.	Mar	huckster	consumption
Ellen Galager	3		Md	Jan		burnt
Ellin Maher	50	W	Irel.	Mar		pleurisy
Conrad Steitz	1mo		Md	Jun		dysentary
Rosella Rickswith?	47	M	Md	Nov		liver compl.
Charlotte Jacobs	19		Md	May	seamstress	consumption
Anthony Henning	23		Ger.	Jul	fisherman	drowned
John Behert	24		Ger.	Oct	shoemaker	liver dis.
Sarah Mathews	2		Md	Jan		consumption
Elizabeth Webster	2		Md	Jun		cat.fever
			18th Ward			
Gertrude Rowland	10mo		Md	Jul		cholera.
William Hughes	2		Md	Jul		teething
John Cloffenger	24		Md	May	RR Engineer	killed RR
Richard Smith	11mo		Md	Jan		pneumonia
Winfield Nace	3		Md	Feb		typhoid
Edward McKinney	35	M	Ire.	Aug	storekeeper	unknown
Joseph Pryor	74	W	R.I.	Apr	cooper	dyspepsia
Richard Pilson	3		Md	Nov		scarlet fever
Thomas Mercer	7		Md	Jan		scarlet fever
Patrick Hibbard	2		Md	Dec		unknown
Ellen Dee	23		Ire.	Jul	dressmaker	consumption
Ann Reisinger	4mo		Md	Jun		whooping cough
John Bathan	21		Md	Mar	RR Engineer	heart dis.
George Moore	14		Md	Feb		spine
Ann Albrecht	8		Md	Aug		whooping cough
Ann Grubell	11mo		Md	Nov		unknown
William Quinn	6		Md	Jul		scarlet fever
Gassaway James	2		Md	Feb		pneumonia
Edward Groomes	2		Md	Jul		cholera infan.
Albert Bathart	10		Md	May		brain fever
Conrad Willig	41	M	Hessedarm.	May	laborer	drowned
Henry Farry	1		Md	Jul		croup
John Evans	9		Md	Aug		croup
Augustus Roock	2		Md	Dec		unknown
Andrew Winter	2		Md	apr		measles
Sophia Arnold	6mo		Md	Mar		croup
Catherine Deitrick	38	M	HesseDarm.	Jan		heart dis.
Mary Dixon	17		Md	Mar		spine dis.
Charles Harker	8mo		Md	Mar		whooping cough
Bridget Bridges	14		Irel.	Dec		typhoid
Lucy Hart	9mo		Md	Aug		typhoid
William Richards	1mo		Md	Nov		unknown

name	age	mar wid	birth place	mon. died	Occupation	cause of death
Ann McKenly	62	W	Ire.	Mar		consumption
Ann Hoffenton	4mo		Md	Oct		cat.fever
Charles Heiser	26	M	Saxony	Aug	butcher	dysentary
Thomas Evans	7		Md	Aug		killed
Mary Head	5		Md	Feb		croup
Ruth Linthicum	31	M	Md	Jan		consumption
Ellenosa Guest	26	M	Md	Mar		child birth
Mary McMeachen	2		Md	Apr		whooping cough
Sarah Sockington	25		Irel.	Mar		lung inflam.
Thomas Talafero	47	M	Md	Oct		stomach cong.
Charles Norris	24		Va.	Jun	merchant	heart dis.
Sarah Armisdon	22		Mass.	Jun		consumption
Emily Andrews	15		Md	Jan		consumption
Edwin Humphries	5		Md	Feb		scarlet fever
John w. Stigars	5		Md	Nov		pneumonia
Prigant? Raabe	37	M	Hessecassel	Mar.	Blacksmith	eresyplis
Ida Kunnard	3		Md	Apr		whooping cough
Emily Gorman	3mo		Md	Jan		pneumonia
Isabella Moore	27		Md	Apr		consumption
Mary Yieldhall	66	W	Md	Nov		lung cong.
Joseph J. Carey	2		Md	Dec		croup
Eliza Bouldin	61	W	Md	Mar		liver compl.
John Arthur	56	M	Irel.	May	laborer	consumption
Laura Wilkinson	2		Md	Jul		water on brain
Marget Richards	2		Md	Oct		scarlet fever
Mary H. Wolf	2		Md	Jan		croup
Grace Mitchell	2		Md	Aug		water on brain
Holland Cook	40	M	Md	Apr	cabinet maker	paralysis
Alexander Reed	41	M	Scot.	Oct	trader	heart dis.
Getron Lepick	30	M	Md	Dec	physician	consumption
Marget Bain	18		Va.	Sep		consumption
Mary E. Shippard	15		Md	Sep		consumption
Thomas Thompson	1mo		Md	Dec		unknown
Frank Towner	12		N.Y.	May		typhoid
George W.Phillips	4mo		Md	Jul		summer comp.
Andw.J.Richards	47		Md	Dec		consumption
Agnes Woodward	1		Md	Jan		heart dis.
Cora Lewis	5		Md	May		gastric fever
Elizabeth Townsend	40	M	Md	Apr		typhoid
Jonathan Parker	67		N.J.	Jul		paralysis
Alfred Crawford	25		Md	Nov	RRConductor	killed on RR
George H. Hall	48		Md	Aug	cooper	lightning
William L. Hall	20		Md		cooper	lightning
Robert Gleason	1		Md	Jul		summer comp.
Ann Grist	28		Md	Jul		drowned
Ida Grist	10		Md	Jul		drowned
Dennis Vaughn	8mo		Md	Aug		teething
Elizabeth White	34	W	Md	Jul		cancer
Louisa Shroft	20		Md	Nov		consumption
James Lang	28	M	Md	Dec	shoemaker	spine dis.
William Moffitt	8		Md	Nov		scarlet fever
Michael Weigert	42	M	Irel.	Feb	drayman	pneumonia
Mary J. Pabst	43	M	Md	Feb		consumption

MORTALITY SCHEDULE OF MARYLAND

persons who died during the year ending 1 June 18<u>60</u>

COUNTY BALTIMORE   DISTRICT 18th Ward

name	age	mar wid	birth place	mon. died	Occupation	cause of death
William G. Freeberger	12		Md	Jan		bil.cholic
John Ramsey	6mo		Md	Aug		summer comp.
Kate King	1mo		Md	Mar		cat.fever
Michael Ridgely	67	M	Md	Jan	chairmaker	dropsey
Thomas A. Riggs	13		Md	Jul		drowned
Henny Tickner	2		Md	Jul		cholera.Infan.
John Myers	1		Md	May		summer comp.
Thomas Reif	2		Md	Mar		croup
John T. Caby	2		Md	Jul		summer comp.
Mary Russell	19		Md	Jul		consumption
Dora Farmer	2		Md	Jul		measles
Connie Bell	2mo		Md	Jul		consumption
David Emmick	53		Md	Jul	shoemaker	kidney dis.
Mary Fisher	27		Md	Jan		consumption
Elizabeth Logan	63		Md	Jul		typhoid
George Robinson	9		Md	Apr		measles
Mary Deiter	2		Md	May		summer comp.
William Bier	10mo		Md	May		summer comp.
James H. Gorman	4		Md	Jul		scarlet fever
John HHenry	24		Md	Feb	huckster	consumption
Kate Duffy	2		Md	May		measles
Samuel Downey	1		Md	Dec		spasms
James McGee	42		Irel.	Aug	shoemaker	apoplexy
Arabelle Lepson	3mo		Md	Mar		heart dis.
Ellen Hartigan	3		Md	Jan		croup
Josephine Winter	7		Md	Jan		typhoid
Robert Smily	85	W	Irel.	Feb		old age
Ambrose Banks	2		Md	Jul		teething
Robert N. Reed	43	M	Va.	Jun	jeweler	kidney dis.
James H. Martin	38	M	Md	Feb	clerk	prneumonia
Charles Brown	23	M	Md	Oct	blacksmith	typhoid
Susan Lee	48	W	Md	Jun		typhoid
Ann Lyman	60	M	Eng.	Jun		burnt
Amos Stocklock	39		Eng.	Feb	upholster	consumption
Augustus Bowersock	50	M	Md	Jul	carpenter	consumption
Charles Byerson	41	M	Md	Apr	laborer	kneumonia
Nelson Naillor	34	M	Md	Nov	carpenter	bowel conges.
Sarah Guiton	6		Md	Aug		croup
Aney McCay	4mo		Md	Jan		bowel inflam.
Alice Graham	3		Md	Dec		throat inflam.
Henry Bassard	50	M	Md	Jun		paralysis
Samuel Church	35	M	Md	Mar	RREngineer	killed on RR
Martha Tipton	1		Md	Sep		thrush
Emily Phillips	1mo		Md	May		croup
Patrick Moore	30	M	Irel.	Oct	laborer	consumption
Sarah Stockdale	63	W	Pa.	Jun		dropsy
Edward Sturgeon	24		Md	Apr	mariner	consumption
Julia Stein	2		Md	May		brain fever
Joseph Walter	3		Md	Jul		whooping cough
Kate Galleger	1		Md	Apr		whooping cough
Marthay Hobins	4		Md	Mar		measles
Joseph Wilson	55	M	Md	Apr	mariner	RR accident

156

persons who died during the year ending 1 June 1860

COUNTY BALTIMORE   DISTRICT 18th Ward

name	age	mar wid	birth place	mon. died	Occupation	cause of death
George Maris	84	M	Pa.	Nov	druggist	debility
Mary Maris	78	W	Md	May		consumption
David Dietrow	8mo		Md	Jun		summer comp.
Mary Winkler	1		Md	Jun		summer comp.
John E. Rupp	6mo		Md	Jan		lung cong.
Murphy Dean	10mo		Md	Aug		whooping cough
William Masly	2mo		Md	Jul		whooping cough
			19th Ward			
Mary McKeever	28	W	Md	Jan		consumption
George Guistchler	25	M	Prussia	Aug		drowned
Susan Clark	64	W	Md	Nov		sudden
Laura Smith	9mo		Md	Sep		teething
Catherine Rupp	64	W	Saxony	Sep		consumption
Charlotte Clemmens	94	W	Md	Dec		old age
John Fritz	39	M	Wirtemb.	Nov	laborer	fits
Josephine Fritz	6		Md	Nov		brain fever
John Stewart	2		Md	Jul		brain fever
Agnes Menick	36	M	Md	Dec		consumption
George Myers	10mo		Md	Jan		bowel infl.
Edward Mercer	31		Md	Mar	baker	RR accident
William Miller	5mo		Md	Oct		head dis.
James Stump	3		Md	Aug		summer comp.
Christiana Simpson	7mo		Md	Aug		scarlet fever
William Adley	40	M	Md	Dec		heart dis.
Julia Cullison	58	M	Md	Dec		heart dis.
Mary Washington	11		Md	Feb		consumption
William Beard	36		Md	Feb	huckster	heart dis.
Andrew Hook	22		Md	Sep	painter	spasms
Margaret Heuisler	10		Md	Dec		typhoid
Lidia Spence	66	W	Md	Dec		consumption
Catherine Wambrook	16		Md	Apr		measles
James Ridgley	8mo		Md	Aug		brain fever
Thomas Hollis	18		Md	May		scrofula
Frank Eichelberger	2mo		Md	May		measles
Gorden Phelps	75	W	Mass.	Oct	shoemaker	pneumonia
Edward Lawrence	2mo		Md	Jan		brain cong.
Jeremiah Henson	8mo		Md	Oct		consumption
Estasia Hood	19		Md	Aug		typhoid
Mary Holmes	6		Md	Mar		whooping cough
George Gasgay	1mo		Md	Mar		spasms
Thomas Deene	2		Md	Mar		disentary
Sophia Baker	2		Md	Apr		cramps
John Estella	38		Md	Feb	butcher	consumption
Mary Gettis	1		Md	Jan		brain infl.
Peter Tindell	30	M	Md	Feb	paperhanger	typhoid
Ann Emick	9		Md	Nov		cramps
Gilbert Casard	3		Md	Jan		measles
Kate Arther	2mo		Md	Mar		cramp
Sophia Appleton	75	W	Mass	Jan		old age
Edward Harkson	13		Eng.	Oct		RR accident

MORTALITY SCHEDULE OF MARYLAND

persons who died during the year ending 1 June 1860

COUNTY BALTIMORE   DISTRICT 19th Ward

name	age	mar wid	birth place	mon. died	Occupation	cause of death
Eugene Hooper	2		Md	Jul		brain cong.
Susan Watts	3		Md	Jul		cramps
Americus Marshall	13		Md	Mar		brain fever
Charlotte Lilly	12		Md	May		consumption
John Loman	5		Md	Aug		consumption
Frank McClenan	3mo		Md	Mar		pneumonia
David Summers	11mo		Md	Aug		pneumonia
John Hall	2		Md	Dec		inflam.Rheumat.
Caroline Miller	2		Md	Dec		brain cong.
Charles Shilling	55		Saxony	Apr	laborer	brain infl.
George Paxton	31		S.C.	Jun		typhoid
Jackson Gallagher	27		Md	Sep		consumption
John Sennet	3mo		Md	Jun		typhoid
Auther Moore	2		Md	Apr		measles
Joseph Hamilton	33	M	Md	Sep	blacksmith	heart dis.
Eliza Lee	20	M	Irel.	Apr		consumption
Rebecca Thomas	26	M	Md	Apr		consumption
Levi Thomas	1		Md	Sep		croup
Cornelia Richards	11mo		Md	Aug		pneumonia
Charles Duncan	1mo		Md	Mar		unknown
Frederick Brawen	9mo		Md	Aug		teething
John Long	62	M	Baden	Jan	laboerer	heart dis.
Harriet Plummer	54	M	Md	Jan		consumption
Mary Blair	2mo		Md	Jun		milk crust
Ann Vance	2		Md	Jun		croup
Septimus Shippley	4		Md	Jan		water on brain
Charles Turner	66	M	Md	Mar	bricklayer	dropsey
George Downing	26		Md	Nov	patrenmaker	consumption
James McGowen	1		Md	Aug		summer comp.
Elizabeth Ruark	48	M	Md	Mar		pneumonia
Mary Cheneworth	42	M	Md	Mar		cancer
Mary Cheneworth	5mo		Md	May		unknown
John Waller	1mo		Md	Dec		spasms
Michael Skeham	6mo		Md	Sep		gastric fever
Mary Shippley	4		Md	Dec		fever
Caroline Klunk	2		Md	Apr		brain infalm.
Francis Stinelean	2		Md	Apr		measles
Mary Eckart	1		Md	Feb		whooping cough
Peter Noting	10mo		Md	Jan		cramps
Anna Matthews	11mo		Md	Jul		teething
William Houser	6mo		Md	Nov		eresiphilas
William Sperry	56		Va.	Feb	merchant	consumption
Eugene Peacock	2		Md	Jul		consumption
John Leas	4		Md	Jul		lockjaw
Bridget Dolan	80	W	Irel.	Oct		old age
John Bummer	8		Md	May		measles
Emily Deer	9		Md	Jan		scarlet fever
Catherine Hemell	82	W	Ger.	Oct		old age
Hannah Rudolph	2		Md	Aug		summer comp.
Elizabeth Romosher	10mo		Md	Jul		consumption
John Nantz	52	M	HesseDarm.	Aug	stonecutter	intemperance
Eliza Wheeler	1		Md	Jan		spasms
Emma Robison	2		Md	Nov		measles

158

MORTALITY SCHEDULE OF MARYLAND

persons who died during the year ending 1 June 1860

COUNTY BALTIMORE   DISTRICT 19th Ward

name	age	mar wid	birth place	mon. died	Occupation	cause of death
Julia Jenett	3		Md	Feb		scrofula
William Clark	40		Md	May	cigarmaker	consumption
Frederick Dearing	11		Md	Oct		accident
Lorence Hobbs	22	M	Md	Mar	cardriver	typhoid
Rose Robison	3mo		Md	Jan		spasms
Alfred McCauley	4		Md	Dec		measles
Jane Roy	18		Md	Jan		heart dis.
Margaret Patterson	1		Md	Sep		summer comp.
Margaret Brill	6		Md	Aug		rheumatism
Sarah Connelly	1		Md	Aug		dropsy
Henry Turner	3		Md	Jan		croup
Kate Krislipp	8mo		Md	Jun		abcess
Martha Keach	68	M	Md	May		pneumonia
Thomas McCork	2		Md	Dec		scarlet fever
Luther Leake	2		Md	May		dropsy
Victoria Bandell	8		Md	Jan		asthma
Elizabeth Armitage	36		Md	Jan	vestmaker	consumption
John Geese	2		Md	Mar		croup
Anna Hogle	2		Md	Mar		consumption
Rebecca Sheets	25	M	Md	Mar		consumption
Mary Osburn	4		Md	Apr		croup
Caroline Shultz	2		Md	Aug		unknown
Jacob Lutz	1		Md	Aug		measles
Lewis Richards	1		Md	Feb		consumption
John Diager	1		Md	Jun		croup
James Johnson	19		Md	Nov	bricklayer	shot at election
Mary Carl	33	M	Bavaria	May		dropsey
Sarah McGall	5mo		Md	May		kator fever
Theresia Burke	18		Irel.	Jun	dressmaker	consumption
Eliza Danehart	2		Md	May		measles
Laura Higgans	1		Md	Aug		consumption
Mary Benson	2		Md	Aug		pneumonia
Lewis Smeltz	6		Md	Dec		lung inflam.
Jane Scott	41	M	Irel.	Oct		consumption
William Lane	4mo		Md	Sep		bowel inflam.
Thomas Matthews	30	M	Md	Feb	painter	consumption
Samuel Linah	72	M	Pa.	Jun	Huckster	disentary
Abraham Linah	41		Pa.	Apr	butcher	dropsy
Barbara Spunir	21	M	Md	Apr		consumption
George Spilman	1		Md	Jul		measles
Sarah Roten	36	M	Md	Jun	shoebinder	childbirth
William Legare	38	M	Md	Mar	machinist	consumption
Elizabeth Justice	41	M	Md	Jan		consumption
Alverta Ray	38	M	Md	May		consumption
Fred Morehart	64	W	Wutemb.	May	laborer	weakness
George Gordshell	6mo		Md	Jun		water on brain
Fanny Ford	75	W	Scot.	Dec		bronchitus
Lucia Gorden	7mo		Md	Jun		colra.infan.
Rachel Scarbough	9mo		Md	Oct		colra.infan.
Charles Gorden	8mo		Md	Jun		colra.infan.
William Fountain	1		Md	Jun		brain inflam.
Phillip Lampbright	5		Md	Jan		spine dis.

159

persons who died during the year ending 1 June 18<u>60</u>

COUNTY BALTIMORE   DISTRICT 19th Ward

name	age	mar wid	birth place	mon. died	Occupation	cause of death
Thomas Robison	70	M	Irel.	Jan	laborer	pleurisy
Robert Hughes	1		Md	Oct		croup
Emma Willis	8		Md	Apr		croup
Laura Handy	30	M	Md	Jun		cancer
Mary Lanner	1mo		Md	Jun		spasms
William Magelton	1mo		Md	Dec		whooping cough
John Lineaweaver	5mo		Md	Feb		heart dis.
John Riglan	23	M	Md	Jul	laborer	consumption
Rebecca Hemick	75	W	Md	Nov		paraletic
Samuel Longley	27	W	Md	Mar	paperhanger	bronchitus
William Cromwell	4		Md	Jan		burned
Margaret Gahan	1mo		Md	Mar		spasms
William Donovan	35	M	Irel.	Apr	shoemaker	consumption
Mary O'laulin	48	M	Irel.	Jan		consumption
Charles Metzell	27		Md	Dec	carpenter	typhoid
William Canten	1mo		Md	Jul		unknown
William Bain	66	M	Scot.	Jan	gardner	sucide
20th Ward						
Dennis Macarty	5		Va	Sep		typhoid
Matilda Bell	70	W	Md	Feb		consumption
Milton Davis	9mo		Md	Apr		pneumonia
Sarah McCoy	43	W	Irel.	Feb		heart dis.
Bennett Fitzpatrick	1		Md	Aug		teething
Charles H. Brown	21		Md	Feb	clerk	consumption
Elizabeth Conway	70	M	Md	Apr		consumption
Otis Henry Conway	2		Md	Jan		cold
Johnson Howard	50	M	Irel.	Oct	horsedriver	cancer
Susan Clarke	63	M	Md	Aug		heart dis.
William Scarf	8		Md	Aug		typhoid
Joseph Lester	1		Md	Aug		spasms
Sarah M. Massey	1		Md	Jan		accident
Margaret Randal	1mo		Md	Nov		spasms
Mifflin Coutier	1		Md	Jan		teething
Ann Addison	28		Md	Feb		heart dis.
John M. Burke	2		Md	Mar		cat.fever
Joseph Sutton	8		Md	Jun		consumption
Rebecca Baker	23		Md	Apr		consumption
Ignatius Barton	9mo		Md	Jun		scarlet fever
Alice Wilson	1		Md	Sep		scarlet fever
Martha Bender	21		Md	Jan		consumption
Samuel Snyder	70	M	Pa.	Jun	farmer	dysentary
Louisa Thomas	75	M	Pa.	May		pheumatism
Henry Gibson	7		Md	Aug		dysentary
Lewis E. Shopley	3		Md	Feb		croup
F.(male)Armbruster	31	M	Ger.	Apr	laborer	consumption
Allen McMahan	65	W	Irel.	Apr		natural decay
George Jacobi	9		Ger.	Sep		scarlet fever
Elizabeth Shultz	62	M	Ger.	Aug		dropsy
Mary Warner	36		Md	Mar		unknown
Elizabeth Denson	2		Md	Jun		measles
Josephine Shaspiski	29		Ger.	Jul		bowel inflam.
Charles Ball	2		Md	Feb		croup
Henry Atkins	2		Md	Mar		croup

persons who died during the year ending 1 June 18_60_

COUNTY BALTIMORE   DISTRICT 20th Ward

name	age	mar wid	birth place	mon. died	Occupation	cause of death
Jacob Conrad	73	M	Ger.	Jul	butcher	consumption
Margaret Noland	3		Md	Sep		whooping cough
Teresa Mitchell	3mo		Md	Jul		unknown
Anna Shipley	2		Md	Jun		measles
Harriet Walker	25		Md	Sep		consumption
Anastasia Ryan	6		Md	Apr		croup
Maria Massay	32		Md	Apr		consumption
Julia Tyland	5		Md	Mar		measles
Adela Greentree	4		Md	Feb		croup
Adaline Floyd	29		Md	Jan		consumption
Nancy Elliot	66	M	Md	May		pneumonia
Calvin Maddon	1		Md	Aug		scarlet fever
Thomas Jones	20		Md	Jul	blacksmith	consumption
Mathew Burns	30	M	Irel.	Apr	laborer	consumption
Benjamin Sheppard	10		Md	Sep		consumption
George McAbee	3		Md	Mar		pneumonia
Robert N. Martin	22		Md	Apr	clerk	consumption
Ida Meistor	3		Md	Apr		croup
Richard H. Lee	20		Md	Nov	student	consumption
Margaret Hisor	64	M	D.C.	Jun		consumption
George W. Geise	6		Md	Jan		scarlet fever
James Bilby	30	M	N.Y.	Mar	notebroker	consumption
Elizabeth Bilby	1		Md	May		whooping cough
Thomas Murphey	80	M	Irel.	May	printer	heart dis.
Ann Foush	5		Md	Nov		croup
Anne Gibson	2mo		Md	Jan		unknown
Henry Wilkinson	5mo		Md	May		summer comp.
Elizabeth Elder	78	M	Md	Feb		pralysis
Jacob Steiner	4		Md	Mar		chokes
George Flagtick	18		Md	Feb		consumption
Ernest Stanback	83	M	Ger.	Jun	shoemaker	old age
Ellinor Pryor	4		Md	May		scarlet fever
Thomas O. Boyd	70		Md	May	farmer	head dis.
Thomas G. Dorsey	6mo		Md	May		lung cong.
Mary I. Hatch	34		Md	May		consumption
Ellen Quake	1mo		Md	Jan		unknown
Eliza Vickers	1		Md	Aug		dysentary
Edward Mooney	6		Md	May		dysentary
Eliza Vincent	1mo		Md	Jul		croup
Marya Diggs	64		Md	Feb		paralysis
Mary Ritter	55	M	Ger.	Jul		consumption
Thomas Mullen	31	M	Md	Feb	butcher	consumption
Robert Sheppard	41	M	Ger.	May	whipmaker	consumption
Catherine Letmate	69		Ger.	Feb		unknown
Anna Miller	6		Md	Apr		croup
Joseph Simmon	67	M	N.Y.	Apr		sorethroat
Catherine Heise	45		Md	Feb		dysentary
Obrian P. Cooper	5mo		Md	Feb		croup
Thomas Shehan	7		Md	Sep		dysentary
John Saberly	17		Mass	Mar		consumption
Cath Heise (male)	45		Md	Feb	agent	dysentary
John Carr	36	M	Md	Mar		consumption

161

MORTALITY SCHEDULE OF MARYLAND

persons who died during the year ending 1 June 18_60_

COUNTY   BALTIMORE   DISTRICT   20th Ward

name	age	mar wid	birth place	mon. died	Occupation	cause of death
Samuel Coon	70	M	Md	Jan		consumption
Raphel Ofer	40	M	Md	Mar	laborer	dropsy
Harriett Steifle	2		Md	Aug		summer comp.
Maria Nash	21		Mass.	Aug		consumption
J.D. Stevenson	1		Md	Feb		croup
Charles Duvall	5		Md	Jan		gastric fever
James H. Warner	2mo		Del.	Oct		unknown
George Morris	84	M	Pa.	Oct		heart dis.
Eve Hurst	35	W	Wurtemb.	Jun		unknown
Margaret Carroll	1mo		Md	Jul		unknown
Sarah Downs	38	M	Md	Sep		consumption
Catherine Fink	8mo		Md	Mar		unknown
Sephia Maynard	38	M	Md	Dec		spinal dis.
Sarah B. Drinker	39	W	Pa.	Mar	teacher	consumption
George A. Simpson	10		Md	Dec		catarrah
Francis Arden	24		Md	Mar	painter	consumption
Hollen Bennett	1		Md	Mar		unknown
Catherine Hays	73	W	Md	Feb		bowel dis.
James Duncan	76	M	Scot.	Jul		paralysis
Isabel Sweeney	50	M	Irel.	Dec		bowel dis.
Stonewald Fulton	19		Md	Sep		bil.fever
Oliva Lent	9		Md	Jun		dysentary
Catherine Shirk	27	M	Ind.	Jan		summer comp.
Joseph R. Hack	3		Md	Nov		unknown
Clinton Biggs	3		Md	Jan		brain fever
Elizabeth Wilhelm	10		Md	Jul		whooping cough
18th Ward						
William Harrison	60	M	Md	Dec	merchant	bil.fever
William Freeberger	11		Md	Mar		bowel comp.
Daniel O'dean	34	M	Irel.	Sep	shoemaker	consumption
William H. Parker	9		Md	Apr		brain fever
Emma Remey	2		Md	Jul		spasms
Adnrew Lewis	6mo		Md	Dec		consumption
James Johnston	46	M	Irel.	Feb	laborer	rheumatism
Adolph Burke	6mo		Md	Jan		brain fever
William Scholfield	2		Md	Feb		consumption
Margaret Weber	2		Md	Feb		teething
Anne ODell	2mo		Md	Jan		unknown
William Howell	26	M	Md	Jun	laborer	heart dis.
Olivia Quail	3mo		Md	Apr		whooping cough
Joseph Jenkins	34	M	Md	Apr	policeman	consumption
Catherine Smith	22		Md	Mar	dressmaker	consumption
George Bolter	34	M	Md	Mar	machinist	consumption
Francis Elshote	76	W	Md	Feb	laborer	old age
Edward Goodman	19		Md	Jun	clerk	consumption
Edward Deems	7mo		Md	Jul		croup
Isaiah Bayless	5mo		Md	Apr		fits
Thomas Stump	48	M	Md	Mar	cooper	unknown
Margaret Schaeffer	28	M	Baden	Aug		spasms
William Goswell	10		Md	Jan		scarlet fever
Charles Williss	4mo		Md	Apr		unknown
William H. Black	3		Md	Apr		typhoid

persons who died during the year ending 1 June 18_60

COUNTY BALTIMORE   DISTRICT 1st.District

name	age	mar wid	birth place	mon. died	Occupation	cause of death
Sarah Jackson	3		Md	Apr		scarlet fever
Joseph Miller	4		Md	Aug		dysentary
Alpha McKinsey	86	W	Md	Apr		old age
Mary Bell	40	M	Md	May		dysentary
James Bateman	25	M	Md	Mar	farmer	scrofula
Eliza Burge	60		Eng.	Mar		asmthma
Bird B.Smith	33		Md	Mar	pysician	consumption
Hennry France	84	M	Md	Jun	farmer	dropsey
Edward Larmer	1mo		Md	Jul		heart dis.
Martha Matthews	20		Md	Jun		consumption
Peter Terry	55		Md	Jan	laborer	brain fever
Mary C. Brooks	59		D.C.	Jul	directress	cancer
Louisa Fisher	2		Md	Jul		whooping cough
Margaret Debot	26	M	Md	Nov		child bed
William Gobner	2		Md	May		croup
Matilda Slager	2		Md	Mar		croup
			2nd. District			
Martin Barton	2		Md	Feb		croup
Harriett Ward	60	M	Md	Aug		bowel inflam.
Josiah Baines	61	M	Md	Feb	carpenter	rheumatism
Thamer Thuse	30		Md	Jan		pneumonia
Kate Stanfield	37	M	Md	Mar		consumption
Mary Naufield	6mo		Md	Jul		consumption
William Steuart	10md		Md	Oct		unknown
Elizabeth Dinal	87	W	Md	Dec		old age
Elizabeth Clay	22	M	Ger.	Oct		typhoid
Sunalta Passmore	4mo		Pa.	Jul		dysentary
Rachael Owings	41	M	Md	Jan		consumption
Elizabeth Claw	22		Ger.	Oct		typhoid
Caleb Peddicord	57	M	Md	Jan	farmer	dyspepsia
Francis N. Worthington	65	W	Va.	Aug		dyspepsia
John Howard	44		Md	Dec	servant	accident
Kate Burkett	6		Md	Oct		throat dis.
Henry Fite	74	M	Md	Apr	farmer	local
			3rd District			
James White	50	M	Irel.	May	laborer	accident
Moses White	26		Irel.	May		cancer
Leah Herbert	28	M	Md	May		unknown
Jacob Smith	18		Ger.	Aug		consumption
Theodore Ritter	9mo		Md	Jul		dysentary
Marcella Super	21	M	Md	May		consumption
Helen Conner	80	W	Irel.	Aug		sudden
William R. Dunn	1		Md	Nov		flux
Hetty Waters	75	W	Md	Feb		dropsey
Edward Miller	33	M	Md	Mar	bricklayer	consumption
Anna Blume	2		Md	Jun		dysentary
Nancy Wilson	75	W	Md	Mar		typhoid
Alice Hutson	1		Md	Feb		consumption
John Gardside	96	W	Eng.	Feb	manufacturer	old age
Margaret Briggs	8mo		Md	Jul		dysentary
Johnsy Pierce	3		Md	Apr		pneumonia
Michael Bowen	36	M	HesseGer.	Dec	laborer	overflow ofBlood

163

name	age	mar wid	birth place	mon. died	Occupation	cause of death
Francis Silver	1mo		Md	May		catarah
Lutery Day	34	M	Md	May		child bed
Lavinia Brown	30	M	Md	Feb		consumption
William H. Farrow	43	M	Eng.	Sep	millright	accident
Ursula Collins	15		Md	Apr		dysentary
Mary Rich	1mo		Md	Mar		fits
James Siran	67	W	Md	Aug		asthma
Peter Bell	54	M	Md	Oct	grocer	consumption
Sarah Smith	79	M	Md	Mar		old age
Eliza Wolf	1mo		Md	Oct		croup
Permelius Hipsly	59	M	Md	Apr	carpenter	consumption
Louisa Lilly	3		Md	May		dropsy
Albert Moss	1		Md	Aug		dysentary
Mary White	20		Md	May		cold
George W. James	52	W	Md	Oct	spinner	consumption
John Summerfield	2mo		Md	Mar		brain infal.
William Hill	2		Md	Mar		water on brain
Michael Lovesta	3		Md	Sep		scarlet fever
Catherine James	1		Md	Aug		pneumonia
Hannah Davis	1		Md	Jun		bowel compl.
John Constine	35		Irel.	Jul	laborer	murdered
Henry Jones	70	W	Md	Dec		consumption
Ellin Dillon	5		Md	Oct		dysentary
Joseph Doyle	2		Md	Nov		lung inflam.
Sarah Garbon	30		Irel.	Feb	seamstress	consumption
Michael Dooley	1		Md	Dec		spasms
Mary A. Sheardon	14		Md	Feb		brain dis.
Julia O. Sheardon	6		Md	Nov		croup
Greenbury Tipton	60	W	Md	Jun	stonemason	consumption
Elizabeth Fowler	70	M	Md	Aug		pneumonia
Ephraim White	16		Md	Jan	farmer	typhoid
Edward Wickins	46		Eng.	Nov	carpenter	paralysis
Bennett Hamilton	26	M	Md	Aug		dropsy
Catherine Smith	12		Md	Aug		unknown
Thomas Fishpaugh	83	M	Md	Nov	laborer	paralysis
Annette Lyman	24		Pa.	Sep		consumption
George W. Gore	46	M	Md	Apr	laborer	cold
Elizabeth Canion	72	M	Eng.	Jan		heart dis.
Mary Ricord	70	W	Irel.	Feb		old age
Mary Snider	34		Ger.	Jun		unknown
William Stockes	45		Md	Jun	paupers	insanity
Elizabeth Watkins	35		Md	Jun		unknown
William Schidell	35		Eng.	Jun	"	unknown
Isabella Wilson	2da.		Md	Jun		unknown
John Fritz	26		Ger.	Jun	paupers	unknown
conrad Attleborrough	9mo		Md	Jun	"	unknown
John Welch	45		Irel.	Jun	"	"
William Watson	34		Irel.	Jun	"	"
John Coulter	48		Pa.	Jun	"	"
Bennett Collins	40		Md	Jun	"	"
Elizabeth Smith	42		Md	Jun	"	"
William Banke	2		Md	Jun	"	"
Michael Clarke	67		Eng.	Jun	"	"

164

persons who died during the year ending 1 June 18 60

COUNTY   Baltimore   DISTRICT   3rd Dist.

name	age	mar wid	birth place	mon. died	Occupation	cause of death
Robert Forrest	55		Irel.	Jul	paupers	unknown
Jane Hendson	22		Irel.	Jul	"	"
John Geddiss	1mo		Md	Jul	"	"
John Shank	45		Md	Jul	"	"
Charles Shamel	7mo		Md	Jul	"	"
John Henry	24		Md	Jul	"	"
Samuel Tinnels	38		Md	Jul	"	"
Christian Kinis	70		Md	Jul	"	"
Margaret Conch	45		Irel.	Jul	"	"
Louisa Andrews	45		Ger.	Jul	"	sundry diseases
George Brooks	67		Md	Jul	"	"
Mary Collins	27		Md	Aug	"	"
John Murray	40		Irel.	Aug	"	"
George Shaw	2mo		Md	Aug	"	"
Frederick Kingten	48		Ger.	Aug	"	'
Catherine McDonald	40		Irel.	Aug	"	"
Christian Bailon	50		Ger.	Aug	"	"
Samuel Thomas	59		Eng.	Aug	"	"
John Daily	39		Ger.	Aug	"	"
Boyd Coning	46		Irel.	Aug	"	"
John Knabb	79		N.Y.	Aug	"	"
Mary Burke	18		Md	Aug	"	"
George S. Canville	68		Irel.	Aug	"	"
Ellen G. Burns	5mo		Md	Aug	"	!
William Wilkins	64		Irel.	Aug	"	"
Mary Butler	74		Md	Aug	"	"
Hugh Todd	50		Irel.	Sep	"	"
George Smallwood	50		Md	Sep	"	"
George W. Tracy	55		Md	Sep	"	"
Elizabeth Benson	19		Md	Sep	"	"
Stephen Smith	54		Irel.	Sep	"	"
Nancy Long	26		Md	Oct	"	"
Mary a. Martin	22		Irel.	Oct	"	"
Michael Mc Colican	68		Irel.	Oct	"	"
Roze Crasner	25		Ger.	Oct	"	"
Joseph Sheplin	44		Ger.	Oct	"	"
Lem Prans	77		Ger.	Oct	"	:
William Fisher	38		Eng.	Oct	"	"
Catherine Engel	55		Ger.	Oct	"	:
Frederick Conner	61		Irel.	Oct	"	"
Robert Green	40		Md	Oct	"	"
John Kuso	14		N.Y.	Nov	"	"
William Atkinson	35		Md	Nov	"	"
Angustus Castule	30		Ger.	Nov	"	"
James Hubbert	66		Md	Nov	"	"
Lummeria Myers	68		Ger.	Nov	"	"
Sophia Frazier	35		Md	Nov	"	"
Henry Cartman	45		Ger	Nov	"	"
Moses white	45		Irel.	Nov	"	"
Frederick English	26		Irel.	Nov	"	"
Dora Geiphin	20		Md	Nov	"	:
John Wagner	60		Ger.	Nov	"	"

165

MORTALITY SCHEDULE OF MARYLAND

persons who died during the year ending 1 June 18<u>60</u>

COUNTY   BALTIMORE   DISTRICT 3rd District

name	age	mar wid	birth place	mon. died	Occupation	cause of death
Eliza Sharp	60		Md	Nov	paupers	various diseases
Ephraim Jay	21		Md	Dec	"	"
Charles E. Gibson	33	W	Md	Dec	"	consumption
Maria L. Wall	22	M	Md	"	"	consumption
Ellen J. Murphy	2mo		Md	"	"	teething
Thomas Strain	60		Irel.	"	Jan	various diseases
Thomas McGrath	46		Irel.	"	"	"
Mary Fay	25		Irel.	"	"	" Baltimore Co.
Lem Brown	60		Ger.	"	"	" Alms House
Conrad Raput	72		Ger.	"	"	"
Logan McClocklin	45		Md	"	"	"
Catherine Conar	45		Md	"	"	"
Conrad Simpson	38		va.	"	"	"
Elizabeth Raley	37		Ger.	"	"	"
Frederick Peters	48		Ger.	"	"	"
Henry Myer	60		Ger.	"	"	"
John Schosler	50		Ger.	"	"	"
Conrad Rollin	30		Irel.	"	"	"
Jane Schidar	25		Ger.	"	"	"
George Creamer	32		Md	"	"	"
Elizabeth Marsy	50		Irel.	"	"	"
Margaret Crego	70		Pa.	"	"	"
Frederick Snider	60		Md	"	"	"
Thomas Trault	65		Md	"	"	"
Joseph Woods	49		Md	Feb	"	:
James Donely	48		Irel.	"	"	"
Elizabeth Frawlon	38		Ger.	"	"	"
Ellen Turner	26		Ger.	"	"	"
Eliza Band	40		Md	"	"	"
Charles Frannick	50		Ger.	"	"	"
Ann E. Calvert	5		Md	"	"	"
Charles McGibbon	22		D.C.	"	"	"
Luke Rogers	40		Irel.	"	"	"
James McGary	40		Irel.	Mar	"	"
Lucy McColister	60		Md	"	"	"
Elizabeth King	33		Va.	"	"	"
Sarah A. Grigley	40		Va.	"	"	"
Mary E. Linsly	35		Md	"	"	"
Michael Lanahan	49		Irel.	"	"	"
Henry Cook	70		Ger.	"	"	"
William Collins	30		Irel.	Apr	"	:
William Albright	30		Md	"	"	"
John Daily	60		Ger.	"	"	"
Maria Thompson	36		Md	"	"	"
George Wilks	3mo		Md	"	"	"
Edward Schirds	40		Irel.	"	"	"
James Taylor	30		Md	"	"	"
Milton Parks	30		Md	"	"	"
Eliza Smith	22		Md	"	"	"
James Ogleman	58		Scot	"	"	"
Samuel Conley	40		Irel.	"	"	"
Thomas Matthews	44		Md	"	"	"
Elizabeth Berry	30		Irel.	"	"	"

persons who died during the year ending 1 June 18_60_

COUNTY BALTIMORE   DISTRICT   3rd Dist.

name	age	mar wid	birth place	mon. died	Occupation	cause of death
Mary Rembord	65		Ger.	Apr	Baltimore Co. Alms House	
George Getty	1mo		Md	"		
Robert Scott	50		Irel.	"		
Hannah Erwin	65		Irel.	"		
Henry Fritz	50		Ger.	"		
Basheyr Mantz	50		Ger.	"		
Dared Cullins	35		Irel.	"		
Henry Brian	2		Md	"		
Elizabeth Williams	35		Md	"		
Maria Joplin	13		Md	"		
Susan Steward	40		Md	"		
James Gray	1mo		Md	"		
Bridget Smith	86		Irel.	"		
Margaret Hammond	40		Ger.	"		
Powell Smith	3		Md	"		
Philipina Keyworth	26		Md	"		
Isabella Cesar	60	W	Irel.	Dec		heart disease
Mary A. Whitman	1mo		Md	Sep		unknown
Mary A. Cockey	68	M	Md	Dec		dropsy
John M. Wise	64	W	Md	Nov	farmer	paralysis
Mary Keener	65	M	Md	Mar		paralitic
Josias Rutter	35	W	Md	Jan	farmer	old age
John Townsend	2		Md	Sep		consumption
John Davis	2		Md	May		unknown
Thomas C. Walker	76		Md	May		cancer
4th District						
Eleanor Cook	59	M	Md	Apr		consumption
Mary Dorsey	6		Md	Aug		water on brain
Susanna Uhler	74	M	Md	Feb		erysipilis
Ann R. Green	2mo		Md	Jan		consumption
Isabel Gore	8mo		Md	Jul		dysentary
George Ebaugh	67	M	Md	Jan	miller	unknown
John W. Oram	11		Md	Mar		water on brain
Rachel Hooker	88		Md	Feb		old age
Isabel C. brown	5		Md	Aug		consumption
Armstrong Painter	2		Md	Feb		cholera
Barbara a. Guinitt	26		Md	Dec		consumption
Jerome Berryman	1		Md	Jul		brain fever
Susan Thomas	5		Md	Aug		bowel inflam.
Philly Beckley	66	M	Md	Mar	farmer	consumption
Julia Long	61	W	Md	Aug		typhoid
Susan Stump	1		Md	May		croup
James M.C.Hanson	73	M	Va.	Apr	M.E.clergyman	paralitic
Hannah Myers	73	W	Holland	Jul		dropsey
Sarah Ermicks	51	M	Holland	Feb		lung inflam.
Mary A. Snackstedt	1		Md	Mar		pneumonia
Susan Groff	55	M	Pa.	Jan		palsy
Mary T. Cipriari	24	M	Md	Mar		child bed
John Dear	74		Ger.	Jun	farmer	old age
William Denise	55		Md	Mar	laborer	pneumonia
Martin A. Young	8mo		Md	Jun		dysentary
Kittie Gore	60	M	Md	Dec		accident

persons who died during the year ending 1 June 18<u>60</u>

COUNTY BALTIMORE   DISTRICT   5th District

name	age	mar wid	birth place	mon. died	Occupation	cause of death
John w. Fowble	8		Md	Dec		bowel inflam.
William Hale	54	M	Md	May	farmer	dropsy
Andrew Martin	1mo		Md	May		unknown
Eli Martin	18		Md	Sep	apprentice	dysentary
Laura V. Myers	4		Md	Aug		dysentary
Elizabeth Martin	20	M	Md	Jan		child bed fever
Lemuel Keller	28	M	Md	Jan	farmer	dropsy
Mary Armacost	56	M	Md	Aug		dysentary
Susan Curtis	6		Md	Jun		measles
Franas Sparks	1		Md	Jun		brain infa.
Angeline Kemp	54	M	Md	Jun		heart dis.
Ellinora Renson	40	W	Md	Jan		pneumonia
Sophia Ensor	19	M	Md	Mar		erysipilas
Trador Gorsuch	1		Md	Jan		scarlet fever
Mathias Wisner	1		Md	Jul		brain infalm.
John D. Williams	44	M	Md	Sep	farmer	jaundice
6th District						
John Stump	15		Md	Feb		typhoid
Mary Matthews	55	M	Md	Apr		head dis.
Julia Morris	15		Md	Jan		consumption
Arabella Jones	2		Md	Sep		throat dis.
George Taylor	52	M	Md	Apr	farmer	typhoid
Eliza Kroh	40	M	Md	Mar		typhoid
Thomas Piece	20		Md	Oct		consumption
Francis Morris	26	M	Md	Feb		consumption
Henry Markey	26		Md	May		consumption
Mary J. Baker	1		Md	Oct		cat. fevet
James Hartley	67	M	Pa.	Oct	farmer	paralytic
Edward L. Gooding	9mo		Md	Sep		throat dis.
John Parker	66	M	Maine	Apr	papermaker	typhoid
Lydia Hampshire	8mo		Md	Sep		brain inflam.
John W. Cross	25	M	Md	Jun	carpenter	gastric fever
Jarvis Masmon	6mo		Md	Mar		spasms
John List	46	M	Baden	Aug	farmer	cholera
Sarah Woods	84	W	Pa.	Nov		oldage
7th District						
Ann Hicks	6mo		Md	May		brain inflam.
Thomas McCormick	3		Md	Dec		scarlet fever
Catherine B. Price	68	M	Md	Jan		rheumatism
Sereptic Ensor	8mo		Md	Sep		brain infl.
Elizabeth Merryman	74		Md	May		heart dis.
Susan Tracy	15		Md	Dec		consumption
Jane Palmer	2		Md	Mar		croup
Samuel Huskey	2		Md	Apr		croup
Jane Harris	60	W	Pa.	Oct		dropsy
John Rutlidge	70	M	Md	Dec	carpenter	stomach dis.
Rebecca Cuddy	74	W	Md	Feb		typhoid
Mary Hunt	105	W	Md	Sep		old age
Margaret Price	22		Md	Feb		typhoid
Gerford Vaughn	77	M	Md	Nov	miller	liver comp.
Seth Daily	5		Md	May		dropsy
James Rogers	1		Md	Nov		dysentary

MORTALITY SCHEDULE OF MARYLAND

persons who died during the year ending 1 June 18<u>60</u>

COUNTY BALTIMORE   DISTRICT 7th District

name	age	mar wid	birth place	mon. died	Occupation	cause of death
Elizabeth Moore	60	M	Md	Jul		dropsy
Hannah Nelson	73	W	Md	Jan		cat.fever
Mary Almong	69	W	Md	Dec		dropsy
Joshua H. Dasey	69	W	Md	Jun		consumption
Barbara Darsey	49	M	Md	none		dropsy
			10th District			
Mary Klinefelter	82	W	Pa.	Feb		dropsy
Aubrey Lions	70	M	Md	Mar	laborer	dropsy
Maranda Price	39	M	Md	Apr		measles
Terese Hartman	22	M	Pa.	Jun		consumption
Elizabeth Richardson	31	M	Md	Mar		confinement
Lazarus Moore	26		Pa.	Jan		killed on RR
George Wolfe	35	M	Ger.	Mar		cancer
John Griffin	66		Md	Mar		stomach dis.
Alpha Ryston	22		Md	Aug		sun stroke
Nicholas Emmery	24		Md	Jun		brain fever
Rebecca Xorman	2		Md	Jun		brain fever
Robert Wilson	67		Md	Jul		heart dis.
			8th District			
Susan Clark	63	W	Md	Oct		unknown
Mary A. Gray	7		Va.	Apr		unknown
Barney McDermon	43	M	Irel.	Jan	laborer	cold
Penelope Bodley	34	M	Md	Jun		pneumonia
Thomas Tool	2		Md	May		scarlet fever
Joseph Tyson	53	M	Pa.	Mar	merchant	consumption
Matilda Jones	2		Md	May		scrofula
John Cadden	9mo		Md	Jun		teething
William Price	83	W	Eng.	Jun	farmer	old age
Mary Fanlin	62	M	Md	Apr		fits
Hester Cross	34		Md	Jan	factoryhand	consumption
Jackson Ferguson	19		Md	Jan	"	consumption
William Gilliland	16		Md	Dec	millright	typhoid
John H. Kidd	41	M	Md	Jan		consumption
James A. Mail	2		Md	Dec		summer comp.
Joshua Matthews	47	M	Md	Oct	farmer	chronic dis.
Sarah E. Rider	5mo		Md	Dec		inflamation
Emma V. Gilland	1		Md	Jun		teething
John F. Brinks	9		Md	May		blow from stone
Morris Tracy	6		Md	Jan		scarlet fever
Aguilla Davis	14		Md	May		cold
Samuel Cockey	69	M	Md	Jul	farmer	hard drink
John Zenck	42	M	Bavaria	Jun	farmer	dysentary
John Kane	1		Md	Mar		cold
Samuel Worthington	36		Md	May	farmer	heart dis.
Ellenor Ensor	84	W	Md	Feb		pneumonia
			9th District			
Elizabeth Zang	3		Md	Jan		typhoid
William H. Douglas	14		Md	Dec		bowel inflam.
George Gildner	6mo		Md	Mar		brain cong.
James B. Badger	92		Md	Nov		paralysis
Dabid B. Badger	1		Md	Dec		consumption
James W. Wardell	8mo		Md	Oct		pneumonia

169

MORTALITY SCHEDULE OF MARYLAND

persons who died during the year ending 1 June 18<u>60</u>

COUNTY   BALTIMORE - CALVERT DISTRICT   9th District

name	age	mar wid	birth place	mon. died	Occupation	cause of death
Sarah J.Walton	2		Md	Aug		bowel inflam.
Susan A. Hammond	50	M	Md	Dec		heart dis.
John T. White	3		Md	Jan		scarlet fever
Richard Hamilton	74	M	Irel.	Jan	hotelkeeper	fall
Michael Bowen	44	M	Irel.	Aug	laborer	cramp
Laura C. Bowen	2mo		Md	May		unknown
Bridget Welsh	4mo		Md	Dec		spasms
Elizaberh Schroder	50	M	CH.Germ.	Aug		dysentary
Mary A. Wright	6da		Md	Feb		convulsions
Maria Conner	2		Md	May		brain cong.
John P. Garguey	1		Ohio	Aug		whooping cough
William Aliman	1		Md	May		water on brain
Emma V. Vogle	1		Md	sep		croup
Frederick Zinhorst	53		Hanover	Dec	surveyor	cramp
Mary C. Flayhart	14		Md	Jul		consumption
Rebecca Maize	71		Md	Apr		old age
John Conan	85		Md	Apr		heart ids.
Richard G. Woods	48		Md	Sep	farmer	dropsy
Joseph W. Shaeffer	3mo		Md	Aug		summer compl.
Thomas Stanton	8mo		Wisc.	Oct		dysentary
Edward Mackan	9mo		Del.	Mar		scalded
Henry Rud	50	M	Md	Jan	cooper	consumption
James H. Butko	20		Md	Jun	laborer	bilious fever
John Liberty	2		Va	Mar		brain dis.
Edward Welch	1mo		Pa.	Aug		dysentary
Joanna Bandon	2		Va.	Jan		brain fever
Mary Orman	2		Md	Nov		brain fever
Sarah Logue	80		Irel.	May		old age
John C. Kelly	1		Md	Jan		heart dis.
Catherine Lewis	70	W	Md	Jul		heart dis.
George Irving	1		Md	Aug		summer compl.
			CALVERT COUNTY	1st.Election Dist.		
Charles Davis	29		N.H.	Nov	carpenter	typhoid
John J. Hollen	21		Md	Feb	farmer	scarlet fever
Ann M. Greeves	19		Md	Feb		scarlet fever
Margaret E. Thomas	8		Md	Apr		scarlet fever
Joseph H. Caster	17		Md	Apr	laborer	scarlet fever
Barbara Caster	12		Md	Mar		scarlet fever
Elizabeth Coster	8		Md	Mar		scarlet fever
George W. Wood	46	M	Md	May	farmer	bronchitis
James A. Wood	11mo		Md	Dec		scarlet fever
Virgil Pitcher	3		Md	Dec		dysentary
Elizabeth 'E.Dixon	7		Md	Feb		scarlet fever
Flora Allen	7		Md	Feb		croup
Mahala Wells	65	W	Md	May		cold
Richard Johnson	5		Md	Feb		scarlet fever
Mary E. Waters	8		Md	Apr		scarlet fever
Chaney Mills(fem)	48	W	Md	Jan		consumption
Mary A. Duke	2		Md	Nov		scarlet fever
Benjamin Fowler	2		Md	dec		scarlet fever
Ann M. Williams	20		Md	Dec		unknown
William Shrives	12		Md	Aug		scarlet fever
Charles M. Fraizer	67	W	Md	May	farmer	heart dis.

170

persons who died during the year ending 1 June 18_60_

COUNTY   CALVERT   DISTRICT 2nd.E.Dist.

name	age	mar wid	birth place	mon. died	Occupation	cause of death
Isaac King	27		Md	Feb	farmer	dysentary
Ernest B. Williams	2		Md	Mar		scarlet fever
Basil S. Dixon	5		Md	Oct		scarlet fever
Elizabeth M. Hutchins	24		Md	Feb		bed fever
Richard H. Hance	4		Md	Jan		scarlet fever
Cassine Weems	35		Md	Jun		consumption
Anna M. Catherton	2		Md	Oct		scarlet fever
Benjamin Grierson	8		Md	Jan		scarlet fever
William H. Bird	42		Md	Apr	farmer	hemorhage
Elizabeth E. Mills	33		Md	Jan		consumption
James W. Monett	12		Md	Jan		consumption
William Hutchins	7		Md	Oct		scarlet fever
Louisa Williams	2		Md	Jan		scarlet fever
Ann K. Leach	9mo		Md	May		spasms
Joseph Blake	2		Md	Apr		scarlet fever
Dorathea Balke	26		Md	Sep		pneumonia
Elizabeth Fowler	2		Md	Dec		scorletina
Susan Morsell	1mo		Md	Feb		convulsion
Rebecca Hance	20		Md	Oct		child bed
John W. Fowler	12		Md	Sep		lung dis.
3rd District						
James Ballings	21		Md	Apr	farmer	heart dis.
Sarah R. Wood	5		Md	Mar		scarlet fever
Agnes Boyd	2		Md	Apr		consumption
Priscilla Young	19		Md	Dec		fever
Sarah Spicknall	16		Md	Dec		scarlet fever
John J. Spicknall	6		Md	Dec		scarlet fever
Dorcas Ireland	25		Md	Nov		typhoid
Frank Ireland	2		Md	Sep		scarlet fever
Allice O. Roberts	1		Md	Jan		scarlet fever
Ella Lyles	2		Md	Dec		scarlet fever
Ann V. Berkhead	16		Md	Sep		typhoid
Ann R. Hance	21		Md	Oct		child bed
James J. Hance	3mo		Md	Dec		diarhea
Wilson Crosby	1		Md	Jul		throat dis.
Eliza Watson	6		Md	Feb		scarlet fever
Samuel Gibson	1mo		Md	Oct		lockjaw
Nathan Norfolk	33		Md	Jan	farmer	pneumonia
Elizabeth Norfolk	7		Md	Dec		scarlet fever
James Wilkinson	41		Md	Mar		intoxication
Thomas Cox	18		Md	Feb	farmer	scarlet fever
Ida Cox	3		Md	Feb		scarlet fever
Isabella Cox	12		Md	Feb		scarlet fever
Isabella Cox	70		Md	Feb		unknown
Sarah Cox	27		Md	Mar		scarlet fever
George W. Lawrence	64		Md	May	blacksmith	tumors.
Richard Hunt	30		Md	Mar	farmer	pneumonia
Mary Talbot	11		Md	Feb		brain inflam.
Elizabeth Kent	33		Md	Mar		consumption
Sarah Kent	1		Md	Mar		scarlet fever
Ann E. Owings	32		Md	Jun		heart dis.
Virginia Allen	3		Md	May		scarlet fever

name	age	mar wid	birth place	mon. died	Occupation	cause of death
James H. Flowers	6		Md	Oct		dropsey
Elizabeth White	75	W	Md	Sep		unknown
Sallie Connelly	3mo		Md	Mar		unknown
Elizabeth Barton	46	M	Md	Dec		liver dis.
Parrent T. Gullitt	1		Md	Sep		whooping cough
Elizabeth Hall	3mo		Md	Aug		summer compl.
William Green	22		Md	Sep	farmhand	bilious fever
Hanah Wilson	33	M	Md	Dec		consumption
John Simpson	5mo		Md	Aug		summer comp.
Ida Onell	6mo		Md	May		unknown
Charles H. Jewell	2		Md	Aug		unknown
Mary Rouse	40		Md	Apr		liver dis.
John Graham	36	M	Md	Mar	merchant	liver dis.
Sarah A. Roe	51	W	Md	May		heart dis.
Alexine Camer	15		Md	Aug		nervous fever
John T. Dill	2		Md	May		summer dis.
Jeremiah Rust	78	M	Md	May	farmer	consumption
Ann Hardcastle	6mo		Md	Jun		summer dis.
Clair Downs	6mo		Md	Aug		whooping cough
James Hubbard	63	M	Md	Sep	carpenter	consumption
James H. Towers	27	M	Md	Apr	farmer	typhoid
Margaret Perry	45	M	Md	Dec		consumption
Robert Benden	8mo		Md	Feb		unknown
				CECIL COUNTY 1st District		
John Ruby	27		Md	Oct	shoemaker	consumption
Ann E. Webb	1		Md	Oct		summer compl.
William H. Lane	1mo		Md	Feb		unknown
Joseph Price	3mo		Md	Aug		unknown
Anna Bassitt	1		Md	Sep		unknown
Ellen Allen	9mo		Md	Mar		brain inflam.
Arthur Morton	1		Md	Aug		brain infl.
Hannah Deacon	68		Del.	Feb		old age
Rebecca A. Hays	1mo		Md	Sep		cholera
Mary Warmsley	42	M	Md	Mar		liver compl.
Eugene Metts	1		Md	Jul		summer comp.
Charles Pearce	10mo		Md	Aug		spasms
G.M.Eldrige(male)	58	M	Md	May	farmer	unknown
E.L.Osburn(male)	40		Md	Jan	farmer	lung congest.
Mary Jemmison	42		Md	Feb		unknown
N.P.Lloyd (male)	44	M	Md	Apr	farmer	dropsy
George Reed	9		Md	Jul		dropsy
				CARROLL COUNTY-Freedom Dist.		
Jonathan Dasey	73		Md	Aug	farmer	dropsy
Edward Rogers	15		Md	Jul		dropsy
John Backer	68		Ger.	Jan	tailor	heart dis.
Mary Charles	70	W	Md	Jan		old age
Charles P. Cook	1		Md	Sep		bowel inflam.
Ann M. Rush	56		Md	Jun		consumption
William Stoddard	2		Md	Nov		croup
Ida Fox	1		Md	Nov		bowel inflam.
Vachel Brown	43		Md	Sep	farmer	dysentary
Thomas Baines	43	M	Md	Feb		bowel inflam.

MORTALITY SCHEDULE OF MARYLAND

persons who died during the year ending 1 June 1860

COUNTY   CARROLL   DISTRICT   Freedom District

name	age	mar wid	birth place	mon. died	Occupation	cause of death
Elizabeth Calvin	30	M	Md	Feb		unknown
Virginia Carter	4		Md	May		bowel inflam.
James Calloway	54		Eng.	Jan	miner	bowel inflam.
G.Wilson(male)	84		Md	Jan		old age
Alice Phillips	2mo		Md	Mar		none
Mary A. Hall	2		Md	Feb		consumption
			Franklin District			
Hannah Linthicum	33	M	Md	Apr		consumption
Kate Lithicum	3mo		Md	Apr		none
Catherine H. Dade	40	M	Md	Oct		none
M. Pool (male)	62	M	Md	Aug	farmer	consumption
L. R. Waters(male)	63	M	Md	Mar	farmer	dropsy
Sarah C. Easton	6mo		Md	Apr		none
William Hooper	1mo		Md	Nov		dropsy
Mary Harkley	43		Md	Mar		dropsy
Carolina Harkley	3		Md	Aug		dropsy
Julia A. Nusbaum	10		Md	Feb		consumption
Elizabeth Franklin	81	W	Md	Sep		dropsy
Sarah Gorsuch	71	W	Md	Mar		cancer
Jacob Farrell	72	M	Md	Jun	farmer	old age
Sarah Smith	10mo		Md	Sep		dysentary
Sarah Clay	61	M	Md	Sep		dysentary
Mary Durvall	2mo		Md	Jul		dysentary
Thomas B. Owings	49	M	Md	Feb	farmer	heart dis.
Rachel Chaney	34	M	Md	Jan		consumption
V. Brown(male)	84	M	Md	Aug	farmer	old age
			NEW Wirdser? District			
Catherine Bail	32	M	Md	Sep		consumption
J. Sherry	84		Md	Jul	farmer	old age
Henry Ellensworth	5		Md	Jul		dysentary
L. Buffington(fem.)	5mo		Md	Jun		dysentary
William H. Yingling	7		Md	Mar		dysentary
Jacob Roop	74		Md	Jun	farmer	old age
Jesse Washington	3mo		Md	Jul		none
Joel E. Roop	3		Md	Dec		ereslypsis
Ann M. Engel	53	M	Md	Mar		"
Elias Grimes	78	M	Md	Mar	farmer	old age
J. H. Norris(male)	3		Md	Jun		consumption
Wesley Durbin	43	M	Md	Nov	laborer	consumption
Rachel Boyle	75	W	Md	Sep		dropsey
			WESTMINSTER District			
Grace H. Gehr	6mo		Md	Apr		dysentary
Ida Pack	4		Md	Apr		dysentary
Samuel Myers	7		Md	Jul		dysentary
William J. Stauch	4		Md	Dec		croup
G. Fowler(male)	60	M	Md	Feb	farmer	consumption
Henry Pinchard	1		Md	Jul		dysentary
Gotlieb Zahn	2		Md	Mar		dysentary
Hannah Sullivan	1mo		Md	Feb		dysentary
Greenville Woodruff	32		Md	Mar	miller	consumption
James Miller	25		Md	Mar	farmer	consumption
James Boggs	10mo		Md	Mar		dysentary
Mary Zacharias	2mo		Md	Sep		consumption

MORTALITY SCHEDULE OF MARYLAND

persons who died during the year ending 1 June 18 60

COUNTY CARROLL   DISTRICT Middletown Dist.

name	age	mar wid	birth place	mon. died	Occupation	cause of death
Ann P. Winemiller	16		Md	Dec		sore throat
Susan A. Winemiller	10		Md	Dec		sore throat
Robert N.F. Winemiller	8		Md	Dec		sore throat
Elizabeth Brown	19	M	Md	Feb		paralysis
Sarah Linn	2mo		Md	Jul		brain fever
Daniel Shunk	72	M	Md	Apr	farmer	throat dis.
Susanna Buffington	57	M	Md	May		palsy
Jesse Coppersmith	2mo		Md	Jul		whooping cough
Tareytown Dist.						
Ann Glosser	5		FRed.Co	May		pneumonia
Mary J. Galt	3		Md	Jan		sore throat
Louisa Woolf	16		Pa.	Aug		scarlet fever
Catherine Mull	83		Md	Apr		consumption
Mary A.B. Fain	2		Md	Nov		unknown
Amos Shilt	11		Md	Jul		typhoid
Elizabeth Hanson	78	M	Md	Mar		old age
Amelia J. Reeves	6		Md	Nov		spasms
Samuel Reindollar	58		Md	Feb	farmer	lung dis.
Eliza J. Hitterluck	25		Md	Jul		typhoid
Benjamin Johnson	64	M	Pa.	Jan	farmer	unknown
John Adlesperger	74	M	Md	Jun	farmer	paralysis
R.T. Redinger(fem)	20		Md	Jul		consumption
MYERS District						
David Myers	56	M	Md	May	farmer	rheumatism
Elizabeth C. Drock	54	M	Md	Aug		disentary
Jacob H. Rish	6		Md	Jan		dropsy
Agnes Ohler	16		Md	Dec		sore throat
Jacob Airhart	72	M	Md	Oct	farmer	consumption
David Lister	89	M	Md	Jul	farmer	palsy
Ma.A. Shuter	6mo		Md	Jul		unknown
C. O. Peterman	1		Md	Feb		lung fever
James Stanisfer	5		Md	Feb		croup
S.M.Lewishumoff	6mo		Md	Apr		croup
John Ruse	8		Md	May		pleurisy
Martin E. Coner	2mo		Md	Nov		unknown
Lazarus Wintree	8mo		Pa.	Mar		lung inflam.
Mary Reiniker	34	M	Md	Mar		consumption
Jacob Maris	70	M	Pa.	Apr		accident
Henry Rontsan	75	W	Md	May		consumption
UNIONTOWN DISTRICT						
Selby Wantz	30	M	Md	Mar	storekeeper	cramp
Heziak Lampart	35	M	Md	Apr	cooper	consumption
Martha Warfield	6		Md	Aug		dysentary
William Flegle	7mo		Md	Sep		dysentary
Louisa Hesson	70	M	Md	Jan		pneumonia
Howard Eckler	2		Md	May		brain inflam.
Adison Whorly	3		Md	Feb		croup
Louis Black	4		Md	Aug		pleurisy
Sarah E. Haines	20	M	Md	Jun		consumption
Elizabeth Haines	4		Md	Jul		brain inflam.
George H. Nelson	2		Pa.	Oct		croup
Ida V. Eckhert	1		Md	Jun		croup
Charles F. Fritz	1d.		Md	Jan		borndead

174

MORTALITY SCHEDULE OF MARYLAND

persons who died during the year ending 1 June 18<u>60</u>

COUNTY -CARROLL   DISTRICT Uniontown District

name	age	mar wid	birth place	mon. died	Occupation	cause of death
Elizabeth Foutz	67		Md	Jul		sudden
Debley Farquhar	60		Md	Feb		dropsy
Rachael Galwick	35		Md	Feb		dropsy
Franklin Galwick	1		Md	Mar		croup
Ann Roberts	85	M	Md	Jun		old age
William Roberts	64	M	Md	Mar	farmer	hung himself
			WOOLERYS DISTRICT			
Margaret Shipley	59	M	Md	May		measles
Amanda Stockdale	7		Md	Apr		scrofula
Ellen Stockdale	5		Md	Mar		scrofula
Moses Barnes	82	M	Md	May	farmer	heart disease
Elias Jordan	58	M	Md	Jul	farmer	liver compl.
Clarisa Panish	62	M	Md	Jan		consumption
James L. Lockert	3		Md	Oct		brain inflam.
Ida E. Grimes	3		Md	Feb		croup
Franklin F. Hoover	5		Pa.	Mar		scarlet fever
Jackson Boyd	30	M	Md	Jan	farmer	bowel compl.
Ann Randal	4		Md	Jan		scarlet fever
Sarah Jones	36	M	Md	Sep		typhoid
Emery U. Uhle	3		Md	Mar		scarlet fever
Elias Taylor	5mo		Md	May		eresipilis
Noah Flatter	6		Md	Jul		dysentary
Susanna Spence	28	M	Md	May		consumption
Nancy Spence	1		Md	Sep		dysentary
Roland Spence	1		Md	May		croup
Margaret E. Rush	60	M	HesseDarm.	Mar		old age
Catherine Taylor	75	M	Md	Oct		consumption
Silas P. Taylor	3		Md	Sep		dysentary
Leonard Taylor	19		Md	Aug	laborer	sudden
Mary Magee	64	W	Md	Feb		typhoid
Jacob Shaver	78	M	Md	Oct		a fall
Margaret Mullen	2mo		Md	Mar		croup
Cornelius Armacott	7mo		Md	Jul		croup
Barbary Wise	71	W	Bavaria	Nov		consumption
Samuel Gettinge	4mo		Md	Dec		pneumonia
Margaret Ham	8mo		Md	Aug		infantism
Thomas E. Bosby	1		Md	Aug		dysentary
			CARROLL CO.Dist.			
William Weekly	32	M	Md	Oct	shoemaker	stabbed
Ann Pugh	62	M	Pa.	Jun		dropsy
George Dreew	61	M	Pa.	Apr	farmer	pleurisy
Peter A.H. Smith	14		Md	Oct	laborer	pleurisy
Elizabeth Forsith	3mo		Md	Jan		croup
Jonah Zimmerman	1mo		Md	Jul		dyrsentary
Jacob E. Warner	2mo		Md	Nov		croup
Elizabeth Utz	69	W	Md	Nov		sudden
John H. Price	1		Md	Dec		measles
Ann Lightenberger	4		Md	Nov		worms
Mary E. Shaffer	1		Md	May		thrush
Jacob Stephenson	38		HesseGer.	Sep	basketmaker	cancer
Cornelius Wantz	5mo		Md	May		lung inflam.
Elizabeth Trailer	78		Md	Aug		dropsy
Julian Roherbaugh	20		Md	May		consumption

175

MORTALITY SCHEDULE OF MARYLAND

persons who died during the year ending 1 June 18_60_

COUNTY -CARROLL - CECIL   DISTRICT

name	age	mar wid	birth place	mon. died	Occupation	cause of death
Allice Sherman	6mo		Md	Aug		dysentary
James Williams	6		Md	May		dropsy
Albert Falkestons	1		Md	Apr		lung inflam.
Morriah Barnes	40		Md	Feb		dropsy
Mary Stansbury	34		Md	Oct		bowel inflam.
Julia Tipton	3		Md	May		lung inflam.
			CECIL COUNTY 2nd	District		
George Walker	31		Del	Sep	sailor	tumor
Sarah Brister	3		Md	Aug		whooping cough
Isabella Carnagy	11		Md	Jan		abcess
Capt David P.Claypool	41	M	N.J.	Dec	SteamerCapt.	consumption
Henry W. Lorain	1		Md	Oct		unknown
Olly Bell Hukill	4		Md	Jan		scarlet fever
John c. Anderson	60		Md	Feb	carpenter	apoplexy
Albert Foulks	6mo		Md	sep		captar
Nathan Blake	89	M	Md	Nov	smith	gout
John H. Alexander	3mo		Md	Sep		whooping cough
John H. Biddle	59		Md	Jan	shoemaker	consumption
Edward O. Scanlin	8mo		Md	Feb		whooping cough
Hanna Francis	7		Del.	Sep		billious
James Kinkaide	1		Md	Feb		croup
Lery L. Boulden	27		Md	Mar		dispesey
Anna R. Hendrich	1		Md	Nov		bowel inflam.
Martha Boyd	2		Md	Sep		unknown
Lewis Roberts	1		Del.	Jul		brain fever
Clara Price	6mo		Md	Nov		dropsy
Mary L. Biddle	19		Md	Jan		heart dis.
Barbary Shrader	30		Ger.	May		unknown
			3rd District			
Rose Fitzsimmons	87	W	Ire.Co.Donn.			old age-d.Feb.
Caroline Brown	58	M	N.J.	Oct		cancer
John Stewart	54		Del.	Sep		rheumatism
Eliza Teal	20		Del.	Dec		typhoid
Mary J. Carter	71	M	Md	Dec		plleurisy
George Boston	82		Md	Mar		consumption
Elizabeth Tull	83	W	Md	Mar		heart dis.
Robert Carter Redefer	4mo		Md	Jun		arcepalius
Ann Short	3		Md	Jan		worms
Robert Conley	2		Md	Mar		worms
Jesse Ottley	77		Md	Jan	carpenter	rheumatism
William Glenn	50	M	Md	Apr	merchant	lung conges.
Joseph Roderick	3		Md	Feb		dropsy
Ann Rozine	40	M	Md	May		consumption
Mary A. Davison	3		Md	Jul		brain inflam.
Elizabeth Miller	62	M	Pa.	Feb		rheumatism
John M. Duncan	40	M	Md	Mar	Presb.Parson	dropsy
John Harvey	61	M	Md	Dec	cooper	heart dis.
Martha Gallagher	82	M	Irel.	May		consumption
Sarah Gallagher	82	W	Irel.	Jul		natural debility
Richard Booth	88	M	none	Jul		bowel inflam.
Palmer C. Ricketts	42		Md	Mar	editor	consumption
Laura Perkins	1		Md	Mar		unknown
Singleton Parker	6mo		Md	May		lung hemorage

persons who died during the year ending 1 June 18_60_

COUNTY CECIL   DISTRICT 3rd.Ward

name	age	mar wid	birth place	mon. died	Occupation	cause of death
James Jewett	45		N.H.	May	shoemaker	apoplezy
Frank Eader	6		Md	Jan		lung
Calvin D. Scott	32		Md	May	printer	suicide
Andrew Lynch	30		Md	Feb		mania Potera
Araminta Ford	40		Md	Apr	milliner	consumption
Thomas Cantwell	50		Md	Mar	smith	consumption
Harriett Alexander	44		Md	Apr		consumption
William McDaniel	56		Del.	Jun	laborer	brain affect.
Martha Worland	58		Md	Feb		consumption
Clara S. George	19		Md	Jan		bowel inflam.
Margaret Lewis	20		Md	Mar		consumption
4th District						
Johnson Phillips	58	M	Md	Oct	plasterer	typhoid
Halber Minner	2mo		Del.	Aug		dysentary
Andrew Gibson	74	W	Irel.	Jul	farmer	apoplexy
Rebecca Holland	80		N.J.	Dec		paralysis
Morgan A. Tyson	60	M	Md	Jun		consumption
Felina W.Young	2		Pa.	Jan		jaundice
Henrietta Kyle	3		Md	Dec		scarlet fever
Charles Young	49	M	Md	Jun	farmer	brain fever
William Marshall	7mo		Md	Jul		cholera
Ann Peterson	77	M	Del.	Dec		erisipilis
Thomas McCane	1		Md	Jul		dropsy
Hugh Feeley	5mo		Md	Jul		dysentary
Samuel Holland	70	M	Irel.	Oct	farmer	throat dis.
Ann Hendrixson	76		Md	Jul		bowel inflam.
John Read	59	M	Irel.	Mar	pumpmaker	kidney dis.
William T. Scott	54	M	Pa.	Dec	carpenter	consumption
Thomas Kirkwood	32	M	Md	Nov	farmer	consumption
Emily Montgomery	6mo		Del.	Mar		diarreah
James Crow	2		Md	Feb		croup
Carlton Janney	1		Md	Feb		scarlet fever
Mary A. Baldwin	45		Md	Apr		consumption
Isabella Jourden	73		Pa.	Dec		paralytic
5th District						
William T. Reynolds	9		Md	Aug		drowned
Virginia McCullough	3mo		Md	Jun		jaundice
A. Deford(male)	1		Md	Apr		teething
Nancy Black	82	M	Md	Apr		old age
Owen Murphy	75	M	Md	Aug		old age
William Gibson	38	M	Md	May	farmer	consumption
James P. Grant	25		Pa.	Mar	carriagemaker	erisyplis
Mary H. Richardson	39	M	Md	Nov		child bed
Charles L. Clark	23		Md	Jun	laborer	consumption
William McMurray	63	M	Del.	Apr	farmer	tesluta
Jane E. Edmund	11		Md	Aug		consumption
Ann E. Lilly	1		Md	Mar		spine dis.
Jacob Halden	62	M	Md	Jul	farmer	heart
Mary Simpson	76	M	Md	Sep		consumption
Catharine McCoddin	66	M	Pa.	Jan		lung inflam
William Vandergrift	42		Pa.	Apr		liver compl.
Benjamin Reynolds	66	M	Md	Apr	farmer	paralytick

persons who died during the year ending 1 June 18_60_

COUNTY -Cecil   DISTRICT   5th District

name	age	mar wid	birth place	mon. died	Occupation	cause of death
James Brister	33	M	Md	Apr		consumption
Ann Grace	65	M	Md	Feb		unknown
Adelade Gladings	7mo		Md	Jul		unknown
Thomas McDowe	2mo		Md	Jul		unknown
Samuel Gladings	4		Pa.	May		bowel inflam.
Rebecca Parner	34	M	Pa.	Mar		consumption
Thomas Roach	73	W	Md	Dec	farmer	old age
6th District						
Ella Brunfield	2mo		Md	Apr		unknown
Annie R. Sharpless	18		Pa.	Nov		consumption
Mercy W. Phillips	23		Pa.	Jul		typhoid
Nancy Reynolds	59	M	Pa.	Oct		typhoid
Margaret Conilson	42	M	Md	May		palsy
Hannah Taylor	74		Pa.	Nov		palsy
Joseph Gracy	1		Md	Sep		brain inflam.
Ann Gallagher	7mo		Md	Jun		brain inflam.
Martha Sergant	18		Md	May		throat inflam.
Elizabeth Maxwell	48	M	Md	May		paraletic
Hannah Devlin	2		Md	Dec		scarlet fever
Sarah J. Tyson	10		Md	Mar		scarlet fever
Rebecca Caldwell	58		Pa.	Jul		asthma
Rachel Richardson	42	M	Md	May		consumption
Charles Smith	4mo		Md	Oct		unknown
William J. Richards	4		Md	Jul		unknown
Hannah Reynolds	21	M	Md	Jan		unknown
Esther J. Moore	3		Md	Jun		gastric fever
William Goesh	82	M	Irel.	Jan	weaver	old age
Mark Balderston	5mo		Md	Jun		unknown
Emma V. Reynolds	3		Md	Jul		head dis.
Charles H. Kraup	29		Md	May	plasterer	liver dis.
George Deal	45	M	Md	Oct	farmer	consumption
Jane Marshall	44		Irel.	Jul		consumption
Sarah Cameron	4		Md	Apr		scarlet fever
Maria Cather	30		Md	Apr		consumption
Rebecca Gillespie	66		Md	Sep		consumption
John Barnes	52	M	Md	Jun	farmer	palsy
Samuel Nichell	62	M	Md	Feb	farmer	consumption
Annie Randolph	81		Md	Sep		old age
Frederick Long	1mo		Md	Oct		unknown
E.J. Rinehart(male)	34	M	Pa.	May	lumber	cancer
Jacob Jennings	1		Md	Mar		pleurisy
Theodore Webb	26	M	Md	Aug	wheelright	consumption
Mary E. Norris	27		Md	Oct		consumption
Harry Moore	6mo		Md	Jul		dysentary
John R. Smith	2		Md	Mar		spine dis.
7th District						
Maggie Cameron	10mo		Md	Nov		brain dis.
Ella Stone	2		Pa.	Jul		measles
Margaret Stone	2mo		Md	Mar		croup
John Worrick	72	M	Md	Sep	farmer	concer
John Madden	31		Md	Feb	painter	paraletic
John Thompson	19		Md	Apr	clerk	consumption
John Walker	36	M	Md	Aug	teamdriver	rheumatism

MORTALITY SCHEDULE OF MARYLAND

persons who died during the year ending 1 June 18 60

COUNTY CECIL - CHARLES   DISTRICT   7thDistrict

name	age	mar wid	birth place	mon. died	Occupation	cause of death
Sarah Knight	68	M	Pa.	Jul		dropsy
Patrick McEnutre	41	M	Irel.	Apr	stonecutter	consumption
Rebecca Ewing	63	M	Md	Feb		arespolis
Rachel Way	63	M	Md	Oct		lung dis.
John Way	30		Md	Jul		consumption
Deborah Broughton	24		Md	Feb		suicide
Elnor Patton	95		Md	Nov		old age
James Evans	62		Md	Apr	farmer	heart dis.
Ellen Stanton	1		Md	Jan		unknown
Mary Jackson	20		Md	Apr		consumption
Sarah Miller	81		Md	Jul		coler morbis
Amos Evans	31		Md	May	merchant	reumatism
Joseph Conden	72		Md	May	farmer	heart dis.
			8th District			
William Bowen	23		Md	Feb	carpenter	consumption
Catherine Derixson	1		Md	Mar		whooping cough
Eliza Moore	74		Md	Nov		old age
Solomon Dixon	1		Md	May		croup
Samuel Gillespie	40		Md	Dec	wheelright	ericipilus
Agnes Bevons	84		Md	Jul		dropsy
John Rowland	4		Md	Sep		dysentary
			9th District			
William Sheaver	54	M	Md	Apr	laborer	heart dis.
Martha Dawson	60	W	Pa.	Aug		dysentary
Sarah Palmer	70	M	Pa.	Jan		palsy
Sarah Rogers	49	M	Md	Apr		consumption
Phillip M. Steel	78		Eng.	Aug	surveyor	bowel inflam.
Susan Taylor	55	M	N.J.	Nov		despepsia
Amy A. Ruder	35		Pa.	Nov	seamstress	despepsia
Kate Stewart	1		Md	Aug		brain inflam.
Lizzie Lee	13da		Md	May		unknown
Mary Benjamin	1		Md	Dec		unknown
Rebecca Crothers	24		Md	Feb		consumption
James F. England	5		Md	May		scarlet fever
Levina M. Pierson	3		Md	Jul		whooping cough
Zilpa England	2		Md	Jan		brain infl.
Rachel J. Smith	27		Md	Jun		consumption
			CHARLES COUNTY-Allens Fresh District			
Jane Hayden	46	M	Md	Jan		fits
Robert Nally	35	M	Md	Jun	farmer	pneumonia
Henry Middleton	25		Md	Feb	collector	consumption
Peter Trihanan	48		Md	Jun	merchant	typhoid
Sarah Lyons	25		Md	Apr	consumption	
Jane Stone	77		Md	Feb		old age
Georgeanna St.Clair	1		Md	Dec		fits
Zachariah Floyd	30	M	Md	Jun	farmer	consumption
George Burroughs	11		Md	Apr		scarlet fever
Benton Burroughs	6		Md	Apr		scarlet fever
Sarah Bally	23	.	Md	May		child bed
Ophelia Bally	3		Md	Mar		pneumonia
James Burroughs	4		Md	Apr		scarlet fever
			Coomes District No.3			
Henry Moore	66	W	Md	Mar	planter	reumatism

MORTALITY SCHEDULE OF MARYLAND

persons who died during the year ending 1 June 18_60_

COUNTY CHARLES   DISTRICT Coomes District No.3

name	age	mar wid	birth place	mon. died	Occupation	cause of death
Mildred Berry	68		Md	Mar		old age
William Pye	1		Md	Jun		cholera
Nathaniel Franan	50		Md	Jul	fieldhand	unknown
Ann Franan	20		Md	Aug		typhoid
Hannah Norris	65		Md	Feb		old age
Thomas Greer	2mo		Md	Aug		unknown
Emily Taylor	2		Md	Jan		burnt
Magruder Tubman	25		D.C.	Dec	planter	consumption
John Brown	62	M	Md	Apr	planter	typhoid
Ann Brown	26		Va.	Aug		dysentary
Mariah Hamilton	48	M	Md	Jun		consumption
Catherine Burnham	23	M	Md	Mar		consumption
William Padget	2		Md	Aug		whooping cough
Samuel Padgett	38		Md	Aug	merchant	typhoid
Benjamin Hamilton	2mo		Md	Jul		spasms
William Brent	49		Md	Aug	physician	heart dis.
William Thomas	10mo		Md	Jul		cholera
Mary Wedding	47	W	Md	Nov		consumption
Henry Wilson	28		Md	Dec	farmer	consumption
Edward Miles	1mo		Md	Apr		cat.fever
Catherine Mudd	39		Md	Jul		pneumonia
Samuel Cooksey	25		Md	Sep	fieldhand	consumption
			Brigantown Dist.No.4			
Elizabeth Knott	65	W	Md	Ovt		unknown
Thomas Gardiner	59	M	Md	Nov	farmer	intemperance
William Goodrich	1mo		Md	Apr		fits
Lothron Hancock	1		Md	Aug		unknown
John Hack	26		Md	Dec		drowned
Phillip Lassen	1mo		Md	Dec		water on brain
Emily Goldsmith	30		Md	Dec		unknown
George Farrell	1mo		Md	Jan		unknown
Ann Watson	39	M	Md	Aug		dropsy
Ann Eatson	5mo		Md	Sep		unknown
			Hill Top District			
Margaret Scott	26		Md	Jun		scarlet fever
Rebecca Stingger	40	W	Md	Jun		pneumonia
Joseph Cooksey	43		Md	Oct	farmer	apoplexy
Joseph Welch	78		Md	Mar	farmer	dropsy
Ann Ward	80		Md	Apr		old age
Joseph Maddox	49		Md	Jun	farmer	colera
Rachel Ulhan	93		Md	Nov		old age
Presly Carter	15		Md	Aug		pleuirsy
William Posey	1		Md	Jul		brain fever
Richard Milstead	26		Md	Sep	laborer	consumption
Nancy Heart	60		Md	May		consumption
Elizabeth Bowie	81		Md	Jan		old age
Walter Murphy	4mo		Md	May		brain fever
Poly Simmons	86		Md	Mar		old age
Charles H. Jenkins	61		Md	Apr	farmer	pleurisy
Vaney Thorp	68		Md	Apr		consumption
Charles Price	2		Md	Nov		croup
Frederick Bowie	8mo		Md	Mar		brain fever

persons who died during the year ending 1 June 18_60_

COUNTY DORCHESTER   DISTRICT 1-12 districts

name	age	mar wid	birth place	mon. died	Occupation	cause of death
Elizabeth North	41	M	Md	May		consumption
Charles North	2mo		Md	Jun		consumption
Mary Raleigh	4mo		Md	Dec		fever
Nancy Ward	49	M	Md	Aug		cysentary
Wdward Carroll	65	M	Md	Apr		consumption
Hester Hirst	64	W	Md	Oct		dropsy
Cademus Hearn	20		Md	Aug		dysentary
Terry A. Pusy	28	M	Del.	May		sore throat
William Kees	11mo		Md	Sep		diarreah
John Wilaby	41	M	Md	Jan	clerk	dropsy
Zadock Ross	60		Md	Apr	farmer	heart dis.
William Wright	33		Md	Oct		consumption
Mary Simmons	27	M	Md	Aug		consumption
Margaret Wright	43	M	Md	Aug		consumption
William Powell	1		Md	Aug		brain inflam.
Thomas Wrightson	58	M	Md	Sep		pneumonia
Laura Riggan	15		Md	Sep		brain inflam.
Thomas Stewart	4mo		Md	Aug		dysentary
William Hurley	3		Md	Sep		lung congest.
William Davis	14		Md	Mar		pneumonia
Ann Carroll	30		Md	Oct		bil.fever
Mary Mills	7		Md	Aug		dropsy
Ann Paul	35		Md	May		dropsy
Minerva Paul	45		Md	Jun		pleurisy
Charles Turner	52	M	Del.	Dec	physician	consumption
Hester Harrington	35	M	Md	Feb		consumption
Mary Harrington	7mo		Md	Mar		cold
Winder Harrington	2		Md	Apr		consumption
Denwood Jones	50	M	Md	Sep	farmer	consumption
Ziporah Travers	26		Md	May		dysentary
Cornelius Richardson	3		Md	May		dysentary
Louisa Fooks	30	M	Md	Apr		consumption
James Courcey	26		Md	Aug		consumption
Neil Mort	55	W	Md	Dec	farmer	pleurisy
Ella Mace	1mo		Md	Sep		unknown
Catherine Thomas	46	M	Md	Jan		consumption
Jane Wilson	20		Md	Jul		typhoid
Charles Stewart	72	M	Md	Sep	farmer	heart dis.
Hester Ann Thomas	23		Md	Aug		consumption
Levin Thomas	20		Md	Jan		unknown
Thomas Spedden	4		Md	Feb		consumption
John Holland	1		Md	Aug		unknown
John Russell	34	M	Md	Apr	farmer	dropsy
Levin Pain	40	M	Md	Jan	daylaborer	pleurisy
William Bradley	76	W	Md	Sep	farmer	consumption
Syphena Houston	52	M	Md	May		dyspepsia
John H. Huston	50	W	Del.	May	farmer	pleurisy
John W. Stacks	28	M	Md	Nov	mariner	pleurisy
Samuel Sewell	75	M	Md	Dec		pleurisy
Mary Robinson	20		Md	Feb		consumption
Henry Tolly	58	M	Md	Jun	mariner	typhus
Matthew Creighton	55	M	Md	Jun	mariner	accident

MORTALITY SCHEDULE OF MARYLAND

persons who died during the year ending 1 June 18 60

COUNTY DORCHESTER -FREDERICK DISTRICT

name	age	mar wid	birth place	mon. died	Occupation	cause of death
Sebastian Cooper	25		Md	Mar	carpenter	brain inflam.
Charles Woodland	2mo		Md	Dec		croup
Brasyilla Slocum	50	M	Md	Aug	farmer	tumor
James C. Geohghan	46		Md	Sep	teacher	bowels.
Bennett Morgan	42	M	Md	Mar	carpenter	kidney dis.
Mary Geohghan	4mo		Md	Sep		diarrhea
Isaac Williams	70	W	Md	Mar		old age
Samuel Travers	72	M	Md	Aug	farmer	dysentary
Susan Cooke	37	M	Md	Mar		consumption
William Keen	11		Md	Mar		unknown
George Penn	7		Md	Aug		dysentary
Gilbert Wingate	76		Md	Jun	laborer	consumption
James Robinson	41		Md	Apr		pleuirsy
William Langrall	47		Md	Feb		pneumonia
Levin Wingate	50	M	Md	Mar	tailor	dyspepsia
Martha Andrews	1mo		Md	May		fits
Ann Lednum	37		Md	Jun		fits
Alice Kirby	5mo		Md	Aug		cholera
Elizabeth McCall	20	M	Md	Feb		unknown
William Lecompt	66	M	Md	Sep		cancer
FREDERICK COUNTY-Buckeye Town Dis.						
Michael O'Connell	3		Md	Jan		burnt
Margaret Detrick	1mo		Md	Dec		spasms
Polly Dixon	69		Va.	May		sudden
Daniel Tingstrum	22		Md	Aug	boatman	typhoid
Mary Nichols	1mo		Md	Sep		unknown
Lynn Cunningham	2		Md	Nov		croup
Mary Cunningham	4mo		Md	Nov		croup
Emmitsburgh Dist.						
David Adams	4		Pa.	May		unknown
Francis Gilson	1		Md	May		typhoid
John Ott	3		Md	Feb		scarlet fever
Mary E. Oler	3		Md	Nov		burnt
Joseph Martin	60		Md	Jul	farmer	cholera
Vincent Weinrick	1mo		Md	Sep		thrush
George Ovelman	59		Md	Jun	farmer	heart dis.
Margaret Ovishotger ?	27	M	Pa.	Mar		unknown
Sarah Shiner	54	M	Md	Jul		quincy
Adaline Eyler	18		Md	Apr		put.throat
Mary J. Eyler	8		Md	Jan		" "
John Cauffman	14		Md	Apr		" "
Adam Cauffman	4		Md	Apr		" "
Thomas Buckingham	12		Md	May		" "
James Myers	7		Md	Jan		" "
Catherine McNulty	9		Md	Mar		" "
Cath.M. Adilsperger	6		Md	Mar		" "
Margaret L. Knott	5		Md	May		" "
William Miles	62		Mass	Nov		dysentary
John Hughes	62		Md	Jul		bowel cons.
John Manning	40	M	Md	Nov	contractor	accident
FREDERICK CITY						
W. Lev. Miller	88	W	Md	Oct	tailor	consumption

MORTALITY SCHEDULE OF MARYLAND

persons who died during the year ending 1 June 18<u>60</u>

COUNTY FREDERICK   DISTRICT Frederick City

name	age	mar wid	birth place	mon. died	Occupation	cause of death
Louisa Craft	1		Md	Oct		spasms
Tobias Ross	4		Md	Mar		scarlet fever
R. Hergsheimer	1		Md	Mar		unknown
Florence Fraley	1		Md	May		chicken pox
Fannie Hafer	1		Md	Aug		teething
Elis Houch	48	M	Md	Jul		consumption
Mary Baker	2		Md	Jul		whooping cough
George Buckley	2		Md	Sep		cold
E.Hofer (fem)	72	W	Md	Aug		cancer
Josephine Hagen	31	M	Md	Sep		brain fever
Ida Davis	1		Md	Dec		thrust
Joseph Thomas	61	M	Md	Feb	laborer	typhoid
Cath.Markle	3		Md	Apr		croup
Jacob Linn	47	M	Md	Jan	cabinetmaker	gastric
Ignatius Hagen	32	M	Md	Jul	hairdresser	cholera
W. Bear	4		Pa.	Jul		bleeding
Emma Swope	2		Md	Apr		cold
Charles Himmel	2		Md	Jun		scarlet fever
George Shaw	1		Md	Sep		bil.fever
Christen Roelly	5		Md	Aug		scarlet fever
Lizzie Duvall	2		Md	Nov		croup
John Overten	3		Md	Dec		croup
Joseph Embury	9mo		Md	Aug		unknown
Lewis Fisher	3mo		Md	Sep		unknown
George Kephart	2		Md	Mar		scarlet fever
Ida Hanna	11mo		Md	Oct		cat.fever
Elli Fisher	113	M	Md	Mar		unknown
Lewis Trail	30	M	Md	Jul	sadler	unknown
Missouri Meise	22	M	Md	Nov		child bed
Ellis Frazier	50	W	Va.	May		unknown
Adikogys Rosenmeigh	14		Md	Jun	student	scarlet fever
W. Hobbs(male)	26		Md	Aug		consumption
George Late Shaeffer	6		Md	Jul		cong.fever
Maria E. Gallagher	52	M	Pa.	Feb		paralysis
Elis Fisher	83	W	Md	Apr		old age
Willie Ashmire	2		Md	Sep		gastric fever
Albert Nolty	32	M	Hanover	Feb	Baker	typhoid
Solomon Weaver	4		Md	Jun		scarlet fever
Amelia Shalts	49	M	Pa.	Feb.		unknown
William Hahn	33	M	Pa.	May	shoemaker	consumption
Thomas Curlin	87	W	Md	Apr		unknown
Henry Stunkle	67	W	Ger	Apr	laborer	drunkedness
Joseph Wilcoxen	1		Md	Sep		whoopingcough
Mary Bear	1mo		Md	Jul		apoplexy
John Legrunge	31		Md	Apr	tobacconist	consumption
William Beam	8mo		Md	Jun		thrush
George W. Dugan	1		Md	Aug		teething
Alex Deater	37	M	Md	Apr	butcher	consumption
Thomas E. Brongle	20		Md	Nov	clerk	consumption
John Noonan	65	M	Irel.	Jan	farmer	cholera
Matilda Cronin	30	M	Md	Sep		brain cong.
Valentine Adams	60	M	Md	Mar	farmer	bil.fever

183

MORTALITY SCHEDULE OF MARYLAND

persons who died during the year ending 1 June 1860

COUNTY FREDERICK   DISTRICT Frederick City

name	age	mar wid	birth place	mon. died	Occupation	cause of death
Thomas Milford	1		Md	Oct		cat.fever
John Hargate	72	W	Md	Nov	farmer	dropsy
Genevieve Stewart	5		Md	Jul		consumption
Tracy Strickle	17		Md	Sep		consumption
Charlette Mercer	20		Md	Aug		typhoid
Milton Cronnin	1		Md	Oct		unknown
Sarah Johnson	50	M	Md	Jul		consumption
Martha Johnson	18		Md	Aug		consumption
George Null	40	W	Md	May	laborer	consumption
Jackson District						
Elizabeth Schlosen	78	W	Md	May		old age
Rebecca Kailor	50	M	Md	Jul		typhoid
Elizabeth Hesson	15		Md	Oct		typhoid
Elizabeth Gross	2mo		Md	Feb		brain dis.
Michael Hoffman	55	M	Va.	Jun	farmer	chronic dis.
Sophia Derr	38	M	Md	Jan		consumption
MIDDLETOWN District						
Henry A. Baer	9		Md	Mar		heart dis.
Jacob Lorentz	73		Md	May	shoemaker	unknown
William M. Rhodenak	4mo		Md	Aug		unknown
Catherine Ahalt	35		Md	Jun		cholera
Stephen Joy	90		Md	Apr	farmer	consumption
Henry Sigler	48		Md	Oct	farmer	palsy
Catherine Songen	55		Md	Mar		unknown
Hanvers District						
Rebecca Seip	48		Md	Jan		rheumatism
Catoctin District						
William S. Green	71		Md	Sep	farmer	paralysis
Peter Grossniakle	80		Md	Oct	farmer	dropsy
Johnstall Elect.Dist						
Mary A. Herrison	61	1835	Md	Nov		cancer
Martha A. Clemson	15		Md	Sep		consumption
Randolph Ballmyer	1		Md	2 Apr		spasms
John E. Brightwell	3mo		Md	Aug		stomach
Anna M. Williar	70		Md	6 Jun		unknown
Martha Crum	16		Md	Aug		typhoid
John D. Clemson	17		Md	Apr		typhoid
Basil Simpson	59		Md	10Jul	retired	paralysis
Abraham Sayler	51		Md	Dec	miller	consumption
R.A.Strasburg	1mo		Md	Dec		unknown
Margaret Rinehart	29	M	Md	13May		confinemanet
Elizabeth Perry	40	M	Md	Sep		confinement
William Diehl	58	M	Md	6Sep	farmer	paralysis
Jacob Diehl	22		Md	24Dec	laborer	accident
Samuel Baker	42	M	Md	May	laborer	typhoid
Jacob Luny	18		Md	4Aug	laborer	dropsy
Mary Birely	42	M	Md	19Oct		dysentary
Isabella Haugh	20		Md	20Oct	seamstress	brain affect.
Susannah Davis	5		Md	12Aug		consumption
Liberty District						
Mary Ecker	48		Md	Aug		consumption
Mary Sappington	1		Md	2Apr		teething
Henrietta Wagner	27	M	Md	May		consumption

184

MORTALITY SCHEDULE OF MARYLAND

persons who died during the year ending 1 June 18_60_

COUNTY FREDERICK   DISTRICT Liberty Electtion

name	age	mar wid	birth place	mon. died	Occupation	cause of death
David E. Biddenger	11		Md	Sep		typhoid
Elizabeth A. Keller	27	M	Md	Jul		consumption
Mary A. Nustanin	34	M	Md	May		floudeny
Susannah Cover	34	M	Md	Jul		apoplexy
G.M.Slugenber (male)	1=		Md	Mar		lung affect.
George Gasther	79		Md	Nov		apoplexy
Josephine Wilson	27	M	Md	Feb		consumption
Thomas H. Wilson	3		Md	Jun		consumption
John Engle	31	M	Md	Mar	farmer	put.throat
Catharine Justice	28	M	Md	Apr		dropsy
John Haines	76	W	Md	Jul	laborer	cancer
L.c. Gitting(fem)	1		Md	Apr		consumption
Thomas Williams	37	W	Md	Oct	blacksmith	accident
George W. Leekins	21		Md	Feb	laborer	consumption
Granville C. Bohn	2		Md	Mar		brain aff.
S.Smith(fem)	68	W	Md	Oct		dropsy
Joshua Norwood	70	W	Md	Dec		yellow jaundice
H.W.Gornell(male)	22	M	Md	Mar	farmer	killed by horse
Singleton Gatrel	54	M	Md	Jun	farmer	dropsy
Minerva A.Martin	29	M	Md	Apr		confinement
Josehine Conelson	21	M	Md	Apr		confinement
Anmatilda Mercer	29		Md	Mar		unknown
A.A.Boston	4		Md	May		put.throat
Anna M. Mercer	9		Md	Feb		dropsy
George W. Miles	14		Md	Feb	laborer	dropsy
Mechanicstown District						
Thomas F. Tinker	1mo		Md	Apr		scarlet fever
James H. Hamet	8mo		Md	May		scarlet fever
Virginia Coon	23	M	Md	Jun		typhoid
Ann Preese	5		Md	May		scarlet fever
Martha Bennett	8		Md	Jan		dropsy
Mary Eyler	1mo		Md	Aug		unknown
John F. Rife	10		Md	May		sore throat
Margaret Graff	54	M	Scot.	Sep		cramps
Mary L. Wayenman	3mo		Md	Dec		scarlet fever
John Simmons	5		Md	Dec		scarlet fever
Susannah Willhide	63	M	Md	Dec		pneumonia
William Freshman	7mo		Md	Jan		scarlet fever
Mary Stans	41	M	Md	Apr		consumption
Sarah Miller	80		Md	Jul		dsropsy
Mount Pleasant District						
Haines Dixon	74		Md	Jun	farmer	old age
John Hallruner	66		Pa.	Jun	farmer	paralysis
Lucy Hallruner	65		Pa.	May		dropsy
Amey Brengle	7		Md	Jan		bowel infl.
Charles Riddlemire	28		Md	Dec	clerk	consumption
Charles Creager	7		Md	Mar		consumption
John Young	2		Md	Aug		bowel inflam.
New Market District						
Caleb Norris	40	M	Md	Jul	dentist	consumption
Elias Wood	31	M	Md	Dec	justicePeace	consumption
Eliz Dean	70	W	Md	Mar		palsy
Kate Duvall	8mo		Md	Aug		bowel inflam.

185

MORTALITY SCHEDULE OF MARYLAND

persons who died during the year ending 1 June 18_60_

COUNTY FREDERICK   DISTRICT   New Market Dist.

name	age	mar wid	birth place	mon. died	Occupation	cause of death
Walter Bevan	3mo		Md	Aug		unknown
John Hannah	33	W	Md	Dec	miller	pneumonia
Mary E. Clary	20		Md	Mar		consumpton
Julia A. Trayer	37	M	Md	Sep		child bed
John Hardesty	66		Md	Mar	laborer	old age
William Sprigg	2		Md	Aug		disentary
John Griffith Jr.	7mo		Md	Feb		scarlet fever
Jack Milesworth	8mo		Md	Apr		teething
Sarah Clary	14		Md	May		heart dis.
Ann Burad	3mo		Md	Jul		dropsy
Petersville District						
Lawson Kam	35	M	Md	Mar	carpenter	tatanus
Clara Biser	16		Md	May		typhoid
John Crum	26		Pa.	Jan	laborer	dropsy
Mariah Weneick	11		Md	Oct		accident
Ida Thrasher	2		Va.	Jul		whooping cough
Mariah Thrasher	1		Md	Feb		unknown
T. Hilliary(fem)	52	M	Md	Aug		bowel cong.
Lydia Drill	6mo		Md	Aug		thrush
James Chidlow	1		Md	Sep		unknown
Caroline Rhodes	37	M	Md	Jun		consumption
N. Hammond	5mo		Md	Mar		croup
Jefferson District						
William Rice	2		Md	Dec		croup
John Hargath	72		Md	Oct		heart dis.
Elizabeth Smith	52		Md	Aug		typhoid
Mary Smith	24		Md	Jan		typhoid
Tilghman Myers	29		Md	Jan	farmer	unknown
Andrew Kessler	91		Md	Jan	farmer	old age
George Ramsburg	10		Md	May		unknown
Urbana District						
Emma Harding	1mo		Md	Feb		croup
Thomas Johnson	73		Md	Oct	farmer	unknown
Mrs. H. Homes	66	M	Eng.	Jun		consumption
L. Lawson(fem)	59	W	Md	Nov		palsy
Benjamin Dudrow	62	M	Md	Apr	farmer	dropsy
Wiliam Turner	66	M	Md	Nov.	laborer	unknown
Richard Dixon	36		Md	May	farmer	paralysis
Emma Dixon	1mo		Md	Mar		croup
WOODSBORO District						
Sarepta Shawk	41	M	Md	Jan		consumption
Margaret Droch	31	M	Md	May		consumption
Sarah Clance	81	W	N.J.	Jan		consumption
Harriet Baker	40	M	Md	Apr		consumption
Jacob Iler	70	M	Pa.	Dec		consumption
John Otto	71	W	Md	Apr	farmer	brain affect.
David Devilbiss	45	W	Md	Oct	farmer	bowel inflam.
John Fogle	2mo		Md	Dec		spasms
Elizabeth Root	5		Md	Feb		euraligy
CREAGERSTOWN district						
Susan R. McDonald	2		Md	May		scarlet fever
Sarah Hefner	2		Md	Apr		scarlet fever

186

MORTALITY SCHEDULE OF MARYLAND

persons who died during the year ending 1 June 1860

COUNTY – FREDERICK-Harford   DISTRICT Craegerstown Dist.

name	age	mar wid	birth place	mon. died	Occupation	cause of death
Mary Patman	6		Md	Jun		lung fever
Elizabeth Graves	60	W	Md	Jul		old age
Mary A. Rice	65	W	Md	Feb		consumption
Elizabeth Hull	4		Md	May		scarlet fever
Irwin Hull	1		Md	May		scarlet fever
Clara Creager	1mo		Md	Dec		scarlet fever
Sarah Erchiltz	2		Md	Apr		cat.fever
Eve Gilbert	72	M	Pa.	Mar		old age
John Delphy	1		Md	Mar		spasms
Ida Miller	5		Md	May		heart afflict.
HARFORD COUNTY– 1st.Dist.						
Ann M. Stephens	20	M	Md	Dec		measles
Catherine Smith	34	M	Ger.	Dec		child bed
Rebecca Mather	70		Md	Oct		consumption
John T. Taylor	1		Md	Oct		cat.fever
Edward Diffenderffer	38		Md	Feb	farmer	apoplexy
George A. Butler	4		Md	Aug		head dis.
Frances Patterson	67	M	Md	Jan		paralitic
Jesse M. Hutton	43	M	Md	Jun	farmer	accident
Mary Susanna Mills	6		Md	Sep		whooping cough
Isabella Price	83	W	Md	Nov		old age
George Alen	1		Md	Mar		cat.fever
John Stu	81	W	Md	App		pneumonia
HAVE de GRACE district						
Elen Gallagher	7mo		Md	Jun		unknown
Hiram E. Donoho	40		Md	Apr	farmer	consumption
Sarah F. Tounsly	1		Md	Jun		whooping cough
Martha Vandiver	19		Md	Jan		consumption
Lame E. Treadwill	43		Conn.	Apr	physician	wheumatism
William H. Allen	2		Pa.	Mar		cat.fever
Lawrence H. Wilson	1		Md	Sep		water on brain
William A. Myers	3mo		Md	Jun		whooping cough
Samuel Russell	43		Md	Jan	merchant	heart dis.
Jane Green	32	M	Md	Oct		confinement
Robert G. Taylor	1		Md	Aug		accident
Joseph L. Kunkle	8mo		Pa.	Sep		consumption
Elizabeth Davis	32	M	Pa.	Jan		consumption
James T. Sullivan	46	M	Md	May	merchant	bil.fever
Jerome Broadfield	1mo		Md	Mar		unknown
Hannah Ephe	69		Bavaria	Feb		old age
John Kean	40	M	Irel.	Apr	laborer	unknown
Elizabeth B. Murphy	15		Md	Jun		consumption
William R. James	4		Md	Aug		croup
William H. Holloway	34		Md	Dec	farmhard	consumption
2nd District Halls-Road						
Sarah Giver	79	W	Md	Feb		old age
Ann Daugherty	78		Md	May		old age
Ann R. Greenlee	34	M	Md	Nov		dropsy
Charles C. Holloway	67	M	Md	May	farmer	consumption
Emily W. Arthur	1		Md	Jul		whooping cough
Ann M. Osburne	22		Md	Jun		consumption
Elizabeth Hanna	20	M	N.J.	Sep		consumption
William H. Figger	28		Md	May	farmer	reulmatism

name	age	mar wid	birth place	mon. died	Occupation	cause of death
J.S. Hall(male)	22		Md	Nov	physician	consumption
George Knight	50		Md	Mar	farmer	pneumonia
Charity Silver	71	W	Md	Jul		dispepsia
Mary L. Strakem	6		Md	Oct		accident
Richard F. Keatly	12		Md	Oct		dysentary
Robert L. Hopkins	2mo		Md	Sep		unknown
Robert Greenland	2mo		Md	Aug		unknown
Sophia Cole	38		Md	Dec		heart dis.
John Stresler	50		Ger.	Jan	laborer	accident
Henrietta F. Smith	62		Md	Feb		consumption
Mary Ann Cole	39	M	Md	Aug		consumption
George Bowser	40		Md	Mar	blacksmith	consumption
Alice James	13		Md	May		diptheria
Catherine Mitchell	96		Pa.	Jun		old age
Fillmore Robinson	2		Md	Jul		consumption
James Baldwin	11mo		Md	Jul		unknown
Osburn Bowen	1		Md	Nov		burnt
Lee Magness	2		Md	Apr		brain dis.
Nancy Jones	65	W	Md	Feb		pneumonia
AmosAnderson	65		Md	Oct	farmer	typhoid
William K. Steiller	76	M	Md	Apr		intemperance
Joseph Kennedy	17		Md	Oct		unknown
Minerva Arthurson	22		Md	May		consumption
Harriet Ewing	38	M	Md	Apr		blood in head
Cyrus Country	71		Md	Nov	farmer	ruptured
Isadore Chisney	2		Md	Nov		accident
Michael Gilbert	50	M	Md	Sep	farmer	dropsy
Thomas Dutten	5		Md	Mar		consumption
Alvin Heinrick Willey	2		Md	Jul		brain fever
John G. Mitchell	2mo		Md	Jan		lung cong.
Noah Spencer	21		Md	Aug	farmer	gastric fever
Anna Baker	2		Md	Sep		dysentary
James F. Knight	5		Md	Dec		measles
Mary McCracken	94		Md	Jan		old.age
Ruth Stevens	35		Md	Nov		dropsy
Ida Sanders	3		Md	May		typhoid
Martha Burley	76	M	Md	Feb		dropsy
3rd Bell Air District						
Helen P. Magan	23		Md	Jun		consumption
Anna J. Hanna	10		Md	Feb		diptheria
Sallie R. Hanna	9		Md	Feb		diptheria
Sarah J. Decker	17		Md	Feb		consumption
Catherine Richardson	71	W	Md	Jan		dropsy
Letitia Cox	66	W	Irel.	Dec		heart dis.
William Cox	1mo		Md	Jan		unknown
Thomas A. Marks	20		Md	Feb	farmer	fall
Walter Scott	31		Md	Dec	farmer	pneumonia
Degustus Jenkins	40	M	Md	Jan	farmer	apoplexy
Jesse Ambler	28		Pa.	Dec		consumption
Meranda Beaumont	29		Md	Nov	seamstress	lockjay
John Kean	96	M	Md	Aug	farmer	bowel afflect.
Ararilla Preston	75	W	Md	Oct		debility

MORTALITY SCHEDULE OF MARYLAND

persons who died during the year ending 1 June 18_60_

COUNTY -Harford   DISTRICT 3rd BelAir Dist.

name	age	mar wid	birth place	mon. died	Occupation	cause of death
George W. Whittaker	38	M	Md	Feb	carpenter	suicide
John Ashton	87	W	Md	Feb		dropsy
Mary J. Grafton	20	M	Md	Oct		paralysis
Margaret Wallace	52	M	Md	Aug		tumor
Anna Way	14		Md	Apr		consumption
Mary E. Grafton	28	M	Md	Mar		pneumonia
Lee H. Morgan	9mo		Md	Mar		pneumonia
William Bull	25	M	Md	Jan	carpenter	consumption
Benjamin Street	75	W	Md	Jun	farmer	paralysis
Susanna Bull	70		Md	Jul	nurse	hemmorage
Isaac Michen	58		Pa.	May	farmer	diareah
Augustus Swietzer	1		Md	Aug		teething
Rosa McCormick	8mo		Md	Aug		dropsy
Naomi T. Robinson	27	M	Md	Nov		consumption
Hannah Forwood	78	W	Pa.	Mar		old age
Margaret S. Forwood	32		Md	Nov		confinement
John w. Forwood	9mo		Md	Mar		unknown
Ann Crissell	65	W	Md	Aug		unknown
Charles Harward	80	M	Irel.	Aug		old age
Lingrum Hulditch	3mo		Md	Jan		whooping cough
Mary Peterson	45	M	Md	Nov		consumption
Sarah T. Clark	17		Md	May		unknown
Thomas Andrews	45		Irel.	May	stonemason	intemperance
Mary Lee	84	W	Md	Apr		old age
Ann Andrews	68		Md	Dec		consumption
G.Albert Miller	3mo		Md	Sep		unknown
Catharine Whitaker	3mo		Md	Oct		dropsy
Rebecca S. Hollingsworth	20		Md	Dec		abcess
Mary A. Norris	20		Md	Oct		accident
James H. Cadow	2		Md	Mar		diptheria
Elizabeth Nelson	58	W	Md	Jan		heart dis.
Daniel H. Loften	50	M	Md	Jun	farmer	cancer
William A. Smith	63	M	Md	Aug	farmhand	consumption
1stDistrict Abingden						
Ann Magniss	76	W	Md	Aug		dropsy
Oliver Eugene Hughett	1		Md	Nov		whooping cough
John V. Shreck	2		Md	Sep		bowel inflam.
Nicholas F. Wilson	3		Md	Jun		unknown
Virginia Yaner	1		Md	Nov		cholera
Hannah Yaner	20		Ger.	May		consumption
John Horn	46		Bavaria	Feb	laborer	consumption
Edward Doyle	30		Irel.	Oct	laborer	intemperance
William E. Cator	3		Md	Feb		measles
Elizabeth Billingate	77		Md	Nov		old age
Franklin Henry	2		Md	Jun		bone disease
4th Marshalls Dist.						
Joseph Knopp	25	M	Pa.	Jun	shoemaker	hemmorhage
Joseph Street	4mo		Md	Mar		unknown
William James Carly	18		Md	Apr	farmer	dropsy
James B. Preston	4mo		Md	May		cong.brain
Priscilla M. Gilbert	13		Md	Mar		measles
Sally Ann Baxter	1		Md	Jan		erysipelas
Ann Craig	3		Pa.	May		unknown

persons who died during the year ending 1 June 18_60_

COUNTY HARFORD   DISTRICT 4th Marshals Dist.

name	age	mar wid	birth place	mon. died	Occupation	cause of death
William H. McMullen	2		Pa.	Sep		measles
Joseph H. Wheller	66	W	Md	May	carpenter	pneumonia
Elizabeth Lambright	26	M	Md	Jan		consumption
Edward Guyten	78		Md	May	farmer	paralysis
Sarah Bull	20		Md	Jun		consumption
William Hutchins	80	W	Md	Jan	farmer	cold
William R. Standiford	54	M	Md	Jan		unknown
Esther A. Chalk	34	M	Md	Apr		consumption
Ellen McGarvil	1		Md	Aug		summer comp.
William H. Beaty	3mo		Md	Jul		whooping cough
Susanna Scarf	2		Md	Oct		croup
Jemima Kennedy	76	M	Md	Nov		pneumonia
Laura V. McCann	8mo		Md	Jul		dropsy
Catherine Gross	65	W	Ger.	May		dropsy
Sarah King	91	W	Md	Nov		old age
Elisha Meads	1		Md	Jun		diarrehea
Mary E. Patterson	6mo		Md	Oct		unknown
Elizabeth Alminy	56	M	Md	Jan		gastric fever
Martha Shane	1		Md	Apr		cat. fever
John F. Wright	31	M	Md	Jun	magistrate	epiliptic fits
Mary Ayres	20		Md	Jun		consumption
Susan Denbo	25		Md	Dec		consumption
Joshua Amos	79	M	Md	Feb	farmer	dropsy
Hannah Kennedy	90		Md	Nov		old age
William H. Price	3mo		Md	Aug		summer compl.
Sarah Devoe	50	M	Md	Jun		dispepsia
William Street	63	M	Md	Jun	farmer	pneumonia
Robert Watt	28		Md	Sep	farmer	typhoid
William Slade	38	M	Md	Oct	farmer	consumption
Joshua Amos	84	M	Md	Apr		unknown
Adam Foland	75	M	Md	Mar		cancer
Rebecca Glenn	94	W	Md	Dec		old age
John A. Thompson	3mo		Md	Jun		diarrhea
Elizabeth Stansbury	30	M	Md	Jun		gastric
John Smithson	75	W	Md	Oct	farmer	dropsy
John L. Heaton	1		Md	Oct		croup
Ramsey M. Rramply	1		Md	Apr		measles
Mary Wiley	1		Md	Sep		dropsy
Rachel Stebbins	45	M	Md	Apr		measles
Ephraim Neal	2		Md	Jan		dropsy
Felix R. Channell	11mo		Md	Feb		inflamation
Sarah Hitchcock	17	M	Md	May		child bed
5th Dublin Dist.						
Margaret Hopkins	16		Md	Jun		scarlet fever
Rachel Bird	2		Md	Mar		liver comp.
Ann Lee	56	M	Md	Mar		gastric fever
Michael Pritchard	2		Pa.	Apr		unknown
Hiram W. Carr	24		Md	Jun		scrofula
Sarah Williamson	23		Md	May		typhoid
Harvey Stokes	83	M	Md	Sep	farmer	gravel
James Trotner	24		Md	May		erysipelas
Blanch Gallion	2		Md	May		brain fever
Syrah Scarborough	23	M	Md	Feb		bowel inflam.

persons who died during the year ending 1 June 18<u>60</u>

COUNTY Harford - Howard   DISTRICT 5th Dublin Dist.

name	age	mar wid	birth place	mon. died	Occupation	cause of death
James Murphy	50	M	Irel.	Mar	laborer	pleurisy
Mary Murphy	8		Md	Mar		bowel inflam.
Elizabeth Biles	38	M	Pa.	Mar		consumption
Julia Street	2		Md	Nov		bronchitis
Mary Cranston	80	W	Pa.	May		debility
Amos Thomas	46	M	Md	Jan	farmer	typhoid
Ida Jane Ashbridge	9mo		Md	Feb		catarrah
Nancy Enfield	48	M	Md	Jan		consumption
Robert Thompson	84	W	Irel.	Sep		unknown
Richard Fox	54	M	Md	Jan	quarryman	penumonia
Ann E. Boyle	33	M	Pa.	Mar		fever
Binnessie Hamilton	22	M	Md	Jul		dropsy
John J.Jones	41	M	Wales	Aug	quarryman	pneumonia
Thomas Howe	71	M	Md	Mar	blacksmith	dropsy
Thomas Stump	64	M	Md	Feb	farmer	gravel
Joseph Hasbands	63	M	Md	Jun	merchant	jaundice
William Simmons	3mo		Pa.	Aug		summer comp.
Walter S. Baldwin	1		Md	Jun		lung affect.
Sarah Ann Miller	23		Md	Nov		typhoid
William Worthington	40	M	Md	Oct	farmer	consumption
Pamela Forwood	31	M	Md	Mar		child birth
Daniel Pritchard	22		Md	Feb	carpenter	consumption
Cordelia Silver	25	M	Md	Apr		consumption
Ruth Quinlan	60	W	Md	Mar		neuralgia
Harriett Richardson	75		Md	Apr		unknown
Benjamin G. Jones	52		Md	Feb		pneumonia
Rachel Kinsey	73	W	Pa.	Apr		consumption
Francis McCater	71		Md	Apr	farmer	dropsy
Joseph J. Pyle	5		Md	Feb		croup
Isaac Street	52	M	Md	Jan	miller	unknown
Ann Rigdon	35	M	Md	Apr		consumption
Robert Griffin	38		Wales	May	slater	pneumonia
Robert Kirk	30	M	Irel.	Jan	laborer	hands of violence
Margaret Stacks	72	M	Md	Aug		dropsy
John P. Roncy	7mo		Md	Nov		unknown
Ann McCausland	57	W	Irel.	Feb		heart dis.
HOWARD COUNTY 2nd Election Dist.						
Ann Frost	83	W	Md	Oct		paralysis
William Hogan	5		Md	Jan		croup
Eugene Karie	15		N.J.	Feb	student	scarlet fever
Remegious Blanc	28		France	Mar	professor	pneumonia
Mark McEllwee	15		Md	Apr	student	erysipilas
Barbara Decker	84		Pa	Apr	servant	old age
Margaret Hickey	10mo		Md	Sep		diarrehea
Mary Jane McBee	27		Md	Mar		paralysis
Ann E. Mitchell	19		Md	Jun		typhoid
Mary A. Gineman	3		Md	May		croup
Mary Ann Swallenback	4mo		Md	Nov		spasms
John P. Dutch	2		Md	Dec		croup
Julia Donnivan	17		Md	Feb		consumption
George E. Hess Jr.	3		Md	Sep		spine disease
D.E. Walker(male)	49		Md	Dec	merchant	insanity

191

MORTALITY SCHEDULE OF MARYLAND

persons who died during the year ending 1 June 18_60_

COUNTY Howard   DISTRICT 2nd.E.District

name	age	mar wid	birth place	mon. died	Occupation	cause of death
Charles Ranney	1		Md	Dec		dysentary
Basil Ray	71		Md	Sep	laborer	old age
Mary Martin	3		Md	Jan		croup
Dorothy Long	26		Ger.	Jan		consumption
William Taylor	49		Eng.	May	storekeeper	unknown
James E. Cassiday	1		Md	Feb		croup
Andrew Yinger	40		Ger.	Sep.	stage prop.	consumption
Emma Mercer	16		Md	Dec		typhoid
3rd Election Dist.						
Mary Carrol	60	M	Md	Dec		typhoid
Jane Bradford	77	W	Md	Jan		pneumonia
Charles B. Hepsley	73	W	Md	May		old age
Frank A. Zink	3mo		Md	Feb		collic
Eliza A. Adams	56	M	Md	Jul	merchant	cancer
1st. Election Dist.						
Anna Zink	1		Md	Sep		unknown
John Cassidy	18		Md	Sep	japaner	dropsy
Bernard Bowers	5mo		Md	Jul		consumption
Catherine Ryne	6mo		Md	Mar		pneumonia
Sally Bryan	74		Md	Apr	seamstress	brain fever
P.F.A.Cooper(male)	29	M	Oldenberg	May	farmer	gout
Charles A. Smallwood	19		Md	Jul	farmhand	consumption
William F. King	61		Eng.	Oct	wheelright	unknown
Joseph Phelps	10		Md	Dec		scarlet fever
William H. Wheeler	21		Md	Apr		heart dis.
Martha Shoemaker	1mo		D.C.	Mar		unknown
Charles Hammond	73	W	Md	Apr	farmer	gout
Jesse Haines	51	M	Md	Aug	farmer	typhoid
Elizabeth A. Rowlis	35	M	Md	Dec		consumption
Nathan R. Shane	43	M	Md	Jan	stonecutter	consumption
Robert Bond	55	M	Md	Feb	miller	consumption
Jonathan Marriott	43	M	Md	Apr	farmer	liver comp.
Martha Newton	35	M	Eng.	Oct		milk fever
Almyra Morrison	4		Md	Aug		unknown
4th District						
Margaret Wayman	60	M	Md	Feb		asthma
Martha Buck	16		Md	Oct		consumption
Patience Day	53	M	Md	Mar		consumption
Eliza Earl	26	M	Irel.	Apr		consumption
Elmore L. Baines	17		Md	Dec		consumption
Thomas Peddicord	73	M	Md	Jan	carpenter	consumption
Nancy A. Burdett	64		Md	May		typhoid
James S. Pickett	1mo		Md	Jun		thrush
Ella McNew	2mo		Md	Jul		unknown
Ann E. Hobbs	25	M	Md	Feb		consumption
Stephen Musgrave	72	M	Md	Apr	farmer	pneumonia
Francis W. Day	15		Md	Mar	farmer	accident
Samuel P. Ridgley	32	M	Md	Feb	teacher	consumption
Margaret Owings	17		Md	Jun		brain inflam.
Edward Dorsey	9mo		Md	Jan	laborer	sudden
William W. Powers	6mo		Md	Aug		bil.disentary
Dr.Davis Hewett	59	M	Md	May	M.D.	sudden

192

persons who died during the year ending 1 June 1860

COUNTY HOWARD - KENT   DISTRICT 4th Dist.

name	age	mar wid	birth place	mon. died	Occupation	cause of death
William Davis	49	M	Md	Jan	farmer	flebitis
Joshua Merrick	1		Md	Mar		croup
W. Buckingham (fem)	54	W	Md	Jan		measles
Ephraim Warfield	63	W	Md	May	farmer	pneumonia
Henry Woodward	1		Md	Apr	carpenter	sudden
Julia Becraft	57	W	Md	Jun		consumption
Matthew Murray	64		Irel.	Jun	private	unknown
			5th Election Dist.			
Richard Brown	60	M	Md	Aug	clergyman	apoplexy
Amril Dorsey (fem)	73		Md	Mar		old age
Margaret E. Zepp	16		Md	Apr		typhoid
Gen.J.W. Tyson	45	M	Philad.	Feb	lawyer	none
Catharine Donnell	1		Md	Dec		whooping cough
Ruth Dorsey	61		Md	Aug		dropsy
Lewis Nicholas	42		Md	Oct	millright	pneumonia
Ada Johnson	1		Md	Jun		heart
Joseph A. Dainhart	2mo		Md	Jul		none
Cora D. Adams	31		Ohio	Dec		consumption
William Willing	21		Md	Sep	physician	consumption
Thomas Z. Blowers	7		Md	Aug		brain inflam.
Margaret J. Cissell	8mo		Md	Oct		bowel inflam.
			KENT COUNTY 1st Election Dist.			
M. E. Hoffman(fem)	28	M	Md	Oct		child bed
E.W. Kennard (male)	1mo		Md	May		unknown
E.Stephens(fem)	9		Md	Sep		pneumonia
Jesse Darby	50		Irel.	Feb	pauper	dropsy
E. Cence (male)	72		MD	May	pauper	heart dis.
L.Newcomb(male)	27	M	Md	Feb	farmer	penumonia
G. Young(fem)	14		Md	May		pneumonia
E. DeCoursey (fem)	9mo		Md	Mar		pneumonia
Thomas M. True	65	M	Md	Dec		apoplexy
Mary T. Ruth	3		Md	Jul		whooping cough
William T.G.Strong	10mo		Md	Aug		bowel inflam.
Samuel H. Bennett	11mo		Md	Jun		whooping cough
Walter Coleman	6mo		Md	Mar		cat.fever
Charles H. Rodney	5		Md	Jul		pt.throat
Emeline Dudley	28	W	Md	Sep		consumption
Sarah Ayres	3mo		Md	Aug		put.throat
Laura Stevens	1		Md	Aug		put.throat
Martha Dawson	49	M	Md	Apr		pneumonia
A.L.Sappington(male)	59	M	Md	Dec		apoplexy
Thomas Wilson	85	M	Md	Oct		dysepsia
Anna Cruikshanks	84	W	Md	Nov		paralytic
Samuel Haines	84	W	Md	Sep		dropsy
James F. Hadaway	7mo		Md	Aug		whooping cough
Alfred Middleton	2		Md	Sep		put.throat
Mary M. Hynson	1		Md	Aug		cholera
William Maslin	85	M	Md	Jan	saddler	old age
Jane Downey	6mo		Md	Jul		cholera
			2nd E.Dist.			
William Morris	5		Md	Jul		convulsions
Sarah L. Miles	4		Md	Jun		whooping cough

persons who died during the year ending 1 June 18<u>60</u>

COUNTY - KENT -Montgomery   **DISTRICT** 2nd.E.Dist.

name	age	mar wid	birth place	mon. died	Occupation	cause of death
Charles Rater	4		Md	Jul		croup
John H. Moody	17		Md	Aug	farmer	neuralgia
			Chestertown dist.			
Thomas E. Earnesh	5mo		Md	Jul		cholera
Anania Simms	30	M	Md	May	milliner	consumption
Alice Avisteato	1		Md	Aug		cholera
Henrietta E. Stokes	1		Md	Jul		dysentary
A.M.Anderson(male)	42		Md	Sep	physician	apoplexy
Samuel C. Hamilton	39	M	Md	Aug	bridgekeeper	dropsy
Eliza Shaw	60	W	Md	Jan		consumption
William W. Dugan	40	M	Md	Jan	carpenter	suicide
Elizabeth Sparks	57	W	Md	Dec		consumption
			3rd Election Dist.			
Daneil Farrell	7		Md	May		whooping cough
Mary J. Stewart	7		Md	Jul		fyphoid
Margaret G. Dillihunt	6mo		Md	Jul		summer compl.
Ella Woodall	6mo		Md	Jul		scrofula
John E. Stewart	43		Md	Sep	blacksmith	whooping cough
Mary A. Rouse	19		Md	Jan		convulsions
Thomas Rouse	3mo		Md	Feb		consumption
Araminta Medders	44	M	Md	Feb		typhoid
Mary L. Mann	31	M	Md	Dec		typhoid
			MONTGOMERY CO.1st Election Dist.			
Joseph Brown	3		Md	Apr		cat.fever
Mary Ellen Brown	4mo		Md	May		bowel infect.
Richard Nicholls	10mo		Md	Jul		bowel inflam.
Michael Henly	34		Md	Mar	laborer	consumption
Kate Worthington	2mo		Md	Jul		unknown
E.P.Etchison(male)	3		Md	Apr		pneumonia
Rachel Wincaster	42	M	Md	Aug		bowel congest.
Ganad Ray	57	M	Md	Jan		pheuumonia
Mary Bowman	55	M	Md	Nov		dispepsey
Nicholas H. Thompson	3		Md	Feb		pneumonia
Warren Adams	53		Md	Feb	laborer	pneumonia
Henry A. Griffith	28		Md	Apr	clerk	cancer
Elizabeth Griffith	39	M	Md	Apr		cholera
Mary E. Price	66	W	Md	Mar		heart dis.
Anna Plummer	7mo		Md	Mar		pleurisy
Sarah Lyon	64	W	Md	Mar		pleurisy
Susan Edmonston	2mo		Md	Jul		pleurisy
G.W. Gittings	1mo		Md	Mar		croup
Maria Beckett	50		Md	Apr		apoplexy
Annie Beckett	2		Md	Apr		whooping cough
Capt.George Carther	79		Md	Nov	farmer	apoplexy
Joseph Gardiner	60	M	Md	Feb	farmer	consumption
			4th Election Dist.			
Sarah Briggs	23		Md	Aug		brain fever
Ferresh A. Griffith	1mo		Md	Apr		pneumonia
Grace Dane	3		Md	Oct		croup
William Lind	70		Ger.	Jan	carpenter	pneumonia
Richard West	19		Md	Apr	farmhand	accident
Mary E. Berry	32		Md	Jun		consumption
A.E.Claggett(male)	27		Md	Dec		consumption

MORTALITY SCHEDULE OF MARYLAND

persons who died during the year ending 1 June 18_60_

COUNTY   Montgomery   DISTRICT 4th.Election Dist.

name	age	mar wid	birth place	mon. died	Occupation	cause of death
Mary E. Jones	28		Md	Jul		consumption
Laura E. Granger	5		Md	Dec		sorethroat
D.H. Higgins	2mo		Md	Apr		unknown
William H. Carroll	6mo		Md	May		unknown
Eloise C. Moore	9mo		D.C.	Aug		cholera
Virginia Carroll	7mo		Md	May		unknown
Aletha Kisner	45		Md	Aug		consumption
James Duffy	40		Irel.	Jul	carpenter	cancer
Louisa Dittrich	2		Md	Aug		dysentary
David Sloan	60		Md	Jan	carpenter	dysentary
James Hawkins	89		Md	Dec		old age
Mary A. Tomlinson	50		Md	Dec		unknown
Alexander Peter	3mo		Md	May		erisypelas
George F. Ricketts	21		Md	Jun	farmer	typhoid
Thomas A. Brooke	1		Md	Apr		cong.fever
Henrietta M. Brooke	74		Md	Apr		pulmonary
Jonathan Fields	40		Md	Dec	laborer	rem.fever
Altha Beckwith	89		Md	Aug		old age
Peter A. Bowie	59		Md	Jan	farmer	consumption
William Braddock	44		Md	Nov	merchant	consumption
Julius West	52		Md	Nov	farmer	pneumonia
Martha Barney	58		Md	none		consumption
R.H.Allen(male)	40		Md	none	painter	sudden
			5th District			
Rachel Moore	3mo		Md	Jan		whooping cough
John Reigle	24		Pa.	Aug	teacher	consumption
Bassil Murphy	53		Md	Jul		unknown
Mariah Fawcett	52	M	Eng.	Dec		cholic.
Ann Soper	45		Md	Jan		ulcers
Benjamin D. Scags	19		Md	Mar		dropsy
Mary Reynolds	87		Md	May		bowel inflam.
Mary Crawford	8mo		Md	Feb		scarlet fever
Deborah Cissel	88		Md	Dec		old age
Eliza Clark	49	M	Md	Apr		bowel inflam.
William Norton	24		Md	Jan	laborer	consumption
Annie Jones	80	W	Md	Nov		paralysis
William Glover	68	M	Va.	Jul	farmer	liver compl.
Thomas Kidwell	48	M	Va.	Feb	farmer	consumption
Charles Stewart	8da.		D.C.	Nov		unknown
Florenton Seigear	1		Md	Mar		whooping cough
Susanna Johnson	2		Md	Jun		unknown
Henrietta Bently	77	W	Md	May		rheumatism
Albert G.Palmer	30		Pa.	Mar	druggist	consumption
Mahlon Kirk	70		Pa.	Apr	farmer	paralysis
Warwick G.Miller	1		Va.	Feb		lung cong.
William Sleighter	3mo		Md	Dec		unknown
Richard White	35		Md	Jul	laborer	cholera
Alfred Walker	55	M	Md	Jul	farmer	paralysis
Edward Davis	70	M	Md	Jun	farmer	dropsey
Tabitha Gittings	72	W	Md	Nov		asthma
Catherine Magruder	21	M	Md	Jul		consumption
Rebecca Shay	60	M	Md	Jan		rheumatism

195

persons who died during the year ending 1 June 18<u>60</u>

COUNTY MONTGOMERY   DISTRICT 5th District

name	age	mar wid	birth place	mon. died	Occupation	cause of death
Josephine Gray	14		Md	May		unknown
Ann Crawford	54	M	Md	May		unknown
Eliza Lagasby	55	W	Md	Oct		typhoid
Thomas Vanby	66	M	Pa.	Nov	farmer	paralysis
			Clarksburg Dist.			
Susan Horton	61	W	Md	Nov		cancer
Samuel Blunt	70	M	Md	May	farmer	heart dis.
Mary Ellen Thompson	28		Md	Jul		childbed
Mary E. Burdett	17		Md	Nov		consumption
William H. Scott	27	M	Md	Jul	farmer	consumption
William Wilson	85	M	Md	Oct	farmer	consumption
Zera Wagner	75		Md	Mar		heart dis.
Matilda Beall	45		Md	Aug		dyspepsia
Sarah E. Johnson	70	M	Md	Mar		paralysis
George B. Cissell	2mo		Md	Dec		unknown
Ruth A. Duvall	52	M	Md	May		consumption
John Watkins	1		Md	Sep		unknown
William H. Danen	45	M	Pa.	Sep	miller	accident
Catherine Nimrod	70	W	Md	Aug		epilepsy
Ella Beall	1mo		Md	Aug		unknown
William R. Mullinix	4mo		Md	Jun		dysentary
Lean E. Lewis	16		Md	Jul		consumption
Henry Smith	52	M	Md	Nov	farmer	consumption
Charles W. Mills	34	M	Md	Apr		consumption
Wellington Day	25		Md	Feb	laborer	consumption
William Burdett	73		Md	Aug		sudden
			MEDLEYS DISTRICT			
Mary Warfield	73	M	Md	May		influenza
William M. Nicholls	59		Md	Jan	farmer	cancer
Mary Nicholls	52	M	Md	Feb		consumption
Bennoni Allnutt	74		Md	Aug	farmer	bil.dysentary
Laurence Allnutt	64	M	Md	Aug	farmer	bil.dysentary
Eleanor Allnutt	57	W	Md	May		pnuemonia
Samuel Dalzell	55		Irel.	May	wheelright	complicated dis.
Ruth R. Bowman	50	M	Md	May		cancer
George Chiswell	1		Md	Aug		pneumonia
Ann R. Norris	58		Md	Feb		palsey
Frances E. Poole	19		Md	Mar		tyhpoid
Preston Siper	1		Md	Feb		pneumonia
S.N.C.White(male)	59	M	Md	Mar	physician	typhoid
Martha Michael	40		Md	Sep		consumption
Albert White	2		Md	Aug		unknown
Wametta Brewer	44	M	Md	Dec		cancer
Nathan Dickerson	82	W	Md	Apr	farmer	pneumonia
Emlina Whalen	30	M	Md	Sep		unknown
Asa Aud	68	M	Va.	Apr	boatman	erysipilas
Henrietta Rollison	48	M	Va.	Nov		typhoid
William Sellman	19		Md	Feb	farmer	typhoid
Thomas T. Austin	26		Md	Feb	farmer	scarlet fever
John Brown	50	W	Md	Aug	blacksmith	consumption
Deborah Orme	37	M	Md	May		paralysis

name	age	mar wid	birth place	mon. died	Occupation	cause of death
John T. Millard	22		Md	May	laborer	consumption
Daneil Diggs	47		Md	May	attorney	dropsey
Amanda Webster	28		Md	May		consumption
Mary Gardiner	3		Calif.	Apr		dysentary
Elizabeth Wilson	39	M	Md	Oct		consumption
Sarah Dudly	24	M	Md	Aug		consumption
Harriet Jones	48	M	Md	Jul		paralysis
			1st Election Dist.			
Jane O'Neale	2		Md	Feb		scalded
Lenard Disney	33	M	Md	Apr	engineer	consumption
Randolph Dorsey	10md		Md	Jul		teething
Edward Keys	7mo		Md	Sep		paralysis
John Chipley	11md		Md	Nov		brain affect.
George W. Chaney	2		Md	Oct		whooping cough
Jane Hodson	37		Eng.	Mar		erexilfisy
Mary P. Emach	82	M	Md	Mar		old age
Elizabeth Walker	78	M	Md	Apr		apoplexy
Frederick Brooke	3mo		Md	May		dysentary
Samuel Botler	55	M	Md	Jan	farmer	dropsy
James M. Duvall	30		Md	Nov	farmer	consumption
Mary Duvall	25		Md	May		tumor
Posela Harby	5		Md	Nov		scarlet fever
Charlotta Beall	84	M	Md	Jul		diarrea
			2nd District			
Clement Hillary	75	W	Md	Sep	farmer	heart dis.
Martha Hopkins	65	M	Md	Aug		cancer
Amelia Howard	92	W	Md	Nov		dropsy
Eliza Sprigg	80	W	Md	Nov		old age
Margaret Baker	11md		Md	Jul		teething
Lawrence Brown	11		Md	May		scarlet fever
Farlton Brown	75	M	Md	Apr		old age
Charles C. Schickels	50	M	Md	Feb	farmer	pneumonia
Thomas Davis	55	M	Md	Feb	miller	pneumonia
Samuel Ervin	62		Md	Feb	farmer	penumonia
Mary E. Owings	23		Md	Sep		dropsy
Elizabeth Grimes	53	M	Md	Feb		consumption
Archibald Magruder	4		Md	Feb		scarlet fever
Alfred Wells	50	M	Md	Feb	farmer	heart dis.
			5th Election District			
Elias Palmer	70		Md	Aug	hotelkeeper	consumption
May E. Hurtt	30	M	Md	Apr		consumption
Joseph R. Kaldenback	1		Md	Jun		teething
George T. Sweeney	64		Md	Feb	laborer	dropsy
Isnatius B. Guyner	29		Md	Oct	planter	typhoid
D.W.H.Guyner(male)	26		Md	Sep	physician	typhoid
Jane B. Guyner	17		Md	Oct		typhoid
John W.W. Kerby	18		Md	Dec	laborer	penumonia
Z.G.Robey	54	M	Md	Nov	planter	pneumonia
John Palmer	84	W	Md	Oct		old age
Stephen Ward	68	M	Md	Jan	planter	consumption
John Townsend	50	M	Md	Nov	planter	consumption
Amelia Suit	33	M	Md	Aug		consumption

MORTALITY SCHEDULE OF MARYLAND

persons who died during the year ending 1 June 18_60_

COUNTY PRINCE GEORGE -QUEEN DISTRICT   5th E.Dist.
ANNES

name	age	mar wid	birth place	mon. died	Occupation	cause of death
George W.W.Hall	23		Md	May	clerk	typhoid
Elizabeth Monroe	45		Md	May		consumption
Clara Robey	88	W	Md	Jul		old age
Eva A. Fayman	1		Md	Sep		cholera
			7th District			
Eliza Mulikin	69		Md	Dec		heart dis.
Elizabeth Howard	2		Md	Mar		braininflam.
Andrew King	9		Hungary	Jun		drowned
Elizins Bowie	78		Md	May	carpenter	dropsey
Richard T. Isaac	24		Md	May		consumption
			8th Election Dist.			
William Trumbull	50	M	Irel.	Sep	planter	appoplexy
Jesse Garner	78	W	Md	Feb	carpenter	old age
Charles H. Sturgiss	5mo		Md	Jan		unknown
John H. Langly	40	M	Md	Apr	laborer	intemperance
Catharine East	44	M	Ger.	May		cancer
Levi A. Proctor	21	M	Md	Apr		paralysis
Susan Cage	67	M	Md	Apr		paralysis
Benjamin Watson	82	W	Md	Mar	planter	old age
G.A.E.Turner(fem.)	27	M	Md	Nov		consumption
William F. Richards	73	M	Md	Apr	planter	consumption
George Brady	1mo		Md	Apr		unknown
William F. Fowler	14		Md	Aug		dysentary
Charles Lynch	52	M	Pa.	Apr	manager	fits
			4th Election Dist.			
Robert Bowie Jr.	38	M	Md	Jan	planter	bowel affect.
Louisa Berg	19		Md	May		consumption
Mary C. Luckett	39	M	Md	Jun		typhoid
Caroline Dorman	43	M	N.Y.	Apr		consumtion
Mary E. Harbin	24	M	Md	May		consumptoin
William Lindsay	36		Md	May		consumption
James E. Goddard	48	M	Md	Aug	carpenter	piles
Eliza E. Thorne	22		Md	Dec	seamstress	injury
William J. Edelin	40	W	Md	Dec	planter	pneumonia
Sarah Medley	70	W	Md	Nov		old age
George W. Clubb	6		Md	Sep		accident
QUEEN ANNES 2nd. Election Dist.						
Eliza W. Roe	3		Md	Mar		whooping cough
Ann Freeman	35		Md	Feb		child bed
William T. Booker	9mo		Md	Sep		brain fever
Mary Dockerty	40		Irel.	Aug		apoplexy
Sarah Knotts	66		Md	May		paralysis
George Finley	12		Md	Nov		bowel cons.
Eliza G. Brown	60		Md	Jun		heart dis.
James Seth	3mo		Md	Jul		sudden
William Holland	27		Md	Aug	farmer	bil.fever
John McKenny	1		Md	Aug		unknown
Samuel Meredith	1mo		Md	Jan		inflam.stomach
Emily A. Cole	33	M	Md	Aug		child bed
James T. Murdock	55	W	Md	Apr	farmer	consumption
Jane Soloway	2		Md	Oct		bil.fever

persons who died during the year ending 1 June 18_60

COUNTY -QUEEN ANNES   DISTRICT   2nd Election Dist.

name	age	mar wid	birth place	mon. died	Occupation	cause of death
Emily A. Cole	33	M	Md	Apr		child bed
James T. Murdock	55	W	Md	Ap	farmer	consumption
Georganna Murdock	5mo		Md	May		unknown
John Shahan	10mo		Md	Jun		unknown
Margaret Smith	17		Md	Nov		typhoid
Sarah Roe	4mo		Md	Aug		unknown
Fletcher Jackson	6mo		Md	May		unknown
John W. Jackson	18		Pa.	Apr		heart dis.
Indianna Jackson	4mo		Md	Mar		unknown
Susan Walls	2		Md	Dec		unknown
Sarah Potts	1		Md	Dec		unknown
Ann E. Camecelt	2		Md	Aug		unknown
William Milburn	1		Md	Sep		unknown
Hannah E. Vansant	35		Md	Jun		consumption
Sarah Cacy	27	M	Md	Jul		consumption
Sarah E. Hasel	5		Md	Jun		lung hemor.
Ann E. Williams	12		Md	Aug		unknown
3rd District						
Daniel Newman	1		Md	Dec		whooping cough
Maria Tilghman	2		Md	Jul		brain fever
L.W. Goldsborough	6mo		Md	Jul		bowel compl.
Rodah C. Banks	6		Md	Oct		fever
John Palmer Sr.	60	W	Md	Mar	clerk	bronchitas
George E. Palmer	48		Md	Jul	farmer	consumption
William Emory	64	M	Md	Jun	farmer	paralysis
Henry e. Wright	63	M	Md	Mar		ereysepilas
Vateria Wright	15		Md	May		consumption
George Turpin	1mo		Md	Aug		cholera
Turbutt Bush	18		Md	Sep		pneumonia
William E. Covington	5mo		Md	Feb		croup
Mary Orrell	9mo		Md	Dec		croup
Rachel M. Parrott	47		Md	May		lung dis.
John Dyott	55	M	Md	Nov	farmer	consumption
4th Election District						
Charles Williss	7		Md	Feb		kidney affect.
Antoinette Hopkins	25	M	Md	Nov		child bed
Tristam Weedon	69	M	Md	Mar	merchant	liver dis.
F.M.E.Earickson(fem)	33	M	Md	Oct		consumption
Richatd Norman	21		Md	Sep		typhoid
Oliver Elliott	40	W	Md	Jan		consumption
Susan E. Hoxter	23	M	Md	Jan		child bed
Roberta Thompson	14		Md	Apr		scarlet fever
Hans Neilson	70	M	Norway	Jun	sailor	dropsy
James Benton	5		Md	Oct		worm syrup
John Lewis	72	W	Md	Apr	farmer	bronchitas
Caroline Lewis	48	W	Md	Apr		consumption
Eliza Walters	57	M	Md	Apr		typhoid
5th Election District						
Josephine Spear	3mo		Md	Oct		whooping cough
Jacob T. Denny	38	M	Md	Aug	farmer	drowned
Solomon R. Wright	23		Md	Jan		marasmus
Philemon Davidson	52		Md	Jan	farmer	pneumonia
William J. Ford	57	W	Md	Jan	farmer	typhoid

MORTALITY SCHEDULE OF MARYLAND

persons who died during the year ending 1 June 18_60_

COUNTY –Queen Annes –St.Marys DISTRICT 5th E. Dist.

name	age	mar wid	birth place	mon. died	Occupation	cause of death
Mary A. Coursey	42	M	Md	Apr		child bed
John W. Dean	23	W	Md	Jan		pneumonia
Frank Chambers	3mo		Md	Nov		thrash
Sarah Bryan	34		Md	Apr		scrofula
Saint Marys County-Leonard Town						
Olevia Camper	1da		Md	May		unknown
Ellen Leigh	3		Md	Jan		unknown
Albert Yates	16		Md	Sep		typhoid
1st E.ection Dist.						
Antonette Freeman	40	M	Md	Nov		inflamation
Margaret D. Joy	5		Md	May		burns
Ellen C. Magill	16		Md	Feb		brain infl.
Samuel Collison	78	W	Md	Nov	baypilot	dropsy
Elizabeth Loker	9mo		Md	Jul		summer compl.
2nd. Election Dist.						
Alex S. Spencer	45	M	Md	Oct	farmer	consumption
E.A. Combs(fem)	16		Md	Dec		consumption
William S.F. Combs	15		Md	Dec		scrofula
Kate Carroll	8da		Md	Apr		infantile fits
Mary Combs	44	W	Md	Nov		pneumonia
Elizabeth Abell	2		Md	Jun		lung cong.
Sarah J. Springer	21	M	Pa.	Jul		heart dis.
Sydney F. Thomas	2		Md	Oct		sorethroat
George W. Pembroke	47	M	Md	Apr	farmer	apoplexy
Joshua Wilson	22		Md	Sep	merchant	rheumatism
Ellen Mathany	56	W	Md	Dec		pneumonia
Thomas Lynch	82	W	Md	Feb	farmer	pneumonia
Edward Henderson	40	M	Md	Oct	pilot	ship fever
Mary A. Gibson	3		Md	Oct		sore throat
John Moore	6		Md	Dec		sorethroat
Sarah Williams	36		Md	Nov	seamstress	unknown
Harriet Thornton	59		Md	Mar	lady	paralytic
Thomas Bell	35	M	Md	Apr	sailor	consumption
Sarah A. Travers	33	M	Md	May		consumption
3rd Election Dist.						
Sophiah Abell	5mo		Md	Sep		whooping cough
Elizabeth Burroughs	3mo		Md	Aug		unknown
Alexander Dyer	27	M	Md	May	sailor	drowned
Mary E. Langley	48	W	Md	Nov	seamstress	rup.blood vessel
Sally Goldsborough	90	W	Md	Nov		pneumonia
Mary A. Drury	3mo		Md	Dec		unknown
Adria E. McWilliams	24	M	Md	Mar	physicians	wife-brain dis.
John Johnson of Len'd.	80	M	Md	Feb	farmer	rheumtism
Edmund Heard	62	W	Md	Apr	farmer	heart dis.
Catharine Stone	63	M	Md	Apr		pneumonia
John S. Peacock	56	M	Md	May		lung inflam.
James S. Edelin	54		Md	Jan		consumption
Elizabeth Greenwell	68	W	Md	Jun	lady	liver dis.
Sophiah Davis	30	M	Md	Sep		consumption
J.F. Jarboe(male)	33	M	Md	Nov	farmer	typhoid
Mary E. Guy	78	W	Md	Jul		old age
Martin B.S. Yates	3mo		Md	Apr		unknown

persons who died during the year ending 1 June 18_60_

COUNTY - Saint Marys -SOMERSET DISTRICT   4th Election Dist.

name	age	mar wid	birth place	mon. died	Occupation	cause of death
Ruth A. Russell	42	M	Md	Jun		consumption
William M. Shanks	2mo		Md	Nov		brain inflam.
Richard Cheseldine	60	M	Md	May	farmer	cholic
Elizabeth Owens	25	M	Md	Jan		pleurisy
Ann Graves	43	M	Md	Jul		brain fever
Mary Long	1mo		Md	Apr		measles
Josephine Neale	18		La.	Jun	lady	dropsy
John E. Payne	9		Md	Dec		accident
Richard Payne Sr.	56	M	Md	Apr	farmer	apoplexy
William F. Long	25		Md	Apr	merchant	measles
Catherine Payne	78	W	Md	Sep		dropsy
Rachael Cawood	4		Md	Oct		stomach
Walter Davis	8		Md	Feb		scarlet fever
6th Election Dist.						
Sarah Russell	32	M	Md	Jul		consumption
Martin Lathrom	22		Md	Jul	farmer	measles
William G. Lloyd	38	M	Md	May	farmer	liver
Edward J. Stone	21		Md	Feb	farmhand	measles
Mary E. Tucker	1		Md	Feb		typhoid
Sarah Wilkinson	83	M	Md	Mar		burned
Joseph S. Stone	18		Md	Jan	farmhand	measles
Ann H. Campbell	62	W	Md	Mar		consumption
Richard Peake	35		Md	Jun		exposure
Mary J. Hooper	10mo		Md	May		diarrah
C.C.Alvey (fem)	9mo		Md	Aug		teething
SOMERSET COUNTY-BARREN CREEK dist.						
George Jenkins	48	M	Md	Oct	farmer	consumption
Elizabeth Lloyd	28	M	Md	Jan		unknown
John Scakese?	60	M	Md	Jun	farmer	lightning
Eleanor Phillips	6mo		Md	Jul		diarreah
Train Lloyd	9		Md	Md	Oct	bil.Fever
Dorothea Sewell	60	W	Md	Dec		dropsy
Ann M.E. Sewell	7mo		Md	Apr		erysepelas
John Lloyd	42	M	Md	Sep	merchant	typhoid
Winder Bacon	19		Del	Aug	carpenter	typhoid
John P. Graham	9		Md	Dep		typhoid
Nancy Windsor	43	M	Md	Jun		diarreah
Elisha T. Bennett	7		Md	Jun		diarreah
Jonathan Bennett	1		Md	Jul		diarreah
Mary A. Darby	8mo		Md	Jul		diarreah
Thomas J. Russell	13		Md	Oct		dorwned
James Huffington	54	W	Md	Apr	farmer	swelling
Ella E. Bounds	1		Md	Jul		cholera
Mary J. Phillips	11mo		Md	Sep		unknown
Alice D. Nilson	4		Md	Aug		diarreah
Lillian Brattan	3mo		Md	May		unknown
Roysten Covington	10mo		Md	Jul		diarreah
George Daris Darby	6		Md	Aug		dysentary
Princess Anne District						
Sally A. Jones	52	W	Md	Jan		consumption
James B. Atkinson	1		Md	Jul		dysentary
Robert T.Ballard	21		Md	Jul	laborer	consumption
Benjamin J.Jones	20		Md	Jan	farmer	consumption

persons who died during the year ending 1 June 18_60_

COUNTY -SOMERSET   DISTRICT   Princess Anne Dist.

name	age	mar wid	birth place	mon. died	Occupation	cause of death
Araminta Moore	16		Md	Feb		consumption
Attaline Lankford	50	W	Md	Nov		consumption
Maria Bromley	40	M	Md	Apr		dropsy
Eleanor Riggin	60	W	Md	Nov		dispepsia
John H.H. Adams	55	M	Md	Jun		consumption
William Hitch	23		Md	Mar	taylor	consumption
John Pollitt	70		Md	Jun	farmer	old age
Isaac Pusey	72		Md	Aug		asthma
Eliza McDaniel	55	M	Md	May		unknown
Samuel Bowland	2		Md	May		unknown
Susan Bowland	67	W	Md	May		cancer
Florence Mills	2		Md	Jun		cholera
Thomas Newman	66	M	Md	Mar	farmer	consumption
HUNGARY NECK DISTRICT						
Parmelia Parks	42	M	Md	May		diarreah
Sarah A. Horner	3mo		Md	Jul		unknown
Charlotte Horner	26	M	Md	Nov		unknown
Levin T. Ross	1mo		Md	Mar		unknown
Matilda Simms	39		Md	Aug		yellow jaundice
SHARPTOWN DISTRICT						
James Brady	65	M	Del.	Apr	shipright	unknown
William J. Marvel	23		Md	Jul	shipright	"
William Bennett	6		Del.	Dec		"
Maria Adams	1mo		Md	Aug		"
James Adams	42	M	Del.	Dec	mariner	"
Ann Collins	2		Md	Sep		"
Winfield Rhodes	1		Md	Jun		"
Margaaret Bayley	33	M	Del.	Aug		typhoid
George T. Bayley	9		Del.	Aug		typhoid
POTATOE NECK DISTRICT						
Amelia J. Beauchamp	30		Md	Feb	seamstress	consumption
Martha A. Revel	38	M	Md	Mar		obstretics
James Parks	45		Md	Aug	merchant	consumption
DUBLIN DISTRICT						
Elizabeth L. Rafield	15		Va	May		consumption
Samuel D. Wilson	4mo		Md	Jul		diarreah
Thomas Milbourne	20		Md	Mar	farmer	unknown
Whittington Polk	90		Md	Sep		unknown
LUNDY DISTRICT						
Garrett Laurance	35	M	Md	Jul	printer	consumption
John Dennis	50	M	Md	Mar	lawyer	consumption
Alice Twilley	2		Md	Aug		typhoid
Maria Connerly	29	M	Md	May		hemmorhage
Charles Humphries	47	M	Md	Mar	farmer	brain inflam.
Charlotte Rhoades	50	M	Md	Aug		consumption
Alice Robertson	7		Md	Sep		typhoid
Samuel Robertson	5		Md	Sep		typhoid
Levin Wallace	21		Md	Jan		pneumonia
Drucilla Smith	33	M	Md	Jul		dysentary
Alpheus Twilly	32		Md	Jan		mania
Benjamin Roberts	50		Md	Oct		typhoid
Vesta Roberts	6		Md	Oct		typhoid
John Eversman	55		Irel.	Nov	tailor	dispepsia

persons who died during the year ending 1 June 1860

COUNTY   SOMERSET - TALBOT   DISTRICT   LUNDY DISTRICT

name	age	mar wid	birth place	mon. died	Occupation	cause of death
Jehu Parsons	80	M	Md	Aug	farmer	old age
Ann R. Chitman	2		Md	Jun		croup
Charles Evans	47	M	Md	Aug	hatter	droppsy
James McHooper	20		Md	Jul		consumption
Emma Thorington	6mo		Md	May		brain fever
Richard Lemon	69		Md	Jul	physician	cholera
William Anderson	30		Md	Jul	tailor	consumption
Edward Humphreys	1		Md	Jul		dysentary
Samuel Somers	77	M	Md	May	farmer	gout
Beanjamin Hearn	60	M	Md	Jun	wheelwright	pneumonia
Mary Williams	1mo		Md	Jul		unknown
			TANGIER DISTRICT			
Henry Windser	25	M	Md	Feb	farmer	unknown
Emily Windser	22		Md	Aug		consumption
Elana Jones	70	M	Md	Oct		unknown
Maria E. Webster	1mo		Md	Sep		unknown
			TYASKIN DISTRICT			
Mansfield Street	62	W	Md	Dec	shipwright	consumption
George Inlois	21		Md	May	mariner	drowned
Algermon L. Dashiell	52	M	Md	Oct	farmer	consumption
William Mezick	17		Md	Sep	farmer	pneumonia
			DAMES QUARTER DISTRICT			
William Webster	16		Md	Sep	mariner	unknown
Sally Shores	29	W	Md	Sep		consumption
Francis Wallace	40	M	Md	Aug	mariner	consumption
Sarah Price	1		Md	Nov		unknown
Elizabeth A. Shores	25	M	Md	May		obstetrics
			TALBOT COUNTY-town of Easton			
Margaret Robinson	63	W	Md	Mar		pleurisy
Elizabeth Wilson	78	M	Md	Feb		paralysis
Thomas L. Goldsburrough	2mo		Md	Aug		unknown
Frances E. Martin	5		Md	Oct		croup
Henrietta Sneed	3mo		Md	Aug		unknolwn
Edith Carmean	1		Md	Aug		unknown
Isaac Atkinson	79	M	Md	Jan		unknown
James Emory	3		Md	Feb		unknown
Mary A. Mason	28	M	Del.	Apr		consumption
John W. Greenhawk	16		Md	Oct		unknown
Ada Tilghman	1		Md	Sep		measles
Thomas Laremore	70	W	Md	Sep		unknown
Bessie Gore	7mo		Md	Jul		brain fever
Henrietta Kirby	23	M	Md	Sep		unknown
Rebecca Eaten	60	W	Md	Dec		asthma
Samuel Gale	3mo		Md	Sep		water on brain
Mary A. Horney	19		Md	Sep		typhoid
John H. Sperry	11		Md	Jul		unknown
Jerome B. Bennett	3		Md	Jul		brain dis.
Jane R. Hughey	38	M	Md	Jan		consumption
Mary Hughey	69	W	Md	May		eresiplas
Sarah B. Leonard	16		SMd	Jan		unknown
Thomas F. Norris	57	M	Md	Jan	farmer	unknown
William A. Abeler	9mo		Md	Jun		teething

MORTALITY SCHEDULE OF MARYLAND

persons who died during the year ending 1 June 18<u>60</u>

COUNTY TALBOT COUNTY   DISTRICT   town of Easton

name	age	mar wid	birth place	mon. died	Occupation	cause of death
Mary M. Harden	37	M	Md	Mar		unknown
Mary McQuay	84	W	Md	Jan		inflamation
Bradford Colburn	5mo		Md	Jul		unknown
Henry Price	62	M	Md	Nov	farmer	apiplexy
Mary Goldsborrough	36	M	Va.	Aug		dysentary
Jacob Faulkner	3mo		Md	Feb		unknown
Joseph Dodds	2		Md	Jun		unknown
Susana Standburg	40	M	Del.	Jul		dysentary
Charles Clark	4		Md	Jun		accident
Robert H. Plummer	18		Md	Dec	laborer	liver inflam.
William F. Hexter	24		Md	Feb	coachmaker	accident
Mary McColister	1		Md	Jul		unknown
Mary E. Leonard	38	M	Md	Dec		pneumonia
Elizabeth Blades	32	M	Md	May		child bed
Rachel Handy	2		Md	Aug		fits
Rebecca Barroll	23	M	Md	Dec		dropsey
Sarah Coney	47	M	Md	Jun		pleurisy
Thomas Laremore	73	W	Md	Sep	blacksmith	unknown
Nancy Sullivan	40	M	Md	Jun		consumption
William Arringdale	55	M	Md	Jun	farmer	paralisas
Lewis Merrick	6		Md	Jun		tumor
Addison L. Harris	6mo		Md	May		yellow jaundice
Lydia Cranch	40		Md	Jul		consumption
Susan Bromwell	60	W	Md	Oct		consumption
Robert Campbell	60	W	Irel.	Apr	timberhaller	dropsey
Percy Jenkins	11mo		Md	Jul		brain fever
Thomas M. Hardcastle	52	M	Md	Oct	merchant	dropsey
Mary E. Cook	27	M	Md	Oct		typhoid
Emily Plummer	46	W	Md	May		consumption
Charles Gordon	1		Md	Oct		dysentary
Jane Simpson	32	M	Md	Sep		consumption
Henrietta Leonard	56	M	Md	Aug		consumption
Susan Wilson	2		Md	Nov		teething
Reuben Simms	50		Md	Sep		unknown
Susan Bromwell	70		Md	Nov		unknown
Mary Morgan	27	M	Md	Apr		child bed
Sarah R. Griffin	24	W	Md	Mar		consumption
Rachel Bond	3da		Md	Mar		consumption
John W. Blades	11		Md	Jun		bowel inflam.
James Lamdin	1mo		Md	Feb		unknown
John P. Middleton	50	M	Md	Aug	mariner	consumption
Susan Middleton	45	M	Md	Mar		pneumonia
James Lecompt	53	M	Md	Aug	engineer	heart dis.
Caleb Griffith	54	M	Md	Mar	farmer	paralysis
John H. Kirby	1mo		Md	Mar		thrush
James Nichols	60	M	Md	Aug	carpenter	gravel
Mary E. Hadaway	4mo		Md	Sep		bronchitas
B. Lane(male)	9		Md	Jul		summer comp.
James Cooper	6mo		Md	May		unknown
Hugh Valiant	67	W	Md	Jul	farmer	pneumonia
William C. Skinner	66	M	Md	Aug		unknown
Ella Hopkins	17		Md	Aug		liver dis.
James Dobson	56	M	Md	May	laborer	paralysis

204

persons who died during the year ending 1 June 18_60_

COUNTY **TALBOT** _ **WASHINGTON** DISTRICT

name	age	mar wid	birth place	mon. died	Occupation	cause of death
Daniel Hoope	76	M	Bavaria	Jun	brushmaker	unknown
George T. Clash	23	M	Md	Nov	farmer	consumption
Hambleton Cecil	17		Md	Feb		accident
Gustave Laramore	4mo		Md	Nov		unknown
Mary A. Wales	61		Md	Oct		unknown
William H. Keifer	11		Md	Jul		drownd
James L. Wrightson	59		Md	Nov	farmer	intemperance
Sarah Cummins	25	M	Md	Nov		consumption
William Dawson	72	M	Md	Aug	farmer	dysentary
Margaret Hunt	36	M	Md	Mar		sudden
George Banning	3mo		Md	Jul		thrush
Matilda Burrows	17		Md	Mar		consumption
Lemuel Roose	16		Md	Nov	laborer	consumption
Jonathan Bartlett	61	M	Md	Jul	farmer	intemperance
Richard Ton	72	M	Md	Jan	shipcarpenter	lung inflam.
Mary E. Right	9		Md	May		typhoid
Sallie A. Bruff	43	M	Md	Jan		consumption
Alice Kemp	60	W	Md	Jul		consumption
John T. Porter	20		Md	Apr	machinist	throat dis.
Elizabeth Lecompt	21	M	Md	May		typhoid
John A. Bruff	1		Md	Aug		summer comp.
Mary A. Hambleton	2		Md	May		rheumatism
Shadrack Warren	4		Md	Dec		scarlet fever
Lenese J. Hampton	4		Pa.	Apr		diptheria
John Merrick	30		Md	Apr	shoemaker	burnt
Henrietta Smith	32	M	Md	Mar		consumption
John Sullivan	53	M	Md	Nov	farmer	unknown
Mary H. Wilkins	15		Md	Sep		unknown
Nelly Neal	7		Md	Aug		convulsions
John R. Piersley	35		Md	Nov	shoemaker	drowned
			WASHINGTON COUNTY-Bronsboro Dist.			
Thomas Martin	73	W	Md	Aug	farmer	dropsy
David Frank	25	M	Md	Mar	carpenter	consumpltion
Mary Arnold	24		Md	Mar		consumption
Michael Rudacil	89	W	Pa.	Oct	farmer	paralysis
Jacob Durnbaugh	82	M	Pa.	Aug	farmer	not known
Magadlma Wolff	8		Md	May		bowel dis.
Jacob N. Etgre	16		Md	Mar	laborer	typhoid
Joseph Bowman	57	W	Md	Apr	farmer	consumption
Amos Rowland	24	M	Md	Mar	farmer	typhoid
Josiah Rowland	5mo		Md	Apr		brain affect.
Aaron Snively	21		Md	May		consumption
Ellenora Netts	71	W	Md	Sep		consumption
Asbery Ecker	1		Md	Sep		fits
Matilday Esterday	1		Md	Jun		croup
Albertis Lewis	2		Md	Jul		throat affect.
			Petersburg Dist.			
Peter Barksdoll	27	M	Md	Aug	blacksmith	consumption
Benjamin F. Martin	9		Md	Jul		brain cong.
Lewis Turney	18		Md	Sep		consumption
George W. Wolff	37	M	Md	Oct	laborer	killed
Ann B. Wagman	13		Md	Nov		child birth

MORTALITY SCHEDULE OF MARYLAND

persons who died during the year ending 1 June 1860

COUNTY **WASHINGTON**   DISTRICT

name	age	mar wid	birth place	mon. died	Occupation	cause of death
Quincy Shepard	20		Md	Mar	laborer	fever
Jeremiah Wampler	46	M	Pa.	Jun	farmer	consumption
Susan A. B. Hartle	8		Md	Feb		unknown
John B. Slick	2mo		Md	Jul		typhoid
Clara E. Bell	13		Md	Feb		brain fever
			CaneTown District			
Eliza Clary	20	M	Md	Mar		consumption
Josephine E. Price	1		Md	Sep		lung fever
Sarah Oswald	67	W	Md	Oct		apoplexy
Margaret Wishard	1		Md	Dec		croup
Jacob B. Batchtel	80	M	Md	Mar	farmer	old age
Jacob Hose	65	W	Md	Jan	carpenter	consumption
William Hose	40		Md	May	laborer	typhoid
Michael Gross	84	M	Pa.	Dec	farmer	old age
			Clear Spring District			
Joseph Snyder	2		Md	Jan		unknown
George L. Truitt	20		Md	Mar	teacher	consumption
Catharine Clopper	54	M	Pa.	Jan		parelitic
John King	40	M	Md	Nov	laborer	bil.fever
Eliza Draper	33	M	Md	Feb		consumption
Levin Reed	31	M	Md	Sep	farmer	brain fever
Samuel Hawer	67	M	Md	Feb		parelatic
David Kretzer	65		Va.	Mar	farmer	dropsy
Ruth Johnson	51	M	Md	Oct		dropsy
Fannie Krepps	64	M	Md	Apr		consumption
Peter Snyder	68	M	Md	Mar	tailor	paraletic
George Hellin	67	M	Md	Nov	farmer	liver comp.
Catharine Rhoads	58	M	Md	Oct		dropsy
			Conororheague Dist			
Ruane Wolford	50	M	Md	Jul		fever
Elizabeth Wolford	10		Md	May		consumption
John Cook	50	M	Md	Mar	laborer	consumption
John Johnson	15		Md	Sep		lightning
Martin Rapp	60	M	Ger.	Aug	farmer	typhoid
Elizabeth Cushman	68	W	Md	Sep		cancer
Eliza Summer	15		Md	Nov		typhoid
Anna Summer	89	M	Pa.	Dec		old age
Ann Summer	49		Md	Jun		typhoid
Jacob Summer	24		Md	Jun	laborer	typhoid
Phillip Neipert	66		Md	Nov	farmer	unknown
Ada Brien	1		Md	Jul		cholera
			Frankstown District			
Elijah Williams	75	W	Md	Mar	cooper	stricture
David Shilling	71	M	Md	May	mason	consumption
Samuel Barber	34	M	Md	Mar	cooper	consumption
Jacob Isemager?	56		Md	Jan	wheelright	consumption
James Rontzan	45	M	Md	Aug	wheelright	consumption
S. Bowen Smith	40		Md	Jan	gilder	bowel affect.
Ellenor Wolff	90	M	Pa.	Dec		rhumatism
Henry Egerly	58	M	Pa.	Aug	farmer	black flux
Ann Witmer	49		Md	Nov		rupture
Sarah Winters	51		Md	Jul		unknown
John M.W. Doub	5		Md	Nov		croup

206

persons who died during the year ending 1 June 18_60_

COUNTY Washington   DISTRICT   Cavetown Dist.

name	age	mar wid	birth place	mon. died	Occupation	cause of death
Margaret M. Wishard	1		Md	Mar		unknown
Jacob Hose	65	W	Md	Jan	carpenter	dyspepsia
William Hose	40		Md	May	laborer	typhoid
Mary Gougher	35	M	Md	Aug		typhoid
Nancy Bowers	21		Md	Apr		unknown
Annie Hershel	80	W	HesseDarm.	Nov		old age
Elizabeth C. Strick	44	M	HesseDar	Mar		typhoid
Nathan Shockley	1		Md	Aug		flux
Ellen Rogers	2mo		Md	Apr		fever
Michael Gross	84		Pa.	Dec	farmer	gravel
Margaret Kale	30	M	Md	Mar		consumption
John H. Stotler	71	W	Md	Apr	farmer	paralysis
Zach Doub	1mo		Md	Sep		unknown
Jacob Bichtell	82	M	Md	Mar		old age
Josephus E. Price	8mo		Md	Oct		pneumonia
Eliza Clay	20	M	Md	Mar		consumption
David Yingling	66	M	Md	Feb	farmer	cancer
William Green	12		Md	Oct		croup
Alex Dinsmore	6mo		Md	Feb		typhoid
Mary Grouf	45	W	Md	Feb		paralysis
Hagerstwon District						
William Bester	57	M	Ger.	Sep	gardiner	consumption
Elizabeth Barber	43		Md	Aug		heart dis.
Catherine Gruber	81		Pa.	Jun		pleurisy
G.W. Baltz	2mo		Md	Feb		croup
Susan Heyser	35		Md	Aug		apoplexy
Sandy Hooks District						
William Moore	6mo		Md	Jul		cholera
Harriet O'Brian	3		Md	Oct		croup
Edward Rice	7mo		Md	Aug		cholera
Barbara Cantham	34	M	Md	Mar		consumption
William Canthram	35	M	Pa.	May	laborer	consumption
Ann Ray	1	M	Md	Sep		consumption
Amanda Dawson	49	M	Va.	Apr		consumption
John Russell	50	M	Irel.	May	laborer	consumption
Hagerstown						
John Heneburger	74	M	Pa.	Sep	cabinetmaker	diabetes
James Flenninger	14		Md	Apr		paraletic
John Albert	82		Pa.	Apr	butcher	pneumonia
Charles W. Bregler	3		Md	Apr		scarlet fever
Helen K. Wright	5		Pa.	Dec		dropsy
Jonathan B.Middledauff	2mo		Md	Aug		birth defect
Mary E. Detrich	57	M	HesseCas.	Feb		burnt
Stephen Parker	71	M	Md	Sep		old age
Elizabeth Brook	14		Md	Aug		fever
Frances Melton	87		Irel.	Jun		paralysis
W.Scott Albert	10		Md	Jun		liver comp.
Eliza Little	37		Md	Apr		pneumonia
Peter Stevens	40	M	Md	Feb	laborer	cramps,fever
Henry Cramer	50	M	Wurtenberg	Jun.	Paternmaker	unknown
Louisa E. Cramer	1		Md	Dec		unknown
Wenton Middledauff	6mo		Md	Aug		cholera
Elizabeth Struck	65		Pa.	Aug		paralatic

persons who died during the year ending 1 June 1860

COUNTY WASHINGTOWN DISTRICT Hagerstown Dist.

name	age	mar wid	birth place	mon. died	Occupation	cause of death
James McCurtin	21		Pa.	Apr	laborer	brain inflam.
Elizabeth Britton	6		Md	Feb		scarlet fever
Daniel C. Miller	64		Md	Mar	farmer	bil.fever
John Hawthorne	59		Irel.	Mar		unknown
Marcus Bennor	63		Wutemberg	Feb	gardiner	suicide
			Hancock District			
John W. Bortman	40	M	Va.	Aug	butcher	bil.fever
Solomon Deckerhoff	35	M	Md	Jun	laborer	typhoid
F.B.Thomas(male)	30		Md	May	farmer	consumption
Samuel Hodges	65		Md	Apr	farmer	consumption
Elizabeth Shivers	23		Md	May	seamstress	typhoid
Elizabeth Giliss	42		Md	Feb	seamstress	typhoid
Otho Shivers	14		Md	Feb	laborer	bil.fever
Mary Shivers	70	W	Md	Jun	farmer	apiplexy
Christian Shivers	28	M	Md	Feb	laborer	bil.fever
			Sharpsburg District			
Elizabeth Detrick	65	W	Md	Nov		paralytic
Mary Myers	31		Md	Sep		heart dis.
William Bowen	41	M	Va.	Mar	farmer	unknown
Harriet R. Diggs	1mo		Md	Apr		unknown
Martha E. Adkins	10		Md	Dec		scarlet fever
Joseph H. Roherback	2		Md	Mar		unknown
John Hoffman	71	M	Md	Nov	farmer	dropsy
William A. Linn	1		Md	Nov		flux
E.McA. Middledauff	11mo		Ill.	Feb		fever
Austin W. Middlekauff	1		Ill.	Mar		bronchitis
John D. Swain	10mo		Md	Jun	carpenter	consumption
Raleigh Bender	25		Md	Jun	boatman	consumption
Thomas Brown	19		Md	Feb	boatman	consumption
Eben W. Hoffman	3		Md	Jan		brain cong.
Kate McMinn	40	M	Md	Nov		consumption
James E. McMinn	5		Md	Nov		unknown
Coleman Shackleford	53		Va.	Mar		consumption
Martha E. Rowe	34	M	Md	May		consumption
Hannah Clifford	73	M	Md	Sep		old age
John Himes	62	M	Md	Feb	carpenter	consumption
Wilfreld Roherback	19		Md	Jun		measles
			Williams District			
Eliza Cunningham	66	M	Va.	Jun		pulmonary
John Ardinger	47	M	Md	Oct		consumption
Ann R. Wient	7		Md	Apr		spasms
William H. Rhoades	1		Md	Mar		sudden
			Pleasant Valley District			
Tobias Brown	83	M	Md	Sep	farmer	old age
Joseph Crampton	26		Md	Nov	physician	consumption
George V. Thomas	60	M	Md	May	laborer	bronkle affect.
Josiah Gauff	25	M	Md	Nov	laborer	accident
			TILMINGTON District			
Adeline Green	1		Md	Jan		cholera
Henry L. Flock	8		Md	Aug		drowned
Sarah Rowland	21		Md	Feb		consumption
			Williamsport District			
Nathaniel Long	41	M	Md	Jul	farmer	killed by horse
Mary Irwin	16		Ohio	Mar		consumption

208

name	age	mar wid	birth place	mon. died	Occupation	cause of death
Edwin Purnell	13		Md	Dec		shot
Virginia A. Johnson	22	W	Md	Feb		unknown
George Brittingham	7mo		Md	Feb		unknown
William C. Beauchamp	3mo		Md	Jun		dropsy
Eliza Smullin	45	W	Md	Jul		dropsy
Susan West	3		Md	Mar		burnt
Virginia Richardson	1		Md	May		bil.fever
			BERLIN DISTRICT			
Zadoc Bowen	57		Md	Sep	farmer	consumption
Joshua Morris	60		Md	Dec	farmer	consumption
Laura Cropper	4		Md	Nov		dropsy
Louisa Connoway	40		Del.	May		neuralgia
Polly Timmons	30		Md	Aug		pneumonia
John Burbage	50		Md	Oct	farmer	suicide
William Bradford	73		Md	Dec		palsy
Ann Nichols	40	M	Md	Dec		child bed
Margaret Brittingham	7mo		Md	Jul		cholera
Lemuel Hall	60		Md	May	farmer	pneumonia
Samuel Johnson	60		Md	May	captain	cancer
Thomas N. Williams	59	M	Md	Apr	carpenter	bil.pneumonia
Eliza Peterson	40	M	Md	Oct		cong.fever
Edward Carey	1		Md	Sep		cholera
Esther Marsh	1		Md	Sep		croup
James Warren	5mo		Md	Aug		none
Hetty Timmons	4		Md	Sep		none
		St	MARTINS District			
Maria Dunnaway	25	M	Md	Feb		consumtion
MaryHamblin	45	M	Md	Sep		fever
Mary Hamblin	5mo		Md	Nov		marasmus
Zippna Tindell	34	M	Md	Aug		consumption
Emma Easham	1		Md	Mar		croup
Elizabeth Mehnay	69		Md	Dec		heart dis.
James Day	7		Md	Jul		hydrophalus
			COSTENS DISTRICT			
Dolly Thornton	2		Md	Oct		dysentary
William Wilson	11mo		Md	Aug		whooping cough
Mary Tull	9mo		Md	Sep		convulsions
Levin Lambdin	43	M	Md	Mar	farmer	consumption
Harriet Schoolfield	21		Md	Jul		consumption
Mary Clark	7mo		Md	Oct		croup
Corine Lankford	1		Md	Jun		measles
Joseph Lankford	3		Md	Jul		measles
Ida Jones	2		Md	Jun		dysentary
James Townsend	5		Md	Aug		dysentary
Maria Watson	40		Md	Jul		cancer
William Truitt	3mo		Md	Jul		cholera
Sally Jackson	75		Md	Feb		dropsy
Mary Hammond	1		Md	Jul		whooping cough
Elmira Jones	1		Md	Aug		cat.fever
			COLBURNS DISTRICT			
Daniel H. Esham	2		Md	Jul		diareah
Johana Shockley	1		Md	Jul		diareah
Henry Dickerson	42		Md	Oct	farmer	consumption

209

persons who died during the year ending 1 June 1860

COUNTY WORCESTER   DISTRICT Colburns Dist.

name	age	mar wid	birth place	mon. died	Occupation	cause of death
Elisha H. Jones	4mo		Md	Feb		unknown
William F. Shockley	11mo		Md	Jun		cholera
Sarah C. Holloway	36		Md	Apr		rosa mania
			NUTTERS DISTRICT			
Richard Hastings	1		Md	May		diarrhea
Kellum Dykes	71	M	Md	Jun	farmer	unknown
Sampson Shockley	50	M	Md	Apr	farmer	manustia
Josephene Bethards	1		Md	Apr		fever
Eleanor Causey	47	M	Md	Feb		consumption
Elizabeth Selby	45	M	Md	Mar		dropsy
Alfred B.Morris	22		Md	Oct	farmer	consumption
John Gunby	48	M	Md	May	merchant	consumption
Emily C. Bussells	3		Md	May		burns
John W. Disharoon	3		Md	Dec		worms
Amanda Morris	1		Md	Sep		unknown
Elijah Ennis	45		Md	Dec	carpenter	dropsy
			PARSONS DISTRICT			
Mary D. Driskill	2		Md	Sep		inflamation
John B. Perdue	51	M	Md	Nov	farmer	paralysis
Marcellus Rounds	19		Md	Mar	laborer	accident
Alexander S. Cathell	36		Md	Sep		diarrhea
Mary E. Brown	31	M	Md	Mar		child birth
			DERRICKSONS ROAD District			
Sarah C. Davis	3		Md	Oct		consumption
John Baker	3		Md	May		burnt
John Parsons	7		Md	Oct		quincey
Mira Parsons	5		Md	Sep		scarlet fever
John Brown	91	M	Md	May	farmer	sudden
Liva Parker	40	M	Md	Feb		dropsy
Clasey Lewis	32	M	Md	May		consumption
Minus C. Littleton	30	M	Md	Jun	farmer	consumption
			SNOW HILL			
Maria W. Nelson	51	M	Md	Aug		consumption
James Knox	78	M	Md	Sep	gentleman	consumption
Nicholas Jenkins	21		Md	May		consumption
Mary A. Wilson	33	M	Md	Oct		consumption
Margaret Spencer	17		Md	Jan		consumption
Julia A. Carey	36	M	Md	Jan		consumption
Alfred Jones	26	W	Md	Nov	gentleman	unknown
Mary E. Jenkins	9mo		Va.	Mar		unknown
Wilmer Taylor	20		Md	May	farmer	brain fever
Josephine Taylor	10mo		Md	May		unknown
William Clavell	62	M	Md	Apr		pneumonia
John H. Holland	67	W	Md	Jun		pneumonia
Elizabeth Richardson	34	M	Md	Jun		consumption
Frederick Richardson	2		Md	Jun		unknown
Charles Powell	4		Md	Jan		croup
Thomas R.Rounds	66	W	Md	Apr	farmer	cong.fever
Mary A. Nock	32	M	Md	Mar		scarlet fever
Emina Holsten	19		Md	Aug		consumption
Eliner Richardson	71		Md	Nov		bil.colic

Carton-123
Carter-2-6-14-22-
28-46-67-68-77-
97-111-123-172-
176-280
Carvill-140
Carlton-98
Carroll-39-63-35-
99-131-139-142-162
181-192-195-200
Carolvalle-147
Carbit-116
Carry-120
Cartman-165
Carnagy-176
Carmichael-58-66
Carson-45-55-58
Cape-37
Carlisle-29
Carmine-30-31-69
Carragan-34
Carl-159
Carovalle-147
Casey-144-150
Case-95-96
Castle-115
Casard-157
Castule-165
Caster-170
Cassidy-135-141-
143-192
Castwart-9
Casho-76
Cather-178
Cateron-6
Catheart-19
Catherton-171
Caton-122
Carther-194
Cathell-23-134-210
Capron-125
Catrup-112
Catlin-106-108
Cator-189
Cauley-44-46
Causey-210-49
Caughey-4
Caufman-182
Caughey-4
Caughers-23
Cavalier-52
Cavenaugh-39
Cave-36
Cawood-201
Cayor-35
Cemer-20
Cence-193
Cesar-167
Chad-92
Chaffin-112
Chaisly-41

Charles-139-172
Charlton-114
Chaplin-113-111
Chaaney-5-27-114
126-127-173-197
Chanceaulme-135
Chanell-190
Chapman-119-127
23
Chambers-20-41-
45-69-139-102-
103-117-100
Chancy-76
Chaffnick-73
Chaffer-17
Challe-19
Chanco-43
Charles-19-13
Chalmer-3-43
Chalk-93-190
Chaulk-67-98
Chamberlain-29
132-152
Chatard-144
Cheny-55
Cheneywith-91
Cheneworth-158
Chelton-107
Cheseldine-105-
201
Chase-15-17-50
143-126
Chew-21
Cheesbrough-16
Chestnut-26
Chesman-73
Childers-4
Chilling-28
Chidlow-186
Chipley-197
Chiswell-196
Chisney-188
Chitman-204
Chister-21-39
Childs-58
Chlers-28
Christopher-
129-137-73
Christ-114
Chum-105
Church-28-29-
139-156
Cinnamond-143
Circle-74
Cissell-193-
195-196
Cisler-125
Cipriari-167
Clanan-66

Claggett-99-134-
146-194-4a-83
Clamince-151
Clapp-58
Clanan-66
Clampitt-27
Clammer-1
Clance-186
Clark-25-31-34-
35-37-53-59-61
83-91-94-98-
1-4-100-111-117
132-136-144-159
160-164-169-177
189-195-204-209
2-4-10-21
Clary-88-129-186
206
Clavill-210
Clay-97-134-163-
173-207
Clarvoe-188
Class-101
Clash-205
Claw-163
Cleary-146
Clem-84-133
Clemson-184
Clemmons-63-80
157
Claypool-176
Cloffenger-154
Clogg-121
Clippinger-122
Clow-100
Cloffenger-154
Clifford-41-208
Cliffe-36
Cline-10
Clickman-38
Clifton-46
Cliao-3
Clother-70
Cloud-26
Closkey-52
Clopper-206
Cloughey-24
Clubb-198
Cluff-108
Cluhen-33
Coale-4
Coath-132
Cochran-83-153
Cockey-39-143-
167-169
Cochran-48-72
Cocklin-97
Codel-22
Coe-28-64-77

Coffner-134
Coffenbagger-25
Cole-4a-12-23-
28-34-54-55-61
70-85-100-188-
198-199-67
Coldazer-125
Coleman-10-26-
132-146
Collett-68
Collentz-88
Collins-6-14-37
48-54-67-82-
106-113-117-
118-119-164-
165-166-202
Collings-119
Collison-112-
142-200
Collond-132
Colton-136-137
Coleson-81
Colwell-60
Collis-62
Coltrider-73
Collier-35-105
111
Cohen-35
Comegges-67
Comeygs-94-134
Colbert-107-115
Conar-166
Coner-174
Conan-170
Conch-165
Condon-44-88-
112-124-179
Coney-2-204
Conelson-178-185
Congan-114
Conner-102-122-
10-13-17-4-56-
133-140-163-
165-170-139-161
182-192-204
Connelley-2-13-
34-41-55-66-97
159-172-34
Conswick-3
Conn-15
Connill-9
Consella-17
Conoway-11-25-
53-128-142-209
Conway-25-160
Conley-166-176
Constine-164
Conkling-40
Conning-165
Coon-162-185

Conn-15
Cooney-9
Cooley-53
Coolhan-144
Coombs-200
Cooksey-80-110-126-180
Connerly-202
Cook-4-8-23-37-42-75-80-81-62-89-101-117-129-134-149-155-166-167-172-182-204
Cooper-17-18-56-63-72-77-83-102-103-106-112-119-118-139-161-182-192-203
Coppersmith-73-174
Cope-79
Cordes-53
Core-27
Cordrey-133
Corbin-97
Corbet-11
Cornish-14-37
Coray-34
Cornelius-24
Cortney-104
Cora-78
Cosgrove-128
Cote-151
Cottingham-121
Cost-22
Cotter-7
Conrad-40-161
Coughts-130
Coutier-160-164
Coursey-101-102-181-200
Country-188
Coulborne-108-204
Cover-185
Covington-80-101-106-119-199-201
Cowan-76-123
Cowman-18
Cowton-1
Cox-44-46-70-80-117-139-171-188
Craig-38-153-189
Craeger-85
Craddick-95
Cragg-122
Craighton-136
Crabblitt-12
Crancer-84
Crasner-165
Crane-100-104-143
Cramer-85-117-207
Craine-85

Crandall-127
Craft-140-183
Craeger-185-187
Cranch-204
Crampton-208
Cranston-191
Crangle-51
Crawford-72-94-95-137-155-195-196-
Crays-3
Createe-35
Cree-110
Creighton-82-181
Crego-166
Creswell-65
Creamer-140-146-166
Crimmon-127
Crist-118-131
Cristy-40
Cripner-43
Crisp-6
Crisap-123
Crissell-189
Croder-52
Crocker-23-135
Crough-140
Crook-99-61-74
Cromwell-20-31-51-85-160
Cropper-118-209
Crockett-107-110-115-149
Crother-70
Cronin-183-184
Crothers-77-179
Crosby-81-70-171-31
Cross-3-69-4a-28-50-168-169
Crosier-104
Crouch-39-76-107
Crouse-24
Cronhardt-34
Crow-56-70-71-79-177-3
Cruse-32
Cruser-49
Cruikshank-193
Cuddy-168
Cullen-35-108-127-128
Cullins-167-52
Culler-116
Cullisnore-132
Culprina-7
Cullison-70-104-157

Culp-12
Culver-70
Cummer-149
Cuney-30
Cummings-53-112-126-129-131-151-205
Cuney-56
Cunningham-91-92-93-114-116-133-182-208-8-31-40-44-66
Curdy-29
Curlin-183
Curry-69
Curlett-22-34-39
Currins-132
Curthrell-37
Curtis-1-34-168
Curvell-31
Cutherenger-141
Cutler-36
Custer-1-78
Cushman-206
Cushing-75
Dabney-143
Dacy-36
Dade-173
Daberry-143
Dager-146
Dail-81
Dailey-39-104-105-142-165-166-168
Dainhart-193
Daley-10
Dallam-136
Dalbon-124
Dale-7-120
Dalzier-96
Dalyrumple-147
Dalzell-196
Daneker-153
Danehart-159
Danen-196
Dannenberg-43
Daniels-69
Darby-193-98-201
Darling-32-136
Dargener-130
Dare-48
Danes-140-194
Danner088
Dartzbaugh086
Darnell-126
Darsey-169
Darrough-22
Darting-35
Dating-100
Daub-33

Dasey-172
Dashiel-49-13-23-106-108-109-110-203-207
Daugherty-90-106-115-187
Davey-19
Davies-143-146
Davis-84-88-89-14-18-19-24-34-43-48-72-9-75-76-78-99-91-93-98-99-103-107-108-109-112-114-119-120-129-137-167-169-181-184-193-195-160-164-170-183-187-197-200-201-210-75-76-78
Davidson-56-61-27-30-124-176-199
Dawson-12-23-111-126-143-179-193-205-207
Day-5-74-93-164-192-196-209
Deacon-172
Deal-28-61-69-143-178
Dean-Deene-4a-54-68-81-82-123-124-157-185-200
Deaver-91
Deater-183
Debot-163
Decker-29-188-191
Deckart-148
Debel-55
Debilus-58
Dee-154
Deabring-147
Deer-Dear-158-167
Deems-51-162
Dearing-159
Deckerhoff-208
DeCoursey-46-193
Deagan-10
Dednick-44
Dearburn-115
Deford-77
Deffendale-34
Deets-31
Dedent-46
Deiter-156
Degory-23
Deitzell-13
Deitzer-129
Deiss-151
Delander-88
Delrist-133
Delphy-187

Goshage-88
Gosnek-55
Gotten-123
Gosman-128
Gott-42-70
Gould-16-28
Gough-21
Gouley-38
Gounce-46
Gowan-7
Grabill-88
Grace-178
Gracy-178
Grader-30
Grady-38
Graham-135-156-
 172-25-45-49-
Graber-45
Grainger-147-
 154-195
Graflin-134
Graff24-185
Graham-79-138-
 153-201
Granby-132
Gramay-40
Grafton-189
Grant-38-67-76
 22-30-122-136
 177
Gray-Grey-6-9-20
 24-39-54-72-72
 96-99-118-119-
 114-126-133-142
 167-169-196
Graty-9
Grantz-117
Gravel-131
Graves-146-187-
 201
Gregory-31
Green-10-16-28-
 29-91-100-130-
 146-165-167-172
 184-187-207-208
Greenwood-94-74
Greenhawk-203
Greenwell-103-104
 200
Greeves-129-170
Greenlee-187-52
Greacy-64
Greenland-188
Greer-180
Greenfield-63
Greentree-161
Griggren-138
Grierson-171
Griffin-6-7-21-
 47-68-110-119-
 145-169-191

Green-1-11-12
 20-34-45-64-
 67-69-70-81
Greenwade-3
Griswould-94
Griffith-26-
 28-45-59-60
 63-65-117-
 186-194-204
Grimes-16-23-
 56-67-99-173
 175-197
Grigley-166
Grimm-153-56
Griscum-62
Grindall-47
Gross-87-148
 151-206-207
Groomes-95-154
Grosh-113
Gross-69-26
Groom-28
Groves-3-138
Grist-155
Gross-43-139
 184-190
Groff-65-167
Grouger-207
Grossniakle-184
Grosscufs-67
Grover-139
Grubbell-154
Gruber-207
Gruin-63
Grub-153
Grunn-91
Grummade-122
Grunfield-133
Grout-129
Gruber-207
Guest-155
Guinn-54-57
Guistchler-157
Guinett-167
Gullitt-172
Guichis-12
Guyton-156-190
Guy-102-200
Gunby-109-210
Gurley-78
Gunton-99
Gunther-153
Gupton-68
Guthrey-118
Guyher-197
Gwinn-45-117
Hacking-85
Hackett-38-110
Hack-162-180
Hadle-117
Haddaway-20-
 193-112=204

Hadley-15-101
Hafner-55
Hagan-85-131
 183
Hager-87-124
Hagard-66
Hagner-54
Hafdy-74
Hahn-118-183
Hafer-183
Hagerman-118
Haines-174-
 185-193-192
Hahn-43-75
Hair-68
Hall-12-35-38
 101-104-107-
 111-119-126-
 133-134-136-
 139-143-155-
 158-172-173-
 188-198-209-
 12
Hale-83-145-
 168
Haller-86-122
Haldenback-99
Hallruner-185
Halleck-136
Haley-114
Halsted-122
Hallows-131
Halpin-143
Halden-177
Halbert-20-28
Hamilton-102-
 140-15-21-40
 65-158-164-
 170-180-191-
 194-
Hamlin-1-52
Hammon-6-29
Hamman-31
Hamet-185
Ham-175
Hammond-4a-5-
 66-70-77-89-
 118-120-125-
 128-167-170
 186-192-269-
Hamburgh-89
Hammpton-53-
 102-205
Hammell-122-128
 137-128
Hammershar-150
Hampshire-168
Hamblin-209
Hammersmith-78
Hammondtree-57
Hane-62

Hancock-80-59-180
Handy-18-54-160204
Hankey-133
Hankins-126
Hamell-131
Hands-133-137-27
Hance-72-172
Han--43
HHanley-31-145-38
Hnway-91
Hannigan-58
Hanson-49-65-127-
 167-174
Hany-128
Hanlon-145
Hanna-Hannah-12-65-
 183-186-188Hannretton-84
Harbaugh-89
Hardesty-186
Harkum-110
Hare-30
Harbeson-65
Hardcastle-172
Harkley-173
Harkson-157
Hartman-54-56-69-
 146-153-169
Hargate-184
Harryman-146-68
Hartigen-156
Hart-154-45-61
Hatch-161
Harley-
Hartley-13-91-127-168
Harney-7
Hartwell-64
Harig-48
Hartzog-39
Hartzell-46
Harrod-36
Harnrus-84
Harman-5
Hanlauf-17
Hartford-21
Harvey-55
Harwood-40-55-144
Harried-148
Harker-135-154
Hardin-5-3-62-29-91-
 112-204
Harman-85-96-154
Harrington-100-110-
 111-144-181
Harding-95-186
Hardy-4a-68-95
Harrison-4a-40-65-96
 105-112-143-136-139-
 163
Harper-28-56-70-113-
 139

219

Hopkinson-97-149
Horn-75-151-189
Hord-5
Horning-19
Horney-10-52
Horman-66
Horris-152
Horner-61-73-95
106-111-134-124
202
Hodges-10-94-99-
114-150-208
Horney-101-111-
112-136
Horsman-106
Hooker-167
Horman-66
Horton-196
Hose-1-206-207
Hosner-56
Hous-130
Houch-183
Houck-61-114
Houser-116-158
Housman-116
Hour-74
Horsley-25
Houck-141-149
Houston-94-181
House-30-28-123
Howden-9
Howe-191
Howart-148
Howard-5-76-79-
86-87-135-143-
144-163-197-198
Howes-95
Howard-103-122-
126-160
Hoxter-111-199
Hoye-2
Hubert-65
Huble-145
Hubbert-165
Huffington-201
Huggins-164
Hubbard-13-81-
112-172
Hughlett-111
Hughs-Hughes-2-
24-37-37-40-47
59-64-66-67-70
92-93-102-106-
154-160-182
Hughey-203
Hughett-189
Hudson-5-10-119
Hukill-176
Hulditch-189
Hulbert-44-94
Hull-30-106-106-
187

Hulton-85
Hulsma-127
Humphreys-50-
105-107-126-
155-202-203
Hunichen-48
Hunt-6-56-59
205-107-148
168-171
Hunter-60-114
Hungerford-71
Hurtt-197
Hurst-7-70-
127-162-37
Hurlock-100
Hurley-96-181
Hurtock-82
Hursley-83
Hutchison-93
Husky-168
Hutchins-80-
171-190
Hutton-187
Hutson-163
Hutman-12
Hutchinson-48
Hush-39
Hyall-89
Hyatt-98
Hyde-129
Hyland-30-37-
76-144
Hyman-133
Hynson-193
Iler-186
Imhoff-142
Ingless-76
Ingraham-142
Inlois-10-203
Innis-38
Instine-133
Irons-2
Ireland-7-40
41-171
Irwin-61-114
208
Irving-170
Iseminger-117
Isemager-206
Isaac-187-132
Isenfeller-13
Jackson-3-30-
60-77-79-92-
106-107-112-
153-163-179
Jacks-127
Jacobs-5-7-8-
21-60-82-124
154-160
James-22-52-59
69-72-117-124
134-135-148-154

Jamey-78
Jameson-36-80
Jarrell-100
Jarvis-135
Janney-127-177
Jarbo-1-103-200
Janeharper-15
Janis-89
Jarman-102-119
Jeffries-2-47
66
Jewett-15-177
Jeinoor-54
Jennett-159
Jemmison-172
Jewell-172
Jerman-145
Jennings-11-14
178
Jenson-71
Jenkins-18-35-
36-39-54-81-
134-149-150-
162-180-188-
201-204-210
Jeans-4
Jeys-151
Jay-166
Joiner-102
Johnson-4a-6-9
12-15-19-20-
2224-26-28-49
50-57-62-71-
80-83-95-97-
108-125-127-
130-132-149-
159-170-184-
186-193-195-
196-200-206-
209
Johnston-162
Johns-134-147
148
Jolley-139
Jones-4a-7-8-
12-16-18-20-
22-23-24-25-
36-37-41-48-
64-67-71-73-
77-79-81-82-
84-91-94-97-
107-108-109-
110-118-119-
123-125-128-
135-148-151-
160-164-168-
185-181-188-
191-195-197-
201-203-209-
210
Jordan-35-98-
120-123-175

James-9-10-14-21
Jourdan-91-144-177
Josephs-124-149
Joyce-Joice-134-
144-40-21
Jubb-126
Judy-122
Juniss-44
Jurgens-21
Justice-159-185
Kailer-87-184
Kaler-146
Kale-207
Kaller-149
Kaldenback-197
Kalputh-128
Kam.186
Kan14-37
Kane-13-136
Kance-14
Kaney-130
Kanklin-23
Karns-122
Karie-191
Kary-111
KKatenkemp-58
Kaun-48
Kaufman-147
Kay-83-113
Keally-188
Keagher-125
Keasy-71
Kean-187-188
Kech-14
Keach-159
Keckett-126
Keegan-50
Keen-33-182
Kees-181
Keep-67
Keenan-144
Keener-167
Keffenberger-5
Keeper-90
Kehune-147
Keil-147
Keifer-205
Keich-79
Keigler-38
Keisler-135
Keller-83-73-185-87-
88-145-168
Kelsey-26
Kelton-42
Kelty-64
Kellick-122
Kelly-10-15-27-33-
43-16-35-36-46-55
67-78-115-117-124
133-170
Kelso-20-107

Kelmyer-139
Kemmell-125
Kemble-32
Kemling-25
Kemper-46-51
Kemp-112-16-
205
Kenly-93-67
Kennard-10
Kent-171
Keniss-26
Kendrick-39
Kennerly-106
Kenman-55
Kennedy-25-43-
44-56-188-190
Kephart-56-84-
183
Kepperwill-142
Keplinger-61-
117
Kepler-87-128
Kersey-107
Kernan-98
Kerly-62
Kerr-14-61-142
Kerby-197
Kerns-50
Kerny-129
Keriman-127
Kessler-186
Kettrick-33
Keyser-152
Keys-25-34
Keyworth-167
Kidd-34-38-78-
138-169
Keirle-39
Kight-3
Kiler-88
Kilfluff-141
Kilgore-150
Killog-130
Killman-110
Killin-11
Kildrick-81
Kimble-77
Kimmell-49
King-2-4-17-19
23-27-35-36-
41-71-97-98-
109-119-125-
132-140-133-
156-166-171-
190-192-198-
206
Kinis-165
Kinkle-187
Kingston-134

Kingten-165
Kinkaide-176
Kinley-14
Kinsey-191-62
Kinsaled-54
Kinkard-77
Kinnamon-82-28
Kinny-62
Kirk-36-78-
142-192-195
Kirkland-129
Kirby-12-30-
98-101-102-
104-126-132
138-182-203
204
Kirth-9
Kinzer-88
Kirkwood-177
Kisner-195
Kissinger-87
Kirvan-82
Kitman-130
Klass-89
Kline-87
Klinefelter-127
Klinefelter-169
Klopsoth-142
Klunk-158
Knadler-117
Knighton-6-7
Knight-5-3-16-
67-92-122-179
188-68
Knabb-165
Knapp-15
Knock-113
Knoleirn-53
Knodle-116-117
Knost-122
Knoble-115
Knoll-43
Knotts-83-103-
138-142-180-
182-198
Knopp-189
Knowles-10-126
Knox-51-118-210
Koke-149
Kolb-38-122
Kolp-20
Kollman-125
Konig-41
Korman-50-149
Kuhnman-140
Kuhn-29
Kulb-60
Kulp-123
Kump-74
Kurtz-43

Kunnard-155
Kuso-165
Kuster-14
Kramer-15
Kraup-178
Krauss-77
Krastol-146
Krepps-206
Kretzer-206
Krietz-153
Krislipp-159
Kroh-168
Kromiller-27
Krotter-127
Krupp-132
Kyles-151
Kyle-47-177
Lackey-67-141
Lackland-78
Lader-46
Labaran-154
Lafatra-27
Lafevre-36
Lafferty-144
Lagg-67
Lague-74
Lagasby-196
Lahwot-10
Laing-38
Lainbright-58
Lake-82
Lainhardt-11
Laley-4a
Lain-94
Lamey-77
Lamden-112-203
Lamdin-126-209
Lamberg-131
Lambert-34-58-
99-148
Lamar-80
Lampbright-159
190
Lampart-174
Lammerick-57
Lane82-159-
172-204
Langrall-182
Lanigan-134
Landers-23-132
Landstreet-148
Lang-147-149-
155
Langley-9-6-
198-200
Langford-108-
109-202-209
Lancaster-26-
80-91-133
Lanhiem-149

Lanier-17
Lanbrack-36
Laner-73
Landen-25
Lancer-12
Langwell-67
Langrell-82
Lanner-160
Lanahan-166
Lanster-138
Lantz-51
Larkins-84-23
Lard-109
Larner-98
Larogue-37
Larrabee-36
Laremore-106-118-
203-204-205
Lassing-133
Lassen-180
Lathberry-119
Lath-10-52
Lathrom-201
Lattan-138
Latimore-80
Laudensleiger-28
Lauer-49-58
Laviller-59
Law-137
Lawrence-31-171-151-
157-202-22
Lawson-19-96-108-
186
Layton-96
Leach-86-104-140-171
Leake-96-159
Leamon-52-95
Leather-86
Leaser-89
Leatherbury-110
Leary-139
Lebby-7
LeBruner-139
Leavis-111
Leddey-33
Lednum-19-31-182
Ledgewood-84
Lee-32-45-51-52-65
66-76-77-161-179-
189-17-29-32-45-144-
Lees-116-158
Leester-127
Leekins-185
LeCompt-182-204-205
Lee-156-158-190
Leehe-44
Legue-151
Lefonte-81
Legg-101
leFeris-114

Legrand-104
Legrunge-183
Lehkill-15
Leigh-200
Leitch-32-72
'126
Lekertt-118
Leipe-152
Lehrol-26
Lemon-146-203
Lent-162
Lennard-193
Lenty-19
Lepick-155
Lepson-156
Leonard-111-203
204
Lenn-141
Legare-159
Leray-138
Leslie-61
Lester-73-160
Letmate-161
Letcher-11
Leugen-146
Leveline-64
LeSounard-148
Lever-126
Levy-50
Leverage-100
Levering-31-48
140
Leverett-100
Lewis-3-62-82-
68-84-102-106-
107-118-123-128
131-134-149-155
162-170-177-196
199-205-210
Lewishomoff-174
Licks-86
Liberty-170
Liday-115
Lide-23
Lidecker-153
Liberkamp-64
Ligge-125
Light-65
Lideke-96
Liggett-88
Lightenberger-175
Lilly-153-158-
164-177
Lightner-33-139
Limon-124
Lind-90-136-194
Linah-159
Lindenberger-37
Linkins-81
Lindle-63

Linenger-90
Lindsey-30-51
Lineaweaver-160
Lneberger-30
Lindall-28
Linn-98-174-
183-208
Linsley-166
Lindsay-198
Linthicomb-5-
125-126-155-
173
Link-33
Linton-110
Lippencott-149
Lippy-130
Lions-169
List-168
Lister-92-174
76
Liston-152
Little-7-75-
207
Littleton-120-
210
Litton-96
Litchfield-54
Littig-20
Liverman-22
Livermore-21
Livingston-29
Lloyd-65-80-28
11-20-24-152-
172-201
Locker-100
Lockerman-150
Lockert-175
LFoffen-189
Logue-51
Logsden-143
Logue-136-170
Logan-64-156
Lohrman-52-83
116
Loker-200
Lomax-15
Loman-112-158
Longfellow-22
101
Lonigrove-28
Longley-160
Long-2-21-62-
79-105-149-
153-158-165-
167-178-192-
201-208
Loons-12
Lord-150
Lorain-176
Lorentz-87-184

Lorrence-104
Lost-79
Louck-70
Louder-131
Louders-4
Love-51-105-
138
Lowe-117-135
18-42-77-97
98-100
Lowndy-98
Lowenkamp-148
Lowman-131
Lowry-19-56-
77-107-116-
4-24
Lovejoy-60
Loyesta-164
Loylis-8
Luby-144
Lucas-80-82
101-103
Luckner-13
Luck-132
Ludman-143
Lukes-153
Ludwick-131
Luigerman-40
Luckett-198
Lunt-16
Lungran-67
Luny-184
Lupner-16
LuLurman-66
Lusby-50-146
Lusbey-30
Lustatz-69
Lutz-159-7
Lutts-35
Lycoff-133
Lynddane-96
Lyers-122
Lyeth-58
Lyon-10-50-
79-105-138-
141-179-194
Lyles-99-171
Lynch-20-26-
42-117-119-
138-177-198
200
Lyman-156-164
Mace-26-68-
109-139-181
Maccubbin-60
Macuby-30
Mackan-70
Maclin-4a
Macklin-91
Macinhammer-20

Macklet-41
Madden-69-153
Maddin-29-59
Mackall-43-99
Maddux-49-109-180
Macarty-160
Maccubins-138
Maddon-91-149-
161-178
Maddens-52
Mae-153
Magan-188
Magill-200
Magnua-123
Magruder-696-123-
195-197
Magleton-160
Magrath-110
Magee-175-75
Magniss-91-189-29
Magnin-28
Maclea-37
Maginder-45
Mahoon-127
Mahoney-77-83
Maguire-60-145
Magness-144-188
Mahan-13
Maher-54
Mahn-33-86-76
Mail-169
Main-133
Maier-135
Majors-106
Malone-110-124-146
Maloney-124-147
Maloy-142-13
Malley-18
Malone-40
Mann-23-95-194-113
Manders-107
Manning-25-42-48-
49-144
Mantle-4
Mandlebaum-147
Mantz-167-85-86
Mansfield-54-138
Mane-55
Marine-24
Marple-50
Mans-48
Marlow-83
Maris-157-174
Marsey-166
Marriott-59-120-192
Marr-21
Marquer-97
Marinder-108
Markle-183
Mariner-41-147

McAbee-161
McAllen-119
McAvoy-51
McAvory-145
McAllister-10-27
    100
McBee-5-191
McBryde-54
McCabe-141
McCahon-87
McCaffery-84-143
McCall-53-182
McCanner-40
McCannon-86
McCartney-87
McCann-124-190
McCan-36
McCaddin-27
McCarthy-145-22
McCauley-159-8-77
McCane-177
McCausland-191
McCarney-144
McCandless-90
McCauley-46-51-68
McCater-191
McCay-104-156
McClanihan-32
McClain-114-135
McClennan-46-60
McClaughlin-151
McClenan-158
McClocklin-166
McClung-152
McClenahan-78
McClester-32
McClellan-50
McClusky-127
McCliston-76
McCluckarty-148
McCloud-126
McColgan-145
McColican-105
McColister-166-204
McCork-159
McCord-134
McCormac-McCormick
    78-91-135-148-168
    189-116-26
McConnell-41
McColigan-39
McCoutt-29
McCoy-114-134-160
McCrady-108
McConiken-39
McCreary-77
McCracken-188
McCoddin-177
McCrutchen-78

McCourt-137
McCullison-148
McCurtin-108
McCurley-55
McCubbin-68-69-
    145
McCullough-33-
    76-77-40-177
McDevitt-139
McDerman-169
McCuenn-59
McCurry-78
McDaniel-2-177-
    202
McDorman-109
McDonald-35-68
    3-114-128-145
    165-186
McDowell-49-135
    144-116
McDonnell-122
McDovott-44
McDowe-178
McDonough-10
McElhaney-141
McEley-7
McEvay-123
McEnutre-179
McEllwee-191
McElroy-44-58
McFadden-93
McFarland-52-111
McFarren-115
McFeely-102
McGall-159
McGarrity-145
McGaw-128
McGarry-136-166
McGlilean-91
McGlinn-128
McGee-44-144-156
McGinn-41
McGarvil-190
McGibbon-166
McGinney-25-112
McGlick-44
McGilton-55
McGirk-60
McGirch-55
McGinnis-43
McGuire-47-81-149
McGrath-120-128-
    166-37-50-53
McGraw-152
McGregor-76
McGowan-158
McGunder-125
McHale-59
McHooper-203

McHearld-55
McInhammer-39
McIntosh-41-46-59
McIntire-McIntyre
    41-109-116
McKay-21
McKenna-62-145
McKenny-127-135
McKinney-41-154
McKinley-20-115
McKinsey-124-163
McKinze-122
McKeever-61-141-
    157
McKenna-139-140
McKernan-145
McKinstry-74
McKinnell-60
McKimmons-52
McKenly-155
McKenny-198
McKeoan-65
McLain-29-53-63
McLean-62
McLaughton-42
McLane-48
McLaughlin-9-29
    37-60-116-126-
    141
McLinday-133
McMahon-131-160
McManus-66
McMillan-56
McMann-63
McMeachen-155
McMurray-177
McMinn-208
McNamara-49
McNelly-49
McNew-192
McNabb-90
McMunz-130
McNara-118
McMullen-78-124
    144-190
McNally-144
McNamee-144
McNoty-63
McNeil-4-48
McNulty-182-16
McPhall-143
McPherson-80-86
    129
McParlin-5
McQuay-204
McQuay-142
McShane-27
McTagart-31
McWilliams-200

Maneau-1
Marker-87-115
March-147
Martin-5-47-48-
62-70-139-142-
143-146-152-
156-161-165-
168-182-192-
203-204
Martenze-117
Marvel-202
Marfield-47
Markey-168
Martell-146
Marsh-71-109-
138-209
Marshall-18-36-
40-61-70-78-81
99-110-128-133
158-177-178
Mark-54-123-
127-188
Maslin-193
Masly-157
Marcellas-43
Maize-170
Mason-4-20-25-
26-86-96-113-
203
Masters-61-114-
137
Masyner-147
Marston-151
Massey-42-160-
161
Masner-65
Masemer-64-75
Masmon-168
Massette-125
Massa-34
Masure-31
Mattingly-105
Matte-16
Matthews-4a-16-
18-35-64-72-80
108-132-142-154
158-159-163-166
169
Manering-72
Mathany-200
Mattingley-79-122
Maugham-24
May-15-117-135-
141-143
Mayentice-34
Mayo-4
Mayhew-116
Mather-187
Maywald-138
Maynard-162
Maxley-130

Maxwell-178
Meads-190
Mears-81
Mealy-55
Medders-194
Medley-198
Medlart-45
Medinger-40
139
Meeks-152
Meekins-94-
154
Meed-85
Meek-8
Mehany-209
Mistor-161
Meise-183
Meir--31
Meisman-33
Melhorn-118
Melehon-46
Melton-207
Menkin-26
Menn-31
Mesick-157
Mencken-43
Meniken-8
Melson-118
Mentzer-75
Merine-154
Meretti-37
Merritt-22-
27-53
Merrill-3
Merchant-60
Mercer-154-
157
Mentzer-90
Merrick-95-
193-204-205
Merket-58
Merridith-25
44-100-101-
198
Merryman-68
64-73-138-
143-151-168
Meseke-66
Messinger-74
97
Mesner-140
Messman-117
Mettee-46
Metzell-45
Metts-172
Meusel-49
Metz-21-140
Metzell-160
Mezick-21-
29-82-106-
107-8

Meyer-138-147
Michen-189-18
Michael-26-34
124-196
Middlekauf-115-
115-207-208
Middleton-16-19
24-98-120-179
193-204
Migalen-122
Milby-71
Miles-95-98-108
180-185-193
Milesworth-186
Milford-184
Milholand-12
Mille-113
Milbourn-51-104
109-199-202-
20-51
Millar-47
Millender-78
Millard-197
Millet-65
Miller-20-21-22
30-31-41-14-17
19-4-13-42-53-
62-66-70-1-5-
9-31-40-57-86-
87-92-96-108-
111-114-115-116
122-127-131-136
137-139-141-146
152-158-157-161
163-173-176-179
182-155-188-191
185-187-189-191
195-208
Milligan-9
Milstead-180
Mills-7-18-27-36
103-135-170-171
181-187-196
Millsock-138
Milstone-84
Milroy-48
Mimey-25
Miney-7-95
Minner-177
Mines-96
Minnock-141
Miflee-29
Mister-109
Misener-85
Mitchell-92-99-
118-139-140-145
150-207-208
45-53-67
Mitchior-43
Mitz-114
Mix-85
Miztler-65

Moale-144
Mobberly-89
Mobly-30
Mockel-38
Moffitt-102-155
Mohiser-34
Moles-66
Molin-12
Moll-129
Molineaux-95
Momford-34
Montgomery-27-31-32
Monohan-145
Montebaugh-117
Monet-171
Monte-45
Montgomery-177
Monroe-143-198
Montigue-66-133
Moody-194-36-77
Mooney-3-32-34-82-
141-161
Moor-27
Moon-3-125
Moore-91-103-124-
154-169-178-202
Moreland-127-149
Moore-96-123-142-155
158-179-195-200-207
4a-10-36-42-54-57-
67-76
Morehart-159
Mora-22
More-156
Morton-150-172-36-68
Mortimer-27-48
Morron-132
Morsell-171
Mornan-17
Moran9-47
Morgan-11-53-64-71-
87-102-113-123-142
192-189-204
Morris-22-71-77-79-
43-120-141-162-168
193-209-210
Morningstar-85
Moreun-41
Morrison-14-15-31-37-
62-64-76-192
Morrow-32
Moriarty-68
Morelston-52
Mort-84-181
Moss-53-125-164
Motler-149
Motter-114
Mould-26
Mounce-125
Mount-89
Mously-114

Monrow-66
Moyer-34
Mudd-29-180
Mugg-103
Mullendore-87
Muller-18-131
Muklemeyer-140
Mull-174
Mulhoffer-37
Muller-90
Mullen-Mullan-
17-30-131-139
142-144-149-
161-175
Mulligan-57
Mullican-96-
111-198
Mullinix-64-
74-196
Munroe-129
Mung-55
Munch-55
Mumford-119
Murdock-38-79
125-198-199
Murphy-3-22-34
47-67-79-80-
92-98-161-166
177-180-187-
191-195
Murray-4a-11-
28-30-56-59-
69-73-75-76-
110-144-165-
193-
Murrell-105
Musgrave-63-192
Myerley-85
Myley-113
Myer-Myers-11-13
17-20-40-47-58
63-65-87-88-89
113-114-115-116
117-143-156-157
165-166-167-168
187-173-174-182
186-208
Nabb-101
Nace-154
Nagle-93
Naillor-156
Nairn-55
Naivore-18
Nader-140
Nally-179
Naley-33
Nantz-158
Nantling-122
Nast-86

Nash-162
Nasse-73
Naufield-163
Naylor-70-89
99
Nealy-111
Neal-Neale-
83-100-123
190-201-205
Neff-87
Neehard-56
Neepier-49
Neipert-206
Neilson-17-
199
Neighbors-111
Nelson-38-92-
93-106-118-
126-140-143
144-169-172
189-210
Neston-44
Netts-205
Neslin-133
Nepotite-17
Neumeir-61
Neucander-114
Neue-113
Nevines-147
Nevill-101
Newbold-18
Newcomb-193
Newell-31
New-130
Newman-10-81
94-101-138-
199-202
Newton-41-77
192
Newnier-26
Nicham-143
Nicaly-2
Nicholas-16-
48-193-132
Nichell-178
Nichols-7-27
86-89-96-106
150-182-194-
196-204-209
Nickell-52-39
Nicholson-4a-
46-97-138
Nicholi-47-48
Nicodemas-75-
88-114
Nilson-90-201
Nimrod-196
Nine-14-17
Nippard-137

Ninegarth-39
Niree-16
Nixon-3
Noble-16-82-
108
Nogle-91
Nock-210
Nollen-9
Noland-161
Nolty-183
Norton-98
195
Norman-143
199
Norrie-147
North-52-81-
148-181
Norfold-72-
171-52
Noonan-132-
183
Norris-7-32-
42-56-60-
69-74-90-
105-155-173
178-180-185
189-196-203
Norton-5-25
Norwood-18-
185
Notter-74
Noting-158
Nowland-77
Noys-86
Null-76-114-
184
Nunbis-92
Nusbaum-75-
88-173
Nustanin-185
Nuttall-136
Ober-149
Oberdick-131
O'Brian-39-
46-50-66-
Och-132
O'cone-144
Ochter-59
O'Connell-182
Oconner-4
O'dean-162
O'dell-162
O'Donnell-91
127
O'Dwyer-62
Oehrig-140
O'Farrell-60
Ofer-7-162
Offatt-96

Ogle-85-57
Ogleman-166
Ohler-174-182
Ohr-5
O'Keefe-142
Olaulin-
Oldham-35
Oldick-6
Oliver-43
O'Leary-19-132
O'Nell-172
O'Neill-O'Neale-50
87-140-149-197
Onion-142
Oram-22-167
Orendorf-15
Orman-170
Orchard-26
Orme-196
Ormsby-66
Orrell-199
Orr-132
Osborn-92-94-116-159
172-187
Oster-116-18
Osler-40-93
Oswald-206
Osbourne-49-53
Ottley-176
Otten-10
O'Tool-124-126
Ott-182
Otto-186
Ousler-51
Ouls-146
Ourspring-66
Overton-183
Ovelman-182
Ovishotger?-182
Owen-Owens-4a-14-19-79-
112-140-152-201
Owings-54-57-163-171-
173-193-197
Ozman-
Pabst-155
Pack-173
Pagenhardt-124
Padgett-80-83-180
Page-33-52
Paine-Payne-105-181-201
Painter-131-167
Pagan-2
Pampillon-51
Pamart-135
Palmer-24-71-96-115-168
179-195-197-199
Panish-175
Papto-66
Parner-178

Raney-29
Raport-152
Raput-166
Rapp-206
Rash-100
Rater-194
Ratigan-145
Ratcliff-58-81
  138-147
Rathelle-72
Raunie-95
Rauch-129
Ravenscroft-1
Ravigneaux-37
Rawlings-17-50
  149
Ray-66-83-96-
  159-192-194-
  207
Raynor-11
Raynis-9
Raysner-87
Raymond-133
Rea-151
Reaner-38
Reany-24
Reahan-43
Reddish-107
Rebensnider-137
Redgrave-51-151
Redefer-176
Rector-151
Redwood-37
Redinger-174
Reel-3
Reed-4-34-50-95
  27-103-132-144
  155-156-172-177
  206
Reid-56-44-58-83
  115-117-150
Rees-131
Reeves-174
Redman-23
Reece-93-101-124
  141-150-24-49
Reidasil-37
Reichert-52
Reef-57
Reintzel-104
Register-134
Reilly-150
Reinaker-140-174
Reinter-147
Reif-156
Reigle-195
Reindeller-174
Reikel-1
Reitgete-1
Reiner-12

Reddish-34
Reilly-20-32-35
  39
Reiheimer-15
Reisenger-157
Reiss-15-146
Reice-22
Relph-116
Rembord-167
Remey-162
Renn-33
Renson-168
Resh-116
Revell-7-105
  202
Reynolds-32-47
  56-71-78-79-
  86-118-135-145
  177-178-195
Rey-58
Rhoads-Rhodes-
  38-79-83-86-89
  97-107-186-202
  208
Rhodeneck-184
Rhodrick-88
Rhule-71
Rhumwalt-137
Rickard-13
Richardson-7-41-
  49-65-77-78-91
  98-103-111-113-
  120-121-126-169
  177-178-181-188
  192-209-210
Rich-145-152-164
Richards-26-34-
  83-99-1-54-79-
  149-154-155-158
  159-178
Rickets-1-35-25-
  47-151-176-195
Rickswith-154
Riddler-149
Ricord-164
Ridout-34
Ridenbough-83
Richey-78
Riddlemeyer-185
Ridgely-1-38-83
  156-157-192
Rice-2-139-186
  187-207
Rider-4-60-90
  105-118-169
Riddle-98-99
Ridenour-89-113
  115-117
Ridgeway-98
Riel-123

Rife-185
Rigley-63
Riggs-2-89-156
Rigdon-93-191
Riley-4a-23-29
  37-44-70-92-
  119-134-143-
  153
Ring-99-135-151
Rine-89
Rinard-92
Rigger-25
Rieves-11
Rieman-46
Riggin-47-50
  107-108-181-
  202
Riglan-160
Rinehart-24-74
  113-178-184
Rimmer-102
Ringgold-55-102
Rinnons-28
Ringler-130
Rineman-73
Rimby-42
Ripley-58
Rish-174
Riston-30
Rishard-114
Rise-59
Ritter-128-161
  163
Rivers-5
Roach-12-34-178
  135
Robb-51-129
Rober-141
Roberts-17-19-
  20-36-53-73-93
  101-107-145-
  171-175-176-202
Robertson-43-202
Roberson-81
Robinson-9-16-23
  24-34-48-63-65-
  82-91-92-105-106
  133-156-188-189
  203
Roby-80-90-113-
  197-198
Robison-114-158
  159-160-181-182
Rockensberg-148
Robelett-20
Rodensen-85
Rode-151
Rodemayer-28
Rodney-51-119-
  192

Rodgers-Rogers-77
  41-22-50-15-114-
  127-140-149-166-
  168-172-179-207
Roderick-176
Roe-22-172-198
  199-71
Roelly-183
Rodinick-115
Rhheter-134
Roherback-208-175
Rogge-41
Roley-80-124
Rollin-33-166
Romney-152
Romosher-158
Roney-133-191
Roten-159
Rontsan-174-206
Rolph-100-101
Rochester-101
Rond-80
Roop-173
Rolllson-196
Roose-205
Root-25-33-186
Rose-56-112-136-
  49
Rosenburg-44-152
Rosenberger-44
Rosengarth-146
Rosentuik-147
Roock-154
Rosenmeigh-183
Rosendale-38
Rosemer-38
Rosenthall-150
Rost-130
Rossman-57
Ross-26-62-69-71
  86-108-117-123-
  125-181-183-202
Rouse-92-100-172
  194
Rossiter-36
Rothrock-54
Rote-73
Rounds-210
Roundtree-30
Rowe-109-115-208
Rowley-17-94
Rowland-117-118-
  208
Rowlinson-102
Roy-57-159
Roysten-149
Rowlis-192
Rozine-176
Ruark-54-120-153-
  158

Ruby-14-77-172
Rudy-87-152
Rudesill-75-205
Ruder-179
Rudolph-17-158
Rud-170
Ruff-25-55-90
Runner-57
Rupp-157
Ruper-58
Rupt-17
Rushmeyer-151
Rusk-129
Rush-172-175
Ruse-174
Ruster-141
Rust-172
Ruth-55-101-192
Rusinger-89
Russell12-48-60
  61-103-106-142-
  156-181-187-
  201-207
Ruther-13
Ruttl-53
Rutter-18-167
Rutledge-136-158
Rye-1
Ryan-46-53-98-
  99-116-149-162
Ryon-86
Ryne-192
Rysten-169
Saberly-161
Saivley-61
Salgues-47
Saltzir-11
Salter-137
Sanders-133-135
Sanks-152
Sanlin-61
Sampson-19
Sands-6-24
Sanehard-71
Sangston-71
Sanner-15-48-104
Santz-147
Sappington-92
  184-193
Sapfel-135
Sarah-6
Sarnoski-152
Satterfield-72-
  111
Satchell-112
Saul-62
Saunders-30-127
  188
Saulsbury-72
Sausman-113
Satz-147

Sayle-17
Saylor-184
Sawner-149
Sax-153
Scales-127
Scanlon-145-176
Scarf-160-190-33
Scaggs-195
Scarf-38-40
Scheckels-137-
  139
Schafler-138
Schafer-149
Schaumteffel-147
Scharitz-13
Schammel-131
Schaffer-12-75-
  162
Schenk-28
Schenter-130
Schettler-31
Scharer-66
Scheron-12
Schiner-182
Schickles-197
Schidel-164
Schirds-166
Schidar-166
Schird-147
Schiminger-140
Schindle-87
Schillenberg-128
Schiefer-148
Schlilt-140
Schock-151
Schopp-150
Schon-130-131
Scholfield-149-
  162-209
Schotts-9
Scherlock-15-52
Schosler-14
Scheckel-6-50
Schow-22
Schleigh-25
Schoenberger-59
Schibeline-63
Schanoffs-64
Schnider-140
Schlosen-184
Schmetz-148
Schmidt-66-126
Schuh-128
Schroeder-42-141
  170
Schuster-142
Schuck-145
Schunk-134
Schwartz-22-63
Schreimer-34
Scotti-135

Scarborough-93-
  119-159-190
Scanlan-79
Schneider-50
Schumel1-5
Scurvey-5
Schults-49-59-73
Scott-91-109-122
  132-159-167-177
  188-180-196
Seabust-130
Seebreese-106
Seikel-1-2
Seinen-12
Seigear-195
Seip-40-184
Seiss-89
Selby-4-5-210
Sellers-71-124
Seller-128
Selvage-135
Sellman-196-75
Selsam-88
Sendes-92
Searley-128
Senson-146
Sennett-158
Septer-90
Sergant-178
Serivner-21
Sessell-138
Seth-198-51
Setz-14
Seiber-14
Seckel-60
Seippper-63
Seltzer-61
Settten-22
Sevann-80
Seward-100
Sewill-6-7-8-
  21-112-150-
  181-201-40
Sexton-122-143
Seymour-58-111
Shackleford-115
  208
Shahan-199
Shaner-75
Shankles-54
Shanklin-67
Shaul-70
Sharpless-178
Shalts-183
Shap-26
Shanin-92
Shane-50-129-
  116-190-192
Shanks-84-115-
  139-165
Shamd-165

Sharp-53-166
Shannon-134
Shanks-118-201
Shaverline-138
Shaw-13-29-58-74
  80-98-115-123-
  165-183-194
Sharp-154
Shanklin-146
Sharer-87
Shaeffer-Shaffer-
  87-118-128-170-175
  183-60-68
Shaspiski-160
Shrader-176
Shalts-183
Sheldon-26
Sheets-89-159
Shay-94-13-55-195
Sheckles-96
Sheatler-131
Shednick-114
Sheardon-164
Sheplin-165
Shehan-161
Shepard-111-137-
  155-161-206
Sherman-176
Sherry-173
Sherriff-56
Shedrick-19
Shertz-67
Sheaver-179
Sherwood-10-32-43
Shelly-65
Shiel-36
Shillinger-144
Sherrity-148
Shilling-11-158-206
Shilt-174
Shirk-162
Shinabuck-114
Shipley-5-37-40-
  59-74-123-124-158
  161-175-89
Shillinberger-57
Shineflow-74
Shields-15-55-69
Shivers-208
Shippard-20-36
Shipman-26
Shoats-117
Sholt-34
Shoder-64
Shockley-40
Sholes-36
Sholman-75
Shorey-30
Shoaf-124
Showell-119
Shosler-166

Steephenson-Stevenson
21-26-49-69-75-98-
129-162-175-10-15
Stephens-115-187-193
Stevens-5-49-57-73-
137-150-151-188-193
2070
Stein-156
Steifle-162
Sterrett-2
Sterhan-79
Stem-74
Steibel-29
Steinman-32
Steinmetz-42
Steigers-40
Steinmaker-40
Stilghman-125
Stickney-144
Stinger-180
Stinelean-158
Stincel-7
Stine-46-38
Stiles-40
Stever-21
Stewers-66
Stigars-155
Stockham-92
Stoddard-57-172
Stockett-23
Stincomb-48
Story-26
Stansbury-125-128
176-190
Stone-75-103-110-
114-150-178-179-
200-201
Stockett-49
Stoufer-116
Stout-21
Stocklock-156
Stockdale-35-156-176
Storm151
Stonebreaker-117
Stotler-207-2
Stokes-190-194
Stocks-164
Stoves-1
Stotner-111
Stonehaker-74-114
Stollemeyer-87
Strank-66
Stratton-3
Straughn-72
Strakem-188
Strawbridge-4a
Strain-106-116
Strasburg-184
Stresler-188
Street-93-142-190-
191-203

Stretehoof-93
Strickle-184
Strick-207
Streibel-29
Stricker-95
Strickland-69
76
Strobel-43-152
Strour-93
Strong-1-193
Stubenger-129
Struck-207
Stuart-Stuard-
121-131
Stumpf-48
Stump22-65
Stutler-74
Stumpenhouse-64
Streaker-4
Sturgeon-136-156
Stump-157-162-
167-191
Stunkle-183
Suit-197
Sullivan-20-40
96-103-105-
173-187-204-205
Sulzer-15-22
Super-163
Sumal-150
Summers-19-54-
149-158-206-84
Summerfield-164
Sutton-3-25-39-
76-104-136-147-
160-185
Swain-208
Swaitz-32
Stans-1-6
Swallenberry-43
Swartz-118
Swallenback-191
Swartsingrover-1
Sweeney-31-45-85
122-162-187
Sweedenbury-62
Swearingen-84-87
Sweitzer-2-66-43
189
Sweitman-2
Swibzler-130
Swope-183
Swormsteat-8
Syinker-15
Syma-44
Tabler-96
Tabman-14
Talafero-155
Taltorn-129
Talbot-28-99-171

Tarrington-27
Tappan-28
Tasher-4
Taner-59
Tatam-47
Taylor-7-9-20
26-30-35-42-
45-49-50-52-
53-62-64-72-
72-74-97-106
122-130-136-
139-141-142-
148-151-166-
168-175-178-
179-180-187-
192-210
Tea-104
Teal-176
Tear-48
Tearel-93
Tliniard-85
Tella-62
Tenison-46
Tenant-34
Tennett-138
Terry-77-163
Teron-67
Tice-86
Tickner-156
Tidings-7-140
141
Tiffany-144
Tigler-132
Tigert-115
Tignor-90
Tilden-94
Tilghman-113-
199-203
Tilman-118
Timely-1
Tindle-119-
157-209
Tinde-118
Timkle-124
Timmons-82-
119-209
Tingstrom-84
182
Tilist-57
Tinnels-165
Tinker-185
Tippett-105
Tipton-156-
164-176
Tiralda-38
Thackery-79
Thayer-23
Thensil-57
Therwick-139
Thorp-72-125
180

Thomas-3-4a-7-10-
13-22-36-41-43-
52-58-62-63-68
72-81-82-84-86-89
90-92-93-101-107
113-134-148-150-
160-165-167-170-
180-181-183-191-
200-208
Thompson-4-4a-11-
12-14-18-27-33-
34-35-41-47-57-
63-68-70-81-82-
87-89-90-92-101-
1-3-104-127-138-
146-155-166-179-
190-191-194-196
199
Thorne-30-198
Thornton-6-57-
200-209
Thorington-203
Thrasher-186
Thorward-131
Thughbright-132
Thurlow-19
Thueston-26
Thurston-26
Thuse-163
Toadvine-120
Tobin-17
Todd-83-89-59-165
Tolly-18-71-181
Tolson-101
Tolinger-6
Tottle-43
Tool-169
Toner-145-161
Ton-205
Tomlison-195
Topkins-131
Torrance-35
Tounsly-187
Towner-155
Towers-172
Towson-53-114-142
Townsend-32-48-118
121-128-155-167-
197-209
Tracy-65-71-105-
141-165-168-169
Tradway-91
Traise-17
Trater-60
Travin-11
Trail-183
Trault-166
Trailer-175
Travish-123
Trayer-186